ANTEBELLUM NATCHEZ

D. CLAYTON JAMES

LOUISIANA STATE UNIVERSITY PRESS

BATON ROUGE

To

Erlene, Sherrie, Ned, Judy,
and Allie Brady James

Acknowledgments

For all of their help, I am deeply grateful to Barnes F. Lathrop of the University of Texas, who patiently supervised my doctoral dissertation on antebellum Natchez, and Professor Glover Moore of Mississippi State University, whose judgment was invaluable in the preparation of my later manuscript which became this book. The archival staffs of the following institutions gave generously of their time in assisting my research efforts: the University of Texas, Louisiana State University (Baton Rouge and Alexandria), Duke University, the University of North Carolina, the University of Virginia, the Library of Congress, the National Archives, the Mississippi Department of Archives and History, and the North Carolina Department of Archives and History. Also helpful were the staffs of the City Clerk's and Chancery Clerk's offices in Natchez. The Natchez Historical Society permitted the use of illustrations from its significant Maurice B. Scharff Collection. Among Natchez residents who gave important assistance were Miss Emma Dorris Bankston, Newell W. Bankston, Mrs. Edith W. Moore, and the late Miss Pearl V. Guyton. My thanks go also to the excellent editorial staff of Louisiana State University Press. Finally I owe a deep debt of gratitude to Miss Karen K. Adams and especially to my wife, Erlene, for help in typing, proofreading, and performing sundry chores essential to the preparation of the manuscript.

D. CLAYTON JAMES

Mississippi State University

Contents

Illustrations

Footnote Abbreviations

AGI   Archivo Generale de Indias, Seville, Papeles y Procedentes de Cuba; transcripts in the North Carolina Department of Archives and History unless otherwise stated.

AHA   *Annual Report of the American Historical Association* with the year of publication stated.

AHR   *American Historical Review*

ANC   Archive Nacionales Coloniale, Paris, series C 13a, in Library of Congress unless otherwise stated.

DAB   *Dictionary of American Biography*

JMH   *Journal of Mississippi History*

JSH   *Journal of Southern History*

LHQ   *Louisiana Historical Quarterly*

LSU   Department of Archives, Louisiana State University, Baton Rouge.

MPAE   *Mississippi Provincial Archives: English Dominion,* edited by Dunbar Rowland.

MPAE Manuscripts. Mississippi Provincial Archives: English Dominion, manuscripts, in the Mississippi Department of Archives and History.

MPAF   *Mississippi Provincial Archives: French Dominion,* edited by Dunbar Rowland and Albert G. Sanders.

MTA   Mississippi Territorial Archives, series stated in each case, located in the Mississippi Department of Archives and History.

MVHR   *Mississippi Valley Historical Review*

PMHS   *Publications of the Mississippi Historical Society*

PMHS *Centenary. Publications of the Mississippi Historical Society, Centenary Series*

PRO   British Public Records Office, Colonial Office Papers, Class V, Library of Congress.

SSA   Secretary of State Archives, series F papers, located in the Mississippi Department of Archives and History.

UNC   Southern Historical Collection, University of North Carolina.

ANTEBELLUM NATCHEZ

Inauspicious
Beginnings

EARLY FRENCH VISITORS TO THE WILDER-
ness of the Lower Mississippi Valley
were impressed by the hostility of the Natchez Indians. The La
Salle voyagers, who in 1682 stopped beneath the steep bluff on
which the tribe resided, were sure that the Indians were plotting
"some evil design" and were "resolved to betray and kill us."[1]
Jesuits journeyed to the Natchez villages soon after the birth of
the Louisiana colony at Biloxi in 1699, but so fruitless was their
work that the mission was abandoned eight years later. The
priests were shocked by the "barbarous" and "vicious" natives.
One Jesuit who stayed five years among the tribesmen concluded
that "they are all thieves and try only to do harm."[2]

Whether the Natchez were more unreceptive to Gallic ways
than were neighboring Indians is moot, but certainly the French
encountered in them a strong and unusual tribe. A century prior
to La Salle's visit the Natchez had established nearly sixty villages and exerted an influence perhaps three hundred miles northward. The Yazoo, Taënsas, and Avoyel tribes had once been part

[1] Memoir of Henry de Tonty, 1697, in Benjamin F. French (ed.), *Historical
Collections of Louisiana, Embracing Many Rare and Valuable Documents Relating
to the Natural, Civil and Political History of That State* (7 vols.; New York,
1846–75), I, 62–65.
[2] François de Montigny headed the Natchez mission, 1699–1701, followed by
Jean-François Buisson de Saint-Cosme, 1701–1706. At least three other Jesuits
visited the tribe during that period. On Jesuit opinions of the Natchez, see
Reuben G. Thwaites (ed.), *Jesuit Relations and Allied Documents: Travels and
Explorations of the Jesuit Missionaries in New France, 1610–1791* (73 vols.;
Cleveland, 1896–1901), LXV, 100–79; Pierre Margry (ed.), *Découvertes et établissements des Français dans l'ouest et dans le sud de l'Amérique septentrionale,
1614–1754* (6 vols.; Paris, 1879–88), VI, 387–433; François de Montigny,
Mémoires historiques sur la Louisiane (2 vols.; Paris, 1753), I, 81–82, 154–57, II,
56–57; *Compte Rendu, Congrès International des Américanistes, 15th Session* (2
vols.; Quebec, 1907), I, 45.

3

of a Natchez-dominated confederation. Although their numbers had since declined inexplicably, in 1700 more than 1,200 Natchez warriors and their families dwelled at seven villages on the bluff and along two nearby creeks.[3]

The Natchez possessed an intense pride nourished not only by memories of former glory but also by a sense of uniqueness born of distinctive social and cultural traits. Their society was ruled by a monarch, or "Great Sun," who was "the absolute master of the goods and life of his subjects."[4] Under him were three divisions of nobility and a large element of "Stinkards," or commoners. Their religion was a version of sun worship with an elaborate ceremonialism. It was rooted in the belief that they were the sun god's chosen people and that their leaders were his descendants; hence the title of "Sun" for a person of royal lineage. Tribal morality was governed by a revered tablet of commandments bestowed by an offspring of the sun god in the misty past. The Natchez remained aloof from the other members of the Muskhogean, their linguistic family. Their superior craftsmanship in ceramics and house construction buttressed this feeling of uniqueness. The haughtiness of the Natchez would make it difficult for them to adjust to the coming of whites, who proclaimed the only true religion, demanded fidelity to another "Sun King," and practiced a morality that astounded the Indians.[5]

[3] Antoine S. le Page du Pratz, *Histoire de la Louisiane contenant la découverte de ce vaste pays* . . . (3 vols.; Paris, 1758), II, 338; Memoir of Sieur de Bienville, 1726, *MPAF*, III, 530–31. Du Pratz, a Dutchman, lived at Natchez from 1720 to 1727.

[4] Du Pratz, *Histoire*, II, 352–53.

[5] *Ibid.*, 393–97; Bernard de la Harpe, *Journal historique de l'établissement des Français a la Louisiane* (New Orleans, 1831), 28; Pierre F. X. de Charlevoix, *Journal d'un voyage fait par ordre du Roi dans l'Amérique septentrionale adressé à Madame la Lesdiquieres* (2 vols.; Paris, 1744), I, 421–23. La Harpe, an army officer, came to Natchez in 1718, and Charlevoix, a Jesuit, visited there in 1721.

Among the many secondary accounts of the Natchez tribe, the better ones include John R. Swanton, *Indian Tribes of the Lower Mississippi Valley and Adjacent Coast of the Gulf of Mexico* (Washington, 1911), 89–108, 167–76; Andrew C. Albrecht, "Ethical Precepts among the Natchez Indians," *LHQ*, XXXI (July, 1948), 569–97; Albrecht, "Indian-French Relations at Natchez," *American Anthropologist*, XLVIII (October, 1948), 321–54; Robert S. Neitzel, *Archeology of the Fatherland Site: Grand Village of the Natchez* (New York, 1965).

Sieur d'Iberville, founder of the Louisiana colony, was "much pleased" with the Natchez locale on a visit in 1700, but wariness of the Indians, together with difficulties at the coastal settlement, led him to postpone his plans for a fort on the bluff. It was 1714 before Governor Antoine de la Mothe Cadillac allowed the brothers Marc Antoine and Auguste de la Loire des Ursins to build a trading post at the landing beneath the bluff. The governor was motivated by several considerations: need for a way station en route from the Illinois country to Louisiana, hope of developing the fur trade of the Lower Mississippi, and suspicion of British influence among the Natchez. The last was confirmed when the La Loires captured a British agent and learned that other Englishmen had been visiting the tribe since 1708.[6]

Already disturbed by the trading post's proximity to their main villages, the Natchez became infuriated when Cadillac on a visit in 1714 peremptorily refused the calumet, the ceremonial peace pipe offered to distinguished strangers, as a supreme proof of hospitality. The Indians retaliated by paralyzing French trade on the river for two years. Several traders were killed, their pelts were stolen, and the La Loire warehouse was pillaged. In 1716 Cadillac ordered Sieur de Bienville, Iberville's young brother, to stop the Indian ravages. Ever at odds with Cadillac over personal and adminstrative matters, Bienville complained that the mission was suicidal since the contingent assigned to him consisted of "thirty-four little raw soldiers, two-thirds of whom are ill, and without provisions."[7] But by chicanery, which included a threat to crush the skulls of the chiefs whom he had invited to a parley and had held as hostages, he wrung satisfactory terms from the Natchez. In addition to returning the stolen goods, they agreed to provide lumber and labor for the construction of a French

[6] Bienville to Count de Pontchartrain, June 15, 1715, *MPAF*, III, 182; Richebourg G. McWilliams (ed.), *Fleur de Lys and Calumet: Being the Pénicaut Narrative of French Adventure in Louisiana* (Baton Rouge, 1953), 160; Verner W. Crane, *The Southern Frontier, 1670–1732* (Philadelphia, 1929), 85–107. André Pénicaut, trader and carpenter in Louisiana, 1700–21, obtained a tract of land at Natchez in 1720.

[7] Bienville to Governor Antoine de la Mothe Cadillac, June 23, 1716, *MPAF*, III, 213–15.

fort on the bluff. Completed by late summer, 1716, Fort Rosalie des Natchez was "merely a plot 25 fathoms long and 15 broad, enclosed by palisades, without any bastions." Despite the small size of the fort, the Natchez did not hamper French traffic for six years thereafter.[8]

John Law's Company of the Indies, which acquired the Louisiana proprietorship in 1717, six years later designated Fort Rosalie as the headquarters of the newly-organized Natchez District. One of nine such administrative units into which the French colony was divided, the district encompassed a triangular-shaped area extending from Fort St. Peter near the mouth of the Yazoo River to a base line running eastward from the Mississippi about forty miles along the 31st parallel. The meager population was located in the rural settlements adjoining Forts Rosalie and St. Peter (the latter constructed in 1719). The Fort Rosalie commandant exercised civil and military jurisdiction over the district. He was appointed by and was responsible to the governor and colonial council in New Orleans, the Louisiana capital as of 1722. In turn, the commandant appointed a three-man committee from the local clerks of the Company of the Indies to administer petty legal and judicial affairs. Bienville protested in vain that at "the Natchez," as the settlement was often called, "these clerks are ordinarily young men very liable to be disorderly, who are not imposing enough for functions of this nature."[9]

As immigration gradually increased, tobacco experts and skilled farmers were sent by the company to several of its Natchez concessions in the hope that the other settlers would imitate their methods and cultivate more tobacco. Convinced that the fertile soil there produced tobacco superior to the tidewater strains, the New Orleans officials offered generous prices of six to ten sols per pound for Natchez tobacco.[10]

[8] Bienville to M. Raudot, January 20, 1716, *ibid.*, 198; McWilliams, *Fleur de Lys and Calumet*, 167–70, 180–82; Du Pratz, *Histoire*, I, 120–28.

[9] Memoir of Bienville, 1726, *MPAF*, III, 506–507.

[10] Committee of Louisiana to the Company of the Indies, November 8, 1724, *ibid.*, II, 398–99; Minutes of the Superior Council of Louisiana, March 23, 1725, *ibid.*, 419–22.

The most extensive concession was that of the commissary general of Louisiana, Marc Antoine Hubert de St. Malo. Worked by a skilled manager and sixty slaves, it contained six hundred arpents planted mainly in tobacco and wheat. Hubert built himself "a quite large house," a water mill for grinding grain, a forge mill for producing guns and tools, and a large tobacco factory. The factory employed thirty Frenchmen and annually produced over 100,000 pounds of finished carottes (cylindrical rolls of tobacco, often used in lieu of hogsheads). A neighbor described the Hubert concession as "very rich" and "one of the most delightful" in the colony. So optimistic was Hubert about the settlement's future that he tried in vain to persuade the company to make Natchez the capital of Louisiana.[11]

Besides tobacco and wheat, the settlers by the mid-1720's were producing small quantities of indigo, silk, rice, cotton, pitch, tar, and "all kinds of dressed timber." With the number of skins obtained along the Lower Mississippi mounting to fifty thousand annually, the trading post at the landing was kept busy. There was also an active trade in horses obtained from the Spanish in Texas. Apparently few of these steeds were retained locally, however, since livestock owned by Natchez residents in 1724 amounted to only "25 to 30 horned cattle, 7 or 8 horses and 30 to 40 hogs."[12]

Hindering the interior trade was an almost complete lack of specie or any regular item of barter comparable to the "made-beaver" (beaver skin) and wampum of the English colonies. Commercial negotiations were transacted informally with no fixed standards of value except on certain company imports. Peltry and lead were most frequently used, but everything from flour and salt to bear's oil and beeswax became mediums of exchange.[13]

[11] McWilliams, *Fleur de Lys and Calumet*, 213–39, 252; Bienville and Sieur de Salmon to Count de Maurepas, April 24, 1741, *MPAF*, III, 745.

[12] Montigny, *Mémoires historiques*, I, 81; Heloise H. Cruzat (trans.), "Louisiana in 1724: Banet's Report to the Company of the Indies, Dated Paris, December 20, 1724," *LHQ*, XII (January, 1929), 122; Bienville to the Company of the Indies, March 23, 1726, *MPAF*, III, 522.

[13] Du Pratz, *Histoire*, I, 331; Montigny, *Mémoires historiques*, II, 56–57.

As the number of independent farms grew, discontent spread among many settlers who felt that the company was neglecting their interests. In 1724 they complained to the company directors that they needed a "workshop for making hogsheads," a new factory "for spinning, rolling or pressing the tobacco," more skilled workers in tobacco production, and more boats for transporting produce to New Orleans. The fort commandant also joined the refrain, accusing the company of retarding development by its refusal to add more warehouses, allocate slaves to concessions that were not Company-affiliated, and rebuild the fort, which was "completely decayed."[14]

Local farmers also complained that the reimbursement they received for their crops was not commensurate with the mercantile prices set by the company, which were 70 per cent above prices at Mobile and New Orleans. Moreover, officers at the fort handled the sale of most incoming merchandise and raised prices as much as 400 per cent above the official levels. Since many colonists cultivated tobacco "to the exclusion of all other products, not even excepting their own food supply," such charges were especially alarming to them. New Orleans authorities duly noted these grievances but by 1728 had done little toward alleviating matters.[15]

In spite of these conditions and largely because of the company's energetic but often exaggerated advertising, the Natchez settlement grew steadily in the 1720's. In 1723 there were 303 inhabitants (including 111 Negro slaves) at the landing, near the fort on the bluff, along St. Catherine's Creek, and at the Terre Blanche concession farther south. Four years later the total number had risen to 713, consisting of 3 officers, 20 soldiers, 180 men, 80 women, 150 children, and 280 slaves. By 1729 the population

---

[14] Petition of Natchez planters to the Company of the Indies, October 17, 1724, ANC, VIII, 227–28; Memoir of Bienville, 1726, *MPAF*, III, 523–24.

[15] Committee of Louisiana to the Company of the Indies, November 8, 1724, *MPAF*, II, 398–99; Father Raphael de Luxemburg to Abbé Raguet, September 15, 1725, *ibid.*, 511–12; La Harpe, *Journal historique*, 293; Nancy M. Surrey, *The Commerce of Louisiana during the French Regime, 1699–1763* (New York, 1916), 164–65, 252.

was probably more than 750. The amount of cleared land grew apace, so that by 1727 there were 6,290 arpents in cultivation. The company concessions at St. Catherine and Terre Blanche had 1,604 and 200 arpents in cultivation, respectively. The remaining land in use was divided among about seventy landholders in tracts up to 300 or 400 arpents.[16]

As the settlement expanded, seeds of hatred were sown among the Indians by incoming Frenchmen. Deeply resented were sexual abuses of the tribe's women, unjust treatment of warriors conscripted as field laborers, encroachments upon Indian farming areas, proximity of the densest French population to the sacred Grand Village on St. Catherine's Creek, and flagrant disrespect for ancient tribal mores. In the fall of 1722 bloodshed began at the concession of St. Catherine. Because of insufficient munitions and an epidemic among his troops, Bienville, now governor, tried to placate the Natchez chiefs with lavish gifts. Several leading officials, including the lieutenant-governor, vehemently opposed Bienville's "leniency." Continuous bickering in New Orleans prevented the formulation of a clear-cut, consistent policy toward the Indians. In the ensuing months more French abuses led to another eruption of warfare. With a force of five hundred troops Bienville marched against the Natchez, razed two of their villages, and imposed upon them laws which, he boasted, they were "faithfully keeping" in 1725. Because of conflicting opinions among officials as to the use of the scanty colonial funds, Fort Rosalie was not repaired despite Bienville's warning that it lay "in ruins" and afforded the colonists no protection.[17]

The arrival of Sieur de la Perier as the new Louisiana governor

---

[16] Louisiana censuses of 1723 and 1727, cited in Dawson A. Phelps, "Colonial Natchez," MS in preparation for publication; Clem G. Hearsey, "The Vengeance of the Natchez," *LHQ*, XII (April, 1929), 273; John A. Caruso, *The Southern Frontier* (Indianapolis, 1963), 174–78.

[17] Lieutenant-Governor Le Blond de la Tour to the Superior Council, August 5, 1723, ANC, VII, 203–205; Bienville to the Natchez chieftains, November 6, 1722, *ibid.*, 300–301; Bienville to the Superior Council, August 3, 1723, *ibid.*, 201–202; Dawson A. Phelps (ed.), "Narrative of the Hostilities Committed by the Natchez Against the Concession of St. Catherine, 1722," *JMH*, VII (January, 1945), 3–10.

in 1726 soon caused tension to mount again at the settlement. Perier entered into a partnership with the heavy-drinking, tyrannical commandant of Fort Rosalie, Sieur de Chepart. Together they planned to acquire and operate a large plantation carved from the rich lands still held by the Natchez. The governor's absorption in this project compelled the company directors to caution him that "the plantation you were bent on developing as soon as you arrived in Louisiana, has taken so much of your time that it has prevented you from watching more closely over things infinitely more important."[18]

Chepart, probably in collusion with Perier, ordered the Natchez to bring him gratis provisions monthly and announced plans to effect the complete removal of the tribe in the near future. In the following weeks the Great Sun, offspring of one of the early Jesuits, held secret meetings with his tribal leaders and possibly with the Yazoo, carefully plotting a response to Chepart's effrontery. On the pretext of bringing chickens for the commandant and begging supplies for a hunting trip, the Great Sun and a party of warriors gained admission to the fort palisades on the morning of November 28, 1729. Suddenly they opened fire upon the surprised soldiers while attacks on the outlying concessions were simultaneously launched. Between 229 and 285 colonists and slaves had died by noon, many being disemboweled or decapitated after trying to surrender. A few men escaped, and about 450 persons, mainly French women and slaves, were spared to be sold to the British or enslaved by the Natchez. On New Year's Day, 1730, the Yazoo joined the uprising by massacring the soldiers and settlers at Fort St. Peter.[19]

[18] Governor Etienne Boucher de la Perier de Salvert to Abbé Raguet, April 25, 1727, MPAF, I, 545; Company of the Indies to Perier, October 11, 1728, ANC, XII, 351; John Delanglez, "The Natchez Massacre and Governor Perier," LHQ, XVII (December, 1934), 636–38.

[19] Father Philibert's register of the 1729 Natchez massacre victims, MPAF, I, 122–26; Perier to Maurepas, March 18, 1730, ibid., 61–70; Mathurin le Petit, Report of the Natchez Massacre by Fra Mathurin Le Petit, S. J., trans. R. H. Hart (New Orleans, 1950). On the massacre, see also MPAF, I, 54–61, 128–29; Delanglez, "Natchez Massacre," 631–41; Charles E. A. Gayarré, History of Louisiana (4 vols.; New Orleans, 1885), I, 396–420; Jean-Bernard Bossu, Travels in the Interior of North America, 1751–1762, ed. Seymour Feiler (Nor-

When a force of French troops and Choctaw allies attacked the Natchez a month later, the tribe escaped into the swamps across the Mississippi. The French pursued the elusive Indians for two years but seldom were able to engage them in battle. Several hundred captives, including the Great Sun, were sent as slaves to the island of Santo Domingo. Remnants of the tribe later joined the Chickasaw in battling the French. The Natchez gradually amalgamated with other tribes, so that by 1743 Bienville could report with relief: "We may regard this numerous nation as totally destroyed as far as we are concerned."[20]

Although the Indian threat was removed, the Natchez settlement was not revived. Memories of the massacre and, more important, alarming financial and administrative disorder in New Orleans militated against renewed promotion of the post. When the French government designated Louisiana a royal colony in 1731, Bienville pleaded for a strong garrison at Natchez and encouragement of immigration there. The value of Natchez to France, he argued, "had become so considerable that the colony has lost one half of its establishment in losing this one."[21] A few troops were kept at the fort, rebuilt from 1730 to 1734, but the Natchez District ceased to function as an administrative division. A French traveler in 1751 found the bluff "uninhabited" except for an "insignificant" number of lonely soldiers. Thus it remained until the termination of the great Anglo-French struggle for North America.[22]

---

man, Okla., 1962), 29–47. Estimates of the total number of victims for the whole district ranged from seven hundred to over one thousand.

[20] Perier to Maurepas, March 21, 1730, ANC, XII, 295–99; Perier's report of the Natchez expedition, March 25, 1731, *ibid.*, XIII, 35–41; Bienville to Maurepas, February 4, 1743, MPAF, III, 776; John A. Green, "Governor Perier's Expedition Against the Natchez Indians," *LHQ*, XIX (July, 1925), 389, 393–97; Louis Juchereau de St. Denis to Salmon, November 2, 1731, in Ross Phares, *Cavalier in the Wilderness: The Story of the Explorer and Trader Louis Juchereau de St. Denis* (Baton Rouge, 1952), 207–13.

[21] Bienville to Maurepas, May 12, 1733, MPAF, III, 592–93.

[22] Bienville and Salmon to Maurepas, February 2, 1732, May 12, 1733, and April 8, 1734, *ibid.*, 562, 592, 662–64; Bossu, *Travels*, 31, 47; Helen H. Cruzat (trans.), "The Concession at Natchez [1731]," *LHQ*, VIII (July, 1925), 389–97; J. F. H. Claiborne, *Mississippi as a Province, Territory and State* (Jackson, 1880), 68, 84–85, 92–93.

As the Seven Years' War with England neared its end, the French without reluctance ceded Louisiana west of the Mississippi and the Isle de Orleans, which included New Orleans, to the Spanish in 1762 at Fontainebleau. In negotiations at Paris in early 1763 the French transferred to the British the area east of the Mississippi to the Appalachians, extending from the Iberville River, then a tributary of the Mississippi below Baton Rouge, to the Great Lakes.

Even in the pre-1729 period when Natchez was one of the most promising French posts in the North American interior, Louisiana as a whole had proven to be a serious economic liability to the home government. Her exports had never approximated the expenses entailed in maintaining the colony. Poor administrators, insufficient troops and supplies, bungling Indian policies, and disappointing trickles of immigrants had characterized the French experience. Except for the immigration factor, Natchez was a microcosm of French ineptitude in the Lower Mississippi Valley.[23]

The British province of West Florida was established in October, 1763, under the famous proclamation which also provided for creation of the provinces of East Florida and Quebec and prohibition of white settlement in the vast transmontane region north of the 31st parallel. But it early became evident to officials at Pensacola, the capital of West Florida, that the key to the province's future development lay along the Mississippi, especially if the border were extended northward to the Yazoo. In the western sector the main tribes, the Choctaw and Chickasaw, were less formidable than the hostile Creek north of Pensacola. The fertile alluvial lands along the great river afforded a sharp contrast to the barren, sandy soil around Pensacola. Also possibilities looked promising for capturing the Illinois fur trade before it got to New Orleans, supplying the backwoods settlers of

[23] Louise P. Kellogg, "France and the Mississippi Valley: A Résume," *MVHR*, XVIII (June, 1931), 16–17; E. Wilson Lyon, *Louisiana in French Diplomacy, 1759–1804* (Norman, Okla., 1934), 13–54. On the role of Natchez in French Louisiana, see also Marcel Giraud, *Histoire de la Louisiane Francaise* (3 vols.; Paris, 1953–66).

the English colonies to the north, and exploiting the Spanish trade along the Mississippi. The dons, who held the west bank, rarely enforced their trade laws forbidding intercourse with the British, and the Paris Treaty gave the English free navigation of the Mississippi.[24]

At the request of Governor George Johnstone of West Florida, the Board of Trade in 1764 issued a supplementary commission authorizing extension of the province's boundary northward to a line running from the conflux of the Yazoo and Mississippi east to the Chattahoochee River. Thus, whereas the border stipulated in the Proclamation of 1763 had been the 31st parallel, now Natchez was included in the domain of West Florida. Later Johnstone obtained a treaty with the Choctaw whereby they recognized this new boundary.[25]

Despite the advantages mentioned, early promotion of settlement at Natchez faced handicaps. After a British army unit was ambushed by Tunica Indians downriver from Natchez, the governor was slow to authorize travel in that region, fearing "an equal Risque of Disappointment and Disgrace." His scheme to lure French and German malcontents in Spanish Louisiana to move across the river failed to materialize. Moreover, bitter internal wrangling among officials, troubles with the Pensacola populace, and growing friction with the Creek made Johnstone reluctant to dispatch troops to the western edge of the province. As late as summer, 1766, the West Florida Assembly reported that the Natchez fort lay "useless and Neglected."[26]

[24] Proclamation of October 7, 1763, in Adam Shortt and Arthur G. Doughty (eds.), *Documents Relating to the Constitutional History of Canada, 1759–1791* (2nd ed., 2 vols.; Ottawa, 1918), I, 163–68; Cecil Johnson, "Expansion in West Florida, 1770–1779," *MVHR*, XX (March, 1934), 481–84; Garland Taylor, "Colonial Settlement and Early Revolutionary Activities in West Florida Up to 1779," *ibid.*, XXII (December, 1935), 351–52; Clarence E. Carter, "The Beginnings of British West Florida," *ibid.*, IV (March, 1918), 314–19.

[25] West Florida supplementary commission, June, 1764, in W. L. Grant and James Munro (eds.), *Acts of the Privy Council of England, Colonial Series, 1613–1783* (6 vols.; London, 1908–12), IV, 668; Choctaw treaty of March 26, 1765, *MPAE*, 252.

[26] Captain James Campbell to Governor George Johnstone, December 12, 1764, *MPAE*, 267; Johnstone to John Pownall, February 19 and May 4, 1765, *ibid.*, 233–34, 280; Alexander Maclellan to Johnstone, December 10, 1764, *ibid.*, 268–69.

Geographic isolation proved to be a major deterrent to the development of a British settlement at Natchez. The journey to Pensacola, necessary in transactions ranging from land claims to criminal trials, involved a tedious trip of four hundred miles. The traveler had to go down the Mississippi to the Iberville, whose course followed what is now known as Bayou Manchac, and the southern-most section of what is now the Amite River, entering Lakes Maurepas and Pontchartrain, and on into the Gulf of Mexico. The return was more difficult, since it entailed travel upstream against the Mississippi's strong current. Poling, warping, rowing, and even sailing were tried, but none was very satisfactory. A poor alternative was to go overland from Manchac, a settlement on the east bank of the Mississippi below Baton Rouge, along a rough wilderness trail that meandered northward to Natchez. Because of the isolated position of Natchez, as well as the province's lack of funds, ships, and troops, it was impossible for Johnstone to maintain close communications with the settlement or to guarantee the security of would-be settlers on the bluff.

He did authorize a detachment of forty-eight Scots Fusiliers to be stationed there in early autumn, 1766. The old French structure was renamed Fort Panmure, but there were no attendant improvements. In order to cut colonial defense costs, however, General Thomas Gage in 1768 ordered the abandonment of the fort, along with Fort Bute at Manchac and several other frontier posts which the British commander deemed dispensable. A protest from Pensacola authorities, stating that the withdrawal would curtail an impending population surge, was to no avail. Montfort Browne, acting governor at the time, did manage to provide a few arms and munitions for the hapless settlers at Natchez.[27]

[27] General Thomas Gage to Lieutenant-Governor Montfort Browne, June 27, 1768, PRO, 5:585, 181; Lord Hillsborough to Gage, April 15, 1768, in Clarence E. Carter (ed.), *The Correspondence of General Thomas Gage with the Secretaries of State, 1763–1775* (2 vols.; New Haven, 1931–33), II, 61–66; Browne to Hillsborough, August 16 and December 1, 1768, MPAE Manuscripts, III, 115, 221–24; Luis de Unzaga y Amezaga to Marqués de Grimaldi, June 8, 1770, in

Despite the area's lack of protection and because of a land-speculation craze that gripped colonists and officials alike, thirty-nine land grants in the Natchez region were approved between May, 1766, and February, 1769. These ranged in size from 20,000 acres, belonging to the Earl of Eglinton, to 140 acres. Other grantees later prominent at Natchez were Daniel Clark, Sr., with three thousand acres, and John Blommart, with one thousand acres.[28] The West Florida governor was authorized to make such grants on generous terms under authority of royal mandamus, the Proclamation of 1763, or by special instruction from the Board of Trade. As elsewhere in the English colonies, land distribution at Natchez was probably accompanied by a considerable degree of abuse and fraud, abetted by the speculative fever. Many grants, including Eglinton's, were not improved, and little effort was exerted by most grantees to attract colonists.[29]

In 1768, Montfort Browne visited Natchez, where he "discovered the most charming prospects in the world." He proposed to the Board of Trade that another province be created for that country with him as governor, that a town be laid out at Natchez, and a road constructed from it to Mobile. But the board turned deaf ears to his enthusiastic outburst, and Natchez continued to languish as a settlement. Its numbers were so inconspicuous that it was not represented in the West Florida Assembly, wherein Mobile and Pensacola each had six delegates and even the unpromising village of Campbelltown had two. Recurring strife and factionalism at Pensacola thwarted any efforts at concerted action in promoting settlement along the Mississippi. In January, 1770, the fortunes of the scantily populated Natchez area sank to a new ebb when a band of rum-crazed Choctaw pillaged a number of farms and wrecked the sole trading post, operated by John

Lawrence Kinnaird (ed.), "Spain in the Mississippi Valley, 1765–1794: Translations of Materials from the Spanish Archives in the Bancroft Library," *AHA 1945*, II, 170–71.

[28] Compiled from "Analysis of Land Grants," in Clinton N. Howard, *The British Development of West Florida, 1763–1769* (Berkeley, 1947), 74–101.

[29] Grant and Munro, *Acts of the Privy Council*, IV, 668–69; Cecil Johnson, *British West Florida, 1763–1783* (New Haven, 1943), 120–22.

Bradley and Henry Fairchild. Most of the settlers fled down-river to Manchac.[30]

Glowing reports by army officers and travelers of the region's potentiality helped to spur a small immigration later that year. Two popular travelogues appeared to dispel the unfavorable picture left by early French writers. In *The Present State of the European Settlements on the Mississippi,* Philip Pittman, an army surveyor in the province, described the Natchez region as "the finest and most fertile part of West Florida." He assured his readers that "the trouble of going up [the bluff] is recompensed by the sight of a most delightful country of great extent, the prospect of which is beautifully varied by a number of little hills and fine meadows."[31] John H. Wynne, another English visitor in the 1760's, argued in his *General History of the British Empire in America* that the government should develop a major colony at Natchez: "If we compare this with the barren deserts of Canada and Florida, what a wide difference is there!"[32]

In mid-1770, seventy-nine settlers and eighteen slaves arrived at Natchez from Fort Pitt. Their claim that one hundred more colonists might be coming shortly prompted Peter Chester, the new governor, to ask London for permission to construct a canal shortening the Natchez–Mobile route and reestablish the military post on the bluff. The British colonial secretary did not object to Chester's encouragement of settlement at Natchez, but no action was forthcoming on the proposed canal or post.[33]

[30] Browne to Hillsborough, June 27, 1768, PRO, 5:584, 147–64; John Bradley to Elias Durnford, February 1, 1770, *ibid.,* 5:577, 233–40; Browne to Earl of Shelburne, July 6, 1768, in Clinton N. Howard, "Colonial Natchez: The Early British Period," *JMH,* VII (July, 1945), 163–70; James A. Padgett (ed.), "The Reply of Peter Chester, Governor of West Florida, to Complaints Made against His Administration," *LHQ,* XXII (January, 1939), 31–46; Moreau B. C. Chambers, "The History of Fort Panmure at Natchez, 1763–1775" (unpublished M.A. thesis, Duke University, 1942), 41, 105–106.

[31] Philip Pittman, *The Present State of the European Settlements on the Mississippi . . . ,* ed. Frank H. Hodder (Cleveland, 1906), 24–25, 78.

[32] John H. Wynne, *General History of the British Empire in America* (2 vols.; London, 1770), II, 401, 407.

[33] Deposition of Daniel Huay, August 25, 1770, PRO, 5:578, 71–72; John Mc-

Undismayed, Chester busied himself in the next three years with numbers of grants at or near Natchez, some being of vast size: for example, 152,000 acres to Anthony Hutchins and his associates from Virginia and the Carolinas; 150,000 acres to the Company of Military Adventurers, a group of Connecticut veterans of the Seven Years' War led by Phineas and Thaddeus Lyman, Israel and Rufus Putnam, and Roger Enos; 25,000 acres to Amos Ogden, a Pensacola justice of the peace and former naval captain who also got 15,000 acres reserved for the New Jersey colonists he promised to attract; 20,000 acres to English brothers John and Richard Ellis; 20,000 acres to a New Jersey group led by Congregationalist minister Samuel Swayzey; and 20,000 acres to a land company headed by Montfort Browne. Most of Chester's grantees failed to settle as much as 15 per cent of their large tracts. Ogden, for instance, could not draw settlers and early sold 19,000 acres to the Swayzey group, whose "Jersey Settlement" on the Homochitto River southeast of Natchez was one of the few successful colonizing ventures of the period.[34]

Two major changes in land policy brought despair and hope in quick succession for Natchez in the years from 1773 to 1775. Noting the free grants issued without surveys in pell-mell fashion

---

Intyre to Governor Peter Chester, July 19, 1770, *ibid.*, 75; Hillsborough to Chester, February 11, 1771, MPAE Manuscripts, IV, 505–506; Eron Rowland (ed.), "Peter Chester, Third Governor of the Province of West Florida," *PMHS Centenary*, V (1925), 58–90.

[34] Survey contract of Amos Ogden, Joseph King, Samuel and Richard Swayzey, June 15, 1772, Benjamin L. C. Wailes Papers, Mississippi Department of Archives and History, hereinafter cited as Mississippi Archives. Survey map of 1789 showing British and Spanish grants to John and Richard Ellis, William N. Mercer Papers, LSU; Thomas Hutchins, *An Historical Narrative and Topographical Description of Louisiana and West-Florida . . .* (Philadelphia, 1784), 49–52; Bernard Romans, *A Concise Natural History of East and West Florida* (New York, 1775), 221–25; Eron Rowland, "Mississippi's Colonial Population and Land Grants," *PMHS Centenary*, I (1916), 405–17; Mark Van Dorne (ed.), *The Travels of William Bartram* (New York, 1940), 344–47; Cecil Johnson, "The Distribution of Land in British West Florida," *LHQ*, XVI (October, 1933), 639–53; W. Magruder Drake, "A Note on the Jersey Settlers of Adams County," *JMH*, XV (October, 1953), 274–75. Hutchins was colonial geographer-general, Romans a Dutch engineer employed in West Florida surveying, and Bartram an English botanist; each visited Natchez about 1772–73.

by governors like Chester, the Board of Trade in 1773 decided to convert ungranted lands into a source of income to meet imperial expenses in America. The new order prohibited further issuance of land warrants except in a few restricted categories. Chester futilely castigated the home government for its indifference toward his province. Fortunately for West Florida's expansion, British officials became anxious to find refuge for fearful Tories along the Atlantic seaboard when the American Revolution exploded. In late 1775 the board advised Chester that the restrictions on grants were to be relaxed for incoming Loyalists. Also their lands, unlike those of earlier grantees, were to be free of quitrents (fixed rent) for the first decade after settlement.[35]

The population of West Florida increased rapidly with the subsequent influx of Loyalists, particularly along the Mississippi where land was most plentiful and rich. Whereas in 1774 about 2,500 whites and 600 Negroes resided in the area from the mouth of the Yazoo to Manchac, the number more than doubled in the next four years and considerably exceeded that of the eastern portion of the province. Infant rural settlements sprang up along the Mississippi at Bayou Pierre, Big Black River, and Walnut Hills, as well as at Natchez and Manchac.

Pursuant to a survey ordered by Chester in February, 1776, an unimposing town was laid out at the Natchez landing. At the end of the year it consisted of "10 log houses and 2 frame houses, all situated under the bluff." The river, which today laps close to the bluff, ran at that time about one-eighth of a mile to the west. Seventy-eight families, most of whom had arrived since 1772, resided at the landing or in the nearby countryside. The settlement was given a justice of the peace, a deputy for affida-

[35] Chester to Lord Dartmouth, November 20, 1775, MPAE Manuscripts, VI, 441–42; Clarence W. Alvord, *The Mississippi Valley in British Politics: A Study of the Trade, Land Speculation, and Experiments in Imperialism Culminating in the American Revolution* (2 vols., New York, 1959), II, 212–15; Peter J. Hamilton, "British West Florida," *PMHS*, VII (1904), 415–26; Clarence E. Carter, "Some Aspects of British Administration in West Florida," *MVHR*, I (December, 1915), 370–74; Wilbur H. Seibert, "Loyalists in West Florida and the Natchez District," *ibid.*, II (March, 1916), 469–74.

vits, and a court of requests. A start had been made, but the residents were disappointed that the garrison was not restored.[36]

As justice of the peace, Anthony Hutchins was well suited to serve as the community's chief magistrate and leading spokesman. After serving with distinction in the Seven Years' War, he had spent several years as a sheriff in North Carolina. In 1772 he had moved with his family to the fertile Second Creek bottomlands southeast of the bluff. Besides being the area's largest landholder and planter, he was also the commercial agent at Natchez for the London commission house of John Miller and Company. A relative described Hutchins as "a man of marked characteristics, courageous, active, of restless and indomitable spirit." Retained on a half-pay colonel's status by the British until 1798, he would be looked to for counsel and leadership by British settlers for many years.[37]

Trade and commerce came soon to the young community. By December, 1776, there were four mercantile stores at the landing, including one owned by John Blommart, a half-pay British army captain, and another owned by James Willing, a well-educated but dissipated young man from an influential Philadelphia family. Both Blommart and Willing also held thousand-acre grants atop the bluff. Louis Le Fleur, father of a celebrated Choctaw chieftain of a later era, operated with handsome profits the main boat shuttle to Pensacola, carrying produce and commodities. Orders for luxury items, including cases of madeira, cognac, and port, as well as fine apparel, were placed with Panton, Leslie, and Company of St. Marks in East Florida. In view of a Spanish estimate in 1776 that 98 per cent of the $600,000 annual commerce of colonial Louisiana went to the English in illicit river

[36] Elias Durnford to Dartmouth, January 15, 1774, PRO, 5:591, 9–32; Minutes of West Florida Council, February 27 and November 8, 1776, *ibid.*, 5:631; Benjamin L. C. Wailes, *Report on the Agriculture and Geology of Mississippi, Embracing a Sketch of the Social and Natural History of the State* (Philadelphia, 1854), 61–62; W. M. Carpenter (ed.), "The Mississippi River in the Olden Time, a Genuine Account of the Present State of the River Mississippi and of the Land on its Banks to the River Yasous, 1776," *De Bow's Review*, III (1847), 115–23.

[37] Claiborne, *Mississippi*, 106–08, 127, 132, 172, 203.

trade, undoubtedly part of the economic growth of Natchez is attributable to its role in this lucrative traffic. The town was also well situated as a focal point for the interior fur trade of the British and for the province's western Indian trade.[38]

The small, motley populace at the landing belied the fact that many settlers preferred to build in the neighboring countryside, especially those who boasted some degree of affluence. By 1776 Hutchins of Second Creek and John Ellis of White Cliffs (later Ellis' Cliffs) south of the fort were already regarded as "large planters." Ellis, a member of the Royal Society of London, owned the region's only sizable library. Bernard Lintot, a recent arrival from Connecticut, was another large landholder south of the bluff; later he would increase his acreage and would also control several mercantile houses. Other settlers living along the outlying creeks included William Marshall, John Turner, Job Routh, and William Vousdan, each of whose families would enjoy prosperity and influence in later times. The principal exports of these men and their neighbors were tobacco, lumber, and indigo.[39]

The Hutchinses and Ellises were few, but the number of those who faced excruciating hardships on the rugged, isolated frontier were many. For example, Mathew Phelps, a retired army captain who obtained a grant above Natchez, started upriver from Manchac in the autumn of 1776 with his family and another household. At Natchez he saw his wife, two of his children, and

[38] A. Strothers to Bernard Lintot, August 6, 1779, William J. Minor and Family Papers, LSU; Account book of Alexander Ross and William Dunbar, entries of March-April, 1778, UNC; Memoir of Francisco Bouligny, 1776, in Alcée Fortier, A History of Louisiana (4 vols.; New York, 1904), II, 25–53; Wailes, Report, 61; Lucy M. McMillan, "Natchez, 1763–1779" (unpublished M.A. thesis, University of Virginia, 1938), 18–46.

[39] Minutes of West Florida Council, January 8, 1776, August 29, 1777, and January 7, 1779, PRO, 5:631, 5:635; Mathew Phelps, Memoirs and Adventures of Captain Mathew Phelps . . . ed. Anthony Haswell (Bennnigton, Vt., 1802), 33–34; Albert C. Bates (ed.), The Two Putnams, Israel and Rufus . . . (Hartford, 1931), 194–202, 237–38; May W. McBee (comp.), The Natchez Court Records, 1767–1805: Abstracts of Early Records (2 vols.; Ann Arbor, 1953), II, 597; Various entries of 1777–78, Adams County Deed Record, Vol. A, Adams County Chancery Clerk's Office Records, Natchez.

the other family die from "fevers." As Phelps moved upstream, the vessel capsized, his other two children drowned, and all of his belongings were lost. For three years he worked to develop a farm near Natchez, but finally quit in dejection and went back to New England. Jedediah Smith, Yale graduate and Presbyterian minister, left his Massachusetts pastorate under pressure from anti-Loyalists and in late 1776 sailed for Natchez with his wife and eleven children. One week after their arrival Smith died, leaving his twelve dependents to fend for themselves. His widow chose to stay and somehow succeeded in rearing most of her children to adulthood. Another immigrant, John Smith, brought his family from Pennsylvania in 1768. After struggling for two years to eke out an existence, he moved to Pensacola. In 1777 he obtained another grant near Natchez, doggedly returned, and by the time of his death in 1804 possessed two thousand acres and nearly a hundred slaves.[40]

The new American government was aware of the strategic value of the growing Natchez region. Proposals to invade the area were studied by the Continental Congress but were dropped because of lack of men and means and an uncertainty of Spain's reaction. Colonel George Morgan, who had visited Natchez, and financier Robert Morris, business associate of James Willing's brother, were among the principal advocates of an American conquest. Most persistent on the matter was Oliver Pollock, wealthy merchant and American commercial agent at New Orleans; he insisted that at least three thousand troops should be sent downriver against the British. Pollock also personally subsidized the provisioning of General George Rogers Clark's forces in the Illinois country. In August, 1776, Captain George Gibson stopped briefly at Natchez on a supply trip to New Orleans, audaciously hauled down the British colors, and raised the Ameri-

[40] Phelps, *Memoirs and Adventures*, 32–35, 163–89; McBee, *Natchez Court Records*, II, 600; Anonymous planter's schedule of agricultural expansion, 1776–86, Mississippi Miscellaneous Papers, Library of Congress; Isabel Calder (ed.), *Colonial Captivities, Marches and Journeys* (New York, 1935), 228–43.

can flag. An alarmed Chester warned Bernardo de Gálvez, Louisiana governor, to halt the Spanish-American collaboration and pleaded with London for vessels in order to station river patrols at Natchez and Manchac.[41]

The only armed incursion by Americans into the area was led by James Willing. Unsuccessful as a Natchez merchant, Willing returned to Philadelphia where he gained a commission as a naval captain, perhaps through Morris' influence. His official instructions, since lost, were probably to carry certain dispatches to Pollock and Gálvez, procure supplies at New Orleans for troops in the Northwest, and confiscate or destroy whatever British property he found along the Mississippi. Leaving Fort Pitt in early 1778 aboard the gunboat *Rattletrap,* he attracted over a hundred frontier adventurers to his expedition by the time it reached the Natchez country.[42]

Willing occupied Natchez on February 19 and proclaimed falsely that Clark would soon follow with a five-thousand-man army. He then forced a committee of large landholders, representing the frightened local citizens, to pledge that they would not "in any wise take up arms against the United States of America or aid, abet, or in any wise give assistance to the enemies of the said States." In turn, the committee secured assurances from Willing, first, "that our persons, Slaves, and other property of what kind soever shall remain safe & unmolested during our neutrality," and, second, "that Capt. Willing shall Engage to send a Flag of Truce to the Choctaw Indians to give out a talk with a Belt, to prevent the Indians falling on the Defenceless In-

[41] Edmund C. Burnett (ed.), *Letters of Members of the Continental Congress* (8 vols.; Washington, 1921–36), II, 445–49; Chester to St. Germain, October 26, 1776, PRO, 5:593, 81; Chester to Unzaga, November 4, 1776, *ibid.,* 113; James A. James, *Oliver Pollock: The Life and Times of an Unknown Patriot* (New York, 1937), 105–16, 127–28; James, "Spanish Influence in the West during the American Revolution," *MVHR,* IV (December, 1917), 193–208; Kathryn T. Abbey, "Peter Chester's Defense of the Mississippi after the Willing Raid," *ibid.,* XXII (June, 1935), 17–18.

[42] John Caughey, "Willing's Expedition Down the Mississippi, 1778," *LHQ,* XV (January, 1932), 9–10; Burnett, *Letters,* II, 565; Chambers, "History of Fort Panmure," 88–90.

habitants."[43] Eighty volunteers from the Natchez country joined Willing's band; many were probably riffraff eager for plunder. The most reluctant person departing downriver with Willing was Anthony Hutchins, who was taken as a hostage after the raiders pillaged his plantation.

En route to New Orleans, Willing's band indulged in widespread plundering, seizing English boats, looting farms on the east bank, and devastating Manchac. William Dunbar, a Scot whose plantation above Manchac suffered heavily, remarked: "All was fish that came in their path."[44] While the raiders were disposing of their loot in New Orleans, the Natchez citizens broke their pledge and frantically urged Chester to send troops. Hearing of this, Willing dispatched a force under Lieutenant Richard Harrison toward the town. On April 16 Hutchins, who had escaped his captors in New Orleans, led a hastily-organized local group which defeated Harrison near Ellis' Cliffs. The retired British officer took great pride in reporting to Chester that "the American colors were soon torn down and now lay dejected at our feet and those of the Britannic Majesty most splendidly appear in triumph."[45] By May, Chester's troops had secured Natchez, and several months later Willing was captured by the British as he tried to flee northward.[46]

Only Hutchins' property was plundered at Natchez, but the inhumanity and lack of restraint exhibited elsewhere by Willing harmed the American cause at Natchez and spread dissension among its residents. Some who had favored American occupation fled to Galveztown, a new settlement immediately south of the Iberville. Governor Gálvez was only too happy to afford "friendly protection to all those that came to the Spanish Ter-

[43] Pledge of the Natchez delegates, February 21, 1778, PRO, 5:579, 177; Phelps, *Memoirs and Adventures*, 111–12. The signers were Isaac Johnson, Luke Collins, William Hiern, Joseph Thomson, Samuel Wells, Charles Percy, and Richard Ellis.

[44] Journal of William Dunbar, entry of May 1, 1778, William Dunbar Papers, Mississippi Archives.

[45] Anthony Hutchins to Chester, May 21, 1778, PRO, 5:594, 475.

[46] Abbey, "Peter Chester's Defense of the Mississippi," 30.

ritory."[47] Of course, the anti-American bias of the Loyalist
majority at Natchez was further confirmed by Willing's outrageous behavior. But a number of citizens, including some Englishmen, vented their wrath against the Pensacola authorities for
neglecting the fort. A British officer who visited the town in
July, 1778, reported that "twenty Men Properly conducted"
could take the place in view of "the total *Want of Discipline*
which at present prevails, and the little Harmony and Confidence
in each other which unhappily reigns too much among the
People."[48]

As consequences of the raid, Chester's forces were reinforced,
a new fort was built at Manchac, the patrol on the river was enlarged, and by early fall a small garrison was stationed at Fort
Panmure. Furthermore, for the first time Natchez was given
representation in the West Florida Assembly, partly because of
its population growth but also because of the government's desire
to placate its malcontents. The Natchez District was created with
boundaries roughly the same as under the French. It was allotted
four delegates to the assembly session at Pensacola in June,
1778—the same number as allowed to Mobile and Manchac
(Pensacola had eight). An assembly resolution was passed
recognizing the gallantry of Natchez delegates Hutchins and
Thaddeus Lyman in the battle at Ellis' Cliffs. The most far-
reaching consequence of the Willing episode, however, was its
revelation to Gálvez that only great weakness on the part of the
Americans had saved the western part of the province for the
British.[49]

Turmoil was destined to continue at Natchez for another six
months. Captain Michael Jackson, who was appointed commandant of Fort Panmure, was already known to the local people
as a horse thief and scoundrel. His rule became so objectionable

[47] Captain Donald Campbell to John Stuart, PRO, 5:579, 131.
[48] James Dallas to Colonel John McGillivray, July 3, 1778, in *AHA 1945*, II,
291–92.
[49] Colonel McGillivray to Governor Bernardo de Gálvez, October 7, 1778, *ibid.*,
308–309; Johnson, *British West Florida*, 99, 108; Abbey, "Peter Chester's Defense
of the Mississippi," 31–32.

that both citizens and soldiers supported a mutiny which Hutchins, Lyman, and Mathew Phelps led. In comic-opera fashion Jackson rallied some men to his side, retook the fort, court-martialed one of the mutineers, and then lost control of the fort again. The chaos did not end until Jackson's superior removed him on misconduct charges and sent Captain Anthony Forster as the fort commandant in January, 1779.[50]

Meanwhile the appointment of Gálvez as Louisiana governor had been followed by a heightening of Anglo-Spanish tensions, featuring seizures of river vessels by both sides. As early as the winter of 1778–79, Gálvez was preparing for war and was taking careful account of "the real purpose" of military movements in West Florida. Finally, when news of the long-awaited Spanish declaration of war against England came in July, 1779, Gálvez was free from "the rule of neutrality that the Court has imposed upon us."[51]

With boldness and speed he struck along the Mississippi in early autumn. Upon his surrender at Baton Rouge, Lieutenant Colonel Alexander Dickson sent word to Captain Forster at Natchez to capitulate. Oliver Pollock, now aide-de-camp to Gálvez, wrote a general letter to the Natchez citizenry urging their friendly cooperation with the "merciful" dons. Fifty-nine residents (but excluding Hutchins) replied in a letter to Dickson that they appreciated his efforts against the Spanish and would welcome the troops of Gálvez, "a brave and generous Conqueror" —plaudits which they knew the governor would read.[52] On October 5, the eighty grenadiers at Fort Panmure meekly surrendered to Captain Juan Delavillebeuvre, who served the next nineteen months as Natchez commandant.[53]

[50] Phelps, *Memoirs and Adventures*, 125–87.

[51] Gálvez to Diego Joseph Navarro, February 5 and March 8, 1779, Galveztown Papers, LSU; Seibert, "Loyalists in West Florida," 470–74; Kathryn T. Abbey, "Efforts of Spain to Maintain Sources of Information in the Colonies before 1779," *MVHR*, XV (September, 1928), 63–68.

[52] Kenneth Scott (ed.), "Britian Loses Natchez, 1779: An Unpublished Letter," *JMH*, XXVI (February, 1964), 45–46.

[53] John Caughey, *Bernardo de Gálvez in Louisiana, 1766–1783* (Berkeley,

The story of resistance at Natchez did not terminate, however, with the easy capture of the fort. Because of his offensive operations against Mobile and Pensacola, Gálvez neglected defenses on the bluff. Delavillebeuvre bewailed "the general wretchedness of everything" at the fort: the roofs leaked so much that "one has to sit on high stools"; thievery was so rampant that "his majesty has now no more than two horses" for the entire garrison; and, most humiliating, "enormous numbers of rats" stole the soldiers' grain—"the cats are even afraid of them." More significant was this comment: "I know of no one faithful in all this district."[54]

Aware of the weak Spanish hold on Natchez, General John Campbell, British provincial commander, tried to instigate an insurrection by sending officer commissions to likely Loyalist leaders. The appointments, which were identical, read: "I do therefore . . . appoint you a Captain or Leader of such Vounteer Inhabitants as you can procure to serve under your Command who prefer the British Government to Tyrannick [sic] despotism and Rule and are willing to risk their lives for the attainment thereof."[55] John Blommart was elected leader of the plot to oust the dons. On April 22, 1781, he and two hundred rebels compelled Delavillebeuvre to surrender after deceiving him into thinking that the fort was undermined with explosives. Those known to have participated included a majority of the signees of the Dickson letter praising the "brave and generous" Gálvez.[56]

No sooner had they occupied the fort, however, than the conspirators splintered into factions. A group led by John and Philip Alston and John Turner demanded execution of the Spanish garrison, raising of the American flag, and division of the spoils taken at the fort. But, probably because of stronger public sup-

---

1934), 149–59; AHA 1945, II, xxix–xxx; Jac Nacbin, "Spain's Report of the War with the British in West Florida," LHQ, XIV (July, 1931), 468–81.

[54] Anna Lewis (ed.), "Fort Panmure, 1779, as Related by Juan Delavillebeuvre to Bernardo de Gálvez," MVHR, XVIII (March, 1932), 542–47.

[55] Quoted in Caughey, Bernardo de Gálvez, 216.

[56] John Caughey, "The Natchez Rebellion of 1781 and Its Aftermath," LHQ, XVI (January, 1933), 57–59.

port, Blommart and Hutchins gained the upper hand. The former assumed military command, while Hutchins, an eleventh-hour joiner in the plot, resumed his former duties as chief magistrate. The Spanish troops were sent under guard to Baton Rouge, the British flag was raised, and the Blommart–Hutchins faction kept a close watch over commissary distributions at the fort.[57]

Then came the shocking news several weeks later that Gálvez had captured Pensacola, with Chester admitting the capitulation of all of West Florida. Recalling the harsh Spanish reprisals against French insurgents at New Orleans in 1768, many of the rebels fled through the forests to Georgia and South Carolina, to the Cumberland region, or to asylum among the Chickasaw and Choctaw. On June 23 the Spanish marched back into the fort without a fight. After oaths of loyalty were administered to 240 residents, the dons imprisoned four ringleaders who had remained at the fort, including Blommart. Gálvez showed surprising mercy, though, and within two years had released the four while offering amnesty to the rest of the rebels. Some who had fled then returned to their homes—including Hutchins, who had led a group of the insurrectionists on a harrowing overland trek to Charleston.[58]

The aftermath of the episode was an uprising along the Mississippi north to Natchez. Led by James Colbert, a roving band of six hundred whites and Chickasaw ambushed Spanish travelers through most of the year 1782. Some of Colbert's key lieutenants were Natchez rebels, including Turner and the Alstons. Prompted by them, the eccentric bandit leader offered Estevan Miró, the new Spanish governor, a number of kidnapped Spaniards in exchange for the Natchez prisoners held in New Orleans, but no deal was consummated. Possibly in an effort to persuade Miró, Colbert confided: "As for the white People that left Notches [*sic*] I much blame them for not Remaining in Peace till war was desided between grat Brittain & Spain." With news of the peace

[57] *Ibid.*, 60–69; Caughey, *Bernardo de Gálvez*, 217–20; *AHA 1945*, II, xxxi–xxxii.
[58] Caughey, *Bernardo de Gálvez*, 220–28.

treaty of 1783, both Colbert and Miró freed their prisoners, and the uprising soon subsided.[59]

Official cognizance indicates that the Blommart and Colbert affairs were considered major menaces to Hispanic control of the Lower Mississippi. Gálvez, who was promoted to captain general of Louisiana and the Floridas in 1781, delayed his transfer to Havana for three months in order to further interrogate Blommart. The next year Miró led reinforcements to Natchez and stayed there five months, personally supervising defensive preparations.[60]

Serious opposition to Spanish occupation ceased at Natchez after the rebellion of 1781, though some Loyalists who moved elsewhere continued to cry in vain for a British recapture. In 1782, preliminary peace talks began in Paris.[61] Unlike the negotiations of 1763, when the colonial town was not a factor in the diplomatic parlaying, the treaties of Paris two decades later were signed only after considerable deliberation and maneuvering that directly involved Natchez. In the preliminary treaty of 1782 between the United States and England, the American boundary was to be fixed at the mouth of the Yazoo (32° 26′) if the British recaptured West Florida before the cessation of hostilities. The definitive Anglo-American treaty, signed September 3, 1783, fixed the southern line of the United States at the 31st parallel despite actual possession by the Spanish up to the Yazoo. It also reserved free navigation rights on the Mississippi for both British and American subjects, again despite Spanish control of the river. On the other hand, the definitive Anglo-Spanish treaty, signed the same day, stipulated that the dons were to "retain" West Florida, whose boundaries were left undefined. The latter document made no mention of Mississippi navigation. Conde de

[59] Ibid., 228–42; Caughey, "Natchez Rebellion," 70–83. On the Blommart and Colbert uprisings, see also letters of Gálvez and Miró in AHA 1945, II, 425–26, III, 8, 15–20, 55, 60, 71–73.

[60] Caughey, "Natchez Rebellion," 83; Juan Manuel de Cagigal to Miró, August 30, 1782, in AHA 1945, III, 55.

[61] Jack D. L. Holmes, "Robert Ross' Plan for an English Invasion of Louisiana in 1782," Louisiana History, V (Spring, 1964), 161–64, 175.

Floridablanca, secretary of state to King Carlos III, tried in vain to get the western line of the United States fixed far to the east of the Mississippi. He also argued that, since England had transferred to America that which was not hers to bestow, Spain would recognize neither the English cession regarding the northern boundary of West Florida nor the clause in the American treaty relating to navigation rights on the river. The next dozen years, which would be fraught with controversy over these treaties, were destined to show how precarious was the Spanish hold on the Mississippi and on its east bank above the 31st parallel.[62]

During the century from La Salle's expedition to the Peace of 1783, each regime that had controlled Natchez made a distinctive contribution toward its later development. The French exterminated the hostile Natchez tribe, without which future settlement would have been most difficult. But after 1729 the tobacco fields again became forests, and no Frenchman remained to speak the language or to claim title to land. The British walked into an area devoid of people. The main feature of Natchez under the Pensacola government, particularly after 1769, was the growing predominance of British settlers. The citizens would continue under the dons to exhibit more interest in the latest English novel than in the death of an Hispanic monarch. The principal Spanish contribution between 1779 and 1783 was the valuable trade linkage with New Orleans, which had been closed to the British. The only American involvement, the Willing affair, left the residents with an unfavorable impression of the infant United States. That view would gradually change, however, as trade and immigration ties increasingly linked Natchez and the American frontier.

Having suffered inauspicious beginnings in 1716 and 1776, Natchez had become a rural community numbering perhaps five hundred persons by 1783. Most of these lived along Second and

[62] Samuel F. Bemis, *Pinckney's Treaty: A Study of America's Advantage from Europe's Distress, 1783–1800* (New York, 1926), 44–65.

St. Catherine's creeks; it is doubtful that the residents at the bluff landing exceeded one hundred. The community's failure to develop as a center of population and commerce comparable to New Orleans, which then had over four thousand inhabitants and a thriving economy, was largely due to four liabilities common to the French and British periods. First, the sway of mercantilism led the Paris and London colonial offices to stress development of those colonies which provided products most needed at home and, in turn, which had sufficient population to afford promising consumer markets for the mother country's exports. Thus French Louisiana and British West Florida were economic liabilities according to mercantilist criteria. If citizens of New Orleans and Pensacola often felt aggrieved, those at struggling interior posts like Natchez suffered even more from the indifference of Paris and London. Second, officials at French New Orleans and British Pensacola rarely possessed administrative competence and experience. Moreover, they continuously faced monumental problems of inadequate revenues and internal dissension. Therefore they, too, paid scant heed to the problems of distant outposts. Third, the Natchez settlement lay isolated in a frontier wilderness. The nearest centers of population were New Orleans and the Cumberland communities. The Gulf was over three hundred miles away by river. The Mississippi's significance was mounting, but it was not yet a major artery for produce and people in an era when towns owed their population and prosperity to their location near the sea or a heavily-used waterway. Fourth, and closely related to the previous factors, neither the French nor the British regime adequately promoted the cultivation of a staple crop which could produce the export needed for the region's sound economic growth. Whether these liabilities to the settlement's progress would be overcome in the Spanish period remained doubtful in 1783 in view of the tumultuous conditions of the dons' first four years of control. The Spanish, moreover, were beset by a problem which the French and British were spared, namely, the task of ruling an alien white population—and one which had alread tried to revolt.

CHAPTER II

Life Under the

Dons

THE FORTUNES OF NATCHEZ WERE MARK-
edly affected by the Spanish-American
frontier rivalry of 1783–98. Up to 1788 the Spanish strategy for
thwarting the southwestward advance of American settlers called
for a monopoly of traffic on the Mississippi and for development
of the Natchez area as a buffer between lower Louisiana and
the menacing American frontier expansion. In 1784 the dons
closed the river to American navigation. In order to gain local
support for Hispanic overlordship at Natchez, officials in Madrid
decided upon a deviation from their traditional colonial policy.
The British at Natchez, even the prodigals of the Blommart revolt, were permitted to remain as Spanish subjects and without
obligation to become Roman Catholics if they would merely
swear allegiance to the throne. Madrid also guaranteed hard
cash and a ready market to the province's tobacco planters, most
of whom lived in the Pointe Coupee and Natchez areas, by
promising to buy two million pounds of their tobacco yearly at
the premium price of ten dollars per hundred pounds. For a
while at least, the Spanish efforts to insure the loyalty of the
Natchez populace seemed to work. Most of the citizens showed
little desire to be under the regime that had sent Willing.[1]

The Spanish Natchez District was similar in its geographic
and administrative lines to the old British district. Its boundary
was approximately the same, and the fort commandant at
Natchez served as the supreme civil and military head of the
district. His sundry duties consisted of those performed in the

[1] Arthur P. Whitaker, *The Spanish-American Frontier, 1783–1795: The Westward Movement and the Spanish Retreat in the Mississippi Valley* (Boston, 1927),
23, 36, 49, 159.

Tidewater colonies by the land registrar, judge, notary public, sheriff, justice of the peace, and garrison commander. The commandant could appoint local citizens as alguaciles, or minor magistrates, to assist him in administering the various district neighborhoods. In 1783 he was allowed only three alguaciles, but by 1797 the number had risen to twelve.[2]

In 1787 Miró accorded the district signal recognition by converting its administration into a "government," which meant, among other things, that the commandant was supplanted as chief official by a district governor with privileges and powers beyond those granted to the military officers in charge of the other district posts in Louisiana. Among the unique privileges of the new position was that of communicating directly with Madrid ministers and the captain general in Havana. That fall Manuel Gayoso de Lemos, a promising forty-year-old lieutenant colonel, was appointed to the post of district governer. Various delays, including his wife's serious illness, made it impossible for him to assume his duties until 1789. In the meantime Carlos de Grand-Pré, a veteran officer and former Natchez commandant, served as the district's supreme military and civil authority.[3]

During his eight years at Natchez, Gayoso won the admiration and affection of both aristocrats and commoners. A widower shortly after his arrival, he married a daughter of planter Stephen Watts in 1792; again a widower five years later, he married her sister. His marriages, together with the fast pace of luxurious entertainment he provided at his sumptuous mansion, "Concord," soon made him the acknowledged leader of Natchez society. Exhibiting wide learning, good taste in manners and wines, and

[2] Jack D. L. Holmes, *Gayoso: The Life of a Spanish Governor in the Mississippi Valley, 1789–1799* (Baton Rouge, 1965), 18–19. Spanish commandants at Natchez were Juan Delavillebeuvre, 1779–81; Carlos de Grand-Pré, 1781–82; Esteban Miró, 1782; Pedro Joseph Piernas, 1782–83; Francisco Collell [Collett?], 1783; Felipe Treviño, 1783–85; Francisco Bouligny, 1785–86; and Grand-Pré, 1786–89. While Manuel Gayoso de Lemos was district governor, 1789–98, Grand-Pré continued as fort commander during most of that period. Acting district governors in 1797–98 were Stephen Minor and Josef Vidal, the latter continuing as Spanish consul at Natchez for awhile after the Spanish evacuation.

[3] Whitaker, *Spanish-American Frontier*, 82; Holmes, *Gayoso*, 26.

a mastery of English, Gayoso proved highly acceptable to the families of wealth, who felt that he was cast from the same aristocratic mold as they. By handling the reins of government with fairness, competence, and tact, he also won the warm regards of most commoners. Respect for Gayoso's ability extended to New Orleans, where Miró considered him best fitted to be his successor; however, Gayoso was not destined to obtain the Louisiana governorship until 1797.[4]

From the beginning Gayoso turned to influential men of property for counsel and assistance. Among them was William Dunbar, who had moved from the Manchac area to a plantation south of Natchez about 1784; it was Dunbar who laid out an upper town on the bluff from 1787 to 1791. John Girault, a skilled linguist and attorney who had migrated from the Illinois country, became interpreter and keeper of the official records. The adjutant major at the fort was Stephen Minor, a native of Pennsylvania and wealthy landholder from whom Grand-Pré had purchased the tract for the upper town. Among the Spaniards on his staff Gayoso's "right-arm" man and secretary was Josef Vidal, an army captain who also speculated heavily in real estate in Natchez and in what was later to become Concordia Parish, Louisiana, across the river.[5]

In 1795 Gayoso organized a cabildo, or citizens' council, and appointed Dunbar, Vidal, Bernard Lintot, and Joseph Bernard as members. The council, which met twice weekly at the "Government House" at the north end of the esplanade on the bluff, was charged with the administration of justice in civil cases involving amounts up to one hundred dollars. It also had jurisdiction over criminal cases in which punishment was thirty days or less. In more serious civil and criminal cases the council submitted preliminary findings to Gayoso, and the final adjudication was rendered by him or the superior tribunal in New Orleans.

[4] Miró to Campo de Alange, August 11, 1792, in Jack D. L. Holmes (ed.), *Documentos inéditos para la historia de la Louisiana, 1792–1810* (Madrid, 1963), 38–39; Andrew Ellicott, *The Journal of Andrew Ellicott* . . . (Philadelphia, 1803), 215–16; Whitaker, *Spanish-American Frontier*, 82; Holmes, *Gayoso*, 120–26.

[5] Holmes, *Gayoso*, 49–51; McBee, *Natchez Court Records*, II, 595.

The council also handled, subject to Gayoso's approval, such petty matters as applications for grants, permits, and passports.[6]

Gayoso inherited with his office serious problems of law and order, created by a minority of unpropertied persons who could be unruly and at times dangerous. According to Francisco Bouligny, Natchez commandant from 1785 to 1786, chief among the "obstacles to the peace" was the origin of the towns-folk: "The greater part of the inhabitants of this town are natives of North America, others are English royalists, a few are French and very rarely there is a Spaniard." Bouligny also noted that the 1,100 whites and 900 Negroes in the vicinity were mostly isolated along Cole's, St. Catherine's, and Second creeks. "All these places have unsettled lands at their rear, and dwellers may thus absent themselves from the district . . . without any news of it reaching the commandant." In addition, gangs of brigands lived among the Choctaw and Chickasaw, and the Indians some-times joined them in raiding district farms. "The greater part of these vagabonds, dregs of Europe and America, are men abandoned to all vices and capable of committing any crime." Bouligny added that his regulations against outlawry had served "neither to give tranquillity to the honorable inhabitant posses-sing property" nor to instill "the slightest fear or respect in the evil-intentioned accomplices and companions of those vaga-bonds." This he attributed to the lack of troops and his own time-consuming absorption in petty administrative chores. Much of the community's disorderliness stemmed from the visits of rural folk who came to briefly transact some business but then spent "the entire day in the town of Natchez where it is the custom, particularly of the common people, to deliver themselves up to drink with the greatest excess." Lastly, Bouligny observed that some citizens became excited by "the slightest move on the part of America" and by "the smallest reason for discontent here, founded or unfounded," and thereupon "set foot on many schemes" which could do "the greatest harm." Bouligny pro-

[6] Jack D. L. Holmes, "Law and Order in Spanish Natchez, 1781–1798," *JMH*, XXV (July, 1963), 200–201.

posed to Miró that "companies of mounted militia" should be formed in each neighborhood, with captains chosen from "that class of decent persons who have wealth."[7]

Apparently nothing came of Bouligny's proposal until Gayoso's arrival, and conditions remained the same. In 1792 the Baron de Carondelet, Louisiana's new governor, wrote Gayoso that he was "weary of the repeated complaints and representations which various inhabitants of that district have made to me concerning the bad effect produced by the excessively free permission to admit to it, without distinction, all kinds of people." He continued, "I have resolved to tell you not to admit, in the future any vagabond, or any Americans other than those who are landholders or who present themselves with negroes or who are recognized by men of integrity."[8] A few months later Gayoso complained that he was still experiencing "great difficulty in preventing the introduction into it [the district] of people of bad conduct, not only real vagabonds but people who live only from stealing cattle and stirring up disputes among the honorable inhabitants, which disorders increase daily."[9]

When a group of "depraved men" began cattle rustling north of Natchez in 1792, Gayoso sent a constable to arrest Benjamin Pyatte, their leader. The bandits' murder of the officer prompted Gayoso to organize a citizens' patrol of thirty men, headed by Natchez tavern-keeper Richard King. Each militia member received two hundred acres plus four rouls per day and rations for every six months of service. Soon Gayoso proudly reported to Carondelet that they had not only apprehended Pyatte and a counterfeiter named Luis Wetasil but had also "stopped the excesses which in other years were experienced from men of Kentucky who were returning to their country, stealing horses, and committing other disorders." He concluded: "The mere name of this company keeps this district in tranquillity, and the

[7] Francisco Bouligny to Miró, August 22, 1785, in *AHA 1945*, III, 136–42.

[8] Baron de Carondelet to Manuel Gayoso de Lemos, May 12, 1792, AGI, legajo 18.

[9] Gayoso to Carondelet, September 15, 1792, *ibid.*, leg. 41.

kind of people who were accustomed to come without a pass-
port depart."[10] This was overly optimistic since, according to
travelers, Natchez under-the-Hill by the 1790's had become infamous as the river's worst den of prostitutes, gamblers, and
rabble-rousers, while the upper town was no more tranquil than
any other frontier community. At least Gayoso was diligent in
his efforts toward insuring law and order and had the strong
backing of the property holders.[11]

Among his other attempts to maintain an orderly society was
a decree of 1791 forbidding the common practice of mortgaging
slaves in Natchez and selling the same slaves later at the Concordia slave mart. Although leaders of counterfeiting rings were
caught occasionally and their plates confiscated, counterfeiting
persisted in Natchez throughout the Spanish era, abetted by the
lack of specie and paper money. Street fighting became so prevalent that Gayoso banned knives and other metal weapons, but
hawkers were soon selling wooden stilettoes. He was also compelled to issue decrees prohibiting some forms of gambling, all
liquor sales to slaves and Indians, and rowdiness in public. Moreover, he strictly enforced curfew hours for the dozen taverns at
the landing in 1792. His proposal to build a $5,000 jail was re-
jected in New Orleans as too costly, so he continued to quarter
prisoners in the decrepit stockade of Fort Panmure (which the
American regime also used for a while). In addition, Gayoso
maintained close supervision over the mobility and business
affairs of his constituents. He required passports for entry and
departure from the district, and he demanded permits for all
forms of commercial operations and building construction in the
town, even to adding a porch to a mercantile store.[12]

[10] Ibid.
[11] Edith W. Moore, Natchez Under-the-Hill (Natchez, 1958), 29–69; Ulrich
B. Phillips, Life and Labor in the Old South (Boston, 1929), 108; Virginia P.
Matthias, "Natchez-Under-the-Hill as It Developed Under the Influence of the
Mississippi River and the Natchez Trace," JMH, VII (October, 1945), 201–203.
[12] Gayoso to Carondelet, June 28, 1792, AGI, leg. 41; John Minor to Gayoso,
December 20, 1794, Minor Papers, LSU; Holmes, "Law and Order in Spanish
Natchez," 189–99.

Gayoso's strictness apparently did not extend to the chief form of public entertainment, horse racing. In 1795 Richard King opened a race track named Fleetfield. The stakes and track maintenance were financed by thirty-nine subscribers, including Gayoso, Minor, Vidal, Dunbar, Watts, and the Catholic priest, Francisco Lennan.[13] As for other pastimes in Spanish Natchez, they were severely limited. Visiting and frequent "socials" partly compensated for the lack of organized entertainment, particularly for the upper echelons of society. Of course, certain recreational activities were enjoyed by nabobs and commoners alike, namely, gambling, drinking, fighting, fishing, and hunting. Game was still plentiful: John Hutchins, Anthony's son, claimed that he killed 107 bears during a single season.[14]

Signs of cultural, educational, and aesthetic interests were generally lacking. As in any frontier society where settlers are primarily concerned with economic survival in a rugged environment, few persons had the interest, time, or affluence needed for cultural pursuits. There were no regularly-established schools, private or public. In 1785 Miró had suggested that three English-speaking Irish priests be sent there to found a church and a parochial school, but, though one was sent to establish a church, no school was forthcoming. A number of tutors were employed by the well-to-do, but some who could afford it, including Gayoso, sent their children to school in New Orleans.[15]

A few homes had been built by the 1790's which in style and spaciousness could be considered mansions. Those in the upper town and its outskirts included Gayoso's "Concord," Vidal's "Airlie," Girault's "Richmond Hill," Daniel Clark's "Hope Farm," William Barland's "The Elms," Pierre Surget's "Cherry Grove," Alexander Moore's "Linden," and Jesse Greenfield's "Cherokee." Most conspicuous in the countryside were Dunbar's "The Forest,"

[13] Grand-Pré to Carondelet, February 29, 1796, AGI, leg. 33; Laura D. S. Harrell, "Horse Racing in the Old Natchez District, 1783–1830," *JMH*, XIII (April, 1951), 123–25.

[14] Charles S. Sydnor, *A Gentleman of the Old Natchez Region: Benjamin L. C. Wailes* (Durham, N. C., 1938), 9–10.

[15] Holmes, *Gayoso*, 128–30.

John Bisland's "Mount Airwell," and Thomas Green's "Spring-field." The better homes were usually built along Spanish and French provincial lines. The town's general appearance, however, probably resembled the unflattering description of English traveler Francis Baily in 1797: "The houses are chiefly framed buildings; but though this country has been settled so long, there is all that inattention to neatness, cleanliness, and the comfort attending thereon, that there is in a country just cleared."[16]

The only known literary work written at Natchez before the American period was John Henderson's *Paine Detected, or The Unreasonableness of Paine's Age of Reason* (1797). The author was a merchant and book dealer who had come from Scotland in 1787 at the age of seventeen. Composed partly in stilted prose and partly in Miltonic verse, his diatribe against Enlightenment liberalism showed a knowledge of English poets and Scottish Calvinism but merited remembrance only because it was the first book printed in the area and because its conservative position typified the sentiments of the propertied class of Natchez society.[17]

Speculating in 1792 on the town's future, Carondelet predicted that, even if Natchez were someday lost to the United States, Spanish influence would remain in the form of the Catholic Church. He was optimistic about the situation at Natchez, "whose inhabitants, even the Protestants themselves, attend church to hear the divine word and send their young children to catechism. Within a few years they will all be Catholics."[18] The Catholics owned in the heart of the upper town a two-story frame church, a priests' home, several valuable lots, and a cemetery. The four Irish priests who served there at various times between

[16] Francis Baily, *Journal of a Tour in Unsettled Parts of North America, in 1796 & 1797* (London, 1856), 283. On the homes of Natchez aristocrats, see Edith W. Moore's articles in Natchez *Democrat* and Natchez *Times*, 1959 Pilgrimage editions; Robert G. Pishel, *Natchez: Museum City of the Old South* (Tulsa, 1959); J. Wesley Cooper, *Natchez: A Treasure of Ante-Bellum Homes* (Natchez, 1957).

[17] Benjamin L. C. Wailes' inaugural address as president of the Mississippi Historical Society, November, 1859, Wailes Papers, Mississippi Archives.

[18] Carondelet to Bajamar, July 25, 1792, in *AHA 1945*, IV, 69.

1787 and 1798 were generally well liked, although at least two of them were notoriously heavy drinkers. As talk of an impending cession of the region to America increased, Gayoso found popular enthusiasm for his church dwindling. He reported in 1795 that the local laymen, "mainly Irish and not the best people of their nation, are of turbulent and intriguing spirits."[19] When the Spanish troops left three years later, so did Father Lennan, the last priest to reside at Natchez for many years. Carondelet's expectations had been thwarted by three countervailing influences: the material engrossment in making a living, which, as elsewhere on the frontier, left settlers indifferent to organized religion; the official policy of religious toleration; and the predominantly Protestant leanings of the minority who professed any religion, which became more persistent after 1794 as the prospect of American occupation brightened.[20]

Some Protestant activity existed in the vicinity, but little in Natchez itself. At the "Jersey Settlement" some fifteen miles to the southeast, Samuel Swayzey, a Congregationalist minister, began the region's first Protestant church about 1774. Swayzey's congregation, which had been meeting in private dwellings, finally disbanded when he died a decade later. Richard Curtis organized a Baptist church at Cole's Creek in 1791, but he antagonized the Spanish and was driven out of the district. A Presbyterian at Natchez described the Baptist evangelists who sometimes ventured into the area as "weak men, of weak minds, and illiterate, and too ignorant to know how inconsistent they act and talk."[21] John Bolls, a Presbyterian elder, was arrested for public preaching and trying to organize a congregation at Natchez. Adam Cloud, a Protestant Episcopal clergyman, preached four years in the Villa Gayoso (Cole's Creek) vicinity before being ousted by Gayoso. Both Curtis and Cloud left in 1795, and both returned after the Spanish evacuation.

[19] Gayoso to Manuel de Godoy, March 31, 1795, AGI, leg. 2354.
[20] Richard O. Gerow, *Cradle Days of St. Mary's at Natchez* (Natchez, 1941), 3–5; *Biographical and Historical Memoirs of Mississippi* (2 vols.; Chicago, 1891), II, 377.
[21] Ebenezer Dayton to Gayoso, August 3, 1795, AGI, leg. 202.

A royal order in 1788 guaranteed religious toleration for non-Catholic immigrants on condition that they confine their gatherings to private homes and refrain from proselyting Catholics. Nevertheless, the restriction on Protestant activities was a continual irritant in Spanish-American relations at Natchez. The Spanish found toleration difficult to practice, and the settlers, including the non-religious, used the occasional ouster of an intruding Prostestant missionary as a pretext for demanding more generous terms from the dons in other matters as well.[22]

The royal order represented a shift in Spanish policy based upon the realization that their efforts to strangle American expansion by closing the river had been unsuccessful. The fringe of American settlements—Kentucky, Cumberland, Holstein, and western Georgia—had over twice the population of Louisiana and was growing at a faster pace. Since 1786 many of these frontiersmen, convinced that the American officials cared little about their needs for Mississippi navigation, had been talking of an independent nation in the transmontane West and of an invasion of Louisiana. Shifting its strategy accordingly, Madrid now planned to exploit the frontier disaffection and lure Americans from the Upper Mississippi Valley to the Natchez country. Besides its liberal provision on religion, the 1788 order also stipulated that non-Catholic as well as Catholic immigrants could obtain free lands in the district simply by pledging fidelity to the Spanish crown. The Mississippi was opened to American boats subject to a 15 per cent duty on downriver shipments; a few years later the duty was reduced to 6 per cent. Furthermore, immigrants to Natchez could bring their belongings free of duty. Despite the

[22] Walter B. Posey, "The Early Baptist Church in the Lower Southwest," *JSH*, X (May, 1944), 161–62; John G. Jones, *A Concise History of the Introduction of Protestantism into Mississippi and the Southwest* (St. Louis, 1866), 13–15, 32; Jesse L. Boyd, *A Popular History of the Baptists in Mississippi* (Jackson, 1931), 18–20; Nash K. Burger and Charlotte Capers, "Episcopal Clergy of Mississippi, 1790–1940," *JMH*, VIII (January, 1946), 59–60; Nash K. Burger, "Adam Cloud, Mississippi's First Episcopal Clergyman," *ibid.*, IX (April, 1947), 88–93; Charles H. Otken, "Richard Curtis in the Country of the Natchez," *PMHS*, III (1900), 147–52; T. L. Haman, "Beginnings of Presbyterianism in Mississippi," *ibid.*, X (1909), 206.

minority of rabble-rousers, who were mostly transients and back-woodsmen, the dons had been well satisfied with their experience in governing the Natchez populace. This was undoubtedly a prime factor in convincing the officials that even larger numbers of non-Hispanic people could be controlled in that district. How much better it seemed to have the volatile, disaffected frontiers-men under close supervision at Natchez than to have them plot-ting irresponsible ventures, possibly against Louisiana, from the distant Kentucky and Cumberland settlements where no national government had much impact.[23]

Ultimately Miró allowed Natchez settlers commercial and land privileges even more liberal than those authorized in the royal order, so intent was he to attract Americans. The Spanish officials at Natchez extended this liberality further, compelling Miró to caution them in 1789 against promising so much to newcomers "lest they be disappointed."[24] Three years later Carondelet was forced to regulate more strictly the entry of American immi-grants, but the door was kept open for bona fide settlers with property.[25]

An increase in immigration to Natchez was evident in 1788, with 89 settlers (including 7 slaves) arriving during ten months of that year. Of these, 51 came from Kentucky and 16 from Cumberland. Fifty-seven vessels with 260 new residents aboard docked beneath the bluff from February through July, 1790. These included 94 men, 12 women, 37 children, and 117 Negroes a typical distribution through the next decade. Thirty-eight of the boats came from Kentucky, fourteen from Pennsylvania, two from Cumberland, and one each from South Carolina, Ohio, and Virginia. In that same period 30 colonists arrived overland from South Carolina and Virginia.[26] As the boats continued to come,

[23] Miró to Josef Valliere, February 28, 1789, AGI, leg. 6; Miró's proclamation of April 20, 1789, *ibid.*, leg. 2370.

[24] Miró to Grand-Pré, April 20, 1789, *ibid.*, leg. 6.

[25] Carondelet to Gayoso, May 12, 1792, *ibid.*, leg. 18.

[26] Benjamin Drake to Miró, July 15, 1788, *ibid.*, leg. 201; *AHA 1945*, III, xxvi; Grand-Pré to Miró, February 23–July 31, 1790, *ibid.*, 299–300, 313–14, 323–31, 336–37, 342–56, 368.

the district population rose from 1,619 persons in 1784 to 1,926 in 1788, 4,346 in 1792, and 5,318 four years later. Although separate figures for the town were not given, Natchez may have constituted one fourth of the district totals.[27]

The growth rate was unprecedented for the region, but the Spanish were disappointed because it did not seriously drain population from the American settlements upriver. The shift in traditional policy in order to lure colonists may have seemed generous to Madrid, but most frontiersmen soon realized that, despite their animosity toward the American government, they would yield certain privileges precious to them if they submitted to Spanish overlordship. At Natchez they would be forbidden to indulge in land speculation, worship publicly as Protestants, and practice local self-rule. For most Americans living in freedom upriver, settling at Natchez meant too great a sacrifice for the little enticement proffered by the dons.[28]

As seen in the arrival figures in 1790, few of those who chose to migrate to Natchez came overland. Roads into the town were few and poorly maintained. Samuel Forman, one of the flatboat arrivals that year, commented on a trip to an inland neighborhood he had made: "Ours was the first four-wheeled carriage that ever passed over those grounds—I can't say roads, for the highway was only what was called a bridle-path—all traveling at that day was on horseback."[29] The best known road was the Natchez Trace, or Trail to the Chickasaw Nation, which existed before the coming of the French. A French engineer who traveled it in 1742 attested to its poor condition, and

[27] Arthur P. Whitaker, *The Mississippi Question, 1795–1803: A Study in Trade, Politics, and Diplomacy* (New York, 1934), 61; Census of the Natchez District, 1792, in Norman E. Gillis, *Early Inhabitants of the Natchez District* (Baton Rouge, 1963), 13–26; Census of the Natchez District, 1796, New Orleans Consular Letters, Diplomatic Division, National Archives; Marcus L. Hansen, "The Population of the American Outlying Regions in 1790," in *AHA 1931*, I, 405. Most important of the arrivals of 1788–90 in later local history were William J. Minor, Lewis Evans, Robert Cochran, and George Winchester.

[28] Whitaker, *Spanish-American Frontier*, 160–61.

[29] Samuel S. Forman, *Narrative of a Journey Down the Ohio and Mississippi in 1789–90*, ed. Lyman C. Draper (Cincinnati, 1888), 57–58.

it was not much improved a half century later. But, as upriver settlements and downriver traffic grew, the Trace was regularly used by boatmen who disposed of their vessels in New Orleans or Natchez and returned northward by horseback. A branch of El Camino Real, the main overland artery between Louisiana and the Mexican capital, ran to the Concordia post (later Vidalia, Louisiana) across from Natchez. Another road, which bore no name, ran from New Orleans and Baton Rouge up the eastern side of the Mississippi to Natchez. In 1785 Miró authorized Benjamin Farrar, a Natchez physician and planter, to construct a new Natchez–Baton Rouge road. Farrar's estimate of costs was $250 for a horse path and $1,000 or more for a wagon road; the former was probably chosen. In 1792 Gayoso appointed overseers for six local road districts, especially for maintenance of the two roads from the town to Cole's Creek and the two which ran to the Homochitto. Ebenezer Dayton was placed in charge of overseeing the town's streets. The most expensive of these proved to be the one running uphill from the landing; it washed badly after every downpour.[30]

The Mississippi River was not a major transportation artery in the 1780's. According to a leading authority, fewer than twenty American flatboats made the trip to New Orleans during that decade (though others terminated their journeys at Natchez). The transformation of the river in the 1790's into a vital avenue of traffic in produce and people was largely a consequence of three developments: the royal order of 1788, which encouraged American trade and immigration; the War of the First Coalition, which pitted Spain against revolutionary France from 1793 to 1795, curtailed much of the trade be-

[30] Surrey, *Commerce of Louisiana,* 88; Holmes, *Gayoso,* 45–48; Robert S. Cotterill, "The Natchez Trace," *LHQ,* VI (April, 1923), 259–60; Dawson A. Phelps, "Travel on the Natchez Trace: A Study of Its Economic Aspects," *JMH,* XV (April, 1953), 155–57; Lena M. Jamison, "The Natchez Trace: A Federal Highway of the Old Southwest," *ibid.,* I (April, 1939), 82–84; Julian P. Bretz, "Early Land Communication with the Lower Mississippi Valley," *MVHR,* XIII (June, 1927), 3–29.

tween Louisiana and Spain, and promoted the colony's trade with the United States; and the large influx of population up-river, which helped to bring statehood for Kentucky in 1792 and for Tennessee in 1796.[31]

The cargoes of the previously-mentioned flatboats arriving at Natchez in 1790 are typical of the river traffic through the rest of the decade. Seventeen of the boats carried tobacco; fourteen, flour; thirteen, meat (usually pork, ham, or "salt meat"); and eleven, slaves (including those for sale and those accompanying settlers). Other commodities brought by the flat-boats included tallow and candles, whiskey, saddles, iron prod-ucts (mainly iron bars, pots, and pans), butter, fur (especially beaver, bear, otter, and wildcat skins), grindstones and mill-stones, liquor stills, wagons, salt, lime, hemp, lard, cornmeal, farm tools, cider, unbleached linen, medicines, and horses.[32] Ap-parently enough corn was raised locally to satisfy subsistence needs. Cattle and hogs were raised in large numbers around Natchez and were supplemented by herds driven overland from the Southwest.

Although many residents and some mercantile establishments had moved to the upper town by the mid-1790's, the liveliest business activity was still at the landing, or Natchez under-the-Hill. Travelers described the waterfront as lined solidly with warehouses, stores, and taverns. Late in the decade some com-mission merchants were reported to be netting $50,000 annually. A pioneer manufacturing enterprise was lumbering, at least three sawmills being in operation as early as 1781. The town became a major supplier of lumber, staves, and naval products for New Orleans. Natchez had at least one brick kiln by the mid-1790's. When Gayoso assumed the Louisiana governorship and moved to New Orleans in 1797, he continued to purchase axes made in Natchez. At least four trained carpenters and three mechanics

---

[31] Whitaker, *Spanish-American Frontier*, 95–106, 171–77.

[32] Grand-Pré to Miró, reports of arrivals, February 23–July 31, 1790, in *AHA 1945*, III, 299–300, 313–14, 323–31, 336–37, 342–56, 368.

were practicing their vocations at Natchez by 1795. Robert Cochran, later a rich commission merchant, and two other men trained in the cordage business were admitted duty-free between 1786 and 1790, in the hope that they would establish cordage factories. Gayoso tried to promote hemp cultivation and cordage manufacturing, but little came of the plan. As for taxes, Natchez businessmen faced no burdens such as the American government would later impose. The Spanish required no local taxes, only a 6 per cent duty on exports and imports.[33]

As the plantation system expanded and agricultural production increased, the demand for slaves rose. In his decree of 1793 Carondelet gave an impetus to the slave trade: "The introduction of Negroes into these Provinces shall be free of all duty; and only the fruits, or silver, which might be extracted to pay for them, shall require the payment of the six percent."[34] In 1784 there were 498 slaves in the district, eight years later there were 1,893, and by 1796 there were 2,110—40 per cent of the total population. The trend of slave prices was distinctly upward. When the slaves of John Alston, an accomplice in the Blommart revolt, were sold at public auction in 1781, two men, ages twenty-eight and thirty-five, brought $330 and $350, respectively; seven women, between twenty-two and thirty-five and averaging twenty-seven, brought an average of $280; and seven children, two to seven,

[33] James Hall, *A Brief History of the Mississippi Territory, to Which Is Prefixed a Summary View of the Country Between the Settlements on Cumberland River & the Territory* (Salisbury, N.C., 1801), 31–32; McBee, *Natchez Court Records,* 23, 106, 594–95; Holmes, *Gayoso,* 104–107. Branch stores of Natchez businesses existed in outlying areas. On Bayou Pierre, for example, was that of George Rapalje, who sold such items as "tubs," plows, axes, and coarse cloth, and bought corn, deer and otter skins, and tobacco. In 1789 Andrew Jackson built a log trading post on the same bayou, purchasing his supplies mainly from Natchez merchant Melling Woolley. Jackson also sold slaves to various district planters. In 1791 he married Rachel Donelson Robards at Thomas Green's "Springfield" nearby; three years later the Jacksons moved back to Nashville. See Notebook of George Rapalje, entry of November 10, 1793, Mississippi Archives; John S. Bassett (ed.), *Correspondence of Andrew Jackson* (7 vols.; New York, 1926–33), I, 8; Bills of goods to Andrew Jackson by Melling Woolley, 1790–91, Andrew Jackson Papers, Library of Congress.

[34] Carondelet's trade proclamation, June 9, 1793, Francisco L. H. (Baron de) Carondelet Papers, LSU.

brought an average of $102. Prices had risen by 1791 when Gayoso purchased four slaves for $1,800, or an average of $450 each. Between 1783 and 1794 John Bisland, the Scottish master of "Mount Airwell," bought or sold twelve men averaging twenty-two years old, for an average price of $437. Between 1797 and 1798 he paid from $400 to $1,450 each for four males aged fourteen to thirty years; the average was $703. A Negro "wench" eighteen years old cost him $425, the price of a good male field hand a decade earlier. In the 1780's slave auctions were usually held at the landing, but by the mid-1790's most transactions took place at the bustling "Forks of the Road" slave mart, located on the Trace at the northeast edge of the upper town.[35]

The keeping of livestock was significant in the economy of the region. In 1784 the district had 3,000 cattle, 1,153 horses, 7,111 pigs, and 117 sheep. A decade later the figures had risen to 14,672 cattle, 5,541 horses, 20,106 pigs, and 5,538 sheep. By 1794 the majority of livestock was held by farmers in the Santa Catalina (St. Catherine's Creek) and Villa Gayoso neighborhoods.[36] The Spanish encouraged livestock raising by enlarging land grants of settlers who brought livestock with them. Gilbert Imlay, a British geographer who visited Natchez in 1796, commented that "no part of the known world is more favorable for the raising of every kind of stock."[37] That same year George H. Victor Collot, a French general, was surprised by the huge herds

[35] Schedule of slave sales from John Alston's estate, July 30, 1781, Spanish Records of the Natchez District, Vol. A, Chancery Clerk's Records; McBee, *Natchez Court Records*, 83; Memorandum book of John Bisland, *passim*, and sundry slave sale and purchase receipts, 1783–99, John Bisland and Family Papers, LSU. Birthplaces of the thirty-three Negroes involved in the Bisland transactions were: Jamaica, six; Virginia, six; Guinea, five; Senegal, five; Natchez District, four; North Carolina, three; Tennessee, two; Kentucky, one; and Maryland, one. The prices and origins of the Bisland slaves were typical for the period in that area.

[36] Censuses of the Natchez District for 1784 and 1794, AGI, leg. 116, 31, Librray of Congress. Villa Gayoso a rural community near Cole's Creek, was laid out in 1791. By the end of 1792 it had 909 persons and ranked next to Natchez in size among district communities. However, it did not continue to grow and had virtually disappeared by 1815.

[37] Gilbert Imlay, *Topographical Description of the Western Territory* (London, 1797), 424.

of cattle he observed around the area, many roaming "wild."[38] According to a distinguished agricultural historian, one of the major differences between the agricultural situation of the Natchez region and that of the Tidewater area at this time was the presence of large numbers of domestic livestock in the former area.[39]

Most of the cattle were of the Opelousas strain, which were originally imported from Spain to the Attakapas Prairie of southwestern Louisiana. A small horse known as a "cane tackey" existed in the region, probably bred from mustangs imported from Texas. French naturalist François André Michaux, a visitor in the 1790's, claimed that Natchez traders, led by Philip Nolan, brought wild horses from as far away as Sante Fe to sell at Natchez for $50 per head. As for other livestock, sheep were of "a scrawny but hardy breed," and the semi-wild hogs of the district belonged to the light-weight type later called "Arkansas Razorbacks" or "Land Pikes." Except for some fine horses imported by Peter Bryan Bruin, Adam Bingaman, Gayoso, and Stephen Minor, pure-bred stocks of horses, cattle, sheep, and hogs were unknown around Natchez until after 1800.[40]

Squabbles between local citizens over livestock led Gayoso to call public meetings in 1793 and 1794 to regulate disposal of stray livestock, fencing, stream pollutions caused by dumping indigo wastes, changes of brands, and bounties on predators. Ezekiel Forman was appointed to handle "money proceeding from the Subscription and sale of stray creatures." Also, "to him

---

[38] George H. Victor Collott, *A Journey in North America, Containing a Survey of the Countries Watered by the Mississippi* . . . (reprint, 3 vols.; Firenze, 1924), II, 64. The first edition was published in London, 1796.

[39] Lewis C. Gray, *History of Agriculture in the Southern United States to 1860* (2 vols.; Washington, 1933), I, 6–7.

[40] François André Michaux, *Travels to the West of the Alleghany Mountains* . . . (London, 1805), reprinted in Reuben G. Thwaites (ed.), *Early Western Travels, 1748–1846* (32 vols.; Cleveland, 1904–1907), III, 245; Jack D. L. Holmes, "Livestock in Spanish Natchez," *JMH*, XXIII (January, 1961), 17–21; Baily, *Journal*, 311–12, 335; George P. Hammond (ed.), *New Spain and the Anglo-American West* (2 vols.; Lancaster, Pa., 1932), I, 231; John H. Moore, *Agriculture in Ante-Bellum Mississippi* (New York, 1958), 61–63.

will apply the Persons, that are duly entitled to rewards for killing beasts of Prey, such as Tygers [panthers?] and Wolves."[41]

The most serious intra-district problem of the Spanish era was
the economic crisis precipitated by Madrid's decision in late 1790
to cut its annual purchases of Louisiana tobacco from 2,000,000
pounds to 40,000.[42] In the previous year two Natchez planters
alone, David Williams and Adam Bingaman, had produced
50,000 and 45,000 pounds, respectively. Over 260 farms in the
district had been engaged in tobacco cultivation, 43 of them
producing in excess of 10,000 pounds. The total district harvest
in 1789 was 1,402,725 pounds. In view of the impending catastrophe confronting the planters, the government at Madrid
agreed to postpone the reduction a year but warned that its annual purchases thereafter would be only 40,000 pounds.[43]

Three principal considerations impelled the Spanish to pursue
this course, which was so contradictory to their policy of attracting settlers to Natchez and developing the district. First, the
tobacco markets of Spain and Mexico were unusually glutted in
1789–90, and the government, whose treasury was already want-
ing, could not afford to pay premium prices at a time when
market prices were depressed. Also, officials in Madrid and
Mexico City had long complained that Louisiana tobacco was
inferior to that obtainable elsewhere, so the glutted conditions
merely afforded an opportunity to curtail a purchasing practice
already undesirable. Third, because of the persuasive influence
of James Wilkinson and others engaged in profiteering in the
Louisiana–Kentucky trade, Governor Miró made the Kentuckians
sole recipients of premium tobacco prices, hoping thereby to lure
them into breaking from the Union and coming into the Spanish
fold. Thus the Natchez economy was sacrificed in the Spanish-

[41] Gayoso's proclamation on livestock, February 28, 1793, quoted in Holmes,
"Livestock in Spanish Natchez," 30.

[42] Caroline M. Burson, The Stewardship of Don Esteban Miró (New Orleans,
1940), 75–84; James A. Robertson (ed.), Louisiana under the Rule of Spain,
France, and the United States, 1785–1807 (2 vols.; Cleveland, 1911), I, 286.

[48] Miró to Gayoso, July 14, 1789, AGI, leg. 6; Grand-Pré to Miró, March 2,
1790, in AHA 1945, III, 305–11; Wailes, Report, 10–12.

American frontier rivalry, while Miró ironically continued to beckon discontented settlers to move to Natchez.[44]

The depression, which hung like a dark cloud over the country for seven years, occasioned a long, acrimonious clash between the Natchez merchant-creditor class and the planter-debtor element. Eleven local merchants in 1790 wailed that their outstanding accounts exceeded $146,000. The planters, in turn, complained of outrageous prices and interest rates charged by the merchants. The latter were most unhappy when Miró declared a three-year moratorium on planters' debts and set a ceiling of 5 per cent on interest charges. The planters were allowed this mercy on condition that they pay one third of their debts each year. In 1791 the merchants howled when tobacco production, now at less than half its former level, did not bring sufficient revenue for the planters to meet their debt commitments. Hutchins penned a memorial to Gayoso, which other large planters endorsed. "When the King declined taking any more tobacco, the merchants combined against us," the memorial stated, "and by agreeing upon a tariff of low prices, have so reduced the value of all descriptions of produce, that it now takes, exclusive of interest, one hundred per cent more of the same produce to pay the same debts than it did four years ago." Unless "equitable prices" were charged, "matters will drift from bad to worse, and the time is not very far distant *when the planter must destroy the merchant, or the merchant must destroy the planter.*" A few days later the merchants, led by Alexander Moore and Peter Walker, retorted that "it is not the design of the creditors to distress or ruin any honest, industrious debtor." The merchants answered the planters' complaint that "they had no encouragement to work, not knowing what value would be allowed them for their crops by their creditors" by posting their prices on produce and consumer items. Their charges included $1.00 a bushel for corn, $6.25 per hundred pounds for beef, and $10.00 per hundred pounds for pork. Since these prices were the same that had prompted Hutchins' memorial, the planters' only consolation was

[44] *AHA 1945*, III, xxvi–xxvii; Whitaker, *Spanish-American Frontier*, 158–60.

that they had compelled the merchants to put their exactions in writing.[45]

In 1792 the debtors again asked for a stay law. In retaliation the disgusted merchants demanded that, if relief were granted, they should be allowed to set up a debts committee to examine each debtor's situation, judge which should be given relief consideration, and attach the property of those who were able to pay but procrastinated. Late that year Carondelet approved another three-year stay on planters' debts; but he authorized Gayoso, not the merchants, to name the members of the debt-liquidations committee and to choose them from both factions. Again in 1795 the planters begged for relief, while the merchants appealed to the Spanish not to extend the stay law. The creditors argued that "a very large majority of the Debtors, so far from exerting their endeavors, to extricate themselves from their difficulties, having no longer the dread of the Law before their Eyes, have become indolent, Dissipated, and Deaf to the calls of their Creditors." The debtors responded that they were being illegally charged 10 per cent and more in interest by the opulent merchants. Another stay was granted, but the merchants continued to demand that "an Annual punctual payment of one fifth with Interest of the whole Debt" was needed to afford the "distressed Creditor" any hope of retrieving even part of "his shattered fortune." The planters, who would constitute the leadership in the revolt against the Spanish two years later, assured Gayoso: "We resolve that they shall not have cause to blush before the Throne; for allegiance is our ambition, we pride in acts of duty and firmness."[46] This seemingly unending controversy was the most important factor underlying the citizens' growing discontent with Spanish rule by 1795 and the origin of political factions in 1797, which bore strong resemblance to the planter-debtor and merchant-creditor alignment.

[45] Claiborne, *Mississippi*, 137–40; Holmes, *Gayoso*, 94–96.

[46] William B. Hamilton, "American Beginnings in the Old Southwest: The Mississippi Phase" (unpublished Ph.D. dissertation, Duke University, 1938 [1937]), 189–95.

In their frustration the planters turned to indigo cultivation, but, for lucrative returns, it required large-scale operations employing huge vats and other expensive equipment. Two types of indigo were produced for export: a pigeon-neck strain with prismatic colors and a light blue variety. Only Robert Dunbar, Gabriel Benoist, Abram Ellis, and Gerard Brandon appear to have found indigo profitable. When a disastrous insect plague obliterated the area's crop in 1792, the planters knew that they must resume their quest for a profitable export.[47]

The failure of the indigo experiment forced a last-ditch gamble on cotton. Because of the inefficiency of the roller gin then in use, which cleaned only seventy-five pounds per day, the efforts of the planters in cotton cultivation would have ended in a fiasco had they attempted to rely on the crop for their principal livelihood before 1795. That year, however, news arrived from Georgia of Eli Whitney's saw gin, which could clean five hundred to a thousand pounds of fiber daily. Before the year's end at least four planters had employed mechanics to build the easily-constructed machines. Because of the lack of iron, hoe blades were often used to make the circular gin saws, which separated the fibers from the seeds. William Vousdan of "Cottonfields" plantation on the eastern edge of town became, in 1796, the first district planter to ship cotton directly to the English markets. Soon gin construction was a thriving business at Natchez, the pioneers being John Barclay, David Greenleaf, and James Bolls, Jr. In 1796 Greenleaf built the first public gin at Selsertown, a hamlet northeast of Natchez, and the next year he constructed the area's first screw press. William Dunbar soon undertook pioneer experiments on the use of imported iron presses and square baling.[48]

The strain of cotton planted in the 1790's was called "Nanking," "Siamese," or, most commonly, "Creole." It was a black-

[47] Wailes, *Report*, 134–39. Robert Dunbar was not kin to William Dunbar.
[48] John H. Moore, *Agriculture*, 22–24; Holmes, *Gayoso*, 99–101; James R. Dungan, " 'Sir' William Dunbar of Natchez, Planter, Explorer, and Scientist, 1792–1810," *JMH*, XXIII (October, 1961), 214–15.

seed, long-staple cotton with a fine lint and brought an average price of 39 cents per pound from 1795 to 1798. But it was difficult to pick and susceptible to worms and plant diseases. Until army worms and a disease called "rot" appeared around Natchez in the early 1800's, however, the Creole variety proved satisfactory enough to obviate the necessity of experimentation in cotton breeding.[49]

Cotton production in the district, which in 1794 had amounted to only 36,351 pounds, rose rapidly in the next few years. By 1798 the district output exceeded 1,200,000 pounds.[50] The largest cotton planter in the region was Stephen Minor, whose nine plantations in 1797 yielded 2,500 bales, worth $51,200 at the prevailing New Orleans price.[51] Another large planter was John Bisland, who also had nine plantations in 1797 with large cotton crops on each. He enjoyed such profits that he ordered large luxury purchases from Liverpool and Glasgow and sent two sons to school in Scotland.[52] By 1798 most of the old tobacco elite had liquidated their debts sufficiently to enable them to engage in large-scale cotton operations. William Dunbar's comment typifies the planters' renewed hope: "We continue to cultivate cotton with very great success. It is by far the most profitable crop we have ever undertaken in this country."[53]

In the French and British eras the liabilities to the development

[49] Anderson, Clayton and Co., "Average Annual Spot Price of Cotton Per Pound: Crop Years 1731–2 to 1957–8," *Anderson, Clayton and Co. Press*, XXXIX (March, 1959), 5; Phillips, *Life and Labor*, 177; John H. Moore, *Agriculture*, 28–31.

[50] Holmes, *Gayoso*, 100–101.

[51] William Vousdan to Stephen Minor, November 8, 1797, Minor Papers, LSU; John Turnbull to Minor, February 27, 1799, Stephen Minor and Family Papers, UNC; Gayetano Valdes to Minor, November 18, 1797, *ibid.*; Minor's crop schedule of 1797, January 16, 1798, *ibid.*

[52] Bisland's memorandum book, various entries of 1797, and notebook, entry of May 27, 1802, Bisland Papers LSU; Beatrice M. Stokes, "John Bisland, Mississippi Planter, 1776–1821" (unpublished M.A. thesis, Louisiana State University, 1941), 11–23, 62.

[53] William Dunbar to John Ross, May 23, 1799, Dunbar Papers, Mississippi Archives. One planter's affluence is seen in William B. Hamilton and William D. McCain (eds.), "Wealth in the Natchez Region: Inventories of the Estate of Charles Percy, 1794–1804," *JMH*, X (October, 1948), 290–316.

of Natchez had included official indifference, geographic isolation, and lack of an export staple. Under the Spanish the situation changed perceptibly. Madrid by 1788 was quite interested in promoting the Natchez region as an attraction to American settlers. Rather drastic alterations in Spanish colonial policy were adopted to suit the Natchez inhabitants. In addition, the district governor who served Natchez during much of the Spanish era was capable and forward-looking and sincerely identified himself with his constituents' problems. Under the American governors some would later lament the region's loss of its remarkable Spanish gentleman, Gayoso. As for isolation, a view of the busy Natchez waterfront in the late 1790's would attest to the fact that the Mississippi River was rapidly nearing its glorious age as the great inland carrier of immigrants and trade. In much of the district the primitive stage of frontier life had passed, especially in the town: population was growing fast, the municipality had expanded atop the bluff, commerce was bustling, and a few signs of sophisticated society were evident. The lack of a staple crop for export had been solved but not without depression and dissension. Considerable wealth from cotton was being realized as the Spanish era ended. But the home government, which had designated the area as a special haven for discontented American frontiersmen, had also contradicted its policy by undermining the area's earlier economic foundation in a desperate effort to exploit disaffection in the American West. With the bestowal of such mixed blessings from Madrid, Natchez became the unwitting pawn in the complicated international rivalry for the Lower Mississippi Valley.

CHAPTER III

Era of Intrigue
and Insecurity

In the 1780's the Natchez region lay like a giant finger pointing upriver—attractive, exposed, and closest of the main Spanish-controlled areas to the path of American settlement. When Miró ordered the Mississippi closed to American navigation, many of the turbulent Kentucky and Tennessee frontiersmen, now over fifty thousand strong, loudly denounced Spain. Aware of the loose hold that the United States government had on its transmontane settlements, Miró feared that irresponsible frontier elements might attempt an invasion of the Natchez District and possibly lower Louisiana. He was also aware that Spanish representation in the province was largely limited to a small force of officials and military personnel. Very few Spanish settlers had come. A large portion of the population south of Natchez, especially the French Creoles, were openly hostile toward their Spanish masters. Miró tried to maneuver the Southeastern tribes against the Americans, but he was never certain of their trustworthiness, particularly of the cunning, influential Creek chieftain Alexander McGillivray. To Miró the relatively calm acceptance of Spanish rule at Natchez since 1781 must have been reassuring, but Natchez was destined to be a target for trouble all too soon.[1]

As the American Revolution ended, numbers of Americans began settling in the Natchez country. One of these was Thomas Green, a zealous patriot who had been a colonel under George Washington. Soon after moving west with his family from Vir-

---

[1] Thomas M. Green, *The Spanish Conspiracy: A Review of Early Spanish Movements in the Southwest* (Cincinnati, 1891), 33–120; Frederick A. Ogg, *The Opening of the Mississippi: A Struggle for Supremacy in the American Interior* (New York, 1904), 400–46; Whitaker, *Spanish–American Frontier*, 26–31.

ginia, Green became infuriated by the Loyalists of the district, who he charged had passively bowed before the "incrochen tyrents" of Madrid. He began organizing a pro-American faction among newcomers in the region. According to Commander Grand-Pré, Green's activities also included slave thefts and sale of gunpowder to American brigands. The Spaniard was, of course, biased against any American agitator, but it is true that Green had been "a maker of powder" in Virginia. The serious trouble began when Green circulated a petition, which was sent to the Georgia legislature, asking that state to extend its civil jurisdiction over the Natchez country.

While Spanish and American officials disputed the territory east of the Mississippi between the 31st and 35th parallels, Georgia leaders continued to claim the Natchez region for their state on the basis of their colonial charter of 1732. Thus the Georgia General Assembly reacted favorably to Green's petition. In 1785 the assembly passed an audacious resolution for the establishment of a western county named Bourbon, whose vast area encompassed Natchez despite the presence of a Spanish garrison and district staff there. A commission was named to go to Natchez, persuade the Spanish to leave, and then set up the new county administration.[2]

That summer, commissioners Nicholas Long, Thomas Green, William Davenport, and Nathaniel Christmas met with Felipe Treviño, Spanish commandant at Natchez. Long, the "young but serious and formal" commission chairman, told Treviño that "there are no treasures that America would not sacrifice in order to obtain this country." But he assured the commandant that the request to evacuate was not to be construed as an ultimatum: "America would never employ other means that those of persuasion and the mediation of the other powers."[3] Though he knew that Spanish policy called for a tenacious hold on the district,

[2] Grand-Pré to Miró, May 26, 1782, in *AHA 1945*, III, 16–18; Edmund C. Burnett (ed.), "Papers Relating to Burbon County, Georgia," *AHR*, XV (January, 1910), 291–98.
[3] Bouligny to Miró, August 28, 1785, in *AHA 1945*, III, 144.

Treviño replied that he must await instructions from Governor Miró. While he bided time for further orders, and hopefully for reinforcements, Treviño conducted an informal local survey of public opinion. His poll showed a strong preference for Spanish rule over that of Georgia. In fact, Richard Ellis and Sutton Banks were jailed after picking a fight with the commissioners. Realizing that Green had exaggerated the extent of support for his petition, Treviño suggested that the commissioners should confer with Miró in New Orleans, to which Long and Christmas were agreeable.

Miró's proposal, however, precipitated a split in the commission and marked the beginning of the end for the entire scheme. Backed by Davenport, Green accused Long and Christmas of "condescension" to the dons and belligerently warned the Spanish that a large force of Georgians awaited his word to attack if the negotiations failed. He also threatened to incite the Yazoo Indians to war against the Spanish. Although Green's subsequent mission to the Yazoo was a failure, word came from the influential Creek chieftain Alexander McGillivray that 2,500 Georgians were en route to attack Natchez—a report later proven false but apprehensively deliberated at the time. Miró thereupon sent Lieutenant Colonel Francisco Bouligny to relieve Treviño and increased the Natchez garrison by 400 men. He also sent Spanish agents among the Creek and Cherokee to persuade them "to infuse terror into the frontiers of Georgia and Carolina," thereby discouraging any passage westward.[4]

Then came word in early November, 1785, that the United States Congress had passed a resolution condemning the Bourbon County action as a threat to amicable relations between Spain and America. The Spanish abruptly ordered the commissioners to leave, and Green, the only one who was a local resident, was imprisoned on charges of inciting insurrection. The embarrassed Georgia legislators castigated the war-like gestures

[4] M. Chachere to Felipe Treviño, August 14, 1785, *ibid.*, 135–36; Arturo O'Neill to Gálvez, July 8 and August 19, 1785, AGI, leg. 37; Gálvez to O'Neill, September 22, 1785, *ibid.*, leg. 37.

of the commissioners, who had instructions not to threaten violence. So ended the Bourbon County affair; but, since the Georgia government stubbornly refused to relinquish its claim to the area, the dons continued to worry about future threats from that state.[5]

Meanwhile, another menace to Spanish sovereignty loomed elsewhere. During the abortive negotiations of 1785–86 between John Jay, secretary of foreign affairs, and Diego de Gardoqui, Spanish minister to the United States, Congress indicated its willingness to postpone the issue of Mississippi navigation for several decades. As the news reached the West in late 1786, an epidemic of disaffection spread. Frontiersmen were further convinced of congressional indifference when American officials meekly accepted the Spanish seizure of three Kentucky vessels at Natchez in December of that year. A rumor spread that George Rogers Clark, who had already confiscated goods from Spanish traders upriver, was amassing a large force to attack Natchez. Miró hurriedly sent reinforcements to the bluff, and the townsfolk braced themselves for the expected invasion. As time passed and no assault came, the rumor subsided, but cries for American acquisition of Natchez continued to echo from Kentucky to Georgia.[6]

In spite of the Spanish catering to American immigrants through the royal order of 1788, the security of Natchez was soon threatened by a new scheme of outsiders desiring control of the area. In late 1789 Georgia sold to several land companies huge tracts in the disputed regions of Muscle Shoals in what is now northwestern Alabama, Chickasaw Bluffs (the present site of Memphis), and the northern part of the Natchez District. The South Carolina Yazoo Company received ten million acres along

[5] Burnett, "Papers Relating to Bourbon County," 135–54, 297–98, 342–45; *AHA 1945*, III, xviii; John R. Alden, *The Revolution in the South, 1763–1789* (Baton Rouge, 1957), 352–53.

[6] Miró to O'Neill, June 20, 1786, AGI, leg. 1445; James Wilkinson to the "Governor of St. Louis," December 20, 1786, *ibid.*, leg. 199; Justin Winsor, *The Westward Movement: The Colonies and the Republic West of the Alleghanies, 1763–1798* (Boston, 1897), 339–50.

the lower Yazoo and down to Cole's Creek. It was the most ambitious of the land companies, planning extensive operations in Indian and slave trading, as well as in land speculation. James O'Fallon, its chief agent, envisioned Walnut Hills near the Yazoo mouth as a United States port of entry and potential trade competitor with Natchez.[7]

When the Spanish seized several ships off the shore of Vancouver Island in 1790, war between Spain and Great Britain seemed imminent. The impetuous O'Fallon consequently began talking of conquering the entire Natchez District, possibly with British aid. Excitement ran high at Natchez when he visited several local residents known to be anti-Spanish, but O'Fallon failed to raise the strong support that he needed. Spanish reinforcements at Natchez, Gayoso's building of Fort Nogales at Walnut Hills, and the Yazoo Company's inability to supply him with adequate funds and men discouraged O'Fallon. When Anglo-Spanish tensions subsided the next year, he abandoned his plans for a colony or an invasion.[8]

During these years, Natchez was often visited by James Wilkinson, who bore news of trading ventures and separatist activities and demands that the dons increase his salary as a secret agent. He and Daniel Clark, Sr., had been influential in getting Miró to encourage the Louisiana–Kentucky trade by subsidies, but their trading firm proved less rewarding than anticipated from 1787 to 1791. By the latter year Wilkinson was back in the United States Army, holding a brigadier general's commission while at the same time continuing to accept $2,000 to $9,000 yearly in secret Spanish pensions. He had many friends in

[7] Miró to Gayoso, July 14, 1789, AGI, leg. 6; Carondelet to Gayoso, January 2, 1791, ibid., leg. 18; Gayoso to Miró, January 17 and March 18, 1791, ibid., leg. 152, 41; American State Papers: Documents, Legislative and Executive [1789–1838] (38 vols.; Washington, 1832–61), Indian Affairs, I, 112–15; Charles H. Haskins, "The Yazoo Land Companies," Papers of the American Historical Association, V (1891), 395–407.

[8] Carondelet to Gayoso, March 29, 1791, and April 17, 1792, AGI, leg. 18, 152; Gayoso to Miró, May 9, 11, 12, 30, and July 26, 1791, ibid., leg. 41; Thomas P. Abernethy, The South in the New Nation, 1789–1819 (Baton Rouge, 1961), 74–101.

Natchez, but few of them associated him or Clark with the tobacco crisis, which the two had actually abetted. Wilkinson's main contacts in Natchez were Gayoso, whose exquisite wine cellar at "Concord" was frequently tapped by the American general; Minor, whose close friends included an associate of Wilkinson's in frontier intrigues, Thomas Power; James White, land speculator, conspirator in league with William Blount, and owner of a large plantation near Natchez; and Philip Nolan, famous wrangler, frontier adventurer, occasional employee of Wilkinson on conspiratorial missions, and son-in-law of Bernard Lintot. Since Gayoso and Minor often acted as "go-betweens" for the upriver schemers and the Spanish officials in New Orleans, Natchez became a favorite meeting place for Spanish-separatist conferences. As late as 1794, two years after Kentucky had achieved statehood, Wilkinson reported at one such gathering that five hundred Kentucky frontiersmen, enraged over Spain's continued obstructions to American trade on the Mississippi, were preparing to attack Natchez.[9] Wilkinson's morsels of information, reliable and otherwise, were swallowed by Natchez citizens, who stayed in a constant state of uncertainty. Gayoso was aware, however, that Wilkinson's conduct was purely the result of personal interest. "I consider his ambition as a favorable circumstance and one from which we can draw advantage," he wrote.[10] Though they may have perceived Wilkinson's motives, the dons continued to reward him handsomely for information

[9] Miró to Gayoso, July 14, 1789, AGI, leg. 6; Gayoso to Carondelet, January 25, 1793, and May 23, 1794, *ibid.*, leg. 152, 2354; Wilkinson to Gayoso, October 12, 1789, *ibid.*, leg. 2373; Abraham P. Nasatir and Ernest R. Liljegren (eds.), "Materials Relating to the History of the Mississippi Valley, from the Minutes of the Spanish Supreme Council of State, 1787–1797," *LHQ*, XXI (January, 1936), 44–45; Lawrence Kinnaird, "American Penetration into Spanish Territory to 1803" (unpublished Ph.D. dissertation, University of California, Berkeley, 1928), xxvi–xxviii; *American State Papers, Miscellaneous*, II, 81; James R. Jacobs, *Tarnished Warrior: Major-General James Wilkinson* (New York, 1938), 137, 152; Thomas R. Hay and M. R. Werner, *The Admirable Trumpeter: A Biography of General James Wilkinson* (New York, 1941), 79–109; William R. Shepherd, "Wilkinson and the Beginnings of the Spanish Conspiracy," *AHR*, IX (April, 1904), 494–95.

[10] Gayoso to Carondelet, May 23, 1794, AGI, leg. 2354.

from which they were seldom in a position to "draw advantage," even when he spoke the truth.

Besides serving as a rendezvous for conspirators, the town was also an important Spanish base for Indian trading and negotiations. Whereas Pensacola served as the meeting place for traders and agents dealing with the Cherokee and Creek, Natchez performed a similar function in the Spanish relations with the Choctaw and Chickasaw. Perhaps the most successful of the Indian agents who went out from Natchez was Turner Brashears. He obtained his bargaining supplies of "rum, powder, and balls" from the merchants at the landing and often made extensive excursions into the Choctaw country. The profits from his personal Indian trade and his employment as Choctaw agent for the Spanish enabled Brashears later to establish himself as a cotton commission merchant.[11]

Spanish-Choctaw relations, which had been strained by increasing outlaw-Indian raids, improved considerably in the early 1790's, thanks to Gayoso's tactful diplomacy. In May, 1792, Gayoso's months of patient suasion of Choctaw chiefs, who had been riled by the building of Fort Nogales, were climaxed by the signing of the Treaty of Natchez. At the town's Church of San Salvador the tribal leaders affixed their marks to the document whereby they ceded the Walnut Hills area to the Spanish. The next year Gayoso's mediation brought a truce to a brief but bloody war between the Creek and Chickasaw. With the sudden death of the pro-Spanish McGillivray, Carondelet ordered Gayoso to arrange a treaty of amity, alliance, and trade with the several tribes as quickly as possible. At Nogales in October, 1793, Gayoso signed such a treaty with the Chickasaw, Choctaw, Cherokee, Creek, Tallapoosa, and Alabama. The document included the Indians' promise of peace on condition that Spain not transfer the Natchez District to another power. Despite his successes with the Indians, Gayoso often clashed with Carondelet over the latter's efforts to incite the tribes against Americans to the north.

[11] Gayoso to Carondelet, February 21, April 3, June 28, July 18, and August 8, 1792, ibid., leg. 18, 41; American State Papers, Indian Affairs, I, 296.

Gayoso admitted that he lived in constant dread that some American agent would be able "to induce the Indians to help them take possessions from the lands we possess," but he feared even more the vengeance of the frontiersmen themselves. His constituents at Natchez likewise lived with these anxieties.[12]

A new threat to Spanish authority arose in 1793 with the signing of an Anglo-Spanish alliance, the declaration of war by Spain against France, and the visit of Girondist envoy "Citizen" Edmond Genêt to the United States. These events set off a reaction of pro-French sympathies in lower Louisiana that reached alarming levels of rioting and open defiance of Spanish authority. George Rogers Clark, with Genêt's encouragement, began recruiting frontiersmen for a march down the banks of the Mississippi to oust the *Ancien Régime* at Natchez and New Orleans. Gayoso stationed a gunboat at the Natchez landing to intercept and search all vessels for copies of the inflammatory "Address to the Brothers of Louisiana," in which Genêt appealed for rebellion against the tyrannical Spanish. Many Louisiana towns witnessed turmoil over the clarion call of "liberty, fraternity, and equality," but, much to Gayoso's satisfaction, the Natchez inhabitants maintained a frigid disdain toward the French Revolution fervor. In fact, some actually opposed it—over three hundred Natchez volunteers journeyed to New Orleans to assist the dons in preserving order in that city. Underlying this seeming loyalty to Madrid, however, was probably a stronger anti-French feeling than a pro-Spanish sentiment. Although the so-called "Jacobin excitement" had lessened by spring, 1794, Gayoso cautioned Carondelet that the causal factors underlying the agitation were still present, especially in Kentucky: "Carried away by their impatience and wearied with watching the results of the negotiations which are pending between our court and the American States, they [the Kentuckians] will embrace any party

[12] Gayoso to Carondelet, July 18, 1792, AGI, leg. 41; Treaty of Natchez, May 14, 1792, *American State Papers, Foreign Relations,* I, 280; Treaty of Nogales, October 28, 1793, in *AHA 1945,* IV, 223–27; Holmes, *Gayoso,* 136–60; Burson, *Miró,* 144–87; Bemis, *Pinckney's Treaty,* 202–208.

which presents itself to them, however violent and improbable it may be, and which promises them immediate success."[13]

Still hopeful of luring Kentucky into the Spanish fold and thus relieving the insecurity of Natchez and New Orleans, Carondelet in 1795 renewed his contrivances with Wilkinson and others in Kentucky, where separatism had been flagging since the achievement of statehood. That fall he sent Gayoso on a mission to Kentucky to promote a revival of disaffection scheming, but this and subsequent projects of the optimistic Louisiana governor proved fruitless. Soon after the return of Gayoso, news arrived of Pinckney's Treaty, which had been signed at San Lorenzo in October. Spanish minister Manuel de Godoy had made the fateful decision, against Carondelet's strong objections, to negotiate with a responsible American government rather than to trust in the governor's intrigues with irresponsible, unpredictable frontiersmen. The treaty did much to dispel western discontent by giving America the east bank of the Mississippi above the 31st parallel, as well as free navigation of the river and the right of deposit at New Orleans.[14]

Gayoso, who felt that Godoy should have had more faith in the separatist intrigues, stated in early 1796 that "it is more than probable that a separation of several states will take place." Concerning Pinckney's Treaty he remarked, "If this union is dissolved one of the contracting parties exists no longer & the other is absolved of her engagements." Gayoso had not lost hope that some turn of events would allow the Spanish to retain Natchez and was convinced that "the Treaty will be reduced to the Navigation of this River." Recalling the non-alienation stipulation in the Treaty of Nogales, Gayoso added: "There are other insur-

[13] Gayoso to Carondelet, May 23, 1794, AGI, leg. 2354; Carondelet to Luis de las Casas, May 23, 1793, *ibid.*, leg. 152; Ernest R. Liljegren, "Jacobism in Spanish Louisiana, 1792–1797," *LHQ*, XXII (January, 1939), 79–83; Frederick J. Turner (ed.), "Carondelet on the Defense in Louisiana, 1794," *AHR*, II (April, 1897), 474–505.

[14] Bemis, *Pinckney's Treaty*, 305–34; Whitaker, *Spanish-American Frontier*, 200–13; Holmes, *Documentos inéditos*, 253–302.

mountable difficulties with respect to the Indians which render impracticable the execution of the part concerning limits."[15]

After ratification of Pinckney's Treaty in April, 1796, Godoy sent orders to Carondelet for its punctual execution. Still convinced that his intrigues would work, Carondelet procrastinated, so Godoy dispatched a more strongly-worded note in August. Before the governor received it, however, Spain had withdrawn from the anti-French coalition and had concluded a defensive alliance with France. In November, Carondelet received not only Godoy's August order but also instructions to attack the British who were supposedly moving into the Missouri Valley. Carondelet hurriedly sent word to Gayoso to cancel preparations for dismantling defenses at Natchez and Nogales. The governor also sent Thomas Power to Kentucky with an offer of $100,000 to anyone who would instigate a secession movement there. Carondelet had dreamed of a new Spanish province in the region from the Ohio to Natchez as a buffer against British encroachments, but Power's mission ended in failure. Since the rumors of British invaders persisted, however, Carondelet felt that they at least provided further excuse for postponing the Natchez withdrawal.[16]

The Spanish-American treaty abetted the interests of Georgia speculators, who pressured the state legislature in 1795 to pass the Yazoo Act, granting nearly thirty-five million acres in the triangle between the Chickasaw Bluffs, Muscle Shoals, and Natchez to four land companies. The Georgia Mississippi Company received the large tract from the Mississippi to the Tombigbee and from the parallel of 31° 18' latitude to that of 32° 40', which included nearly all of the Natchez District. Governor George Mathews and United States Senator James Gunn of Georgia were

[15] Gayoso to Daniel Clark, Sr., January 17, 1796, New Orleans Consular Letters, National Archives.

[16] Juan Morales to Carondelet, March 16, 1797, AGI, leg. 90; Carondelet to Conde de Santa Clara, April 22, 1797, *ibid.*, leg. 1502; Gayoso to Santa Clara, June 5, 1798, *ibid.*, leg. 1502; James R. Jacobs, *The Beginning of the U.S. Army, 1783–1812* (Princeton, 1947), 203–205; Whitaker, *Mississippi Question*, 51–56. In his will Stephen Minor bequeathed several small islands off the Mississippi coast to Thomas Power's children. Adams County Will Record, I, entry of January 8, 1816, Chancery Clerk's Records.

among the main backers of this company, which paid only $155,000 for the land. No sooner was the act passed, however, than a strong public reaction set in, culminating in the Rescinding Act of 1796, which undid the work of the previous legislature. But, since much of the acreage had already been sold by speculators, the rescision created pandemonium in the matter of land titles. Zachariah Cox of Kentucky, James White of North Carolina and Natchez, William Blount of Tennessee, and Mathews of Georgia each concocted schemes for profiteering in the area claimed by the Georgia Mississippi Company, in spite of the rescision. All four speculators were in Natchez at various times from 1796 to 1798, pursuing their sundry plans. Long before Georgia finally renounced her claims to the region in 1802, however, all of these projects had collapsed. But confusion over land claims would continue around Natchez for decades.[17]

The final fourteen months that the Spanish flag flew over the town were a stirring climax to the tensions that had been manifested many times during the previous fifteen years. Land fever, western separatism, Spanish defensiveness, American aggressiveness, and Natchez factionalism blended into a maze of misunderstanding, machination, and duplicity in 1797–98.

With new urgings from Godoy as well as pressure from General Anthony Wayne, Carondelet in February, 1797, reluctantly dispatched a note to Gayoso to begin dismantling the fortifications at Natchez and Nogales. But shortly after the courier's departure upriver, the governor received orders from Madrid to postpone the evacuation. Godoy was planning talks with American officials about alterations in Pinckney's Treaty while simultaneously negotiating with the French for the retrocession of Louisiana. Carondelet's second messenger arrived at Natchez with the countermanding order a few days after the coming of an American commissioner, who was bent upon forcing the evacuation of the district.[18]

[17] Juan Nepomuceno de Quesada to Las Casas, February 10, 1795, AGI, leg. 1438; Abernethy, *The South in the New Nation*, 136–91.
[18] Isaac J. Cox, *The West Florida Controversy, 1798–1813: A Study in Ameri-

Andrew Ellicott was the scholarly, irascible Quaker whom President Washington had selected to negotiate the demarcation of the boundary between the Spanish Floridas and the United States. He was also instructed to persuade the Spanish to withdraw from Natchez. A small army escort and two dozen woodsmen accompanied Ellicott on the trip downriver from Fort Pitt (now Pittsburgh), and Lieutenant Percy Smith Pope's unit moved to the Chickasaw Bluffs to reinforce Ellicott if necessary (the Spanish having evacuated the fort there). After stopping several days at the Bayou Pierre plantation of Peter Bryan Bruin, a leader of the American faction in the district, Ellicott and his band docked at Natchez on February 24, 1797, and encamped on a knoll overlooking the bluff and the town esplanade. At Patrick Connelly's tavern atop the elevation the Americans brazenly hoisted the United States flag, which was clearly seen by the Spanish in the fort at the south end of the esplanade. A demand that it be removed, said Ellicott, was met "with positive refusal, and the flag wore out upon the staff."[19]

With new instructions from New Orleans that the evacuation be delayed, Gayoso and his garrison of sixty regulars adamantly refused to budge. In fact, Gayoso ordered some dismantled artillery pieces at the landing to be hauled back up the hill to the fort. The Spaniard politely informed Ellicott that his orders were to hold Natchez and Nogales indefinitely. At one time or another Carondelet and Gayoso gave four reasons for Spain's delay in withdrawing. First, there were recurring rumors of an imminent attack on Natchez by the British from Canada. Also, the Spanish feared Indian retaliations against the local people if they yielded the area in violation of the Nogales treaty. Third, Madrid authorities objected to the clause in Jay's Treaty of 1794 whereby America gave England navigation rights on the Mississippi.

can Diplomacy (Baltimore, 1918), 32–44; Franklin L. Riley, "Spanish Policy in Mississippi after the Treaty of San Lorenzo," *PMHS*, I (1898), 50–66; Riley, "Transition from Spanish Rule," *ibid.*, III (1901), 261–67.

[19] Ellicott to Gayoso, March 31, 1797, AGI, leg. 1500; Ellicott, *Journal*, 37–44; Pearl V. Guyton, *Connelly's Tavern on Ellicott's Hill* (Jackson, 1942), *passim*.

Lastly, Gayoso deeply resented Ellicott's disrespectful, antagonistic approach—for example, his charge that the Spanish were imprisoning men because of their American sympathies. To this Gayoso piously retorted: "There is but one single individual imprisoned in this entire district, and that upon a criminal charge."[20]

Sending sometimes three notes a day to Gayoso demanding withdrawal, Ellicott seemed determined to hold his encampment behind Connelly's tavern until the dons furled their flag. Tension mounted when Ellicott addressed a circular to the "Residents of the Natchez country and Warriors of the Choctaw Nation" to join him in pressuring the Spanish to leave. In New Orleans, Philip Nolan and American vice consul Daniel Clark, Jr., vainly tried to convince Carondelet of the rightness of Ellicott's position. In late April, "Crazy" Percy Smith Pope's troops arrived to reinforce Ellicott, while another American unit, commanded by Captain Isaac Guion, took its station at the Chickasaw Bluffs and prepared to move down to Natchez if it became necessary.[21]

Realizing that neither side possessed a preponderance of military strength, Gayoso also appealed to the local people for support. In late March he issued a proclamation emphasizing protection of life and property as the main reason for postponement of the evacuation. He also shrewdly declared a moratorium on planters' debts for the current season.[22] In May, Carondelet penned a proclamation which was to be "published & posted up in all the districts of the Government of Natchez in the usual places." In it he blamed the troubles at Natchez on "some evil

[20] Gayoso to Ellicott, March 31, 1797, in Claiborne, *Mississippi*, 164; Carondelet to Las Casas, January 30, 1797, AGI, leg. 153; Ellicott, *Journal*, 101–103. The Spanish evacuated their Chickasaw Bluffs and Tombigbee forts in March, 1797.

[21] Daniel Clark, Jr., to Ellicott, March 14, 1798, New Orleans Consular Letters; Clark to Timothy Pickering, March 17, 1798, *ibid.; American State Papers, Miscellaneous*, I, 710; Ellicott, *Journal*, 67, 96–98. Daniel Clark, Jr., was a nephew of Daniel Clark, Sr., of Natchez. On Nolan's activities, see also Edward E. Hale, "The Real Philip Nolan," *PMHS*, IV (1901), 281–329; *DAB*, VII, 543–44.

[22] Ellicott, *Journal*, 65–67; Whitaker, *Mississippi Question*, 59–60.

disposed Persons who have nothing to lose." They were trying to lead the citizens "into improper measures whose disagreeable consequences would only fall on those possessed of Property whilst the perturbators of the public Peace would screen themselves by flight." His references were obviously to Ellicott and his intruders, but the governor refrained from mentioning names. As for the evacuation and the start of the boundary demarcation, Carondelet claimed that their suspension had been due to "the imperious necessity of securing lower Louisiana from the hostilities of the English." He held the "well grounded hope" that during this period of uncertainty the citizens would "behave with the same tranquillity & entertain the same affection" as they had shown "on all occasions previous." The governor concluded with a tactless plea for public support of "the Spanish Government, which will not without feeling in the most sensible manner see itself forced to destroy a settlement which it has been at so much pain & Expense to form & protect." That same month Nolan, in New Orleans, wrote Ellicott that Carondelet was ready to "give the Americans lead and the inhabitants hemp."[23]

Carondelet had grounds for hoping that the inhabitants at Natchez would support the Spanish regime against Ellicott. They had remained loyal during the Bourbon County incident of 1785, the O'Fallon scheme of 1790, the Jacobin excitement of 1793, and, most recently, the enigmatic ventures of Blount and other speculators. Gayoso himself was a valuable asset: his honesty, competence, aristocratic demeanor, and tactfulness had won admiration, especially among the wealthy and influential at Natchez. Of vital interest to the citizens were their land titles and claims, which would remain secure under the dons but might be in jeopardy if the United States took the area. In addition, the introduction of the saw gin and of large-scale cotton production after 1794 had enabled many of the debt-laden planters to forecast economic success for the years ahead.[24]

[23] Carondelet's proclamation to the citizens of the Natchez District, May 26, 1797, New Orleans Consular Letters, National Archives; Ellicott, *Journal*, 85.

[24] Hamilton, "American Beginnings in the Old Southwest," 427–28; Whitaker, *Mississippi Question*, 60–62.

On the other hand, Ellicott also had reason to expect strong local backing. Seven out of eight residents, by his estimate, were United States citizens or were Britishers who favored American occupation, while "about eight persons, including some officers," supported the Spanish. In May, 1797, Pope sent a report to Guion which was overly optimistic: "The inhabitants are anxiously awaiting a change of government, and to a man, are warmly attached to the United States."[25] It is probably true that the overwhelming majority of settlers during the previous decade were Americans by birth. Also, many of the citizens of longer residence were now resigned to the impossibility of a return of the British flag and had come to look forward to passing under the Federalist regime, which was thought to champion British and propertied interests. Most settlers, old and new, chafed under the regulations against land speculation, self-government, and public Protestant worship. Though the shift to cotton had brought hope, many people were still suffering from the consequences of the tobacco crisis and blamed their woes on the Spanish.[26]

The factional alignments of the citizens in 1797 have been variously delineated. Daniel Clark, Sr., who was a leader of the merchant-creditor group, former business partner of Wilkinson, and close personal friend of Gayoso, saw two distinct groups opposing the Spanish by June. First, there were those—such as Anthony Hutchins, Thomas Green, and Peter Bryan Bruin—who felt that Gayoso had "insulted, wronged, and refused to grant land to them." Second, there was the frontier-rabble element, which "was in general composed of low characters inured to the practice of murdering and plundering."[27] On the other hand, Cato West, Green's son-in-law and a spokesman of the planter-debtor faction, analyzed the Natchez factions in this manner:

[25] Ellicott to Pickering, April 14, 1797, Correspondence of Andrew Ellicott, Library of Congress; Pope to Guion, May 2, 1797, John F. H. Claiborne Papers, Vol. D, Mississippi Archives.

[26] Whitaker, *Mississippi Question*, 62–63.

[27] Gayoso to Carondelet, June 2 and 7, 1796, AGI, leg. 23.

"For a long time prior to the arrival of the American Commissioner two parties had actually existed in this Country—the Planters, Mechanics &c. chiefly Natives of the United States constituted the one party." The other group was composed of "a number of miscellaneous characters including informers and a train of Court Sycophants who had been long in the habit of corrupting the Officers at the expence of the honest and undesigning subject." These were the men who had been favored by the Spanish with lucrative army supply contracts, government positions, and land grants approved after Pinckney's Treaty but dated earlier. Conspicuous among these types were Moore, Minor, Vidal, and Dunbar.[28]

The most significant element in the factionalism at Natchez, however, seems to be that which was rooted in the old creditor-debtor debacle. The rural-debtor group tended to rally behind Pope, who was convinced that the dons would not leave without "being first damnably flogged." He thus favored an open attack on Fort Nogales, which, he thought, could be easily taken in view of its poorly maintained fortifications and few defenders. Hutchins and Green were particularly bellicose. The latter recruited two hundred armed men from Cole's Creek for an assault, but Gayoso arrested him before the attack was launched. Green escaped from the fort brig, however, fled to Tennessee, and returned to the Natchez melee that summer. Most of the merchant-creditor group lived in the town and feared damages to their large property investments there if fighting occurred. Consequently they supported Ellicott, who differed with Pope and preferred forcing the Spanish departure by threats, bluffs, and constant pressure on the beleaguered Gayoso. The many differences between economic and national interests, together with personal feuds, produced strife almost daily in the ensuing months. Added to the confusion of 1797 were mysterious visits to Natchez by Mathews, Blount, Power, and Cox in connection

[28] Cato West's committee to Winthrop Sargent, August 26, 1799, in Clarence E. Carter (ed.), *The Territorial Papers of the United States*, Vols. V–VI, *The Territory of Mississippi, 1798–1817* (Washington, 1937–38), V, 72.

with separatist or speculative schemes, which multiplied the excited rumors over the town's fate.[29]

In the late spring of 1797 several itinerant Protestant ministers suddenly appeared on the scene, inciting those who would listen to overthrow the despotism of Rome and Madrid. On June 9 some irate Irish Catholics mauled Barton Hannon, an outspoken, drunken shoemaker and lay Baptist preacher who was damning the papacy and recruiting volunteers for a revolt. Gayoso's arrest of Hannon for disturbing the peace triggered an outbreak of disturbances in the next few days. On June 12 over three hundred armed men assembled at William Belk's tavern on the Trace to organize a rebellion. With Pope encouraging the plan and Ellicott discouraging it, no massive assault occurred, but everyone was wildly excited for days. There were a few isolated cases of violence, and on the night of the fourteenth a small band of rebels, upon Pope's instigation, tried to capture an elevation near the fort but were repelled by Spanish fire. Amidst the confusion a band of Choctaw wandered into town and, becoming thoroughly inebriated, caused further disorder and alarm. The situation was ominous enough to compel Gayoso and his family to flee from "Concord" to the safety of the fort. Knowing that he was on the defensive and sincerely fearing for the safety of his constituents, Gayoso released Hannon and agreed to a citizens' meeting, suggested by Ellicott, for the purpose of electing a council to help restore order.[30]

The fateful meeting at Belk's tavern on June 20 marked the

[29] Pope to the Natchez citizens, June 12, 1797, AGI, leg. 1500; Pope to Guion, May 2, 1797, John F. H. Claiborne Papers, Vol. D, Mississippi Archives; Ellicott, *Journal*, 70–74, 147; Cox, *West Florida Controversy*, 44–63. William Dunbar, who had moved from the Manchac area to a plantation south of Natchez after the American Revolution, became a major speculator in Natchez real estate during Gayoso's rule. Fearing he might lose a real estate opportunity in 1797 if the Americans took the town, he persuaded Gayoso to grant him about twenty-seven acres on a valuable site near the fort as compensation for his earlier services in "laying off & measuring the lots of this City." Dunbar to Gayoso, April 4, 1797, and Gayoso to Dunbar, April 19, 1797, Dunbar Papers, Mississippi Archives.

[30] Ellicott, *Journal*, 97–100; Diary of Captain Manuel de Lanzo, entries of June, 1797, in Holmes, *Documentos inéditos*, 318–55. See also the correspondence of Gayoso, Carondelet, Pope, and Ellicott, June 12–17, 1797, AGI, leg. 1502.

virtual end of Spanish control over Natchez. A large body of
local citizens were present, as well as Ellicott, Pope, and Gayoso.
Hutchins, whom Gayoso described on this occasion as one "who
had formerly been violent in his measures against our government," presided. "Foreseeing that these riots would result in rob-
bery and disorder," the Englishman "began to fear for his own
property and sincerely joined the party of moderation."[31]

A temporary committee was elected to assist Gayoso in re-
storing order and to draft resolutions which epitomized the
citizens' chief grievances. The committee consisted of Hutchins,
Lintot, West, Bernard, Gabriel Benoist, William Ratlif, and Isaac
Gaillard. Hutchins, now eighty-two years old and a leader of the
first revolt against the dons in 1781, polled the most votes and
became chairman. The committee promptly prepared four resolutions on behalf of the citizenry and sent them to Gayoso:
First, the citizens should not be prosecuted or injured because of
their neutral position during the period prior to official American
occupation. The citizens should also be exempt from militia
conscription except in cases of riot and Indian attack. Third,
the "laws of Spain" should be continued only if executed "with
mildness & moderation;" no citizen should be tried outside the
district. Finally, the committee, in turn, would "endeavor to
preserve the Peace & promote the due Execution of Justice."
Though presented to Gayoso as recommendations, probably out
of respect to him, the action really amounted to an ultimatum.[32]

Gayoso's dilemma was such that he could not extricate himself
without more aid from Carondelet, which was not forthcoming.
So he submitted gracefully and approved the resolutions in a
meeting with the committee on June 24. Vidal and Benoist were
delegated to carry the document to New Orleans. Carondelet approved it with the reservation that capital crimes were to be
tried in New Orleans. The *de facto* government was now the
committee, working in conjunction with Ellicott and Pope. The

[31] Gayoso to Carondelet, June 23, 1797, *ibid.*, leg. 1502.
[32] Citizens' committee to Gayoso, June 20, 1797, *ibid.*, leg. 1502; Gayoso to
Carondelet, June 21, 1797, *ibid.*, leg. 1502.

next month Gayoso received word on his promotion to the Louisiana governorship and assumed his duties at the capital on
August 5. He left Stephen Minor, his adjutant major, in charge
of Spanish affairs at Natchez.[33]

No further rioting or violence occurred that summer, but the
Cole's Creek group refused to recognize the agreement until the
committee threatened to use force against them. Meanwhile,
maneuverings for power and bitter jealousies at Natchez led to
two changes in the committee plan. A second and permanent
committee, often called the Committee of Safety, was elected in
July. Thanks to energetic campaigning and pressuring by the
Ellicott faction, those elected were largely merchants and pro-
Ellicott men, led by Bernard, Clark, and Bruin. Enraged,
Anthony Hutchins wrote Gayoso that "widespread fraud" was
evident in the balloting. The venerable British colonel, whom
Ellicott called "Squeaking Tony, long and bony," mounted a
counter-offensive that won enough popular support for another
election in September. The new committee was dominated by
the planter-debtor group and was headed by Thomas Green,
father-in-law of Hutchins' daughter. Minor and the second committee would not recognize the new committee, but the latter
remained active through the next spring. At the end of September, Minor reported to Gayoso that, despite the presence of two
citizens' committees, the people seemed relatively tranquil, and
Blount's latest visit had met with "hostility in every quarter."[34]

However, the town was in turmoil again within a few weeks.

[33] Gayoso to Hutchins, June 24, 1797, Mississippi Miscellaneous Papers,
Library of Congress; Gayoso to citizens' committee, June 22, 1797, AGI, leg.
1502; Ellicott and Pope to Gayoso, June 22, 1797, ibid., leg. 1502; Gayoso to
Pope, August 18, 1797, ibid., leg. 1500; Gayoso to Wilkinson, August 19, 1797,
ibid., leg. 1500.

[34] Carondelet to Gayoso, July 1, 1797, ibid., leg. 2354; Gayoso to Santa Clara,
September 24, 1797, ibid., leg. 2354; Minor to Ellicott, September 8, 1797,
Ellicott Correspondence; Ellicott, Journal, 140–49. The citizens' committee
elected in July, 1797, consisted of Joseph Bernard, Daniel Clark, Peter Bryan
Bruin, Gabriel Benoist, Philander Smith, Roger Dixon, Isaac Gaillard, and
Frederick Kimball. The extra-legal committee elected in September included
Thomas Green, Chester Ashley, Daniel Burnet, James Stuart, Landon Davis,
Justice King, Abner Green, and Dr. John Shaw.

Blount, who had been expelled from the United States Senate in July on charges of plotting with the British, Creek, and Cherokee to attack the Spanish, met with Ellicott on several occasions early that autumn, leading Gayoso to charge complicity between the two. Ellicott, in turn, accused Hutchins of conspiring with Blount. The bombastic Hutchins roared that he would expose Ellicott's illicit sexual life, though he never came forth with the sordid details he promised. In November, Hutchins' group sent a petition to Congress asking for the removal of Ellicott on grounds of duplicity and mishandling the Natchez situation. But the paper was stolen from the courier before he left the district. A loud popular outcry was raised, prompted by Hutchins' charge that the thief was hired by Ellicott. Frantically endeavoring to avert a recurrence of violence, Minor sent his troops from house to house in quest of the stolen petition and the identity of the culprit. The blame was finally centered upon Silas Payne, who had written pamphlets for Ellicott. Whether a trial took place is not known, but the clamor for it renewed public excitement. Meanwhile Ellicott had been savage in his remarks about Hutchins, and coincidentally a rumor began circulating about a plot to assassinate the latter.[35] William Vousdan, Hutchins' son-in-law, wrote Minor in early November that, in view of the strong public feelings, "if Col. Hutchins is murdered I am induced to say that Mr. Ellicott may be the next victim, for retaliation will have no bounds when once begun."[36] No attempt was made on Hutchins' life, but the rumor persisted for weeks. Minor reported to Gayoso about this time: "Generally speaking the People are getting heartily tired of all party business, and American politicks is now becoming an old thing. . . . I could raise as great a party at present in favor of [Spanish] Government as could be raised

[35] Gayoso to Carlos Martinez de Yrujo, October 20, 1797; Gayoso to Santa Clara, October 20, 1797; Minor to John Girault, November 23, 1797; John Burnet and William Brocus to Minor, November 24, 1797; Minor to Gayoso, November 26, 1797; and Gayoso to Santa Clara, December 13, 1797—all in AGI, leg. 1500. On Blount's activities, see also William H. Masterson, *William Blount* (Baton Rouge, 1954), 286–323.

[36] William Vousdan to Minor, November 8, 1797, Minor Papers, LSU.

on the opposite side." Later Minor commented: "God send a speedy determination of things, otherwise they will all run mad, with memorials, certificates, circular letters, &ca."[37]

Two other November events contributed to the tenseness of the situation. News came that Gayoso was sending Grand-Pré as the new district governor. Grand-Pré, who was well known at Natchez, did not command as much respect as did Gayoso among the local citizenry. Futhermore, the people feared the appointment meant a reassertion of Spanish authority. As far as they were concerned, Minor, who was an American and the acting district head, was sufficient Spanish representation, especially since he made no effort to exercise more than titular authority. The Committee of Safety sent a hotly worded note to Gayoso warning him that the arrival of Grand-Pré was certain to spark a new explosion. Gayoso discreetly decided to keep Grand-Pré as Baton Rouge commandant.[38] The people were again in a dither the next week when word spread that Pope was preparing to attack the fort. The attempt, if such were contemplated by Pope, was not made, but Minor and Vidal convinced Gayoso that the plot was real. The Louisiana governor sent a sharp warning to Pope and Ellicott that their recklessness could lead to serious international repercussions.[39]

In early December, Captain Isaac Guion arrived with a larger unit of troops and promptly took command of all United States forces in the district despite protests from Pope and Ellicott. The officer then called a meeting of the various factional leaders to try to work out their differences, but became so disgusted with their bickering that he stormed out of the room. Guion's forceful, truculent disposition and, more important, his preponderance of military strength kept the situation tense but orderly in the following months. Another citizens' committee was elected later, but Guion continued to hold tightly the reins of authority.[40]

[37] Minor to Gayoso, November 26 and 29, 1797, AGI, leg. 1500.
[38] Ellicott, *Journal*, 161; Whitaker, *Mississippi Question*, 65.
[39] Minor to Gayoso, November 29, 1797, and Gayoso to Santa Clara, December 13, 1797, AGI, leg. 1500.
[40] Ellicott to Pickering, February 10, 1798, Ellicott Correspondence; Vousdan to Guion, May 9, 1798, John F. H. Claiborne Papers, Vol. D, Mississippi Archives.

On March 30, 1798, Ellicott recorded in his journal that at 4 o'clock that morning he went to the fort "and enjoyed from the parapet, the pleasing prospect of the galleys and boats leaving the shore, and getting under way: they were out of sight before daylight. The same day our troops took possession of the works." Ellicott then packed his bags and departed to undertake the long-postponed boundary demarcation. Since the survey teams included some of the participants in the late events at Natchez— among them Minor, Power, Dunbar, and Daniel Burnet—it is no wonder that the wrangling continued on the boundary project. Ellicott complained that his colleagues used their energy to "disorganize and talk politics." When Gayoso came for the ceremonies marking the official start of the demarcation on May 31, his unexpected and public embrace of Ellicott prompted a disgruntled comment by the American commissioner: "I had not been shaved for two days. Men's kissing I think a most abominable custom."[41]

Congress on April 7 created the Mississippi Territory; its bounds encompassed the Natchez District and the region eastward to the Chattahoochee. Vidal, who had earlier succeeded Minor as the supreme Spanish official at Natchez, continued from April to August as Spanish consul there. The last dispute between the Spanish and Americans at Natchez occurred in June when Vidal and Guion became embroiled in a hassle over authorization to issue passports, during which Guion threatened "to throw Vidal out of town." No longer backed by military force, Vidal was forced to retreat on the issue.[42]

President Adams' selection of George Mathews as territorial governor raised such a storm of protest in Congress and at Natchez that his name was withdrawn. Instead, Adams appointed

[41] Ellicott, *Journal,* 176; *American State Papers, Miscellaneous,* I, 710–11; Ellicott to his wife, June 19, 1798, in Catherine V. C. Matthews, *Andrew Ellicott: His Life and Letters* (New York, 1908), 159. On Ellicott, see also *DAB,* III, 89–90.

[42] An Act for the Government of the Mississippi Territory, April 7, 1798, in Carter, *Territorial Papers,* V, 18–22; Guion to Vidal, June 10, 1798, and Vidal to Gayoso, July 10, 1798, AGI, leg. 1502.

Winthrop Sargent, a Massachusetts Federalist and former secretary of the Northwest Territory. Relative calm existed at Natchez when Sargent arrived on August 6, 1798. Three weeks later the town was visited by the new over-all commander of the United States Army, General James Wilkinson, who was en route to Fort Adams on the river just above the 31st parallel, recently established as the official point of entry into American territory.[43]

Prior to sending Guion downriver the previous year, Wilkinson had briefed him on the situation at Natchez, which he referred to as "an extensive, opulent, and polished community, agitated by a variety of political interests and opinions." The general predicted: "The moment the Spanish domain terminates they [the townsfolk] will find themselves without laws or magistrates, and the bonds of society being dissolved, more or less irregularities may ensue."[44] Disorder had already characterized political conditions at Natchez before and after the revolt of June, 1797, with nearly every thread of the Spanish-American frontier rivalry woven into the complicated tapestry. Whether "irregularities" would continue to plague the community depended largely upon the regime which the territorial governor would institute. The era of international intrigues had passed, but the uncertainties about the future that had long gripped the minds of the Natchez people were still present.

[43] Commission of Governor Winthrop Sargent, May 7, 1798, in Carter, *Territorial Papers*, V, 28–29; Pickering to George Mathews, May 8, 1798, *ibid.*, 31.
[44] Wilkinson to Guion, May 20, 1797, John F. H. Claiborne Papers, Vol. D, Mississippi Archives.

CHAPTER IV

No Cobwebs
on City Hall

FOR THE FIRST EIGHT MONTHS OF HIS GOVernorship Winthrop Sargent ruled Natchez, the territorial capital, by personal decree. He antagonized many townsmen by his tactless, tyrannical behavior and by his favoritism toward the community's creditor faction, most of whom now styled themselves Federalists. When Adams and Pickering counties were created in 1799, Natchez became the seat of the former. For the next three years municipal as well as county affairs were handled by the justices of the peace, who comprised the Court of General Quarter Sessions and the Court of Common Pleas. With the arrival in 1801 of Republican William C. C. Claiborne as the second governor and the ascendancy of the rural Republicans in the new territorial assembly, the capital and county seat were moved to Washington, an infant village six miles to the east. Incorporation was then pushed by the townsfolk living on the bluff. Since Natchez was the only sizable town for over a hundred miles in any direction (it numbered some 1,400 inhabitants), the move seemed justifiable even to those who despised its coterie of opulent creditors.[1]

The General Assembly incorporated Natchez in March, 1803, providing for a municipal government with "extensive and summary" powers. An early authority on the town's history, John Monette, says that if this arrangement "leaned to the despotism of monarchy, it resulted from the nature of the circumstances under which it was enacted," namely "the number of lawless

[1] Sargent to James Ross, October 17, 1798, in Dunbar Rowland (ed.), *Mississippi Territorial Archives, 1798–1803* (Nashville, 1905), 66; Proclamation of Sargent, April 2, 1799, *ibid.*, 126–28; Presentments of the Grand Jury of Adams County, June 6, 1799, in Carter, *Territorial Papers*, V, 63–66; Natchez citizens to Sargent, March 28, 1801, *ibid.*, 122–23.

adventurers and boatmen from the Ohio region which annually infested the city and habitually defied the municipal authorities."[2]

The Common Council, or municipal governing body, was to consist of six appointed officials and nine elected ones. The governor would choose a mayor, city clerk, marshal, and three aldermen, while the citizens would elect annually a treasurer, assessor, collector, and six assistants to the aldermen. The council could create and fill certain subsidiary posts, such as market clerk and city printer. The mayor, the city clerk, and the three aldermen would be given authority also as justices of the peace. In addition, a Mayor's Court, or municipal judicial body, would be provided, consisting of those five magistrates.[3]

Two weeks after the act was passed Claiborne announced his six appointments. Merchant Samuel Brooks, whose daughter had married Anthony Hutchins' son but who had not been involved in the bitter factionalism of previous years, proved to be a wise selection as the first mayor. After the election of the other officials the Common Council met for the first time on April 9, drafting eleven rules of procedure for future meetings.[4]

At the first session of the Mayor's Court three weeks later eight attorneys were admitted to practice, eighteen tavern licenses were granted (twenty-six by the year's end), and ten "defaulting jurors" were fined. Civil suits, however, would soon occupy a large amount of the court's time, the number of cases rising from 37 in December, 1803, to 144 in April, 1805.[5]

The Mayor's Court had jurisdiction over criminal cases in which the punishment did not exceed one month in jail, a fine

---

[2] John W. Monette, *History of the Discovery and Settlement of the Valley of the Mississippi* (2 vols.; New York, 1846), II, 359–61; *Ordinances of the City of Natchez with the Acts of the Legislature of the State of Mississippi in Regard to Said City* . . . (Natchez, 1829), 3.

[3] Edward Turner (comp.), *Statutes of the Mississippi Territory, Digested by the Authority of the General Assembly* (Natchez, 1816), 347–53.

[4] Common Council Minute Book, I, entry of April 9, 1803, Records of the City Clerk's Office, Natchez.

[5] Mayor's Court Minute Book, I, entries of May 3, 1803, December 5, 1803, and April 4, 1805, City Clerk's Records; City Treasurer's Reports, I, entry of December 9, 1808, City Clerk's Records.

of $50, thirty-nine lashes "on the bare back," six hours in the public stocks, or three hours in the public pillory. It also had authority over civil cases which involved up to $100. If the amount were $21 to $99, the defendant could ask the court to empanel a jury. Major criminal and civil cases had to be referred to the territorial court.[6]

The legislature conferred additional powers upon the Mayor's Court in 1805, including jurisdiction over civil cases involving sums up to $500. In 1814 the territorial assembly abolished the court.[7] Monette claimed that "the arbitrary proceedings of this court at length became so oppressive that public opinion was roused against it, until it was denounced in a public meeting, and finally made the object of a presentment by the grand jury, 'as a public grievance,'" In his historical notes Edward Turner, a city magistrate at that time, said that the court was "too summary for debtors—hence the outcry."[8]

The Mayor's Court was reborn in 1852 on a more modest scale. The mayor, or president—either title was used by the 1850's—and the city constable constituted the judicial body, which met briefly each weekday. The mayor rendered the final judgments; he was empowered to levy fines up to $10 and order jail sentences up to twenty-four hours for violators of municipal laws.[9] There was no recurrence of the old animosities against the city court.

The city charter was amended in 1809, changing the governing body to a seven-man Board of Selectmen. The treasurer, assessor, collector, marshal, and selectmen were to be elected by the qualified voters; the president, as the mayor was henceforth called, and the city clerk were to be elected by and from the

[6] Common Council Minute Book, I, entry of May 13, 1803.

[7] Harry Toulmin (comp.), The Statutes of the Mississippi Territory, Revised and Digested by the Authority of the General Assembly (Natchez, 1807), 129–34; Turner, Statutes of the Mississippi Territory, 347.

[8] Monette, Valley of the Mississippi, II, 360; Historical notes of Edward Turner, Wailes Papers, Mississippi Archives; Natchez Mississippi Messenger, July 19, 1805.

[9] Laws of the State of Mississippi Passed at a Called Session of the Mississippi Legislature, Held in the City of Jackson, October, 1852 (Jackson, 1852), 191–93.

Board of Selectmen. City elections were to be held on the first Monday of each January, with all terms being for one year. The act also set the municipal boundaries at one mile from the Catholic chapel in each direction except, of course, to the west where the line extended to the river.[10]

The basic administrative structure of government at Natchez underwent few changes during the four decades after Mississippi's admission into the Union in 1817. The president was elected by the citizens after 1850, but otherwise the number and terms of elected officials remained the same. The selectmen continued to appoint a market clerk and a city printer each year. Beginning in 1847, however, the markethouse which the city had operated since 1806 was leased to William J. Minor, a prominent planter and son of Stephen Minor. The market clerk's function was by that time relegated to collecting a percentage of Minor's profits from the operation. The compromise with laissez-faire was lucrative for the lessee and the city: municipal revenues from this source often exceeded $225 a month.[11]

Although amendments to the city charter were rare, a significant growth in city governmental activities occurred between 1818 and 1860. It is evident not only in the more frequent meetings of the selectmen (they assembled sometimes twice a week), but also in the development of new programs as the town passed from the frontier stage to that of a mature community. The selectmen annually appointed a board of street commissioners, a police board, a health board, and a board of trustees for the Natchez Institute, a large public school which the city established in 1845. The various board appointees were usually civic-minded townsmen who were not city officials at the time and received no remuneration. By 1849 the number of permanent committees of the Board of Selectmen itself stood at eight: roads, health, accounts, finances, landing, safety, enrolled bills, and "proposals

[10] *Ordinances of the City of Natchez,* 3; George Poindexter (comp.), *The Revised Code of the Laws of Mississippi* . . . (Natchez, 1824), 624–26.
[11] Board of Selectmen Minute Book, IV, entries of December 27, 1848, and November 20, 1850, City Clerk's Records.

and grievances." A decade later a committee on gas street lighting and one on public property had been added. Besides the
elected officials, the city payroll by 1850 included the following
positions: solicitor, health officer, counselor, printer, "city guard"
captain and four watchmen (for fire and epidemic watches),
surveyor, "town clock attendant," street contractor, nursery superintendent, cemetery caretaker, two constable assistants, four
janitors, and eight Institute teachers. For the most part, the
commissions and committees were active, and their reports suggest a remarkable degree of efficiency and dedication. This was
true also of the regular meetings of the selectmen where attendance of all magistrates was frequently recorded.[12]

By 1812 the city had already constructed on the public square,
which was two blocks east of the bluff commons, a firehouse,
city hall, public cistern, jail, city markethouse, pillory, stocks, and
whipping post. Funds for capital construction in the early period
were obtained through public lotteries, which the magistrates
conducted after receiving public sanction at town meetings. The
old fort blockhouse was moved to the public square to serve as
a "city gaol" until two lotteries later, when adequate funds were
gained for a new jail. The firehouse, with the public cistern
beneath it, was erected in 1807 with lottery money. When the
first volunteer fire company was organized seven years later, the
engine house promptly burned to the ground. A new one was
built in 1816, and $2,000 worth of "engines, buckets, hooks, and
other instruments" were provided after the city fathers had presided over still another public lottery. By 1840 the town had the
Phoenix Independent Fire Company, the Hook and Ladder
Company, Achilles Engine, Neptune Engine, Protection Engine,
Water Witch Hose Company, and Relief Hose Company. The
lottery system by then had been abandoned in favor of bond
issues when capital funds were needed. Normal costs for fire
protection, such as equipment and maintenance, were provided

[12] *Ibid.*, IV, entries of July 14, 1847, June 3, 1849, and January 5, 1858; *ibid.*,
V, entry of January 24, 1860.

through city tax revenues, with such expenditures exceeding $8,000 a year by 1853.[13]

The city markethouse was a handsome brick and frame building, first constructed in 1806 with several later additions. Produce stalls were located on its lower level with a carriage drive through the center and some city offices on the upper level. During certain hours each weekday when the markethouse was open, usually 8 to 10 A.M., venders were prohibited from selling produce in other parts of the town. The produce that could be sold in the markethouse's eight stalls included "meats of all kinds, meal, flour, fish, wild game, poultry, cheese, butter, eggs, suet, lard, tallow, wax, fruits, and vegetables of all kinds." The city officials appointed the market clerk and paid him a monthly salary. He, in turn, set prices, collected a percentage from the sales for the city coffer, and—until Minor got the leasehold in the 1840's—generally supervised market operations and building maintenance.[14]

Besides the structures on the public square, the city maintained a powder magazine, signal cannon, ferry, nursery, and cemetery, as well as an ever-growing number of streets. The powder magazine was built in 1814 in anticipation of a British attack and was later used mainly by local militia units. The cannon, perched on the bluff's edge, was used to signal steamboat arrivals after 1810; to salute special occasions, such as the popular anniversary of Jackson's triumph at New Orleans (January 15); and to dissuade riotous boatmen at the landing. Beginning in 1804, the ferry rights across the river to Vidalia were leased by the city to the highest bidder at an annual public auction. The city also em-

[13] Common Council Minute Book, I, entry of July 3, 1805, and Appendix A; City Record of Accounts, I, entry of May 22, 1807, City Clerk's Records; Selectmen Minute Book, I, entry of February 1, 1814; *ibid.*, II, entry of February 15, 1816; Fiscal report for 1853, quoted in *ibid.*, V, entry of January 11, 1860; Natchez *Courier*, February 23, 1842.

[14] Record of Accounts, I, entry of May 19, 1812; *Mississippi Herald and Natchez Gazette*, May 27, 1806; Selectmen Minute Book, IV, entry of October 27, 1847.

ployed a man "for crying the ferry . . . and for warning and attending on Selectmen."[15]

The city not only maintained a tree nursery from 1806 onward but also promoted city-wide campaigns to get the townsfolk to plant its free "Trees of China" [chinaberry] on the theory that such would "contribute as well to the health as beauty of the city." After years of legal controversies with several landowners the city in 1815 finally got title to the "public burying grounds" on the north end of the bluff. Paupers and Negroes were interred at the south end.[16]

Street surveys and repairs were frequent items on the selectmen's agenda. In the 1790's the town expanded from two or three streets at the river's edge to the top of the bluff, with eight streets running eastward and perpendicular to seven north–south streets. By 1810 the so-called "Williamstown" area of fifteen blocks extended from the northeast edge of the original grid. The older streets stretched out in irregular patterns across the bayous and ravines of the outskirts. Houses appeared along routes that formerly had run only to secluded homes of the elite. Narrow side streets branched off the main roads to Woodville, Washington, and Pine Ridge, as well as the upper and lower river roads along the bluff's edge. Nearly two thirds of the city ordinances in the 1820's dealt with new streets or repairs on old ones. As early as 1822 the city records note that "paving," or gravel surfacing, was used in some downtown areas, including "paved sidewalks." From 1826 onward a street surveyor and a street contractor regularly appeared on the municipal monthly accounts.[17]

[15] Common Council Minute Book, I, entry of February 11, 1804; Selectmen Minute Book, I, entries of February 18, 1812, January 24, 1815, and January 1, 1816. According to an entry of December 31, 1813, the selectmen excused Stephen Carter, the ferry operator, for two years' tardiness in paying the ferry rental, accepting his explanation that he had not known "where to find the City Treasurer or his Deputy."

[16] Common Council Minute Book, I, entry of February 11, 1806; Selectmen Minute Book, I, entry of April 4, 1815; *ibid.*, V, entry of February 1, 1860. The burial area for paupers and Negroes washed into the river after a bluff cave-in about 1818. Thereafter some of them were buried in the main cemetery.

[17] Common Council Minute Book, entry of August 28, 1805; Selectmen Minute

Water carriers were forbidden in 1819 to sell water taken from the river's edge where boats were liable to dock and make the stream "filthy." That same year the Natchez Water Company was incorporated "for the purpose of introducing water into the city of Natchez, by means of leaden or wooden pipes." The company was capitalized at $200,000 and could sell stock at $100 per share. It was one of the few public services which the city did not monopolize. The company's charter officials, including Edward Turner, president; Samual Postlethwaite, II, a future president; Lewis Evans, assessor and former sheriff; and Charles B. Green, later a city counselor, however, were closely linked with the municipal administration. The water was tapped from artesian wells sunk at Natchez-under-the-Hill.[18]

Through county and city "overseers of the poor" the Natchez magistrates and the county justices of the peace cooperated in administering relief to orphans, destitute widows and minors, and epidemic-stricken families. Samuel Brooks served simultaneously as the first mayor and as chief justice of the Adams County Orphans Court. From 1803 to 1817 almost a third of the city's annual expenditures were for "relief of the sick poor."[19] Such entries in the city records do not appear in later decades, possibly indicating that state and county programs had supplanted the city's efforts in the area of relief.

A small and inadequate hospital had stood on the edge of the commons since the early 1790's. Popular pressures for a new one and a successful subscription drive by Natchez citizens culminated in the legislature's incorporation of the Natchez Hospital

Book, II, entry of February 18, 1818; *ibid.,* IV, entry of September 22, 1857; Record of Accounts, II, entry of February 5, 1822.

[18] *Ordinances of the City of Natchez,* 278–79; Poindexter, *Revised Code of the Laws of Mississippi,* 643.

[19] Adams County Orphans Court Minutes, I, various entries of 1803–1804, Chancery Clerk's Records; Guardian's Bonds, I, 62, Chancery Clerk's Records; Letters of Administration, I, 421–81, Chancery Clerk's Records; Common Council Minute Book, I, entry of May 7, 1806; Treasurer's Reports, I, sundry entries under "relief of the sick poor," 1803–17; Helen P. Armstrong, "Public Welfare and Private Programs Administered in Natchez and Adams County, Mississippi, 1798–1822" (unpublished M.A. thesis, University of Chicago, 1943), 32–39.

in 1805. The incorporating act stated that the new institution was "for the reception and relief of indigent boatmen, and paupers of every description in this territory."[20] But, in actuality, it also served the local citizenry. The land was donated by Stephen Minor, and merchant George Cochran inaugurated the campaign for funds with a gift of $1,000. A three-story brick building which could comfortably accommodate seventy patients was constructed. Some territorial funds were provided for its operation, and after 1817 it received state appropriations of $4,000 or more per year. Its name was changed to the State Hospital of Mississippi in 1836, but the act stipulated that the Natchez mayor was to continue as chairman of its board of trustees, a post he had held since the hospital's founding. City funds were not expended in its support, but the hospital board usually included several municipal officials. Its staff consisted of several town physicians, who served the hospital on a part-time basis.[21]

When an epidemic of yellow fever struck the community in 1817, the Board of Selectmen, one of whom died in the scourge, "resolved that it is expedient in the present state of things to employ a city watch for fifteen days from this date [October 1], to consist of four men in whom implicit confidence can be placed."[22] Their job was to guard the town day and night during the crisis and to quickly isolate persons found on the streets in a stricken condition. In later years the "city guard" was made permanent and its duties expanded to cover fires, cholera, and smallpox, as well as watches during the "Yellow Jack" season. The city often spent $200 or more per month on such salaries.[23]

[20] Turner, *Statutes of the Mississippi Territory*, 241–42; Poindexter, *Revised Code of the Laws of Mississippi*, 641; *Mississippi Herald and Natchez Gazette*, April 29, 1806.

[21] Anderson Hutchinson (comp.), *Code of Mississippi: Being an Analytical Compilation of the Public and General Statutes of the Territory and State, with Tabular References to the Local and Private Acts, from 1798 to 1848* . . . (Jackson, 1848), 295, 305–306; Joseph D. Shields, *Natchez: Its Early History*, ed. Elizabeth D. Murray (Louisville, 1930), 51; Julia Ideson and Sanford W. Higginbotham (eds.), "A Trading Trip to Natchez and New Orleans, 1822: Diary of Thomas S. Teas," *JSH*, VII (August, 1941), 388.

[22] Selectmen Minute Book, II, entry of October 1, 1817.

[23] *Ibid.*, IV, entries of November 15, 1854, and April 12, 1859.

The magistrates also tried to combat yellow fever by passing an ordinance in 1828 forbidding excavations and gradations, which were believed to unearth the seeds of the dreaded disease: "It is the opinion of this board, that the work of graduating the uneven surface of the city . . . has been the principal, if not the sole cause of the melancholy change that has taken place in the salubrity of our city." As late as 1854 a contractor was fined for violating the ordinance.[24]

In 1818 the legislature had established a board of health for Natchez. It was to consist of five local citizens and a "health officer," who must be a qualified doctor; these were to be appointed by the selectmen. Dr. Frederick Seip became the first health officer. At its first meeting, less than two weeks after its founding, the board set up several regulations, violators of which were subject to stiff fines. First, stagnant water on city lots was to be drained, and wells and cisterns were to be covered. Boats with diseased hands aboard were to be prohibited from docking, while empty flatboats and other vessels at the landing were to "be scrubbed or set adrift." Alley filth was to be removed. Lastly, "privy-houses" were to have "vaults at least 12 feet deep" and were to be cleaned regularly.[25]

A small quarantine hospital was built at Bacon's Landing, two miles downriver, in 1818. Another was constructed on the edge of the upper town in 1854. Although violations of quarantines and health regulations were frequent, as were damnations of the health commissioners by some disgruntled businessmen, the Natchez board remained active in the ensuing decades. Indeed, public health efforts at Natchez were among the earliest and most enlightened anywhere along the Mississippi. In contrast, New Orleans did not have a permanent and effective board of health until 1855, so vigorous had been the merchants' opposition to quarantines and the consequent curtailment of business activities.[26]

[24] *Ordinances of the City of Natchez,* 102–103.
[25] Poindexter, *Revised Code of the Laws of Mississippi,* 631–41; Board of Health Minute Book, I, entries of February 14 and 25, 1818, City Clerk's Records.
[26] *Ordinances of the City of Natchez,* 40–44; Board of Health Minute Book,

The magistrates' tight control over the town's economic life was manifested in various ways. Permission had to be obtained from the Board of Selectmen for any construction, even the shingling of a shop roof. To cut down fire hazards, the city fathers ordered wooden chimneys removed and sundry building alterations in numbers of old structures. They appointed inspectors of flour and lumber after 1821, giving them power to regulate the size and quality of bread and of finished lumber manufactured in the town. In 1819 and again in 1828 city ordinances were passed regulating the kinds of commodities and produce that could be sold by grocers and shopkeepers, with free Negroes prohibited from keeping "tippling shops and victualling houses." In 1829 the city forbade persons "to butcher any meat, cattle, sheep, hogs, or other animal, for sale within the limits of the city," a fine of $20 being the penalty for violation. The harbor master, a position created in 1821, had the authority to decide which vessels could dock, where they could tie their lines, how long they could stay, and what fees they were to pay the city. Five landings were designated at Natchez-under-the-Hill: steamboat landing; flatboat landing; raft, shingle, fire and cord wood landing; Peter Creyon's landing for flatboats, keelboats, barges, and steamboats; and livestock landing. A complicated system of fees was set up, the levies depending on which landing was used, size of the vessel, and length of stay.[27]

Municipal revenues were obtained from a variety of sources, the types not varying greatly between 1803 and 1860. A property tax of 12½ cents per $100 valuation was levied in the territorial era; later it was raised to 25 cents. From 1811 onward the city imposed a tax of $6 per year on drays, carts, wagons, and other vehicles. Taxes were placed on the tonnage of boats, the number of hands, and the sale of slaves as early as 1804. In one day's revenue in 1806, well before the busy times of steamboating and

various entries of May, 1822, and July, 1855; Selectmen Minute Book, IV, entry of October 18, 1854; Gordon Gillson, "Louisiana: Pioneer in Public Health," *Louisiana History*, IV (Summer, 1963), 214–27.

[27] Selectmen Minute Book, IV, entries of October 27, 1847, and April 26, 1848; *Ordinances of the City of Natchez*, 45–63, 90–92, 126–49, 283.

the interstate slave trade, the city treasurer recorded receipt of $83.25 "from 333 hands in navigating boats at 25¢ ea." and $79.75 "for tonnage on boats and taxes on slaves." An ordinance of that year also set heavy license fees for "visiting entertainers." Included in the revenues from this source in the next four years were $75 from "Davenport and Street for exhibiting wax figures," $72.96 from Charles Thomas for his showing of "The Invisible Lady" (whomever she may have been), and $20 from "Noah Hampton for exhibiting a tiger." Ordinances in 1810 and 1823 substantially increased the license fees for "exhibitions of public shews." Tavern keepers were required to pay $20 per year for licenses, while venders paid $10 annually. By the late 1840's the city enjoyed an income from nonresident tuition fees at the Natchez Institute, which ranged in yearly totals from $285 to over $1,000. Leaseholds on the markethouse and ferry also brought some income. Another revenue source was the sale of cemetery lots, which brought an average of $546 into the city coffer each year in the 1850's.[28]

Of the amounts received in fines, most came from violations of the ordinances against "public nuisances" and gambling. The fines seem to have been levied arbitrarily and inconsistently, with discrimination against the lower classes and transients. For example, a man at the landing was fined $4.50 in 1812 for "selling liquor to Indians," whereas two years later a resident of the upper town paid only a 58-cent fine for the same misdemeanor. Most nuisance fines were for street fighting, which was almost as common in the upper town as in the lower one. But the nuisances cited in the city records include a number of shenanigans, as exemplified in an entry of 1814: "On account of nuisance under the hill produced by halling [sic] the carcase [sic] of an alligator

[28] Adams County personal tax rolls, 1802, 1805, 1807, and 1812, MTA, Series A; *Mississippi Herald and Natchez Gazette,* June 24, 1806; Treasurer's Reports, I, entries of February 19, 1806, May 6, 1808, April 11, 1811, and December 28, 1823; Common Council Minute Book, I, entry of February 10, 1806, and Appendix B; *Ordinances of the City of Natchez,* 195–97; Selectmen Minute Book, I, entry of July 2, 1814; *ibid.,* V, entry of January 11, 1860 (quoting fiscal report for 1853); *ibid.,* entry of February 1, 1860.

before Isaac Evans House by 3 Negroes, $4.50."[29] The "gaming" ordinances outlawed some forms of gambling which were most popular at the landing, such as roulette, while permitting other types of betting in the upper town, as on horse races. Christian Schultz, a river traveler in 1808, observed an incident at Natchez-under-the-Hill in which a boat hand was arguing with "a spy of one of the ministerial officers of the tribunal." The two agreed to decide the "trifling dispute" by the toss of a dollar. "The boatman lost his wager fairly; but what was his surprise when he afterwards found himself arrested upon the information of this very villain and fined either twenty or fifty dollars for gambling."[30]

Despite the variety of revenue sources and the obvious affluence of some citizens, the city government operated on a tight budget and was continuously in debt after 1820. From 1803 to 1817 city revenues averaged $1,726 annually and expenses $1,245. Although tax receipts were up to $8,092 in 1821, expanding municipal operations forced the city to borrow $5,000 in 1821 and $3,000 the next year from the Bank of the State of Mississippi. A major expense by 1847 was the public school: $9,105 of the city's total expenses that year went toward the Natchez Institute's operation. By the early 1850's costs for the school, gas lighting, and street improvements, as well as increased salaries, compelled the city fathers to turn to bond issues. The gap between income and expenses had widened alarmingly by 1853, when city expenditures were $40,584 and receipts amounted to only $13,134.[31] Indicative of the mounting fiscal problems is the report of the city treasurer for 1859:[32]

[29] Treasurer's Reports, I, entries of November 5, 1812, and July 2, 1814.
[30] Christian Schultz, Jr., *Travels on an Inland Voyage through the States* . . . (New York, 1810), 136–37.
[31] Compilations from Treasurer's Reports, I, and Record of Accounts, I, 1803–17, in D. Clayton James, "Municipal Government in Territorial Natchez," *JMH*, XXVII (May, 1965), 165; Selectmen Minute Book, IV, entries of April 19, 1848, and October 18, 1854; *ibid.*, V, entry of January 11, 1860.
[32] Selectmen Minute Book, V, entry of January 11, 1860.

LIABILITIES OF THE CITY

Old warrants ....$ 341.05
Warrants of 1859 not presented on
    General Account 527.93
Warrants of 1859 not presented on
    Institute Account 952.75
Bonds & warrants due Feb. 1860 .... 3,200.00

Total liabilities ....$ 5,021.73

CITY EXPENSES

Salaries of city officers ....$ 5,167.68
Streets and roads 3,271.74
Fire engines 9,318.46
Gas and lamps 1,934.10
Contingent expenses 4,843.70
Pavements 3,524.97
Gravel bar & Landing 344.17

Total expenses $28,404.82

Amount of taxes not collected 5,267.03
Amount in Treasury Jan. 1, 1860 .... 5,710.55

NATCHEZ INSTITUTE EXPENSES

Salaries of teachers $11,302.10
Janitor 462.00
Repairs 188.78
Collector & treasurer 572.86
Other expenses 350.58

Total $12,876.26

RECEIPTS

Balance on hand Jan. 1 ....$ 1,617.78
Taxes 13,443.71
Tuition of non-residents 950.00

Total $16,011.49

Amount in treasury Jan. 1, 1860 .... 3,467.87
Amount of taxes not yet collected 2,439.68

As might be expected, none of the city fathers earned enough from his public position to devote full time to official duties. In the territorial period the mayor and city clerk each received $250 per year, and the assessor $90. In 1810 the city clerk was also allowed 25 cents per 100 words of minutes, whereupon the minutes became markedly more voluminous. The selectmen were paid small sums for each meeting attended. The collector got a 3 per cent commission (4 per cent by 1811) on city taxes collected. The marshal, in addition to a meager salary, obtained some income from disposing of stray dogs and dead horses. Dog licenses of 25 cents per year were required after 1812, and the marshal earned as much as $82 a month extra by killing unlicensed strays. Since horses frequently died on the commons, he was paid $5 per head for hauling off their carcasses.[33]

Municipal salaries increased appreciably from 1818 to 1860, particularly in that last decade. In 1847 the mayor's salary was $600; twelve years later it had been raised to $1,000. During the same period the city clerk's salary rose from $450 per year to $600. In 1821 the collector received $601, his commission having been upped to 7.5 per cent. By 1853 his commission exceeded $750. Salaries and commissions of other officials were proportional to these in their rises.[34]

The tax burden which the citizens were willing to bear was closely related to the public attitude toward the city officials. This affinity can be better understood by a look at voting habits and the causal factors underlying election-time behavior. Suffrage requirements, of course, were not so strict as to bar most white adult male residents even in the territorial era. Up to 1817 the right to vote and hold office was given to two groups of free white males twenty-one years old and over: those who had been city residents for six months and were listed on the city tax

[33] Common Council Minute Book, Appendix B; Record of Accounts, I, entry of January 23, 1817; Treasurer's Reports, I, entries of February 26, 1804, February 19, 1806, July 19, 1811, and November 4, 1816; Selectmen Minute Book, I, entries of August 20 and December 11, 1813.
[34] Selectmen Minute Book, IV, entries of October 27, 1847, April 19, 1848, April 21, 1852, and April 12, 1859; Treasurer's Reports, I, entry of April 10, 1824.

assessor's rolls, and those living in the county who owned $100 worth of city real estate upon which current taxes had been paid. The state constitution of 1817 permitted suffrage for white adult males who had resided in Mississippi one year and in Natchez six months and who belonged to the state militia or had paid city taxes at least six months prior to election time. The last major change in suffrage requirements came in 1832 when voting and office-holding eligibility was opened to any white adult male of one year's state residence and four months' city residence, the restriction on tax payment being dropped.[35] The only white adult males excluded before 1832 were foreign nationals, transients, and poor whites, who together constituted a small minority centered mainly at the landing. After 1832 no sane white adult male of reasonable residence and American citizenship was barred.

Despite such lenient suffrage requirements, however, voter apathy was prevalent from territorial times onward. Eligible white adult males of Natchez numbered 492 in 1810 and 670 in 1820. Only 36 of these voted in a special election for treasurer in 1815; and, when seventeen candidates ran for the Board of Selectmen in 1817, a mere 172 men went to the polls. There were but 301 ballots cast in the city elections of 1838, 627 in 1843, and 374 in 1848—although the number of white adult males had risen to 1,341 by 1840. In 1850 the white adult male population was 1,572; a decade later it was 1,709. The proportion of these who went to the polls in the January elections, when all elected city officials were selected, sank to new ebbs in the final antebellum decade. In 1850, 317 votes were recorded; the next year 422 voted. For unknown reasons the turnout in 1853 was comparatively strong, with 580 men casting ballots, but no other figures of the decade came close to one third of the white adult male totals. In 1858 the vote was 398 and in 1860 only 269.[36] If

---

[35] Poindexter, *Revised Code of the Laws of Misissippi*, 627; Hutchinson, *Code of Mississippi*, 25, 41.

[36] Selectmen Minute Book, I, entry of March 27, 1815; *ibid.*, II, entry of January 6, 1817; *ibid.*, IV, entries of April 18, 1848, November 20, 1850, January 3, 1853, and January 4, 1858; *ibid.*, V, entry of January 2, 1860; Natchez *Courier*

figures were available for other antebellum towns of similar size, perhaps the percentage of those exercising their right to vote would not seem appalling. But in Natchez, where city affairs were administered with efficiency and zeal admirable even by today's municipal standards, the public apathy must have been most discouraging to the city magistrates.

The overwhelming majority of voters in municipal contests were of the middle class, as is clearly shown in comparisons of data in voter registries and manuscript census returns. In the city elections of January, 1853, when the turnout was a near-record 580, a sampling of 100 names on the registration list indicates that the typical voter was a store employee or artisan who was under thirty-five years of age, owned few or no slaves, and possessed less than $1,500 worth of real and personal property. The names of many wealthy men known to have been residing in the town are conspicuously absent. If only about one out of four white adult males generally went to the polls, the ratio of rich residents who cared enough to vote seems to have been worse.[37]

The voters, as well as the men they consistently elected to city posts, seem to have been representative of the majority of the white citizens. The magistrates usually came from two bourgeois categories. First, there were the young lawyers who had recently arrived or had been practicing only a few years. These neophytes tried to use city politics to spread their names and sometimes to serve as a springboard into state affairs. Second, there were the rising entrepreneurs, many of whom were formerly yeoman farmers. These included small merchants, tavern keepers, saddlers, smiths, sawmill operators, printers, and various other artisans. In 1809 thirty businessmen of modest means banded together in a fraternal organization known as the Natchez

and Journal, January 5, 1838; William R. Hogan and Edwin A. Davis (eds.), *William Johnson's Natchez: The Ante-Bellum Diary of a Free Negro* (Baton Rouge, 1951), 421, 768, hereinafter cited as *Johnson's Diary;* U. S. Censuses (1820–60), MS population schedules.

[37] Selectmen Minute Book, IV, entry of January 3, 1853; U. S. Census (1860), MS population schedule.

Mechanical Society, which remained active through the years and functioned as an early version of a chamber of commerce. At times every member of the Board of Selectmen belonged to the society. Although its actions were largely restricted to resolutions, the society, through its members who were journalists, inveighed against the closed doors to economic opportunity and the concentration of wealth in the hands of the large commission merchants, planters, and established professional men who resided in the local mansions.[38]

National party alignments figured little in city politics, but all of the pre-1820 magistrates whose party loyalties are known were Republicans. The wealthy of that period were predominantly Federalists; later they leaned toward Whiggery. Had the large property holders tried to wrest control of the city government from the bourgeoisie, a lively party battle might have ensued. As it was, however, the situation was not that the rich tried for office and were defeated; very few of them even offered as candidates. Less than a dozen of over 420 candidates for city offices from 1803 to 1860 were of the well-to-do class.[39]

The territorial mayors were all men of small incomes and Republican sympathies. Samuel Brooks, who served in 1803–1809, 1811, and 1814, was a mild-mannered merchant and popular Republican leader. John Shaw, president in 1810, had helped to stir up anti-Spanish sentiment in 1797. Quite versatile,

[38] Turner, *Statutes of the Mississippi Territory*, 355; Natchez *Chronicle,* December 11, 1809; Poindexter, *Revised Code of the Laws of Mississippi,* 604; Hutchinson, *Code of Mississippi,* 153. Early leaders of the Mechanical Society were printers Timothy Terrell, John Shaw, and Andrew Marschalk, inn-keepers Samuel Purviance, William Beaumont, and William Parker, and merchants James Foster and Samuel Patterson.

[39] Only four known men of wealth served on the city council, 1803–60. Lyman G. Harding, a lawyer-planter who built the Georgian mansion "Auburn," was an alderman in 1803–1804. Andrew Brown, a wealthy sawmill owner, served as selectman in 1837–38. John P. Walworth, a planter whose real and personal property was valued at $326,000 in 1860, was a selectman in 1839 and 1858–60. Thomas C. Pollock, a merchant with $133,000 worth of real and personal property in 1860, was on the Board of Selectmen in 1849–51. At least four other wealthy men were candidates for city posts. Their fate was typified by that of John Perkins, a planter, who lost in the assessor's race in 1838 to Jacob Byers, a carpenter, 250 to 51. Cf. city minutes and census returns for the above years.

he was a physician, attorney, and journalist, making little money from any of his practices. He edited the Natchez *Halcyon* and later the *Mississippi Republican* and ardently championed the Republican opposition to the Federalists in territorial politics. Anthony Campbell, president in 1812–13, was a shopkeeper and militia captain. By the 1830's he had turned to journalism and was one of the state's most active Jacksonian propagandists. Edward Turner, who held the presidency from 1815 to 1819, was at that time a young lawyer and staunch Republican who owned three slaves and twelve acres in the country.[40]

Howell Moss and Samuel Postlethwaite, II, served as presidents in the 1820's. In 1824 Moss announced in a local newspaper that, since he was losing $720 a year by trying to practice law in a town with twenty-six other attorneys, he was entering the mercantile business and advised other struggling lawyers to do the same. Though he was the nephew and namesake of a large merchant, Postlethwaite was himself in the small-merchant class, owning five slaves and $3,500 worth of real estate in 1830. Josiah A. Lyle, who served several presidential terms before his death in a duel in 1839, was a shopkeeper and owner of eight slaves. Samuel Cotton and John R. Stockman, presidents in the 1840's, were both small merchants. Cotton owned twenty slaves and Stockman none in 1850; their real-estate valuations were $4,000 and $5,000, respectively. Lyle, Stockman, and Cotton were Democrats. Of twelve post-1820 presidents whose political affiliations are known, eight were Democrats.[41]

All four of the municipal presidents in the 1850's were middle-class merchants. The dates of their terms, their slaveholdings,

[40] Thomas M. Owen, "Federal Courts, Judges, Attorneys, and Marshals in Mississippi, 1798–1898," *PMHS*, II (1899), 151–53; Dunbar Rowland, *Courts, Judges, and Lawyers of Mississippi* (Jackson, 1935), 17–18; Carter, *Territorial Papers*, V, 377–79; *DAB*, X, 60–61; James D. Lynch, *The Bench and Bar of Mississippi* (New York, 1881), 84–87; U. S. Census (1820), MS population and slave schedules.

[41] Natchez *Mississippi State Gazette*, April 30, 1824; *Ordinances of the City of Natchez*, 102, 104; *Mississippi Free Trader and Natchez Gazette*, November 5, 1839; Natchez *Courier*, January 8, 1842; Certification of Natchez municipal elections, January 3, 1848, SSA, Series F; Selectmen Minute Book, IV, entry of May 26, 1847; U. S. Censuses (1830–50), MS population and slave schedules.

and their real-estate and personal-property valuations in 1860 are
as follows: Benjamin Pendleton (1850–51), nineteen, $15,000
and $20,000; George I. Dicks (1852–53), nine, $16,000 and
$13,000; Robert W. Wood (1854–58), seven, $3,000 and $7,000;
and John Hunter (1859–61), twenty-seven, $8,000 and $28,000.
Their economic status was a marked improvement over that of
most of their predecessors in office, but the general economic
situation of the community had moved upward in the 1850's,
leaving them still in the category of small merchants. The other
twenty-nine men listed as merchants in 1860 had an average of
twenty slaves, $24,044 in real estate, and $20,130 in personal property.

The economic level of the other members of the Board of
Selectmen was usually somewhat lower than that of the presidents. The twelve most active selectmen of the 1850's, judging
from committee chairmanships, attendance regularity, and lon-
gevity in office, on the average possessed four slaves, real estate
valued at $6,916, and personal property valued at $9,250. This
group included an editor, a store clerk, a cabinetmaker, a carpenter, an auctioneer, a tanner, an attorney, and five merchants.

Perhaps part of the explanation for the activeness of the city
fathers, as well as for their economic status, is found in their ages
and origins. The twenty-four presidents and selectmen previously mentioned averaged thirty-seven years of age when first
elected to city office. Only two of them were born in Mississippi,
while the others hailed from New England, Pennsylvania, New
York, Maryland, Kentucky, Ohio, Ireland, France, and the
Germanic state of Württemberg. Only one half of them are listed
in the census returns for Natchez prior to their terms in office.[42]
The fact that, for the most part, the city officials were relatively
young men who were not of local parentage or long residence in
Natchez may have contributed vigor, fresh ideas on local government, and some freedom from provincial notions to their han-

[42] U. S. Census (1860), MS population and slave schedules; Selectmen Minute
Book, IV, entries of November 20, 1850, April 21, 1852, October 18, 1854, and
March 29, 1859.

dling of municipal affairs. On the other hand, the same factors may have militated against harmonious relations with some of the established citizens. Moreover, they help to explain the magistrates' economic status, which, although probably comfortable, was far from that of the town's wealthy residents.

Several of the city fathers who served before 1818 moved on to greater distinctions. Brooks became the first state treasurer. Turner later distinguished himself in such state positions as attorney general, house speaker, chancellor, and chief justice. Thomas B. Reed, an early selectman, was elected to the United States Senate. The busy traffic in land claims made Natchez a mecca for lawyers, some of whom were very able in both law and politics. But after 1820 none of the town's attorneys who achieved acclaim beyond the local level served as city magistrates. Lawyers from Natchez occupied the Mississippi governor's chair for fifteen of the first seventeen years of statehood. Five city attorneys served on the state supreme court in the 1820's, two of whom, Edward Turner and John Taylor, became chief justice. Two attorneys who practiced in territorial Natchez later served in the United States Senate. But of this talented group only two, Reed and Turner, participated in the municipal government.[43]

The successes of Natchez lawyer-politicians in state and congressional contests decreased as the influence of the eastern and northern Mississippi counties grew in the following decades. After 1830 only two local attorneys were elected to the state house speakership; one served as governor; one won appointments to a presidential cabinet and a territorial governorship; three went to Washington as Senators; and three served as United States Representatives.[44] But not one of these men served as a city official; none even ran for a municipal post. Perhaps,

[43] Dunbar Rowland (ed.), *Official and Statistical Register of Mississippi, Centennial Edition, 1917* (Madison, Wis., 1917), 176, 187–88, 413–14, 420–21, 448–49; *Biographical and Historical Memoirs of Mississippi*, 109, 113–14, 122, 285, 416–17, 419–20.

[44] Rowland, *Official and Statistical Register, 1917*, pp. 188, 414–15, 421–22, 449.

like the two best-known politicians that Natchez produced, John
A. Quitman and Robert J. Walker, they realized that the day had
passed when an aspirant could exploit his identity with Natchez
for political gain. Too, by the 1830's the local attorney with
talent and ambition often married into the gentry class and felt
no need for whatever assistance city office might afford him in his
rise. Moreover, as was true of some local nabobs, his attitude
toward the middle-class magistrates may have been more hostile
than indifferent.

From the earliest years of the city government the officials
seem to have antagonized the wealthy residents. In 1805 the
Common Council appointed a committee to go to the legislature
"to enter a protest against the destruction or attrition of the
charter of this city which is prayed for by a petition which has
been clandestinely circulated by a few discontented persons."[45]
The malcontents were a large group of wealthy merchants and
planters who had complained that a disproportionate amount
of city revenue was derived from their vested interests and activities. A small but rankling issue was the municipal tax on
vehicles, which fell mainly on their "pleasurable carriages" and
wagons used in hauling cotton to the commission merchants'
warehouses at the landing. The property tax, as well as the taxes
on boats and slaves, was also a source of grievance to the elite.

The city fathers seemed to capriciously relish pleas for tax relief from men of means. In 1806, for instance, the Common
Council answered a relief petition of John Girault of "Richmond
Hill" by raising his tax valuation by $5,000. In 1812 Stephen
Minor, who owned "Concord" and was probably the wealthiest
citizen of Natchez at the time, was given a refund of $10 when
he begged the authorities for tax relief. The selectmen flatly refused to accede to a similar plea by him the next year. Harman
Blennerhassett, a wealthy Ohioan who had come with the expedition of Aaron Burr in 1807 and had remained to become a cotton
planter, was curtly refused relief from city taxes in 1815.[46] In

---

[45] Common Council Minute Book, I, entry of July 23, 1805.
[46] Ibid., entry of February 3, 1806; Record of Accounts, I, entries of July 16,

fact, the small refund to Minor was the only one granted by the city magistrates for two decades, although there were many petitions by the gentry "praying relief" from municipal taxes.

It was the large merchants who made the most strenuous objections to the health board's quarantines; for it was they, of course, who stood to lose most heavily in their lucrative trade with New Orleans when boats were prohibited from docking and all traffic to and from the community came to a standstill. Some of the town elite joined the county gentry in a long and bitter feud with the city officials to get the titles to the public square and town commons turned over to the trustees of Jefferson College, an institution located at nearby Washington. Also, the principal opposition to the establishment of the Natchez Institute came from a coterie of wealthy men who did not want their taxes used to promote public education.[47]

Another element antagonized by the magistrates was the populace of Natchez-under-the-Hill. The tavern license hit the landing folk especially hard since, until the late antebellum years, many of the taverns were situated there. The prohibition on vending while the city market was open and the levies on incoming vessels were also objectionable to them. But their loudest complaints were against the ordinances which seemed to discriminate against their pleasures. The ban on gambling at Natchez-under-the-Hill was particularly galling when the horse-racing season opened each year at the well-kept Pharsalia race course on the outskirts of the upper town. There affluent planters like William J. Minor and Adam L. Bingaman could race their imported thoroughbreds, and wagers amounting to many thousands of dollars passed hands, including some selectmen's hard-earned dollars.

The license required of "visiting entertainers" was another cause of discontent at the landing. The tawdry performances

1812, November 13, 1813; Selectmen Minute Book, I, entry of March 29, 1815.
[47] Board of Health Minute Book, I, sundry entries of May, 1822; Common Council Minute Book, I, entry of March 24, 1804; Carter, *Territorial Papers*, V, 181–82, 333–39, 426–27, 447; *Annual Reports of the Board of Visitors and the Board of Examiners of the Natchez Institute, 1854* (Natchez, 1854), 3, 11.

and exhibitions which came to enliven the commoners' life were few and far between and usually were staged on flatboats or in taverns at the landing. More than one troupe moved on down-river upon learning of the stiff license fee. On the other hand, several of the city officials were instrumental in organizing the Natchez Theatrical Association, which sponsored amateur dramatics and occasional professional performances. The city council exempted the organization from the entertainment fee and passed a resolution commending its "laudable purpose of improving the manners and morals of the citizens."[48] To the landing populace this must have seemed to be official catering to the tastes of the middle and upper classes.

Ironically, many persons of the territorial era who lived in the outlying areas, especially around Washington and Greenville, looked askance at Natchez as a town completely dominated by rich Federalist planters and large merchants. The Republican yeomen's dealings with the town on the bluff were limited to occasional visits to negotiate with opulent creditors who often charged outrageous interest rates, or to sell their cotton to large commission merchants who paid as little as possible for their crops, or perhaps to visit a relative whose "dogtrot" cabin lay within sight of a resplendent mansion where yeomen were not welcome. The images most likely to be imprinted upon the memory of the yeoman visitor from his brief experience in Natchez were those of exploiting creditors and elegant homes. Likewise in the later antebellum decades, the piny-woods people of the eastern and northern areas of the state carried on the stereotype of aristocratic Natchez, by then reputed to be a stronghold of Whig nabobery.[49] However, the image of patrician dominance of the town bore semblance to reality only in a qualified economic sense. As for local government and municipal affairs, it was an illusion. The political consequence of the illusory but persistent aristocratic reputation of Natchez was the demise of the town's influence in state affairs.

[48] Selectmen Minute Book, I, entry of July 2, 1814.

[49] Ibid., entry of November 25, 1811; Sydnor, Wailes, 36, 68; James P. Shenton, Robert John Walker: A Politician from Jackson to Lincoln (New York, 1961), 11.

CHAPTER V

Federalist-Whig
Stronghold?

THE IMAGE OF NATCHEZ AS A CENTER OF aristocratic political dominance originated in the early days of the Mississippi Territory. However, the old creditor–debtor rancor persisted after 1798 under Federalist and Republican labels. Bold and open was the favoritism shown by Governor Winthrop Sargent toward men of means who espoused Federalism. As his key advisers he chose such powerful creditors as Daniel Clark, Stephen Minor, William Dunbar, and John Girault. His despotic rule and his contempt for commoners brought loud wails from various interest groups of Jeffersonian suasion. Among these were most of the region's yeoman farmers, many of the planters who were heavily in debt or whose land claims were in jeopardy, and the small-merchant and mechanic class of Natchez. David Ker, a minister-educator and zealous Republican who moved to Natchez in 1801, wrote that fall: "The oppression of the Spanish government & even of our first territorial government has served to inflame the love of Republicanism . . . [among the] country people." As the foremost Jeffersonian leaders he mentioned Anthony Hutchins, Thomas Green, and Cato West, who had been the nemesis of the creditors for years. Edward Turner, another Republican arrival of that year, found that "the leaders of the turbulent and disaffected, of whom Col. Hutchins was always considered the chief, were active in their opposition and determined if in their power that the Governor should be deposed."[1]

The Republicans complained chiefly of the need for debtors'

[1] Mary L. Thornton (ed.), "Letter from David Ker to John Steele [1801]," *JMH*, XXV (April, 1963), 136; Turner's historical notes, Wailes Papers, Mississippi Archives.

relief, the lack of popular government, and the uncertainty over land titles. The last issue, which remained unsettled for two decades, probably caused the greatest concern. The lands were often shingled over by British, Spanish, and Georgia Colony grants, so that few residents—especially the new ones, who were mostly Republican yeomen—could be sure of their titles. Moreover, Minor, Dunbar, and other Sargent cronies had acquired large tracts through antedated Spanish grants, i.e., grants certified after Pinckney's Treaty but dated before it. The dissidents led by Hutchins and Green, always a thorn in Gayoso's side, had not been so favored. Thus they were bent upon getting their henchmen into the important posts of the land office which the federal government was soon to establish.[2]

In 1799 the Adams and Pickering County grand juries, packed with Republicans, drafted presentments condemning Sargent's regime as more tyrannical than that of the Spanish. A few months later a committee of prominent Republicans headed by West sent a memorial to Congress "protesting against the improper and oppressive measures of the Territorial government, and praying for a legislative assembly."[3] In May, 1800, the territory was granted a general assembly, control of which went to the Hutchins—Green faction in that summer's elections. With Jefferson's victory in November and his subsequent choice of William C. C. Claiborne, a Tennessee Republican, as the second governor, the rural opposition to the Natchez-centered Federalist minority went to work in earnest. As noted in the preceding chapter, Natchez was stripped of both the territorial capital and the

[2] *American State Papers, Public Lands*, I, 79–80, 99–102, 125–26, 601–609; Robert V. Haynes, "The Disposal of Lands in the Mississippi Territory," *JMH*, XXIV (October, 1962), 226–41.

[3] Petition to Congress by Committee of Inhabitants, October 2, 1799, in Carter, *Territorial Papers*, V, 78–82; *Papers in Relation to the Official Conduct of Governor Sargent, Published by Particular Desire of His Friends* (Boston, 1801), 47–51; Rowland, *Mississippi Territorial Archives*, 22, 310, 382; Claiborne, *Mississippi*, 210. For a major cause of grievances, see also William D. McCain (ed.), *Sargent's Code: A Collection of the Original Laws of the Mississippi Territory Enacted 1799–1800 by Governor Winthrop Sargent and the Territorial Judges* (Jackson, 1939).

county seat. In addition, two federal establishments were awarded to Washington—Fort Dearborn and the important land office west of the Pearl River. Pickering County now was renamed Jefferson, and the new counties of Wilkinson and Claiborne were created, the former being carved from the southern half of Adams.[4]

Jeffersonian strategems were concocted by a close-knit group of party leaders who organized as the Mississippi Republican Society, with headquarters at Villa Gayoso. The most prominent members of the society were Green, Hutchins, West, Ker, Turner, and John Shaw. The latter three were Natchez men and were linked with their cohorts by family as well as party ties. The Natchez group felt that a coalition with the Hutchins—Green faction was the best way to combat the Federalists and offset Washington's growing influence. The two leading Natchez newspapers of the time were Republican: Samuel and Timothy Terrell's *Mississippi Messenger,* and Andrew Marschalk's *Mississippi Herald.*[5]

In spite of their preponderance of wealth, the Federalists had no comparable organ or political society. Furthermore, in order to elect their assembly candidates they had to rely heavily upon

[4] An Act for the Government of the Mississippi Territory, May 10, 1800, in Carter, *Territorial Papers,* V, 95–98; Territorial election returns, July 29, 1800, MTA, Series A; Sargent to John Marshall, November 12, 1800, in Rowland, *Mississippi Territorial Archives,* 303–11; Toulmin, *Statutes of the Mississippi Territory,* 14; U. S. Congress, *Statutes at Large of the United States . . . 1789–1873* (17 vols.; Boston, 1845–73), II, 230; *Acts Passed at the Third Session of the General Assembly of the Mississippi Territory* (Natchez, 1802), 27–40.

[5] Hamilton, "American Beginnings in the Old Southwest," 566–81; Robert V. Haynes, "A Political History of the Mississippi Territory" (unpublished Ph.D. dissertation, Rice University, 1958), 121. In the *Mississippi Herald,* September 28, 1802, Andrew Marschalk, editor, lampooned the political situation with this bit of rhyme:

> In Natchez town, and country round,
>   Are demo's, feds contending;
> Good Lord, what fun it is to *some,*
>   Who laugh behind the curtain.
> What is the ground on which they found
>   So great an opposition?
> Is it mere fun, measures, or men,
>   Gives rise to this contention?

Adams County rather than Natchez votes. Natchez, whose average property valuation in 1810 was less than half that of the county whites, tended to give Republican majorities in territorial elections. The Federalist cause was also handicapped by the continued presence of Sargent, who married a wealthy Natchez widow, bought "Gloucester" southeast of town, and became a cotton planter. By 1805 he had already amassed 11,802 acres and 342 slaves. Refusing to retire from the political arena, he failed in bids for a seat in the legislature in 1811 and 1821, finishing fifth of six candidates in the latter year.[6]

Republican unity was short-lived. Claiborne and a Republican coterie at Washington opposed West's move to get the territorial capital transferred from Washington to Greenville, which was located on the Natchez Trace in Jefferson County about thirty miles northeast of Natchez, in 1802. Turner tried to rally his townsmen behind the West proposal, but the Natchez Republicans were split on the issue, as evidenced in the *Herald's* support of Claiborne and the *Messenger's* backing of West. Marschalk felt that any further acquiescence in Greenville's leadership would cost Natchez all of its influence in territorial affairs. Turner, whose appointment as land registrar had been strongly opposed by Federalists and reluctantly accepted by Claiborne, charged also that the governor was swayed in his policies by Dunbar and Girault, who "are both deep designing men, of plausible manners, very capable of imposing upon those who are fond of flattery, and may be considered at the helm of the federal party in this Territory." Turner and his colleagues won some satisfaction when Claiborne left in late 1803 to govern the Orleans Territory, and West became acting governor for the next sixteen months. But the capital stayed at Washington.[7]

[6] Adams County personal tax rolls, 1805, 1810, MTA, Series A; Territorial election returns, August 4, 1811, *ibid.*; Adams County election returns, August 7, 1821, SSA, Series F.

[7] Turner to John Breckinridge, November 2, 1803, in Carter, *Territorial Papers*, V, 264–78; Natchez *Mississippi Herald*, September 28, 1802, and May 28, 1803; Natchez *Mississippi Messenger*, September 8, 1805; Laura D. S. Harrell (ed.), "Diary of Thomas Rodney, 1804," *JMH*, VII (April, 1945), 111–16; Haynes, "Political History of the Mississippi Territory," 121–22; Mack B. Swear-

Two disputes involving Jefferson College illustrate the hostile and sometimes ridiculous aspects of the factional struggles. For years the school would be known as a stillborn child with the politicians of Natchez, Greenville, and Washington serving as muddled midwives. Not long after the college was chartered, the Hutchins–Green members of its board took advantage of a poorly attended meeting of the trustees in March, 1803, and passed a motion to locate the college at Greenville. Claiborne, the board chairman, and the irate Washington trustees who had been absent got the action rescinded at the next meeting and then accepted a gift of land at Washington for the college site. The disgruntled Hutchins–Green faction reneged on its pledges, causing the college's opening to be postponed eight years for want of funds. In the meantime, however, the board, with a coalition of Washington Republicans and Adams County Federalists in the majority, became embroiled in a legal fight with the Republican city fathers of Natchez. In 1802 Congress had granted the college two lots and a thirty-acre tract of public property in Natchez for revenue purposes, the sites to be chosen by the governor. The next year Claiborne picked the public square as the two lots, and West, acting governor a few months later, selected the commons as the large tract. Perhaps more than anything else, this action convinced Brooks and many of the town's Republicans that the flirtation with Greenville boded ill for Natchez. The property dispute was heated, and the issue was not settled until 1816 when the city won "permanent and clear title" to the contested plots, the college getting $6,000 in settlement.[8]

ingen, *The Early Life of George Poindexter: A Story of the First Southwest* (Chicago, 1934), 58–60. On William Claiborne's political career, see also Joseph T. Hatfield, "The Public Career of William C. C. Claiborne" (unpublished Ph.D. dissertation, Emory University, 1962); and Vivian V. Volstorff, "William Charles Coe Claiborne: A Study in Frontier Administration" (unpublished Ph.D. dissertation, Northwestern University, 1932).

[8] Journal of the Proceedings of the Board of Trustees of Jefferson College, entries of January 3 and July 25, 1803, Jefferson College Papers, Mississippi Archives; Report of committee to select site for Jefferson College, March 14, 1803, *ibid.*; J. K. Morrison, "The Early History of Jefferson College," *PMHS*, II

Other Republican rifts developed when Robert Williams, a North Carolina Republican, was appointed governor in 1805. Disappointed that the post was not tendered to West, the Hutchins–Green faction made life miserable for Williams, among other ways, by repeatedly accusing him of conspiring with the Federalists. The new governor's attempts, real or supposed, to usurp the authority of certain officeholders provoked a rising group of Republicans centered at Washington. They included such territorial officials as Cowles Mead, George Poindexter, Thomas Rodney, Ferdinand L. Claiborne, and William B. Shields, and their influence in territorial politics soon eclipsed that of the Greenville Republicans. Rodney, an astute and venerable judge, concluded in 1808: "The Conduct of the Govr. Indeed is like That of a Man whose mind is deranged."[9] Meanwhile in Natchez many Republicans and even some Federalists followed Thomas H. Williams, a promising newcomer to the local bar. Though no kin to the governor, he supported Robert Williams' policies and opposed both the Greenville and Washington Republicans.

The assembly elections of 1808 saw the terms "country ticket" and "city ticket" in vogue, the former referring to the Mead–Poindexter candidates and the latter to the governor's supporters, mainly of Natchez. Poindexter defeated Thomas Williams for congressional delegate, carrying Adams County 273 to 40 but trailing in Natchez by a count of 34 to 176. The legislature, however, was so evenly divided between the two Republican factions and the Federalists, who had profited from the opposition's disunity, that a virtual impasse existed in the sessions of 1808 and 1809. Finally Ferdinand Claiborne, house speaker and broth-

(1899), 183–85; Common Council Minute Book, I, entry of March 24, 1804; Selectmen Minute Book, I, entry of July 20, 1816; Carter, *Territorial Papers*, V, 203, 333–49, VI, 535–36, 735–36.

[9] Thomas Rodney to George Poindexter, October 20, 1808, in Carter, *Territorial Papers*, V, 654–57; Robert Williams to Thomas Jefferson, March 14, 1807, *ibid.*, 529–30; Ferdinand L. Claiborne to James Madison, October 25, 1807, *ibid.*, 563–67; William B. Hamilton, *Thomas Rodney: Revolutionary and Builder of the West* (Durham, 1953), 83–85.

er of the former governor, circulated a petition asking for the governor's removal, an act which got the endorsement of a majority of the legislators. In 1809 President Madison dismissed Governor Williams and appointed as his successor David Holmes, an agreeable Virginia Republican.[10]

An incident that heightened political tensions during Williams' administration but accomplished little else was the Aaron Burr conspiracy. In late 1806 word reached West, acting governor at the time, that Burr was leading an armed flotilla down the Mississippi, probably to commit some form of treason. West mobilized the territorial militia under General Ferdinand Claiborne, appointed Poindexter and Shields as aides-de-camp, and arrested Dr. John F. Carmichael, a prominent Federalist and former port collector at Natchez who had reputedly conspired with Burr. Of course, Burr's true intent was as enigmatic then as now. Thomas Freeman, surveyor general, commented that "the whole of Burr's schemes, plans and movements are doubtless better known in Washington [D.C.] than here. . . . Yet there are many friends of his here."[11]   The strange expedition docked above Natchez on January 10, 1807, whereupon Claiborne arrested "the restless spirits" on the flatboats, few of whom had even long rifles. Burr was released under bond, which was paid by Natchez Federalists, while Judge Rodney busily set about empaneling a grand jury and making preparations for the arraignment proceedings. Meanwhile Burr visited in the home of Federalist planter Benijah Osmun, enjoyed the gay life of high society in Natchez, and found time to court a local maiden. He also persuaded Lyman Harding, a Federalist attorney at Natchez, to prepare his case. Late that month Governor Williams returned and, though personally convinced that Burr was an honest but

[10] Territorial election returns, August 3, 1808, MTA, Series A; Rodney to C. A. Rodney, December 24, 1807, in Simon Gratz (ed.), "Thomas Rodney Letters," *Pennsylvania Magazine of History and Biography*, XLV (April, 1921), 57. On Holmes, see also William B. Horton, "The Life of David Holmes" (unpublished M. A. thesis, University of Colorado, 1935).

[11] Thomas Freeman to Peter Hagner, December 30, 1806, Peter Hagner Papers, UNC.

unfortunate man, felt compelled to go along with Rodney's plans to try him.[12]

A large crowd assembled at Washington on February 2 for the opening of the case which Rodney called "The United States v. Col. Aaron Burr." Territorial Judge Peter Bryan Bruin, later ousted as a sot, sat with Rodney on the bench. Poindexter, then attorney general, in a surprise move asked for dismissal on the grounds that the territorial court lacked federal jurisdiction. The Republican ranks were thrown into confusion. His motion lost, but the grand jury refused to find Burr guilty of any crime. Indeed, the jury's presentment was sharply critical of Mead and "the late military arrests made without warrant." Former Vice President Burr interrupted to say that he heartily agreed. The Federalists roared with delight at the sight of the chaotic bungling of the Republican officials. Long after Burr had fled with the aid of some Natchez Federalists, the Republicans were still hurling epithets at each other over the handling of the "case." Williams was so irritated that he dismissed Mead as territorial secretary, Abner Green as treasurer, and Claiborne as militia commander. These ousters, in turn, precipitated the resignations of nearly a dozen Republican militia officers. Reflecting on the abortive case, Rodney sadly concluded that "the Mountain has surely brought forth a Mouse." But the "Mouse" had intensified Republican-Federalist animosities, further splintered the Republicans, and hastened Williams' departure.[13]

[12] Gideon Granger to Robert Williams, December 20, 1806, Robert Williams Papers, Mississippi Archives; Williams to Colonel John Fitzpatrick, February 10, 1807, *ibid.;* Cowles Mead to John Dearborn, January 19, 1807, in *American State Papers, Miscellaneous,* I, 478; Natchez *Mississippi Messenger,* January 20, 1807.

[13] Presentment of grand jury, February, 1807, in Dunbar Rowland (ed.), *Third Annual Report of the Director of the Department of Archives and History of the State of Mississippi* (Nashville, 1905), 101; Rodney to C. A. Rodney, February 11–12, 1807, in Gratz, "Thomas Rodney Letters," *Pennsylvania Magazine of History and Biography,* XLIV (July, 1920), 299–302. Among the best of the many accounts of the Burr episode in Mississippi are Thomas P. Abernethy, *Burr Conspiracy* (New York, 1954), 199–226; Abernethy, "Aaron Burr in Mississippi," *JMH,* XV (February, 1949), 9–21; Walter F. McCaleb, *The Aaron Burr Conspiracy* (New York, 1936), 230–31.

The political feuds between Natchez, Greenville, and Washington factions quieted after the coming of Governor David Holmes, who proved to be a fairly popular compromise, catering to some interests of all of the major groups. Also people's minds were increasingly diverted toward problems associated with the Anglo-American differences that threatened war. Jefferson's embargo and consequent vindictive trade restrictions by both sides severely curtailed commerce in the southwest as elsewhere. Cotton and slave prices sank alarmingly as depression settled over the region between 1808 and 1814. The War of 1812 and the Creek uprising, though little affecting the Natchez country beyond excited rumors of British or Indian attacks, also helped to keep political quarreling at a minimum. Contributing to this same end were the deaths by 1811 of the most vitriolic of the older generation of politicians—Hutchins, Dunbar, and Green.[14]

The most important factor in the diminution of political hostilities in the Natchez region was the common threat posed by the increasing eastern population of the territory. As early as 1803 easterners had agitated for a division of the territory, arguing that their needs were seldom considered at the territorial capital. Since 1805 the eastern section had a vigorous, able champion in Territorial Judge Harry Toulmin. Between 1809 and 1814 nine new counties had been created, six of them east of the Pearl. By 1815 Indian cessions had quadrupled the size of the territory, immigrants were pouring into the piney-woods eastern region, and a new movement was under way to divide the Mississippi Territory.[15]

Contrary to an erroneous notion long propagated in Mississippi histories, the positions were reversed by 1815, with Natchez leaders pushing the need for division. They feared not only the

[14] Poindexter to Rodney, August 15, 1810, George Poindexter Papers, Duke University; Carter, *Territorial Papers*, VI, 339–40, 385, 584–91; Robert V. Haynes, "The Southwest and the War of 1812," *Louisiana History*, V (Winter, 1964), 46–51; Eron Rowland, "The Mississippi Territory in the War of 1812," *PMHS Centenary*, IV (1921), 7–156.

[15] Haynes, "Political History of the Mississippi Territory," 215–40; Sydnor, *Wailes*, 18–19; Claiborne, *Mississippi*, 297–98.

loss of their influence in territorial affairs but also the heavier tax burden that loomed ahead if the easterners grew strong enough to control the assembly. Already Natchez alone bore 14 per cent of the territorial tax load; Adams County (including Natchez) paid 32 per cent of the taxes, and the seven counties of the old Natchez District bore 74 per cent of the total. Between 1808 and 1809 Poindexter had led a successful western effort to block Toulmin's attempt to get division, since at that time the population scales still tipped in favor of the river country. But in December, 1816, James C. Wilkins, Natchez merchant and a Republican leader in the territorial house, prepared a memorial to Congress asking for division and statehood for the western sector. Twelve legislators signed it, including eight from Adams County (six of whom were Natchez men) and four from Franklin, Jefferson, and Claiborne counties. The memorialists argued that "between those sections of Country [east and west] there is no natural or Commercial connection; no community of Interests or pursuits. . . . The Revenue derived from the Wealth and Industry of the Inhabitants of the Counties near the Mississippi, would be expended in a Section of the Country with which they could have only a forced connexion." A month later fifteen legislators, mostly from the eastern counties, signed a memorial advocating "admission of the Territory with its present limits."[16]

The Wilkins proposal won the nod of Congress, and on March 1, 1817, President Madison signed the act dividing the territory along the present lines of Mississippi and Alabama and authorizing a constitutional convention for the western portion. Four months later forty-seven delegates from the fourteen Mississippi counties convened in the tiny Methodist church at Washington. Sectional bitterness was evident from the first rap of the gavel to the last. Since nearly 70 per cent of the delegates were from the former Natchez District, representatives from the interior

---

[16] Washington *Republican*, February 14, 1816; memorials to Congress by members of the territorial legislature, December 6, 1816, and January 8, 1817, in Carter, *Territorial Papers*, VI, 732–35, 744–46; Swearingen, *Poindexter*, 94; Richard A. McLemore, "The Division of the Mississippi Territory," *JMH*, V (April, 1943), 79–82.

counties realized that they faced an uphill fight to get any voice in the deliberations. The distinguished eight-man delegation from Adams County included six Natchez men: attorneys John B. Taylor, Edward Turner, John Steele, Christopher Rankin, Josiah Simpson, and merchant Wilkins. David Holmes, who maintained residences in Natchez and Washington, was easily elected convention president.

Differences were so strong that a motion to reconsider the crucial question of organizing a state was lost by a tie vote on July 15. Thereupon Poindexter, who now represented Wilkinson County after previous residences in Natchez and Washington, was elected chairman of the committee to draft a constitution. He, Taylor, Rankin, and Wilkins were the most influential delegates in floor debates and actual drafting. With the delegates from the river counties victorious on all major issues, the final document was the most conservative constitution of any state admitted after the War of 1812. The backwoods representatives fought in vain against an appointive judiciary, property qualifications for voting and officeholding, apportionment on the basis of taxation, and the lack of an amendment provision. The constitution went into effect on the day it was signed, August 15, with no plebiscite on ratification.[17]

On the surface it may seem strange that this Republican-dominated convention could have produced a document so conservative in nature that it might have been penned by the Federalist nabobs. But the key figures behind its formulation were persons of considerable property according to Mississppi standards of that time. Poindexter in 1815 owned 2,800 acres, forty slaves, and several Natchez lots. Taylor owned 2,000 acres, fifteen slaves, and a valuable tract on the north end of the bluff in Natchez. Rankin, whose holdings are unknown, was the law

---

[17] *Journal of the Convention of the Western Part of the Mississippi Territory, Begun and Held at the Town of Washington, on the Seventh Day of July, 1817* (Port Gibson, 1831), *passim.* See also Dunbar Rowland, "Mississippi's First Constitution and Its Makers," *PMHS,* VI (1902), 79–90; and W. Magruder Drake, "Mississippi's First Constitutional Convention," *JMH,* XVIII (April, 1956), 79–110.

partner of Charles B. Green, who enjoyed one of the most lucrative practices in Natchez. Wilkins in 1815 held 4,678 acres and
277 slaves, but his principal wealth was derived from his large
cotton-commission business at Natchez. John F. H. Claiborne,
who knew Wilkins well, later wrote that "he controlled for a
long time the commerce of Mississippi, and nearly all the cotton
it produced." Such men probably had more in common with the
wealthy Federalists than with the Republican backwoodsmen,
who were mostly small farmers with few or no slaves.[18]

The future of Natchez in influencing state affairs looked bright
as Mississippi entered upon statehood. The town was selected
as the first state capital, and the Bank of the State of Mississippi,
located at Natchez, received a charter granting monopolistic
control over state banking for twenty years. Adams County was
allotted four representatives in the lower house, which was one
sixth of that chamber's constituency and equalled the representation of four eastern counties. In population and commercial activity Natchez had no rival among other Mississippi towns;
Vicksburg and Jackson in the 1820's were insignificant villages,
whereas Greenville and Washington were declining rapidly.
Moreover, Natchez attorneys virtually controlled the early state
judiciary. Three of the first four chancellors were from the bluff
town: John A. Quitman, Edward Turner, and Robert H. Buckner.
Two of the first four chief justices were Natchez men: John B.
Taylor and Turner. The other two, William Shields and John P.
Hampton, had law offices in the town. In addition, six other
Natchez men served on the state supreme court during its first
decade and a half. Joseph G. Baldwin, a Mississippi lawyer,
author and humorist of the 1830's, and later a California supreme
court justice, praised the Natchez-led state bar in these words:
"It may well be doubted if so able and efficient a bar existed at
any one period of the same duration, in a Southern state."[19]

[18] Adams County personal tax rolls, 1815, MTA, Series A; Claiborne, *Mississippi*, 352–55.
[19] Poindexter, *Revised Code of the Laws of Mississippi*, 465–72; Sydnor,
Wailes, 80–81; Lynch, *Bench and Bar*, 22–78, 84–89, 99–113, 126–32, 140–46,
151–66, 189–98, 211–45; Rowland, *Official and Statistical Register*, 1917, 170,

From 1818 to 1830 most of the town's leading attorneys with political ambitions were affiliated with the powerful Natchez Junto, the nearest thing to a political machine in the state. The Junto's aim was to maintain the political supremacy of Natchez by de-emphasizing its aristocratic reputation, stressing the Jacksonian Democratic sympathies of its majority, and thereby winning support from the ever-growing eastern populace. The key Junto men were Wilkins, Robert H. Adams, and brothers Duncan S. and Robert J. Walker. The main financial backers of the Junto were wealthy planters Adam L. Bingaman and Stephen Duncan and merchants Alvarez Fisk and Wilkins. John Claiborne, a young Democratic aspirant who abhorred the Junto's duplicity, wrote in 1829 that its leaders "with their understrappers and hirelings are all Jacksonians and great intriguers." Local opposition supposedly came from "Dr. Duncan, Col. Bingaman, A. Fisk, and the great body of the Second Creek planters, who are all friends of John Quincy Adams." Claiborne added, however: "They oppose the 'Natchez Junto' upon the Presidential question, but *unite* with them in everything else, as the members of the two parties are mostly connected with one another. In conjunction they form a powerful Aristocracy of wealth and official power. The talent belongs principally to the Jacksonians." He concluded: "The 'Natchez Junto' is not therefore entitled to credit with the people of Mississippi. . . . [Its members] are one and the same with the old Natchez Federalists, who have so long attempted to domineer over the state."[20] All but Claiborne's final statement seems to have been true; none of its Jacksonians had formerly been Federalists.

Nevertheless, for about a decade the Junto's influence was telling. It sponsored the successful candidacies of four of the state's first five United States Senators: Thomas Williams, Holmes, Thomas B. Reed, and Adams. Five of the first seven

183; Joseph G. Baldwin, *The Flush Times of Alabama and Mississippi: A Series of Sketches* (New York, 1953), 179.

[20] Notebook of John F. H. Claiborne, political notes of 1829, John F. H. Claiborne Papers, Library of Congress.

elections for the state's sole seat in the United States House
of Representatives were won by Christopher Rankin and Thomas
Hinds, who had Junto backing. Also affiliated with the Junto
were five of the state's attorneys general: Reed, Harding, Turner,
Buckner, and Richard M. Gaines, all Natchez lawyers. Five of
the state's seven house speakers before 1830, as well as two of
the first four governors, Holmes and Gerard C. Brandon, were
linked with the Junto.[21]

As men with vested interests were learning after 1820, the
rising common man counted for more at the polls than did
wealth, and newly settled areas challenged the supremacy of
the old. Eleven new counties were formed in Mississippi during
the 1820's as the Choctaw yielded more of their lands. The eastern and northern sectors were being rapidly settled by yeomen.
Their delegates to the legislature presented a united front against
the southwestern representatives on issues ranging from internal
improvements and banking to Indian removal and slave trading.[22]

One of the first victories of the backwoodsmen came in 1821
when the legislature voted to move the state capital from Natchez. After transferring it temporarily to Columbia, and later to
Monticello, the legislature in 1822 awarded it to Jackson, a village which had been laid out that year. Sir Charles Lyell, an
English visitor in the 1820's, undoubtedly expressed the sentiments of Natchez leaders in his sarcastic commentary on the
transfer. Because Natchez was "the metropolis of the state,"
"a center of communication," and a "natural and convenient"
meeting place of the legislature, he wrote, "the Democratic
party could not be expected to put up, for many years, with an
arrangement of affairs so reasonable and advantageous." The
legislature accordingly "gave orders to a surveyor to discover the
exact geographical center of the state," which he found was "in
the middle of a swamp, accessible only by a canoe." "This was

---

[21] Bela Metcalfe to Poindexter, August 5, 1819, John F. H. Claiborne Miscellaneous Papers, Mississippi Archives; Edwin A. Miles, *Jacksonian Democracy in
Mississippi* (Chapel Hill, 1960), 28–32; Sydnor, *Wailes*, 70–71; Rowland, *Official
and Statistical Register, 1917*, 187, 374, 413–14, 420–21, 448–49.

[22] Miles, *Jacksonian Democracy in Mississippi*, 20; Shenton, *Walker*, 11.

welcome news," continued Lyell; "all might now be placed on a footing of equality, the spot being equally inaccessible and inconvenient for all." It was finally decided to locate the capital on "an adjoining rising ground," which, Lyell charged, was "a serious abandonment of principle."[23]

Oddly enough, by the mid-1820's the Junto was in retreat on all fronts except state elections. In 1825 the backwoods legislators almost succeeded in pushing through a bill to annul the charter of Jefferson College, considered by them a school for aristocrats' sons. A compromise was reached whereby the governor and lieutenant governor were made trustees and the legislature would fill future vacancies on the college board. A year later the last state governmental body was removed from Natchez when the supreme court was transferred to Jackson. Also in 1826 the Natchez–Adams County representation in the lower house was cut in half. A revision of the judicial districts two years later ended the paramount influence of Natchez attorneys on the dockets of circuit courts in the interior counties. The old district had extended from Natchez eastward to Lawrence County, whereas the new First Judicial District ran northward from Natchez to the Yazoo, thus pitting the river county lawyers only against each other. Moreover, despite the sharp rise in backwoods population the southwestern river counties (Wilkinson, Adams, Jefferson, Claiborne, and Warren) bore nearly 70 per cent of the state tax load in 1830 although only 34 per cent of the white population of Mississippi lived there. The tax burden of Natchez and Adams County was about one third that of the river counties.[24]

A harbinger of the Junto's future was the resounding defeat of Thomas Reed by Powhatan Ellis in the United States Senate race of 1827. Ellis, a Wayne County politician, was a popular champion of the piney-woods folk. Two years later Reed man-

[23] Sir Charles Lyell, *A Second Visit to the United States of North America* (2 vols.; New York, 1849), II, 161–62.

[24] *Mississippi House Journal*, 9th Session (1826), 117–18, 143–44, 169–70; *ibid.*, 11th Session (1828), 72–75; *Natchez*, May 22, 1830; Shields, *Natchez*, 244.

aged to win the state's other Senate seat but died a few months after his victory. Robert Adams, also a Junto politician, was then elected to the post, defeating Poindexter. It was a hollow victory for the Junto, however, since Adams also died shortly, and Poindexter was elected as Senator. Adams' election proved to be the last important victory of the Natchez Junto.[25]

The machine's climactic defeat came in a contest for United States Representative in 1830. The five candidates from counties outside the river country centered their attacks upon the Natchez candidate, who was Wilkins, the Junto "king." The most intensive campaign was waged by Franklin E. Plummer, a piney-woods legislator with a colorful personality and a backwoodsman's vocabulary. While Wilkins refused to engage in stump oratory in the eastern counties, Plummer not only kissed the yeoman families' babies but also picked red bugs from their bodies to the parents' grateful satisfaction. Plummer won easily in an impressive triumph for the piney-woods region, and Wilkins finished a weak third. The Junto found little consolation in the fact that Plummer polled less than 2 per cent of the vote in Natchez and Adams County. It was shockingly apparent that the Junto's attempt to disassociate Natchez from the aristocratic label had failed, not in the least because its politicians refused to put hayseed in their hair.[26]

In the 1830's the political influence of Natchez was further buried by the pell-mell growth of the northern half of the state. Between 1833 and 1836 thirty new counties were created from lands recently ceded by the Choctaw and Chickasaw. No small amount of the northern growth represented migrations from the southern counties, thirteen of which declined in white population between 1830 and 1840. With both houses of the legislature more than doubling in size during that decade, Natchez and Adams County's two seats in the lower house and one in the upper

---

[25] Miles, *Jacksonian Democracy in Mississippi*, 27–29; Foote, *Bench and Bar*, 25–28.

[26] Woodville *Republican*, June 26, 1830; *Natchez*, July 31, 1830; Adams County election returns, August 13, 1830, SSA, Series F.

chamber were like three frogs on a bayou lined with croakers. Reflecting upon the new balance of legislative power with over half of the state's population in the northern section, a river-county editorialist moaned that "the Choctaws and the Chickasaws had broken upon the deliberations of the legislature, and greater confusion would not have ensued if they had broken into the hall armed with tomahawks and proposed to scalp the old members."[27]

John A. Quitman, an ambitious young politician of Natchez, foresaw the impending engulfment by the "Indian" counties and shrewdly joined in a mounting popular refrain for a more democratic constitution. Alert to the mistakes of the now impotent Junto, Quitman sensed that the voice of Natchez in such proceedings would soon be inaudible if the convention were postponed much longer. Known as an outspoken anti-Jackson man since his arrival from New York in 1821, he had, nevertheless, enjoyed a meteoric rise in political and legal circles. Quitman's popularity was due partly to his marriage into the Turner family, to his outstanding work in state-wide Masonic and militia activities, and to his fervent crusade as a nullificationist during and after the controversy over South Carolina's Nullification Ordinance of 1832. In 1827 he had won an upset victory over the Junto in a contest for representative in the state's lower chamber. When a constitutional convention was called in 1832, Quitman was serving as state chancellor and head of the Mississippi States Rights Association, which he had founded. He and the wealthy Stephen Duncan, both of whom would soon be among the founders of the state's Whig party, won convention seats possibly on the basis of their popular nullificationist views.[28]

At the constitutional convention in Jackson, Quitman headed the important judiciary committee, but he and the other southwestern delegates were powerless in trying to preserve the con-

[27] Vicksburg *Register*, October 19, 1837; Miles, *Jacksonian Democracy in Mississippi*, 32.
[28] Diary of John A. Quitman, VI, various entries of 1826–29, John A. Quitman Papers, UNC; Quitman's certification as state chancellor, 1828, John A. Quitman Papers, University of Virginia.

servative features of the old constitution. The eastern and northern delegates overrode their wishes on one issue after another.
Early in the proceedings Quitman wrote his wife: "I fear much
upon the whole our [convention's] labors will result in great in-
jury to the state."[29] Among the sections of the new constitution
which Quitman, Duncan, and their conservative colleagues vainly
endeavored to block were popular election of the state judiciary,
abolition of property qualifications for voting and office-holding,
and reaffirmation of Jackson as the state capital. The two Natchez
men and eight other delegates voted against the final draft of
the document, but it was easily approved with thirty-eight affir-
mative votes, mainly from northern and eastern delegates. Duncan was convinced that the convention had gone too far, un-
wisely creating a constitution "much more democratic than any
other in the U.S."[30]

Organization of new counties from the Indian cessions of
1830–32 was one thing, but seating of their legislators was another. When the lower house decided to admit representatives
from sixteen new northern counties in 1835, the southwesterners
reacted swiftly. Quitman, who was senate president and would
serve briefly as governor later that year, spearheaded a drive to
void the house's action. Under his leadership the senate audaciously declared the entire lower chamber an "unconstitutional
body." After two more stormy weeks Hiram G. Runnels, the
governor, a Jacksonian yeoman, reluctantly adjourned the legislature. But at the next session the "Indian" representatives were
quietly seated, while their opponents inexplicably assumed an
attitude of resignation.

Two years later, however, representatives from ten counties
created from the Chickasaw cession of 1832 sought admission,
and a new "battle of seats" erupted. This time John T. McMurran
of Natchez and Seargent S. Prentiss, both Whigs, led the opposi-

[29] Quitman to his wife, September 16, 1832, Quitman Papers, UNC.
[30] Stephen Duncan to Levin Wailes, September 14, 1832, Wailes Papers,
Mississippi Archives. See also *Journal of the Convention of the State of Mississippi Held in the Town of Jackson* (Jackson, 1832).

tion. The former was Quitman's law partner, and the latter had earlier been a member of the Natchez bar. Their efforts were checkmated, however, when Adam L. Bingaman, Natchez Whig and senate president, unexpectedly advocated recognition of the northerners. Bingaman's motive in making this move, thought by all to be against his town's interests, remains an enigma. Nevertheless, it is known that he was a competitor rather than a supporter of Quitman, disagreeing mainly over the states' rights fetish. McMurran and several other legislators resigned in protest when the northerners ultimately took their seats.[31] So ended the frustrating, ineffectual battles against the upstate representatives. The retreat before the northern hordes was henceforth to continue almost without interruption.

To make matters worse for Natchez in the 1830's, its bar and consequently its political reservoir suffered seriously. For one thing, local representation on the state's highest court nearly vanished after 1832 when the judiciary became elective. Only Edward Turner and Joseph S. B. Thacher were elected as supreme court justices in the last three antebellum decades. Moreover, Vicksburg, the comparatively new town rising in the Nogales–Walnut Hills vicinity, began to rival Natchez in attracting the best legal minds. Among the talented lawyers who left Natchez to practice in Vicksburg were Prentiss, Joseph E. Davis (brother of Jefferson), William Gwin, and William L. Sharkey. Jackson also drew attorneys involved in state affairs and in litigation over the former Indian lands to the north. Even the little town of Woodville in Wilkinson County lured some of the ablest members of the Natchez bar, including Poindexter, Abram Scott, and John Henderson, Jr. In 1833 Wilkinson residents held the governor-

[31] James H. McLendon, "John A. Quitman" (unpublished Ph.D. dissertation, University of Texas, 1949), 88–91; Dallas C. Dickey, *Seargent S. Prentiss: Whig Orator of the Old South* (Baton Rouge, 1945), 92; William H. Sparks, *The Memories of Fifty Years* (Philadelphia, 1870), 351–52; Joseph D. Shields, *The Life and Times of Seargent Smith Prentiss* (Philadelphia, 1883), 97–98; John F. H. Claiborne, *Life and Times of Gen. Sam Dale, the Mississippi Partisan* (New York, 1860), 222–23.

ship, seats in both houses of Congress, and a state supreme court justiceship.[32]

At Vicksburg a Democratic clique known as the Mississippi Regency was formed in the mid-1830's, supplanting the defunct Junto as the state's principal political machine. The Regency resembled its predecessor in that some Junto men, especially Walker, were prominent in its maneuverings, and its aim was to control state politics by exploiting the popularity of Jacksonian Democracy. It differed from the Junto in that its key leaders were two ex-Tennesseans, Samuel and William Gwin, and its emphasis was upon party rather than sectional domination of Mississippi politics. Like Wilkins' affinity with the Junto, chief strategist William Gwin's relation to the Regency was that of a shrewd manager rather than a frequent candidate for office. In addition to successfully promoting politicians like Walker and Alexander J. McNutt, the Gwins gained quick fortunes in a land-speculation syndicate. James Wilkins, Robert J. Walker, Samuel Davis, and Levin R. Marshall, all of Natchez, were the other members of the syndicate, which manipulated lucrative schemes in Arkansas, Texas, and Mississippi.[33]

The man who became the best-known Democrat of Natchez was Robert J. Walker. Short in stature and weighing barely one hundred pounds, Walker was physically unimpressive but possessed an excellent mind and an insatiable urge for fame. A law graduate of the University of Pennsylvania, he married into the distinguished Bache family of Philadelphia. He arrived in Nat-

[32] George Caolter to Nathan G. Howard, January 27, 1833, Nathan G. Howard Papers, Mississippi Archives; George L. Prentiss (ed.), *A Memoir of S. S. Prentiss* (2 vols.; New York, 1855), I, 139; Howard S. Fulkerson, *Random Recollections of Early Days in Mississippi* (Vicksburg, 1885), 99–100; Sydnor, *Wailes*, 24–30; Miles, *Jacksonian Democracy in Mississippi*, 26.

[33] Claiborne, *Mississippi*, 430–46; DAB, IV, 64–65. William Gwin moved to California in 1849, was soon elected to the constitutional convention, and later represented that state in the U.S. Senate, 1850–61. He distinguished himself as a champion of expansionism. On Gwin's career, see also Joseph W. Whitwell, "The Public Life of William M. Gwin in Mississippi" (unpublished Ph.D. dissertation, University of Texas, 1930); and Hallie M. McPherson, "William Mc-Kendree Gwin, Expansionist" (unpublished Ph.D. dissertation, University of California, Los Angeles, 1931).

chez in 1826 with influential connections already established. His brother Duncan was Edward Turner's law partner; wealthy Stephen Duncan was a cousin; and the Walkers were long-time family friends of the Minors and Wilkinses, who had come from the same region of Pennsylvania. Walker soon joined Dr. Samuel Cartwright and John Claiborne in editing the *Statesman,* a local Jacksonian newspaper. He became a respected backstage manipulator in the Junto but held no political office until the mid-1830's. Partly because of the Junto taint, Walker was defeated for United States Representative in 1832. Much of his time was spent in building his legal practice and in wild gambles in land speculation that nearly led him into bankruptcy in 1834. In fact, only shrewd maneuvering saved him from charges of fraud arising fron a Senate investigation of some questionable deals of the Chocchuma Land Company, which Walker, Quitman, and the Gwins had formed.[34]

Walker's quick advance to political fame began with the United States Senate race in 1836. The candidates were Walker, Plummer, and incumbent Poindexter, none of whom was palatable to the Natchez Whigs. Never accepted into the town's elite society because of his uncouth ways, Poindexter had condemned Natchez in general and its aristocrats in particular after his move to Wilkinson County. Although they had shuddered at Plummer's defeat of Wilkins earlier, the local Whigs wined, dined, and bribed the unpredictable hayseed orator until he agreed to desert the Democrats and promote Whig interests if elected. As for Walker, the Whigs portrayed him as "the caucus nominee of the Van Buren Regency," the epitome of the "mobocracy" marching across the country "with the stride of a drunken and infuriated giant, trampling down constitutions and laws."[35] Walker had strong backing from the Regency, and Anthony Campbell, now

[34] *American State Papers, Public Lands,* VII, 494–506; Jackson *Mississippian,* September 25, 1835; Shenton, *Walker,* 9–17; Gordon T. Chappell, "Some Patterns of Land Speculation in the Old Southwest," *JSH,* XV (November, 1949), 474–77; Magdalen Eichert, "Some Implications Arising from Robert J. Walker's Participation in Land Ventures," *JMH,* XIII January, 1951), 41–46.
[35] Woodville *Republican,* March 21, 1835, and February 11, 1837.

one of its main journalists, circulated reprints of a letter from President Jackson endorsing Walker. Meanwhile Walker, upon Regency advice, moved his residence to Madison County on the grounds that Natchez was "politically contaminated." As the election drew near, tempers exploded. A duel between Samuel Gwin and Poindexter's law partner sent both men to their graves. In the long-awaited senatorial election of January, 1836, the legislature chose Walker on the fifth ballot. Quitman groaned, "We are . . . chained to the car of Van Buren for six years."[36] That fall Poindexter permanently crippled himself in a fall from the upper gallery of the Mansion House, a Natchez hotel. Most of his remaining days were spent in the taverns of the town he despised—Natchez. A witness to his tavern behavior claimed that "neither the rattle of dice, the lucky run of cards, nor the jests and gibes of low associates, brought a smile to his lips."[37] Having prostituted himself before the chortling Whigs, Plummer also sank into oblivion.

Walker, whose ambition far outweighed any concern for the town where his political acumen had been nurtured, was never again closely associated with Natchez. Though his term was undistinguished in the service of his state's interests, he won re-election to the Senate over Prentiss and five others by lauding Jackson, intensively wooing the northern counties, extolling nullification, and exploiting the popular reaction against state banking in the wake of the Panic of 1837. In the Senate he became known as an expansionist, states' rights advocate, and clever opportunist. President James K. Polk, a man of similar views, selected him as his Secretary of the Treasury in 1845. After a brief term as Kansas territorial governor under President James Buchanan, Walker practiced law in Washington, D.C., until his death in 1869. The townsmen of antebellum Natchez boasted of him as one of the community's famous sons, but Walker's rise had been possible only because he totally aban-

[36] Quitman to his wife, January 10, 1836, Quitman Papers, Mississippi Archives; Shenton, *Walker*, 17–21.
[37] Claiborne, *Mississippi*, 414; *Johnson's Diary*, 146.

doned his identity with the town on the bluff which most yeomen held in contempt. His efforts to restore the town's political influence or to further its economic growth were nihil.[38]

Except for Walker's triumphs, Natchez politicians fared poorly in contests for state and national posts after the mid-1830's. In the fall of 1836 Quitman, bidding for a seat in the United States House of Representatives, was badly defeated by an opponent who had championed the seating of the northern representatives the previous year. John Claiborne, elected as a United States Representative in 1834, was unseated in a hotly disputed election in 1837. Turner, now converted to Whiggery, lost in a bid for the governorship in 1839, and Bingaman was decisively beaten that year in the election of a United States Representative. Claiborne and Turner, like Walker, had tried to cast aside their identity with Natchez by moving temporarily to the piney-woods region before their campaigns. No Natchez man—indeed, no politician from the counties of the old Natchez District—won a seat in the United States Senate after Walker. The town could claim only John D. Freeman and Quitman among the Congressmen from Mississippi after 1837. Quitman's brief gubernatorial terms in 1835–36 and 1850–51 were the only times a local man sat in that chair during the last three antebellum decades. Largely for his political future's sake, Quitman found it expedient by the mid-1840's to switch into the radical Democrats' camp.[39]

[38] On Walker's career, see also George J. Leftwich, "Robert J. Walker," *PMHS*, VI (1902), 359–72; William E. Dodd, *Robert J. Walker, Imperialist* (Chicago, 1914); H. Donaldson Jordan, "A Politician of Expansion: Robert J. Walker," *MVHR*, XIX (September, 1933), 363–76; Frank H. Tick, "The Political and Economic Policies of Robert J. Walker" (unpublished Ph.D. dissertation, University of California, Los Angeles, 1947); Edwin A. Miles, "Robert J. Walker— His Mississippi Years" (unpublished M.A. thesis, University of North Carolina, 1949); A. B. Morris, "R. J. Walker in the Kansas Struggle" (unpublished M.A. thesis, University of Chicago, 1916).

[39] Natchez *Mississippi Free Trader*, October 29, 1835; *Mississippi Free Trader and Natchez Gazette*, August 6, 1839; *DAB*, XIX, 60–61; John F. H. Claiborne, *Life and Correspondence of John A. Quitman, Major-General, U.S.A., and Governor of the State of Mississippi* (2 vols.; New York, 1860), I, 162; Jackson *Mississippian*, October 11, 1839; Alfred Cox to Quitman, April 8, 1838, Claiborne Papers, UNC; James B. Ranck, *Albert Gallatin Brown, Radical Southern Nationalist* (New York, 1937), 18. On John Claiborne as a politician, see also Frederick

The impact of the multiplying northern counties' population upon the declining influence of the Natchez region is apparent from an editorial appraisal in 1846. The Natchez *Courier and Journal*, a Whig organ, found that the nine southwestern counties paid $103,239 in state taxes, and the nine northernmost counties paid only $68,806. But the southwestern group's legislative delegation consisted of twelve representatives and three senators, while that of the northern group was twenty-five representatives and seven senators.[40]

The northern legislators that year rammed through a legislative apportionment change which further increased the political impotence of the southwestern counties. Whereas United States Representatives had previously been elected at large, the new measure provided for four congressional districts, only one of which was in south Mississippi. Thus the river counties were pitted against the Pearl River counties. As the Englishman Sir Charles Lyell observed: "I met more men of property in Mississippi who spoke as if they belonged to an oppressed class, governed by a rude, ignorant, and coarse democracy than in any other part of my tour."[41]

A rankling reminder of the northerners' political supremacy was the opening of the University of Mississippi at Oxford in 1848. Both Whigs and Democrats from Natchez in the legislature from 1844 to 1848 protested against locating the school in isolated Lafayette County. George Winchester, Benjamin Pendleton, Ralph North, and Robert Stanton were Natchez legislators who at various times in the 1840's led in opposing the

---

D. Williams, "The Congressional Career of J. F. H. Claiborne," *JMH*, XVII (January, 1955), 24–42; Williams, "The Career of J. F. H. Claiborne, States' Rights Unionist" (unpublished Ph.D. dissertation, University of Indiana, 1953); William B. Hamilton and Ruth K. Nuermberger, "An Appraisal of J. F. H. Claiborn, with His Annotated 'Memoranda' [1829 –1840]," *JMH*, VII (July, 1945), 131–55; Franklin L. Riley, "Life of Col. J. F. H. Claiborne," *PMHS*, VII (1903), 217–44.

[40] Natchez *Courier and Journal*, October 30, 1846.

[41] Hutchinson, *Code of Mississippi*, 167; Lyell, *Second Visit to the United States*, II, 163. See also John F. H. Claiborne, "A Trip Through the Piney Woods [1841]," *PMHS*, IX (1906), 487–538.

location of the state university at Oxford. They wanted either a southern site or four state colleges in lieu of the single university. Neither proposal, of course, was seriously entertained by the northern legislators.[42]

In 1846 the Woodville *Republican* announced its support of the Natchez *Courier's* proposition that the southwestern counties should secede from Mississippi and join Louisiana where "rule by gentlemen" was still in vogue: "There is scarcely a reason why we should remain linked (like the living to the dead among the Romans) to the dead carcass of northern Mississippi." Echoing the sentiments of many disgusted persons of the Natchez region, the editorialist continued: "There is little sympathy between us, and no benefit derived by us from the State government, unless to pay the chief taxes and to have little or no representation in the legislature, and to be cursed with all the evils of local legislation made exclusively for the northern part of the State's benefit." The aroused writer wanted a committee to contact Louisiana authorities immediately and urged his readers: "We say, go ahead—let us off—off from Brownism, demagogism, toadyism, repudiation, taxation without representation."[43] Since nothing more appears on this matter in either paper, the movement is assumed to have been stillborn.

The term "Brownism" referred to the radical Democratic policies of Albert G. Brown, a coarse but cunning backwoods demagogue who seized the helm of state Democratic leadership in the early 1840's. He won the governorship as well as a United States House seat in the 1840's and was an outspoken champion of the southern nationalist movement of 1849–51. Even Quitman cast his lot with "Brownism," and the principal Natchez newspaper, the *Mississippi Free Trader,* applauded his desertion of Whiggery. Stumping on a states' rights platform in 1849, Quitman soundly defeated Luke Lea, a Whig, for the governorship. But

[42] *Mississippi Session Laws* (1844), 227–28; *ibid.* (1846), 98–104; *ibid.* (1848), 153–55, 177–79; Edward Mayes, *History of Education in Mississippi* (Washington, 1899), 125–34; Hutchinson, *Code of Mississippi,* 227, 230, 235–38.
[43] Woodville *Republican,* June 27, 1846.

Lea carried Adams County where the conservatives still had a majority. On the other hand, Quitman as a Democrat carried the Natchez vote, a feat which as a Whig he had been unable to accomplish since his first candidacy in 1827.[44]

In the mid-1850's Natchez was briefly swept by the fever of Know-Nothingism. The essentially anti-foreign, anti-Catholic ideology of the Know-Nothing, or American, party had little relevance to the basic issues of Mississippi politics. But it gained strong support from disillusioned Natchez Whigs, who saw their national and state party organizations crumbling as sectional controversy in the nation flared anew over the Kansas–Nebraska Act. For many Whigs the frustrating flight into nativism and chauvinism was preferable to an alliance with the Brown Democrats, who seemed to be as adamantly opposed to Natchez and propertied interests as to abolition. When Quitman ran for United States Representative in 1855, most Natchez Whigs as well as other conservatives of the river counties threw their support behind the candidacy of Giles M. Hillyer, the Whig *Courier* editor who now preached Know-Nothingism. A witness reported that a Natchez rally for Hillyer in July drew "an enormous crowd."[45] Thomas Botters of Holmes County wrote his merchant friend Absalom F. Dantzler, who had just returned to Natchez from the California gold fields, "I fear your strong Whig prejudices have misled your judgment as well as that of other good men as to the true interests of our common country." Expounding in detail upon the fallacies of Know-Nothing doctrines, Botters concluded that "the means proposed by the Know Nothings will actually create the danger against which they seek to protect us. Believe me, there is wild ferocity and blind fanaticism moving in this matter."[46] Nevertheless, Adams County gave

[44] Ranck, *Brown*, 44–45; Quitman to Walker, February 14, 1842, Robert J. Walker Papers, Mississippi Archives; Natchez *Courier*, November 19, 1849. See also James H. McLendon, "John A. Quitman, Fire-eating Governor," *JMH*, XV (April, 1953), 73–89.

[45] Diary of Benjamin L. C. Wailes, entry of July 14, 1855, Wailes Papers, Mississippi Archives.

[46] Thomas Botters to Absalom F. Dantzler, September 6, 1855, Absalom F. Dantzler Papers, Duke.

Hillyer a majority, while Quitman carried Natchez and the Congressional district, the aggregate vote being 6,558 to 4,543 in Quitman's favor. In 1857 he won re-election, with the voting pattern remaining roughly the same despite the subsidence of Know-Nothingism at Natchez.[47]

At President Buchanan's inaugural banquet, Quitman contracted a severe case of food poisoning, from which he never recovered. He died in July, 1858, at "Monmouth," his Natchez home. With his passing the Natchez region lost the last of its influential politicians. Gwin and Walker had moved out of the state in the 1840's. Henry S. Foote of Vicksburg, former Whig governor and spokesman of moderation, left the state in disgust when the radical Democratic "fire-eaters" surged to new power after 1852. At "Longwood," his wife's family residence on the edge of Natchez, Prentiss died in 1850, and Poindexter, long in obscurity, died three years later. Bingaman, who had ranked next to Quitman in the first decade of Natchez Whiggery, moved to New Orleans with his Negro mistress. Bereft of adroit politicians in the critical late 1850's, both Whigs and Democrats at Natchez seemed to acquiesce as the radicals rushed the state toward disunion. In the election for United States Senator in 1857 Brown carried not only Natchez but also Adams County and the rest of the counties along the Mississippi.[48]

One factor which is helpful in interpreting the political trend is the comparison of the circulation figures of the local newspapers. In the decade preceding the Civil War the state's largest and most outspoken secessionist organ was the *Mississippi Free Trader*. A study of its subscription lists shows clearly that its subscribers were largely the middle-class commercial men of Natchez. Less than 100 on the list for 1852 appear to have been residents outside the town. On the other hand, the *Courier* catered to the large merchants, bankers, well-to-do professional

[47] Natchez *Courier*, December 26, 1855; Fourth District election returns for U. S. representative, 1855 and 1857, SSA, Series F.

[48] McLendon, "John A. Quitman," 348–52; Dickey, *Prentiss*, 396–401; *Johnson's Diary*, 47; Reuben Davis, *Recollections of Mississippi and Mississippians* (Boston, 1889), 324.

men, and planters of the county as well as the town. Since Whiggery purported to represent commercial, propertied, and Unionist interests, obviously the *Courier* attracted interest among some
of the middle-class capitalists as well. But in 1850 the Democratic *Free Trader's* circulation was 2,980, second largest of the
state's newspapers, while that of the *Courier* was only 1,158. In
the next decade the margin between them widened until by 1860
the *Free Trader's* circulation was 4,250, over three times that
of the *Courier*.[49] It is difficult to believe that the consistent
Democratic position of the *Free Trader* and the *Courier's* equally
consistent Whig stance were contradictory to their readers' views.

Through the years the competent as well as the incompetent
historians who have mentioned the political make-up of Natchez
have unanimously agreed that the town was an aggressive Federalist–Whig stronghold. The origins of the contention are
three-fold. First, the stereotype was deliberately promulgated
during the antebellum period by eastern and northern Mississippi
politicians in order to garner votes and unify the ranks of the
Democracy. In view of the ostentatious display of wealth by
the nabobs of Natchez and Adams County, it was not a difficult
image to portray. The Natchez "gentlemen's conspiracy" to run
the state was as popular a target before 1861 as the vote-getting
stereotypes of "Lily-whites" or "Goldbugs" would be for later
generations. Of course, during and after Reconstruction the
image of aristocratic Natchez served the new purpose of glori-
fying the Old South's superior civilization. Also, Natchez contributed a number of talented politicians who won acceptance as
leaders of the state's Whig party. On the other hand, Democratic
politicians from Natchez were generally less able and lacked
distinction within the high ranks of the state party, which were
tightly controlled by popular representatives of the backwoods
majority. Third and most significant, researchers examining the
state's pre-1861 voting patterns have always stopped with county
totals. A study of precinct returns would have revealed some

[49] *Mississippi Free Trader and Natchez Gazette* subscription record book,
1848–52, Duke; U. S. Censuses (1850–60), MS schedules on social statistics, VI.

interesting differences in Natchez and Adams County voting behavior.

Even without precinct voting data, enough evidence is available to substantiate a denial of Federalist-Whig dominance. First, as stated in the previous chapter, the city magistrates were usually entrepreneurs of the middle class who were Republicans and later Democrats. Second, there was no major opposition organ to the town's succession of Republican and Democratic newspapers up to 1825, chief of which were the *Herald, Messenger, Republican,* and *Statesman.* In 1825 the *Ariel* was founded but went out of business four years later and was followed in quick order by two more financially unsuccessful anti-Jackson newspapers. By 1835 the journalistic competition had narrowed to the Whig *Courier* and the Democratic *Free Trader,* of which the latter's circulation was consistently larger. Third, if, as some authorities on southern Whiggery have contended, there was generally a close correlation between Whig strength and high property values, the strength lay with the county white populace and not with the townsfolk. Since this will be expounded upon later in more detail, a single example will be cited here. In 1850 one out of twelve whites in Natchez owned slaves. The average town slaveholder that year owned four slaves, whereas the average slaveholder in the county owned eight-two.[50] Lastly, the roll of Natchez men elected to territorial, state, and national offices is clearly led in numbers by Republicans and Democrats. Of those whose political affiliations are known, only five of fourteen territorial legislators from Natchez were Federalists. The town sent six Republicans and Democrats to the state's lower house between 1817 and 1833 and three National Republicans and anti-Jackson men. Of the state representatives from Natchez after 1833 eleven were Democrats, eight were Whigs, and one was a Know-Nothing. As for state senators, the town's successful candidates from 1817 to 1833 included four Republicans and Democrats, and two National Republicans. In the period 1834–

[50] U. S. Census (1850), MS slave schedules.

60 Natchez sent four Whigs and four Democrats to the state senate. Those who served as United States Representatives were the Republican Rankin and three Democrats, Claiborne, Freeman, and Quitman. Natchez men who won United States Senate seats were Republicans Williams and Holmes, and Democrats Reed, Adams, and Walker. United States Representatives and Senators were not decided by local returns, of course, but it is revealing that none from Natchez were National Republicans or Whigs.[51]

Precinct returns from Natchez and Adams County were found for twenty-one elections ranging from state and national contests to constitutional and secession conventions. Unfortunately a majority of elections were reported only in county aggregates. But the available precinct returns strongly indicate that the political make-up of Natchez has been misjudged by reliance upon county totals. In certain contests, such as in the case of a Natchez candidate opposing one from the piney-woods counties, a fair indication of local party strength cannot be ascertained. But some precinct returns will be offered which are typical of others in revealing town—county differences and local party alignments.

In the election of six territorial representatives from Adams County in 1815 all posts were won by Natchez Republicans. Those who finished in the last six positions were county residents, five of whom are known to have been affiliated with the Federalists earlier. The voters were permitted to select any six names on the ballot.[52]

[51] Miscellaneous election returns and certifications, 1803–1860, SSA, Series F, and MTA, Series A. Determination of a candidate's political affiliation is based here, as elsewhere in this chapter and the preceding one, on evidence of participation in party rallies, committee memberships, and outright identifications by ticket listings in contemporary Natchez newspapers and in the election data in MTA and SSA. In no case has a candidate's party identification been accepted solely from statements in secondary works. Of course, the affinity of politicians and parties is complicated by the fact that some men changed parties. The most conspicuous cases are those of Quitman, a Whig who became a Democrat, and Turner and Wilkins, Democrats who joined the Whig party.

[52] Twelve other candidates received votes, most of them one each and the highest getting six votes. Adams County precinct returns, May 22, 1815, MTA, Series A.

	Natchez	Adams Co.	Total
Nathaniel Swayzey	399	93	492
James C. Wilkins	399	24	423
Nathaniel A. Ware	397	25	422
Edward Turner	396	22	418
William D. Baker	397	17	414
Anthony Campbell	352	19	371
Peter Bisland	16	352	368
David Greenleaf	15	350	365
Jesse Carter	21	342	363
Samuel Montgomery	12	343	355
Alexander Covington	11	328	339
John Wood	8	276	284

Nine candidates ran in 1818 for four seats in the state house of representatives. Voters in Natchez could select two, and county voters could pick two, with the seats going to the four with the largest number of votes. Eight were regular Republicans, and seven were Natchez residents. Grayson of Washington had earlier been a Federalist and would later be a Whig; at the time he was probably a Quid. He and Sessions were the only ones not from Natchez.[53]

	Natchez	Adams Co.	Total
Edward Turner	201	54	255
Joseph Sessions	33	184	217
John B. Nevitt	108	45	153
William B. Jackson	96	28	124
Anthony Campbell	72	13	85
Beverly R. Grayson	7	42	49
Charles B. Green	11	2	13
Christopher Rankin	5	2	7
William D. Baker	2	0	2

In the election of two state representatives in 1827 Quitman and Bingaman were National Republicans, while Green was the

[53] Six other candidates received one vote each. Adams County precinct returns, August 5, 1818, SSA, Series F.

Jacksonian candidate, backed by the Junto. All were Natchez residents. The town and county voters could select two. Notice that Green was first in the town and last in the county.[54]

	Natchez	Adams Co.	Total
John A. Quitman	251	338	589
Charles B. Green	267	241	508
Adam L. Bingaman	62	269	331

None of the candidates for United States Representative in 1832 was from Adams County. Guion was a Democrat from Warren County, Plummer represented the Jacksonians of the eastern counties, and Cage was a National Republican from Wilkinson County.[55]

	Natchez	Adams Co.	Total
John I. Guion	248	303	551
Harry Cage	187	286	473
Franklin E. Plummer	47	56	103

Bingaman and Turpin were National Republican candidates in the race for two state house seats in 1832. The others were Democrats. All were Natchez residents except Turpin of Washington. The aggregate votes given to the Democrats in Natchez exceeded that polled by their opponents.[56]

	Natchez	Adams Co.	Total
Adam L. Bingaman	207	83	290
William Vannerson	187	54	241
White Turpin	62	64	126
Amos Alexander	24	58	82
Thomas M. Green	66	16	82

Likewise, in Bingaman's re-election in 1833 the Democratic vote was divided, its aggregate surpassing his totals in Natchez

[54] Adams County precinct returns, August 6, 1827, *ibid.*
[55] Adams County precinct returns, August 7, 1832, *ibid.*
[56] *Ibid.*

and in the county. As in the previous election, voters could select two names on the ballot.[57]

	Natchez	Adams Co.	Total
Adam L. Bingaman	177	101	278
William Vannerson	163	106	269
F. L. Claiborne	100	109	209

Between 1830 and 1836 the South Carolina nullification controversy and the Jackson-Biddle "bank war" led some local Democrats to switch into Quitman's Whig states' rights movement. Still the Natchez vote in presidential elections remained Democratic: in 1832 the Jacksonian electors led 165 to 62, and in 1836 the Van Buren electors polled a majority in the town, 171 to 143. It is true that the aggregate Adams County vote in presidential elections from 1840 to 1852 returned Whig majorities. A diligent search for precinct returns for these elections produced only those of 1852. Natchez voted 366 to 334 in favor of the Scott electors over the Pierce electors, or 52 per cent for the Whig presidential candidate. Adams County voted 58 per cent in Scott's favor, or 148 to 108. The fact that a large number of Natchez men had served with Quitman in Scott's Mexico City campaign in 1847 may have been decisive in the margin he received over the New Hampshire Democrat. This may also have been a significant factor in 1848 when General Taylor carried the county.[58]

As mentioned earlier, when Quitman ran for governor as a radical Democrat in 1849, he at last carried Natchez, obtaining 241 votes to 178 for Whig Luke Lea. But Quitman trailed in the county returns, 247 to 275, giving Lea a majority of the Adams County aggregate vote, 453 to 448. These returns offer a prime example of the tendency to identify Natchez with the overall county returns, thus stamping the town as Whig. That same year Natchez elected L. Madison Day, a Democrat, as its

---

[57] Adams County precinct returns, November 6, 1833, *ibid.*
[58] Adams County precinct returns, November 3, 1852, *ibid.*; Adams County aggregate returns, presidential elections of 1840, 1844, and 1848, *ibid.*

state representative, while Adams County sent Alexander K. Farrar, a planter and Whig, to the state's lower house. By then Natchez and Adams County each had one representative, elected in separate contests by the respective sets of voters.[59]

In the gubernatorial race of 1853, Whig Francis M. Rogers' tally in the aggregate vote of Adams County was larger than that of radical Democrat John J. McRae (415 to 341). Again, however, the precinct returns for Natchez gave the Democratic candidate a majority of 214 to 199. But, when the final test of loyalty came in the vote for delegates to the secession convention of 1861, Natchez dissented from disunion, as did a number of other southern commercial centers with strong northern trade ties. Natchez voted 426 to 161 in favor of cooperationists, whereas Adams County's vote was 106 to 70 for cooperationists. Thus the secessionists polled 27 per cent of the town vote and 40 per cent of the county vote. Josiah Winchester, a Natchez Whig attorney, and Alexander Farrar were sent to the fateful convention, both men dedicated to opposing secession.[60]

Not all elections where precinct returns are available can be explained by the alignment of Republican–Democratic Natchez against Federalist–Whig Adams County. A case in point is the election of three delegates to the convention called in 1832 to draft a new constitution. The winners were Quitman and Duncan of Natchez, and Spence M. Grayson of Washington, all National Republicans and later Whigs. The other three candidates were Democrats, two of them from Natchez. Those elected were all active in the Mississippi States Rights Association, and, though they carried Natchez, the county support for the three far exceeded their town backing.[61] Did the voters select men most likely and able to fight for protection of propertied interests and preservation of the conservative features of the old constitution? Was party a more significant factor than personality?

[59] Adams County precinct returns, November 7, 1849, ibid.
[60] Adams County precinct returns, November 9, 1853, and December 22, 1860, ibid. Edward M. Blackburn of Natchez and George M. Marshall of Adams County were the other candidates for seats in the secession convention.
[61] Adams County precinct returns, August 7, 1832, ibid.

Such questions must remain unanswered. Moreover, two sets of precinct returns for state house elections in the 1840's showed Whig majorities in the town's voting. Do the other eighteen precinct reports typify the general trends of Natchez voting behavior?

Even with allowance for gaps and inconsistencies, the available evidence is adequate to draw certain conclusions. Natchez was not a center of Federalist–Whig predominance. Indeed, except for the brief period of the Junto's successes, no Natchez political clique can justly be considered aggressive in the sense of being militant, domineering, or assertive. The townsmen usually favored Republican–Democratic candidates, while the county voters generally supported Federalists and Whigs. A minority of the town vote and a large majority of the county vote was often sufficient to give conservative candidates an aggregate majority in Adams County. Thus was born one of the oldest and most persistent illusions in Mississippi history.

CHAPTER VI

Introducing the
Nabobs

The term "nabob," which has come to mean "man of great wealth," more aptly describes the type of aristocrat bred at Natchez than any other word. The town's privileged class was separated from the masses primarily by distinctions of property and economic power. Very few of the aristocrats could claim their privileged status of gentility on grounds of birth, local or elsewhere. Nor could they claim it on a political or cultural basis. The aristocracy's political dominance has been shown to be largely illusory, but its economic pre-eminence is no myth.

The town nabobery consisted of about forty families whose men were prominent in agricultural, professional, and commercial vocations. Although most of the landed gentry lived on their country estates in Adams County, some planters with large holdings preferred to live in Natchez where the pleasures of high society were more readily accessible. There they joined the large merchants and established professional men to form a small, close-knit aristocratic clique. The three groups were economically interdependent. Affluent merchants and professionals often owned extensive cotton acreage, sometimes acquired to settle agrarian debts owed them. In turn, the planter dealt frequently with men who shipped his cotton, defended his land titles, treated his slaves, and lent him money for more lands, slaves, and cotton. The groups were also socially related, enjoying the same lavish parties and balls to the exclusion of the rest of the town's society but often including the county gentry. Some men of wealth lived in both town and country. For example, Jonathan Thompson, a large planter, maintained urban "Green Leaves" and rural "Hawthorne," retreating to the latter mainly during late summer and early autumn when the threat of yellow fever was prevalent. Intermarriages among and within the three groups, as well as with the outlying families of gentility, occurred so frequently that the proverbial Philadelphia lawyer would have been baffled by the complex family relations. One such clan included the closely related Surget, White, Wilkins, Bingaman, Lintot, Minor, Vousdan, and Chotard families, each of which held title to vast cotton domains.

During the territorial era when the town was passing through the transition from frontier to civilized community, social structures had been loose, and mobility was common on the basis of property. By the 1830's, however, the growth of urbanization had produced not only some degree of order and sophistication at Natchez but also a tendency toward class stratification. The aristocracy was entering its second and third generations, and the urge for status among the aspirants for the genteel level could no longer be fulfilled merely by the acquisition of wealth. Blood kinships and established family connections had become significant. To European visitors, especially those of nobility, the claims of certain Natchez families to an aristocracy of heredity must have seemed rather artificially contrived. But in the little world of the nabobs the sense of uniqueness and separateness grew until, by the late antebellum years, the aristocrats had recoiled within their restricted sphere, almost oblivious to the lower classes.[1]

[1] A partial list of the Natchez aristocracy was jotted down by William Johnson, the free Negro barber, in consequence of having seen a surprising number of "the most wealthy and inteligent [*sic*] part of this Community" downtown on December 12, 1837, probably for the opening of the winter racing season at Pharsalia:

Gov. McNutt	Judge P. Ellis	Dr. S. Duncan
Gov. Reynolds	Mr. A. Cox	Maj. Jas. Surget
[Runnels]	Cap. Frank Surget	Capt. J. B. Nevitt
W. B. Gov. Dr.	Maj. Shotard	Mr. Saml. Davis
Morgan	[Chotard]	Mr. J. F. Gelespie
Maj. A. Miller	Pres. E. B. Marshal	[Gillespie]
Mr. Ventress	[Marshall]	Judge Guion
Col. Bingaman	Col. Harris	Mr. J. Turnbull
Capt. T. G. Ellis	Maj. Shields	Dr. Gwinn [Gwin]

John A. Quitman sensed something of the increasing aloofness of the aristocracy when he proposed to the daughter of Henry Turner, a well-to-do merchant and brother of Edward Turner. Quitman had to sign a lengthy contract prior to the marriage in 1826, assuring the family of his bride-to-be that her "said lands and Negroes . . . shall go to the Heirs and personal representatives of the said Eliza Turner, and not to the Heirs or personal representatives of the said John A. Quitman." When Quitman acquired spacious "Monmouth" as a home, purchased four plantations and 40,000 acres on speculation, and achieved distinction in legal and political circles, the local nabobs gradually accepted him into their select society.[2]

Harry Lee, another enterprising young man who came to Natchez, found the road to acceptance among the gentry quite rough when he courted the daughter of Nathaniel Ware, who, in turn, had acquired wealth and status by marrying into the affluent Percy family. After Lee had been discouraged by the father because of the young man's lack of well-bred forebears, Eleanor Ware wrote her suitor: "I shall speak to my Father, earnestly. . . . I shall plead as for my life. . . . My Father is wayward and of a franker disposition, but not cold hearted, or unfeeling." Perhaps recalling his own similar entreaties before Charles Percy many year before, Ware yielded and permitted the marriage.[3] That same year, 1840, Negro barber William Johnson commented in his diary upon the recent marriage of nabob Louis Bingaman to a New York girl: "The N.P. [newspaper] speaks of

Brigadeer [sic]	Maj. Young	Mr. Reynolds of
Gen. Quitman	W. S. Elliott	New Orleans
Capt. W. B. Minor	Dr. S. Gustine	Mr. L. Bingaman

Johnson's list includes a fair sampling of prominent aristocrats although some were not Natchez residents at that time, for example, Runnels. *Johnson's Diary* 209–10.

[2] Quitman-Turner marriage contract, 1826, Quitman Papers, University of Virginia; B. A. Crawford to Quitman, September 29, 1848, *ibid.*; Mrs. Edward Turner to the Quitmans, August 10, 1837, Quitman Papers, UNC; Henry Turner to Quitman, June 27, 1843, *ibid.*; Quitman to George Turner, December 20, 1841, Quitman Papers, Mississippi Archives.

[3] Eleanor Ware to Harry Lee, 1840, Eleanor Percy Ware Lee Letters, LSU.

the wedding Dress Costing $2000 And of the marriage Contract or Settlement $100,000—Not bad to take."[4] Not only was it difficult to marry into the aristocracy, but for one unfortunate plebeian an attempt to gain the acquaintance of a genteel young lady almost resulted in a duel with her father. Rebecca, the teen-age daughter of merchant-planter Henry D. Mandeville, related the "humiliating" experience that she and her sister Josie underwent: "He had come up along side of Josie who heard him distinctly say, 'good evening Misses Mandeville shall I have the pleasure of your acquaintance.' I do not known the man's name though he frequently attends our Church [Presbyterian]—it seems he knew ours, which only makes his impudence the more gross—to dare to insult a Mandeville! How my blood boils at the thought."[5]

The most intimate insight into the life and outlook of the Natchez aristocrats is found in the interesting Reed–Watson letters. Late in 1831 Julius A. Reed, a recent graduate of Yale's theological school, left his native Connecticut to become a tutor in the home of planter-judge John Perkins. One of the wealthiest and most socially prominent of the nabobs, Perkins owned 18,000 acres of cotton plantations in Mississippi and northeast Louisiana, maintaining homes at Somerset, Louisiana, Columbus, Mississippi, and "The Briers" at Natchez. Recipient of Reed's letters was Henry Watson, Jr., his uncle in Connecticut, who seems to have been about the same age as Reed, perhaps twenty-five.[6]

Reed's initial impressions of his new environment were not particularly unfavorable. In February, 1832, he wrote Watson that "the society is good but too gay for me." Of the Perkins family he said: "Mr. P. is a man of his word of stern integrity & benevolent but too anxious about money tells his sons it is the

[4] *Johnson's Diary*, 310–11.

[5] Diary of Rebecca Mandeville, entry of June 24, 1848, Henry D. Mandeville Papers, LSU.

[6] MS introduction to the Reed-Watson letters, by Mattie Russell, Henry Watson, Jr., Papers, Duke; Percy L. Rainwater (ed.), "Memorial of John Perkins," *LHQ*, XX (October, 1937), 974–78; Robert D. Calhoun, "The John Perkins Family of Northeast Louisiana," *ibid.*, XIX (January, 1936), 70–88.

main thing. Mrs. P. is a plain woman but kind intelligent sensible & quite a favorite with me The boys are pleasant scholars but give me *some* trouble." Concerning the judge he added: "He is very particular & expects me to dress genteely."⁷ By April, however, the hypersensitive young tutor was becoming disgusted:

I dont like your expression *"our slaves"*—I have no such property. I hear of no insurrectionary spirit now—great fears were entertained last fall before my arrival but were probably groundless. That "folly shews itself more openly at the south" I fully believe & cannot say there is not "less hypocrisy" If there is—it is owing to the fact that virtue is less creditable here. I have no where seen so foolish & trifling a set of young men—quissing [*sic*] is so fashionable that it is impossible to know when the truth is spoken by them. Conversation with them is like beating the air. I have more than once sat still & in disgust listened to their nonsense till I could have turned up my nose at them. As I do not join in their froth I am no favorite—I am merely on speaking terms with a single native out of the family. Of the ladies I can speak less decidedly—some of them talk forever & in so loud a tone as to be heard throughout the house others appear pretty well. There have been balls & *parties* without number but I have not been invited—and the family takes no pains to introduce me into company. From my conversation they must know I am not extravagantly fond of their routs but that does not account for their not sometimes taking me with them. I dont know whether they think my occupation degrading or myself not fashionable enough—although I care *very* little for the *parties* my pride is a little wounded—& it is somewhat problematical whether I shall continue a second year with this family. There is no accounting for tastes You think the south better than the north— The more I see of the south the more I love the home of my childhood. . . .

We are to have a large party on the 5th more than 100 invitations have been issued—I have been out getting evergreens for trimming the saloon [*sic*]—how pleasent I shall fine [*sic*] it (if I get an *invitation*) I know not. I can do as young Dr. Smith of Baltimore who is here says

⁷ Julius A. Reed to Henry Watson, Jr., February 11, 1832, Watson Papers, Duke.

he did last night introduce himself to & amuse himself with a fine house dog. He thinks of the young gentry here just as I do.[8]

Later that month Reed reported the following incident to Watson:

Judge P. &c. I conclude do not intend to treat me as an equal. Several weeks since a neighboring lady paid us a call—she invited me to call often & without formality—to breakfast dinner or tea as might be convenient, in the presence of Mr. & Mrs. P. not long after the *family* was invited to spend the evening socially—The family went—not a word was said to me except that they were going "to spend the evening out." Next morning Mrs. P. said "Mrs.—expressed some disappointment at your absence but I did not tell her *you* were not invited." . . .

Judge P. says Mr. Reed we will excuse you at any time you wish & sometimes lest I forget what my wishes are sends the boys away before all the courses are served. The uniform deportment of the family is of a like tenet. It is galling—whether I will endure it circumstances will determine. They have taken me with them or rather *after* them but once—then none were invited—Perhaps you would like this place—If so possibly I will yield to you.

The consequence of such treatment on the part of the family is that I am similarly treated by others & that I am scarcely invited anywhere—Indeed from the above you may collect the sum total of my invitations. As for the society in itself considered I care little—but the neglect I cannot away with. . . . We shall leave for Columbus between the 21th [*sic*] & last of May. I expect to drive a waggon with one of the boys & some baggage for company—I dont expect to drive to suit Jud. P.[9]

After an arduous trip overland to Columbus the family traveled northward that summer for a vacation at Tyree Springs, a fashionable resort near Nashville. Taking Reed along as a sort of valet, the Perkinses continued to ignore his existence socially. While there Reed wrote his sympathetic uncle: "All will whirl away to the spring & leave me in solitude & returning make an

[8] Reed to Watson, April 3, 1832, *ibid.*
[9] Reed to Watson, April 14, 1832, *ibid.*

uproar with their nine pins before my door."[10] On the return trip
southward Perkins began construction of a mansion outside
Columbus, which he named "The Oaks." By now "burning with
rage" at the family's ostracism of him, Reed threatened to quit as
tutor but was persuaded to stay a little longer. That autumn
Reed was with the family at their Somerset residence but was
calculating how much he would have to save to move to Illinois
where he owned a small parcel of land.[11] While in Louisiana,
Reed uncovered a new point of friction between himself and
Judge Perkins:

> I hear so much slang about the Tariff & such vile slander heaped
> upon men for whom I entertain profound respect that I am ready to
> consent that the South should cut loose from the Union. I am highly
> gratified that my native state voted for Mr. Clay. . . . Last night I
> withstood the whole family on the character of J. [Jackson] till they
> became so loud in his praises & the abuse of Mr. Clay that I left the
> room. The Judge says the Vote shall have the best frame he can get
> & shall occupy a conspicuous place in his house.[12]

Reed left to take a tutoring job at the tiny settlement of
Amsterdam in Hinds County. But the pay was so paltry that he
lost $150 in expenses over income while there in early 1833. On
March 15 he began his letter to Watson: "I am again at the
'Briers' in my own comfortable room." No sooner was he back in
Natchez than he again began to criticize the young aristocrats:
"The morals of the young men are precisely what you might expect them to be, intercourse with blacks is hardly disreputable."[13]
By April he had again quarreled with the Perkinses and had
taken a room in town while working as a clerk for Alvarez Fisk's
cotton-commission firm: "I feel more at home & more contented
than I have before since I left Connecticut." He quit after several
weeks, though, and boarded a steamboat for Illinois where he
had longed to be throughout his sojourn in Natchez.[14]

[10] Reed to Watson, July 12, 1832, *ibid.*
[11] Reed to Watson, September 21 and November 7, 1832, *ibid.*
[12] Reed to Watson, December 13, 1832, *ibid.*
[13] Reed to Watson, February 12 and March 15, 1833, *ibid.*
[14] Reed to Watson, April 12, 1833, *ibid.*

In his last letter from Natchez to Watson, Reed delivered a parting salvo at the "cold and corrupt" aristocrats who had never accepted him:

I do not like the people and did you know the Southrons as well as I do I think you would damn them with faint praise. I have hardly found the first young man of whom I would make an associate Some of whom I have been disposed to think well I find are low and dissolute—I have one now in mind who was vain I knew, & was not possessed of such intellect as to command profound respect but as I gave him credit for integrity & unblemished morality I was inclined to cultivate his acquaintance but you cannot conceive my disgust when returning here last winter I found that he had been caught in the embraces of the "fair sec." [*sic*] and this when judging from his own language you would suppose he entertained the highest regard for virtue & morality His feats are notorious still he is received in the first circles & he had the effrontery to deliver in the young mens Lyceum a lecture on the *morality* of music in which *he* is something of an adept. . . .

There is today a great race near here all classes & characters have gone and large sums will be lost and many will advance a step in the road of vice and drunkeness all to improve the breed of horses.

This final letter from Natchez also contains an ironical twist which shows that even the pious young abolitionist from New England momentarily dreamt the dream that motivated the materialistic aristocrats he despised: "Could I enjoy health here I could make a fortune to a certainty I could start with a salary of 1000 dolls. [as bank clerk] & eventually get 3000 or 4000 from which I could go to planting and soon make my 100. bales per year but the risk is too great the objections to the mode of life are insurmountable & slave holding must not be thought of."[15]

The lure of "my 100. bales" for all types of men was also noted by another New Englander, Joseph Holt Ingraham, who joined the Jefferson College faculty in 1830 and later entered the Episcopalian ministry:

[15] *Ibid.*

A plantation well stocked with hands, is the ne plus ultra of every man's ambition who resides at the south. Young men who come to this country, "to make money," soon catch the mania, and nothing less than a broad plantation, waving with the snow white cotton bolls, can fill their mental vision. . . . Hence the great number of planters and the few professional men of long or ancient standing in their several professions. As soon as the young lawyer acquires sufficient to purchase a few hundred acres of the rich alluvial lands, and a few slaves, he quits his profession at once, though perhaps just rising into eminence, and turns cotton planter. . . . Physicians make money much more rapidly than lawyers, and sooner retire from practice. . . . Even editors have an eye that way.[16]

Rather showy exhibitions of personal wealth were obvious at almost every turn in Natchez and the vicinity. The nabobs' effective imitations of the English landed gentry impressed Canadian visitor William Kingsford, who found boxed gardens "cut into quaint figures as was the fashion of the last century" in England.[17] By 1860 there were at least forty large, expensive homes in and near the town which could be considered in the mansion class. Britisher Sir Charles Lyell, who was accustomed to visiting in the mansions of the English gentry, described the Natchez aristocrats' dwellings as "elegant" and "charming."[18]

Life in the sprawling "big houses" which dotted the local landscape usually passed at a slow pace, marked by frivolity, complacency, and haughty oblivion toward the commoners. According to the diary she kept at "Monmouth" in 1855, Quitman's daughter Rosalie faced two major crises that year: her advancing age as a spinster and a "duel with a LIZARD that had paid us a visit & was actually on our Bar." At nearby "Linden" another crisis was encountered when the unmarried sister of David Ker, II, was left a handsome bequest by a rejected suitor who died. Ker advised her: "Should you, after having accepted diamonds or

[16] Joseph H. Ingraham, The South-West, by a Yankee (2 vols.; New York, 1835), II, 84–86.
[17] William Kingsford, Impressions of the West and South during a Six Weeks' Holiday (Toronto, 1858), 46.
[18] Lyell, Second Visit to the United States, II, 153.

any other jewels from Dr. Provan, marry, I would advise you to sell, or give away, that jewelry and wear none but what your husband may select." Katherine Minor of "Concord," widow of Stephen Minor, also had some advice for her son James, who was in New Orleans: "Avoid as much as is possible *low* company, associate with the refined for your manners soon tell what company you keep. Recollect, dear Son, you have a name to preserve."[19] Random though they are, the above comments are quite typical of those found in other aristocrats' diaries and letters. Manners and appearances absorbed their interests to the exclusion of concern for the community's general welfare, exchanges of ideas, or attention to national problems.

The commoners' resentment against the nabobs' ostentation and indifference is difficult to assess, but gleanings from the city minutes, William Johnson's diary, voting behavior, bourgeois correspondence, and newspaper items suggest that the aristocrats were not appreciated as much before 1861 by the town's majority of whites as they would be during the later glorification of the Old South. In a frank comparison of the value of small farmers and large planters to the area, the *Free Trader* observed in 1842:

They [the small farmers] would crowd our streets with fresh and healthy supplies of home productions, and the proceeds would be expended *here* among our merchants, grocers and artisans. The large planters—the one-thousand-bale planters—do not contribute most to the prosperity of Natchez. They, for the most part, sell their cotton in Liverpool; buy their wines in London or Havre; their negro clothing in Boston; their plantation implements and supplies in Cincinnati; and their groceries and fancy articles in New Orleans. The small planter has not the credit nor the business connections to do this; he requires the proceeds of his crop as soon as it can be sold; and he purchases and pays for, cash in hand, almost every necessary wanted during the

[19] Diary of Rosalie Quitman, entry of September 11, 1855, Quitman Papers, UNC; David Ker to Mary Ker, March 7, 1859, Mary Susan Ker Papers, UNC; Katherine Minor to James Minor, December 21, 1839, Minor Papers, UNC. On James's premature death Ralph Waldo Emerson, a close friend of the Minors, wrote a moving letter of sympathy. R. W. Emerson to W. J. Minor, March 4, 1860, Minor Papers, LSU.

year, in the same market where he sells his cotton. The small planter hoards no money in these times; he lends none at usurious rates of interest; he buys up the property of no unfortunate debtor for a few dollars; but he lays it all out for the purchase of supplies, and thus directly contributes his mite to the prosperity of our city.[20]

From time to time the Democratic *Free Trader* roundly assailed the local families of great wealth who did not show the slightest interest in civic or charitable activities in Natchez and paid little in city, county, and state taxes. Particularly vulnerable was the Surget clan. Frank and James Surget, sons of the French immigrant Pierre Surget who had come in the 1780's, possessed vast stretches of alluvial land west of the Mississippi, ranging from southern Arkansas to the Louisiana sugar country. In 1855 an Arkansas newspaper attacked Frank Surget for holding 11,000 acres near Batesville for two decades without making improvements or being willing to sell or lease to settlers: "Rich as Croesus; a nabob of Natchez, Mississippi; making his five or six thousand bales of cotton a year; he appears to care for nothing for the wants or desires of the people."[21] Howard S. Fulkerson, an employee of the Woodville Manufacturing Company, found that the Natchez aristocrats "could illy brook contradiction and opposition from their equals." "Indeed they were slow to regard any as their equals except those of their own class," he added.[22] Thomas Taylor, a Pennsylvania Quaker who visited Natchez in 1847, described the local aristocracy thus:

Many of the *chivalric gentry* whom I have been permitted to see dashing about here on highbred horses, seem to find their greatest enjoyment in recounting their bear hunts, "great fights," and occasional exploits with revolvers & Bowie Knives—swearing "terribly" and sucking mint juleps & Cherry Cobblers with Straws. . . . The "patriarchal institutions" and Turkey buzzards, tho' not the most agreeable, are

[20] Natchez *Mississippi Free Trader*, April 14, 1842.
[21] Little Rock *Arkansas State Gazette and Democrat*, February 16, 1855.
[22] Fulkerson, *Random Recollections*, 15.

certainly among the chief characteristics of this region,—They shock & disgust you on every side.[23]

Frederick Law Olmsted, then a New York *Times* correspondent and late a reknowned landscape architect, visited the Mississippi town in 1854. A yeoman whom he interviewed south of Natchez commented on what Olmsted might expect as he neared the community:

> Big plantations, sir, nothing else—aristocrats; swell-heads I call them, sir—nothing but swell-heads, and you can't get a night's lodging, sir. . . . A man might die on the road 'fore he'd get a lodging with one of them. . . .
> Must have ice for their wine, you see . . . or they'd die; and so they have to live in Natchez or New Orleans. . . .
> Good God! I wouldn't have my children educated, sir, among them, not to have them as rich as Dr.—, every one of them. You can know their children as far off as you can see them—young swell-heads! You'll take note of 'em in Natchez. Why, you can tell them by their walk; I noticed it yesterday at the Mansion House. They sort o' throw out their legs as if they hadn't got strength enough to lift 'em and put them down in any particular place. They do want so bad to look as if they weren't made of the same clay as the rest of God's creation.[24]

Before Olmsted reached Natchez he met several groups of aristocrats. "Marble-like in propriety, looking stealthily from the corners of their eyes without turning their heads," some genteel ladies in a carriage passed him, completely oblivious to other travelers. A wagon full of young "swell-heads" later ran over Olmsted's dog. As he approached the outskirts of town, he found that "every inch of the land" had been "bought up by the swell-heads on purpose" to keep immigrants away.[25] Unknown to Olmsted, he had been passing many large tracts owned by Natchez men ever since he left Baton Rouge. The

[23] Edwin B. Bronner (ed.), "A Philadelphia Quaker Visits Natchez, 1847," *JSH*, XXVII (November, 1961), 519.
[24] Frederick L. Olmsted, *A Journey in the Back Country in the Winter of 1853-4* (New York, 1860), 27–28.
[25] *Ibid.*, 33, 35–36.

depletion of their lands through soil exhaustion, erosion, and wasteful farming practices had led Natchez aristocrats as early as the territorial period to explore Louisiana tracts for possible extension of their plantation holdings. Before 1817 Concordia Parish had become a planting province of the nabobery of Natchez and Adams County. Over 81 per cent of the lands there were owned in 1860 by absentee landlords, most of whom lived in the bluff town across the Mississippi. By that time 91 per cent of the parish's population consisted of slaves. A number of Natchez aristocrats, such as Dr. John Ker, D. L. Rivers, and Lemuel P. Conner, maintained residences both on the bluff and at Vidalia. Natchez men constituted a majority of the board of directors of the Mechanics and Traders Bank of Vidalia, established in 1833, and Conner headed the Concordia courthouse building committee in 1856.[26]

In the 1820's the Natchez nabobs began extending their holdings to include cotton lands from Pointe Coupee to Madison Parish and sugar-cane lands from Ascension to Terrebonne Parish. A New Orleans newspaper declared in 1827 that during a recent week over $50,000 worth of cane acreage in Lafourche Parish had been purchased by Natchez men. In 1860 two clans from Natchez and its vicinity, the Bislands and Minors, had a total investment of $1,793,600 in real and personal property in three parishes of the sugar country. John Routh, a cotton planter who lived in Natchez, had property in Tensas Parish worth $1,214,000. By 1860 seventy-two men of Natchez and Adams County held fifty or more slaves on plantations in Louisiana, and forty-five of these planters possessed real and personal property in that state valued at $150,000 or more. In addition, several of the wealthier Natchez planters had large landholdings in the Yazoo-Mississippi Delta region of northwest Mississippi, in southeastern Arkansas, and in East Texas, although lands in the last

[26] Vidalia *Concordia Intelligencer,* January 12, 1850; Joseph K. Menn, *The Large Slaveholders of Louisiana, 1860* (New Orleans, 1964), 2, 73, 97. See also Robert D. Calhoun, "A History of Concordia Parish," *LHQ,* XV (January, 1932), 44–67; XV (April, 1932), 214–33; XV (July, 1932), 428–52; XV (October, 1932), 618–45; XVI (January, 1933), 92–124.

two locations were usually bought for speculation. Quitman, for example, had 40,000 acres in Texas, and Frank Surget owned 50,000 acres in Arkansas.[27]

Olmsted's observations in 1854 regarding the aristocratic domination of the agricultural area around Natchez were correct. The number of large farms in Adams County increased steadily from 1820 to 1860. The tendency was accelerated in the final antebellum decade: in 1850, 70 per cent of the farms had 200 or more acres of improved land; in 1860, 78 per cent were in that category. Farms with 500 to 999 improved acres grew from 18 per cent to 31 per cent in that same period, and those with 1,000 or more acres of improved land increased from 11 per cent to 14 per cent of the county's farms. In contrast, Tishomingo County, which was typical of the northeastern section of the state, had only 0.4 per cent of its farms in the 1,000-acre class. The average for all Mississippi counties in 1860 was 2 per cent for farms with 1,000 or more improved acres. The number of non-slave landholdings in Adams County decreased from 48 to 22 between 1850 and 1860, but slaveowners' farms rose from 133 to 209. In cotton production slaveholders in Adams County produced 27,993 bales in 1860, and the non-slaveholders produced 2,028 bales. Exact figures are not available, but the Natchez nabobs appear to have invested more heavily in Louisiana than Adams County acreage, with resident county planters controlling most of the large tracts in the latter location.[28]

The leadership of the county gentry changed little from 1798 to 1860. Throughout the era such clans as the Ellises, Dunbars, Hutchinses, Farrars, Bislands, and Brandons stood pre-eminent in landholdings, slave ownership, and social prestige. Such was not the case in Natchez where economic conditions were less static and the nabobery more varied, encompassing commercial and profesional aristocrats as well as the landed gentry. According to

[27] New Orleans *Louisiana Courier*, April 7, 1827; Menn, *Large Slaveholders of Louisiana, passim;* Herbert Weaver, *Mississippi Farmers, 1850–1860* (Nashville, 1945), 109–11. See also P. A. Champomier, *Statement of the Sugar Crop Made in Louisiana, 1854* (New Orleans, 1855).

[28] Weaver, *Mississippi Farmers,* 74–79, 101.

the personal tax rolls of 1807–12, the leading men of wealth residing in Natchez or on its outskirts included merchants James Wilkins, Samuel Postlethwaite, Abijah Hunt, and Alexander Moore; attorneys Lyman Harding, Charles Green, and John Perkins; physicians John Carmichael and Frederick Seip; and planters Winthrop Sargent, Christopher Miller, Adam Bingaman, Stephen Minor, John Girault, William Vousdan, Jonathan Thompson, Lewis Evans, and Job Routh. Regardless of vocation, all of these men were engaged in cotton planting. Sargent was the wealthiest, owning 11,802 acres and 342 slaves in Adams County, as well as over 20,000 acres in Ohio and Virginia. By 1860 the list of the men of great wealth was drastically changed and enlarged. Only the Bingaman, Minor, and Routh families still ranked high in holdings. Some of the early leaders had moved elsewhere, like Perkins; others had died without leaving a direct lineage, such as Thompson, who succumbed to yellow fever along with his entire family in the early 1820's; and still others had split their estates among their children as they reached maturity, as Moore did. Though, of course, a relatively small element of the town's population, the Natchez nabobs by 1860 ranked with the wealthiest in the entire South.[29]

Because of the complex holdings outside Adams County which the Natchez nabobs had acquired by the late antebellum period, estimating their wealth is an elusive business. A look at some individual holdings, however, may be more interesting and enlightening than further generalizations about the aristocracy. Several authorities on the Old South nominate Stephen Duncan as probably the nation's largest cotton planter and slaveholder by the 1850's. His plantation records show that in 1851 Duncan owned six cotton plantations and two sugar cane estates, on which he had 1,041 slaves. In addition, he kept twenty-three house servants at "Auburn," his Natchez residence. His lands were in Issaquena, Jefferson, and Adams counties and in the Attakapa Prairie of south-central Louisiana. That year they

[29] Adams County personal tax rolls, 1807–12, MTA, Series A; U. S. Census (1860), MS population and slave schedules.

produced 3,177 bales of cotton and 3,234 hogsheads of sugar, besides an unknown quantity of molasses and minor subsistence crops.[30] Five years later Duncan, who had come to Natchez in 1808 as a young physician from Pennsylvania, conservatively estimated that his estate was worth $1,909,407: $829,907 in slaves; $400,000 in lands and improvements thereon; $479,500 in bonds and stocks; and $200,000 outstanding in personal notes due to him, mostly by planters (including $25,360 owed by Wade Hampton of South Carolina). His northern securities that year were as follows:[31]

Columbus & Indiana Rail Road Bonds @ 7%	$25,000
Chicago & Aurora Rail Road Bonds @ 7%	20,000
Hartford & New Haven Rail Road Bonds @ 6%	50,000
Galena & Chicago Rail Road Bonds @ 7%	10,000
Northern Indiana Rail Road Bonds @ 7%	10,000
Hudson River Rail Road Bonds @ 7%	1,000
New Jersey R. R. & Transportation Bonds @ 6%	$26,000
Erie & Kalamazoo Rail Road Bonds @ 7%	30,000
Watertown & Salem Rail Road Bonds @ 7%	2,000
New Albany & Salem Rail Road Bonds @ 10%	15,000
New Albany & Salem Rail Road Bonds @ 8%	26,500
New Albany & Salem Rail Road Bonds @ 7%	15,000
Evansville & Bransfordville Rail Road Bonds @ 7%	60,000
New York Central Rail Road Bonds @ 6%	500

[30] Journal of Stephen Duncan, entries of 1851, Stephen Duncan Papers, LSU. Duncan's plantations, slaves, and production in 1851 were as follows:

	Slaves	Cotton	Sugar	Crop Value
Homochitto	89	188		$ 8,234.75
L'Argent	111	678		21,616.32
Oakley	160	416		14,388.40
Carlisle	127	673		20,718.05
Reserve	115	493		16,137.13
Duncanais	117	729		23,259.58
Oxford	154		1,134	65,000.00
Camperdown	168		2,100	(Included with Oxford)
	1,041	3,177	3,234	$169,354.23

[31] Manifold of Duncan's securities held by Charles P. Leverich, April 18, 1856, Duncan Papers, LSU; memorandum on financial affairs of Duncan, December 4, 1857, *ibid.* See also Paul W. Gates, "Southern Investments in Northern Lands before the Civil War," *JSH*, V (May, 1939), 155–85.

New York Central Rail Road Bonds @ 7%	2,500
Atlantic Dock Co. Bonds @ 7%	16,000
Bank of New York Stock 50 shs. @ $100 Ea.	5,000
Pennsylvania Rail Road 350 shs. @ $100 Ea.	50,000
Terrehaute & Richmond Rail Road 1,000 shs. @ $50 Ea.	50,000
Michigan Central Rail Road 500 shs. @ $100 Ea.	50,000
New York Central Rail Road 300 shs. @ $100 Ea.	15,000
	$479,500

Duncan's investment in real and personal property in Issa-quena County jumped from $75,000 in 1850 to $1,340,700 in 1860. Apparently about half of his cotton production was concentrated in that county by the time of secession. In 1859 Duncan was ranked as a "4,000-bale planter" despite the fact that several years previous he had started dividing his domain, with his son Samuel receiving several Louisiana plantations. Even the Civil War did not seem to curtail his production seriously; in 1863 the Confederate government issued Duncan a receipt for $279,008 worth of his property confiscated or destroyed in Issaquena, including 2,080 cotton bales burned by retreating Southern troops.[32] Duncan's start on the road to wealth came through his lucrative medical practice, shrewd land speculation, and discreet marriages—first into the Ellis family and later into the Bingaman clan. Like nearly all of the nabobs, he showed little interest in town affairs; but, unlike his aristocratic colleagues, he was concerned about state and national affairs.[33] He served as president of the Bank of the State of Mississippi, delegate to the constitutional convention of 1832, president of the Mississippi Colonization Society from 1831 to 1839, and vice president of the American Colonization Society in 1850. An

[32] Duncan's journal, entry of July 19, 1852, Duncan Papers, LSU; Confederate receipt for property confiscated or destroyed, 1863, ibid.; New Orleans Picayune, February 19, 1859; U. S. Censuses (1850–60), MS population and slave schedules, Adams and Issaquena counties.

[33] Duncan to Leverich, November 6, 1843, January 20 and February 12, 1844, Charles P. Leverich Papers, Mississippi Archives; Duncan's journal, sundry entries of 1857, Duncan Papers, LSU.

active Whig, he was a close friend of Henry Clay, whom he entertained on several occasions at his lavish home. During the Civil War Duncan moved back to his native Pennsylvania where he died soon after the hostilities ended.[34]

Among the most complicated and vast of the Natchez planting domains was that of the Surget family. Frenchman Pierre Surget acquired a Spanish grant of 2,500 acres just southeast of Natchez, built "Cherry Grove" mansion in 1788, and began to extend his holdings. After his death in 1796 Catherine Surget, his enterprising wife, efficiently managed plantation affairs and built up the family acreage to 7,090 by the time of her death in 1805. Sons Frank, James, and Jacob then took the helm, expanding their operations steadily and benefiting from strategic marriages into the Bingaman, White, and Minor families. Frank and James Surget ultimately controlled huge amounts of rich farm land in southern Arkansas and in Louisiana as well as in Mississippi. John Claiborne called Frank Surget "the most extensive and successful planter ever known in Mississippi." Frank became well known not only for his vast wealth but also for his pioneering efforts in horizontal plowing. In addition to 50,000 acres that he owned in Arkansas, Frank left his sons 8,010 acres in Concordia and Madison parishes, valued at $685,600 (slaves as well as real estate), besides $154,000 worth of property in Wilkinson County and $633,000 in Adams County. James held nine plantations in Louisiana and Mississippi and had 453 slaves. His son, James, Jr., reputedly inherited nearly 1,000 slaves. By the mid-1850's Frank and James Surget were both 4,000-bale planters and together controlled perhaps 93,000 acres, although about half of this acreage was bought for speculation and lay unimproved. In 1850 James Surget retained sixteen house servants at his "Cherry Grove" residence, while Frank had twenty-two at palatial "Clifton," which he had purchased from the Postlethwaites.

[34] Charles S. Sydnor, *Slavery in Mississippi* (New York, 1933), 219–31; Robert C. Weems, Jr., "The Makers of the Bank of Mississippi," *JMH*, XV (April, 1953), 150–54; Natchez *Democrat*, 1959 Pilgrimage edition.

Jacob, the third brother, had moved to New York but still held at least one large cotton plantation in Adams County.[35]

One of the most affluent Natchez clans was the Davis family. Patriarch Samuel Davis migrated from Philadelphia in the 1790's and married a daughter of well-to-do Josef Vidal. By 1811 Davis was a large planter and was the only one at Natchez bold enough to ship his cotton aboard the *New Orleans* on the first steamboat voyage down the Mississippi. By 1860 his sons Samuel M., George, Alfred V., and Dr. Frederick Davis were masters of a sizable agricultural domain on the flatlands west of the bluff and maintained homes in Natchez and in Concordia Parish. Their total holdings in Louisiana in 1860 included 14,649 acres, on which they produced 6,639 bales of cotton, and 843 slaves. Alfred ranked among the ten largest slaveholders in Louisiana that year, while his brother Samuel was rated in the "top ten" of cotton producers in that state. The aggregate valuation of real and personal property held by the Davis clan in Adams County and in Louisiana was $1,696,000 in 1860.[36] Of all slaveowners that Sir Charles Lyell met on his American tour, Samuel Davis the elder impressed him the most because of his humanitarian concern for his Negroes. The English traveler found Davis' slave cabins "all neatly built and well whitewashed. Even in this cursory view we could perceive how much the comfort and bodily wants of the slaves had been attended to."[37] Davis' interest in his slaves as persons, however, was probably exceptional among the Natchez nabobs, who generally were concerned with their colored people mainly as chattel investments.

[35] U. S. Census (1860), MS population and slave schedules, Mississippi and Louisiana; Claiborne, *Mississippi*, 141; Weaver, *Mississippi Farmers*, 106, 108; Natchez *Democrat*, 1959 Pilgrimage edition; Paul W. Gates, *The Farmer's Age: Agriculture, 1815–1860* (New York, 1960), 149. Frank Surget apparently commanded considerable cash besides his landed and chattel holdings. He made a cash purchase, for example, of $108,805 worth of railroad stock in a single transaction in 1850. Nathaniel Coit to Robert Cochran, September 19, 1850, Robert Cochran Papers, Mississippi Archives.

[36] Menn, *Large Slaveholders of Louisiana*, 105, 108–109, 177–78, 202–203; Shields, *Natchez*, 85.

[37] Lyell, *Second Visit to the United States*, II, 155.

William J. Minor, son of colonial planter Stephen Minor, spent most of his autumns and winters at "Concord" in Natchez. The rest of the time he spent at his several residences in the Louisiana "Sugar Bowl," where he operated three estates in Terrebonne, Assumption and Ascension parishes. For the years 1855–61 the three plantations averaged an annual total of 1,218 hogsheads of sugar; in 1860 real and personal property valuation for the three was $1,153,000. In addition, Minor owned a Concordia cotton plantation and over $185,000 worth of property in Adams County. Minor was widely recognized as one of the finest turfmen in the South and was a pioneer in introducing organized cricket competition into the Southwest, the Natchez Cricket Club's matches being held in his "Concord" pasture. His brother John, who lived at "Oakland," owned property in Adams County and Ascension Parish valued at $555,600 in 1860.[38]

Another of the great planters whose cotton production was 4,000 or more bales per year by the 1850's was Levin R. Marshall. A grandson of Stephen Minor, he married first into the wealthy Chotard family and later into the Dunbar clan. At the time that he bought "Richmond Hill" as a residence in 1832, he had five cotton plantations in Adams County and Louisiana. In 1860 he owned 817 slaves on 14,400 acres of plantations in the two states, another 32 servants at his home, and over 10,000 acres in Arkansas. His livestock herds were among the largest in the Natchez region. Marshall also dabbled in town real estate, owning at one time the fashionable Mansion House hotel. Other than his presidency of the Commercial Bank of Natchez in the late 1830's, his only known participation in community activities was in 1825 when he headed the welcoming celebration on the oc-

[38] William J. Minor to Leverich, January 10, 1841, Leverich Papers, Mississippi Archives; Joseph F. Lewis to W. J. Minor, March 31, 1849, Minor Papers, UNC; J. Carlyle Sitterson, *Sugar Country: The Cane Sugar Industry in the South, 1753–1950* (Lexington, 1953), 56–60, 65, 79, 179–80, 188, 205. On Minor's holdings, see also J. Carlyle Sitterson, "The William J. Minor Plantations: A Study in Ante–Bellum Absentee Ownership," *JSH*, IX (February, 1943), 61–73; C. L. Wingfield, "The Sugar Plantations of William J. Minor, 1830–1860" (unpublished M.A. thesis, Louisiana State University, 1950).

casion of the Marquis de Lafayette's visit. His son George married a daughter of nabob David Hunt and received "Lansdowne" mansion and plantation just north of town as a wedding gift from his father-in-law. In 1860 George Marshall's property in Adams County and Louisiana was valued at $319,000.[39]

Haller Nutt, who lived at "Longwood" on the southern edge of Natchez, listed his holdings in 1860 as 800 slaves, including 32 house servants, and 42,947 acres on twenty-one plantations from Adams County to Terrebonne Parish. He figured his net profit from cotton and sugar that year at $228,320. His father, Rush Nutt, had won fame for his experiments with cotton hybrids, developing the popular "Petit Gulf" strain in 1833; the son continued seed breeding and produced a successful strain known as "Egypto-Mexican" in 1841. Between 1859 and 1860 Haller Nutt was occupied with the construction of a second "Longwood," designed by Philadelphia architect Samuel Sloan and patterned after a Moorish castle which Rush had sketched while abroad many years earlier. In August, 1860, 99 columns, 143 pedestals, and hundreds of other expensive furnishings and construction items arrived from France on a specially-chartered vessel. However, due to the outbreak of war, Nutt's house, certainly the most unusual structure in the area, was never completed.[40]

The Stanton clan, of which there were seven separate households in Natchez by the 1850's, may have been one of the wealthiest in the area, but unfortunately little is known of the holdings of five of the families. Brothers Frederick and David Stanton seem to have led the clan in affluence. The former, who lived at "Cherokee" prior to building "Stanton Hall" in 1857, came to Natchez from Northern Ireland as a physician but soon estab-

[39] Theodora B. Marshall and Gladys C. Evans (eds.), "Plantation Report from the Papers of Levin R. Marshall of 'Richmond,' Natchez, Mississippi," *JMH*, III (January, 1941), 45–55; New Orleans *Picayune*, February 19, 1859; *Johnson's Diary*, 110; Weaver, *Mississippi Farmers*, 50, 99; U. S. Census (1860), MS population and slave schedules.

[40] Inventory of Haller Nutt's plantations, 1860, Haller Nutt Papers, Duke; Samuel Sloan to Nutt, July 30, 1860, *ibid.*; invoice of Nutt's goods aboard the *Ville France*, August 27, 1860, *ibid.*; Rodney *Southern Telegraph*, September 12, 1838.

lished a lucrative partnership with ex-attorney Aylette Buckner in the cotton-commission business, eventually expanding into planting. By the time of his death on the eve of the Civil War, Frederick Stanton owned 444 slaves and 15,109 acres in six Louisiana and Mississippi plantations, producing over 3,000 bales of cotton yearly. Most of his property was in Concordia, but he had $102,000 invested in Adams County real and personal holdings. David Stanton, who bought "The Elms" in Natchez, owned $122,000 worth of property in Adams County in 1860, including thirteen house servants. Like his brother, David was engaged in the cotton-commission traffic at Natchez as well as in Louisiana cotton production.[41]

In the early territorial period Abijah Hunt, an enterprising New Jersey immigrant, built up a highly profitable chain of stores and gins from Natchez to Port Gibson. Though his firm engaged mainly in cotton brokerage, its activities ranged from selling white hats and ladies' "delicate shoes" to hauling logs and cotton bales. He also became a cotton planter, owning one plantation of 3,645 acres in Adams County and even larger acreage in Jefferson and Claiborne counties. Hunt, an outspoken Federalist, was killed in a duel with Poindexter in 1811. His nephew David then took over his business, gradually converting most of the mercantile assets into lands and slaves. By 1850 David Hunt owned nearly 1,700 slaves and twenty-six plantations in Adams, Jefferson, and Claiborne counties and in Tensas Parish. He kept residences in Natchez and near Cole's Creek, spending most of his later years at "Woodlawn," his country home. The houses and estates in and near Natchez which he gave to his children as they married included "Lansdowne," "Fatherland," "Oakwood," "Homewood," and "Argyle." Since his sons Andrew, Abijah, Dunbar, and George received approximately equal portions of land and slaves worth about $350,000, and since his three daughters were given lesser but still considerable shares of his estate when they married, their father's total

---

[41] U. S. Census (1860), MS population and slave schedules, Mississippi and Louisiana; Gates, *Farmer's Age*, 148; Natchez *Democrat*, 1959 Pilgrimage edition.

assets before these divisions in the 1850's must have been at least $2,000,000. Moreover, David Hunt is known to have owned real estate in Ohio and invested widely in railroad securities. A thorough check of his Mississippi and out-of-state investments might show that he was the Old South's wealthiest individual.[42]

John A. Quitman, whose career is normally associated with politics, was also a large planter. At "Springfield" Plantation, in Adams County, he produced 546 bales in 1833 on 2,000 acres of improved land. By 1841 he owned a plantation in Coahoma County and one in Warren County, the latter valued at $350,000 that year. In addition, he owned 40,000 acres in eastern Texas and a sugar cane plantation on Bayou Grand Caillou, Terrebonne Parish, Louisiana. He expanded his Grand Caillou estate from 3,600 acres to 7,500 in the years 1845–57; in 1860, two years after his death, it was valued at $385,000.[43]

Rivaling James Wilkins, whose opulence has been mentioned earlier, as the most influential merchant-financier in Natchez by 1840 was ex-Bostonian Alvarez Fisk. After practicing law awhile he purchased several cotton plantations in the 1820's and simultaneously entered the cotton-commission business. Soon he expanded his operations by opening a brokerage house in New Orleans and was on his way to a sizable fortune. In 1833 Julius Reed, who worked in his counting room at Natchez, reported: "Their books are kept like the Bank books, & their transactions are almost as extensive, the balance sheet of the house in N. Orleans for the quarter ending Sept. 30th shewing an amount exceeding six hundred thousand [dollars]."[44] Fisk was the most

[42] Abijah Hunt to Robert W. Gray, November 11, 1800, Abijah and David Hunt Papers, Misissippi Archives; Abijah Hunt's petition to import London merchandise, May 2, 1806, *ibid.*; David Hunt to William Lindsey, April 4, 1816, *ibid;* MS biography of David Hunt by son Dunbar Hunt, Dunbar Hunt Papers, in private possession of the family of the late Pearl V. Guyton, Natchez. See also David Hunt Papers, LSU.

[43] "Springfield" plantation book, sundry entries of 1833, Quitman Papers, UNC; Henry Turner to Quitman, June 27, 1843, *ibid.;* Quitman to George Turner, December 20, 1841, Quitman Papers, Mississippi Archives; B. A. Crawford to Quitman, Quitman Papers, University of Virginia; William Wood, *Autobiography of William Wood* (2 vols.; New York, 1895), I, 460.

[44] Reed to Watson, March 23, 1833, Watson Papers.

active of all the aristocrats in commuity affairs, playing a prominent role in educational, philanthropic, and church activities until his death in 1853; in fact, he may be best remembered as the "father" of the Natchez Institute.[45]

The manuscript federal census returns of 1860 for Adams County and Louisiana show seventeen other Natchez residents whose real and personal property holdings were valued at more than $300,000. (A check of their properties in other Mississippi counties and in other states might gain for even more Natchez nabobs nominations as antebellum millionaires.) Of the seventeen, seven were planters, three were attorneys, two were bankers, and five were merchants. A significant commentary on the growth of Natchez commerce as an avenue to wealth is the fact that, whereas in 1820 only Wilkins and Postlethwaite were merchants of great wealth, nearly half of the most opulent in 1860 were of the commercial class. As evidenced again and again in this analysis of holdings, of course, large merchants tended to channel their surplus profits into landed and chattel investments just as readily as did the full-time planters. Charles G. Dahlgren, for example, operated one of the town's largest plantation-supply firms while at the same time controlling 6,100 acres of cotton lands in Tensas Parish. Moreover, having married into the Routh family, he managed part of their large landholdings in Adams County. Like a number of other nabobs, Dahlgren could be classified with both the commercial and agricultural elements of the Natchez aristocracy.[46]

On the eve of the Civil War Natchez boasted probably one of the largest concentrations of men of great wealth of any town in the South. The notion of "wealthy Natchez" was created largely by the presence of this nabobery. The aristocrats' contributions to the local economy, however, are debatable, for in

---

[45] *Annual Reports, Natchez Institute, 1854,* 11–12; Alvarez Fisk to B. L. C. Wailes, March 28, 1845, Wailes Papers, Mississippi Archives; Joseph B. Stratton, *Memorial of a Quarter-Century's Pastorate* (Philadelphia, 1869), 50–52.

[46] U. S. Census (1860), MS population and slave schedules, Adams County, Mississippi, and Tensas Parish, Louisiana; Natchez *Courier,* July 17, 1859; Natchez *Democrat,* 1959 Pilgrimage edition.

many instances their principal holdings lay outside the town and county. Some paid almost all of their taxes to the Louisiana government; few seem to have added much to the tax coffers of Natchez and Adams County. In shipping and importing they usually dealt with the wealthy local commission merchants or directly with the factors of Liverpool, New York, or New Orleans. Thus the downtown middle-class businessmen did not profit greatly from their proximity. The gentry's shadow over the community was also a continual deterrent to immigration because such aristocratic predominance economically suggested to ambitious entrepreneurs and yeomen that the local avenues of opportunity were monopolized. Furthermore, as was true of the southern aristocracy generally, the possibilities of manufacturing suffered from the absorption of investment capital in lands and slaves. The role of the men of great wealth in the Natchez economy may be compared with that of certain Northern coal magnates, who, mainly for social reasons, chose to keep their residences in a town long after their laborers had exhausted the local resources and had moved on to more lucrative strip-mining elsewhere.

Urban historian Richard C. Wade's study of the early development of cities in the Upper Mississippi Valley indicates that where rapid growth and prosperity occurred for the community as a whole the far-sighted and dedicated leadership of large numbers of the most influential local citizens were involved. He maintains that "it requires the united influence of many individuals and various interests and the concurrence of a diversity of circumstances to give impulse to the healthy growth of a town." Wade concludes: "Many settlers came across the mountains in search of promising towns as well as good land."[47] Antebellum Natchez lacked such conditions for sound urban development.

When the dons abandoned Natchez in 1798, the town had no serious rival in population or commerce between New Orleans and Cincinnati. But by 1860 Natchez had fallen far down the

[47] Richard C. Wade, *The Urban Frontier: The Rise of Western Cities, 1790–1830* (Cambridge, Mass., 1959), 33–34.

list of southern municipalities in size and trade activity. It is true that the town had grown gradually during the period, but its progress verged upon insignificance in comparison with the surging municipalities elsewhere along the Mississippi and Ohio rivers. Memphis, for example, had jumped from 46 settlers in 1820 to 22,632 four decades later, while Natchez had risen unspectacularly from 2,184 to 6,612 inhabitants. The total value of manufactures at Memphis in 1860 exceeded $4,230,000, whereas for Natchez the figure was less than $214,000.[48]

Needless to say, the workings of geographical, demographical, economic, political, and social factors in the rise and decline of towns may never be explained satisfactorily. But there seems to be more than a coincidental relationship between the unique concentration of nabobs at Natchez and the fact that the town was the only one of any size in the Mississippi Valley in 1800 that did not become a considerable population and trade center later. Of course, no way is known to prove conclusively the causal affinity, but the general accumulation of evidence surely points toward an indictment of the "swell-heads." Except for a rare individual like Fisk, the weight of aristocratic wealth and talent was never directed toward bettering the town's economic status. Although it may be merely idle but interesting conjecture, one cannot help but wonder how the community would have progressed if no nabobery had arisen or, on the other hand, if a concerted effort had been made by the aristocrats toward municipal development.

[48] U. S. Censuses (1820 and 1860), MS population schedules; Rowland, *Official and Statistical Register, 1917*, 731–35; Gerald M. Capers, Jr., *The Biography of a River Town: Memphis, Its Heroic Age* (Chapel Hill, 1939), 45–47, 83, 101, 103, 185; Robert R. Russel, *Economic Aspects of Southern Sectionalism, 1840–1861* (Urbana, 1924), 226–29. The growth rate of Natchez was unimpressive when compared not only to Memphis but also to other transmontane Southern municipalities, viz.:

	1820	1860
Natchez	2,184	6,612
Louisville	4,012	68,033
Nashville	1,639	16,988
Mobile	1,017	29,258

CHAPTER VII

There Were
Other People

NATCHEZ COULD NOT KEEP PACE IN POPU-
lation with urban centers like Memphis
and Louisville, but at least its growth rate was greater than
Adams County's. Between 1810 and 1860 Natchez enjoyed a
393 per cent increase in population, which represented a rise from
1,684 inhabitants to 6,612. On the other hand, the county (excluding Natchez) grew 163 per cent, or from 8,318 residents to
13,553. County population actually declined in numbers during
the last two antebellum decades, having reached its zenith in
1840 at 14,608 inhabitants. Natchez grew steadily and claimed
an ever-increasing percentage of the aggregate population of
Adams County. In 1810 the town's populace constituted 16.8 per
cent of all persons in the county; by 1860 the figure had grown
to 32.8 per cent. Nevertheless, the rate of population increase at
Natchez was meager when compared to that of the state, whose
population in 1860 was over ten times that shown in the federal
census of 1820.

Contrary to a general trend of declining slave populations in
southern urban centers, slavery at Natchez was climbing rather
rapidly in numbers during the years 1810–60. From 459 in 1810
the town's slave population had grown to 2,131 by 1860, an
increase of 464 per cent as compared with a county rise of 289
per cent. In 1810 fewer than 8 per cent of all slaves in Adams
County lived in Natchez, whereas a half century later the town
had 15 per cent of the total. Much of the increase in urban slaveholdings occurred between 1830 and 1860. In the former year
there were 76 slaveowners in the town, 56 of whom owned five or
fewer slaves, while 13 had six to twenty slaves, and 7 held over

twenty. The number of slaveholders in 1860 was 382, of whom 257 owned less than six slaves, 113 held six to twenty, and 12 had over twenty slaves. The increase in town slaveholdings occurred particularly among middle- and upper-class commercial men. In 1850 the two largest slaveholders were Andrew Brown, a sawmill owner who had thirty-three slaves, and George Weldon, a merchant who held thirty. In 1860 A. C. Britton, a banker and cotton broker, led the list with thirty-seven slaves, and gunsmith Stephen Odell ranked next with thirty-six. Obviously the large planters who lived in town retained only house servants although, as previously pointed out, some of them kept considerable slave retinues at their mansions. Even with the surge in slaveholdings at Natchez, however, the average owner in 1860 held only five slaves.

By 1840 Adams County and Natchez together had 283 free Negroes, which was nearly half of all the "free persons of color" in Mississippi. Most lived on small farms in poor-soil areas near Natchez, such as the edge of Butler's Swamp; only 101 actually resided in the town. Various attempts were made by white groups to discourage the continued residence of free Negroes in the area, including a so-called "Inquisition" beginning in 1841. But two decades later 208 of the 225 free Negroes in Adams County were living in Natchez. By that time most of the increase was through reproduction rather than manumission, the latter declining sharply as northern abolitionist fervor rose after 1830.

As most frontier towns grew in size and sophistication, the early preponderance of white males tended to decrease. But at Natchez the ratio of white males to white females remained about the same from 1810 to 1860. Males consistently comprised 58 per cent to 63 per cent of the white populace. In 1810, for example, the town had 626 white males and 395 white females, while in 1840 the figures were respectively 1,831 and 1,163, the males constituting 61 per cent of the total whites in both censuses.[1] In view of the long establishment of the community, it may be that by 1810

[1] U. S. Censuses (1810–60), MS population and slave schedules.

Natchez had already lost some frontier traits, including this demographic characteristic.

Data on the origins and migrations of the inhabitants of Natchez between 1800 and 1817 are available for 320 whites, mostly of the middle and upper classes. Of this group, which represents about one fourth of the white population of the time, 17 per cent moved to the town in 1800–1801, 52 per cent in 1802–17, and the rest prior to 1800. Nearly half of the residents were foreign-born, with 86 per cent of them from the British Isles and the rest from nine other nations, especially France and the Germanic states. Of those born in the United States 33 per cent were natives of Virginia and 22 per cent natives of Maryland, with Pennsylvania, Massachusetts, and New Jersey ranking next in that order. Only 8 per cent were natives of Adams County. As for places of residence immediately prior to moving to Natchez (excluding birthplaces), 42 per cent came from Pennsylvania, 17 per cent from Virginia, 16 per cent from Georgia, 14 per cent from Kentucky, and 10 per cent from Tennessee. No residential colonies of immigrants existed in Natchez, but in outlying areas some families who had migrated together settled in the same neighborhoods. The more significant groups were the Marylanders, including the Covington, Magruder, and Wailes families, who moved to the Washington area between 1807 and 1811, and the North Carolinians of Scottish and Scotch-Irish descent who migrated to Union Church, northeast of Natchez, between 1805 and 1809.[2]

In 1850 Natchez still retained its colorful cosmopolitan atmosphere although much of the notoriety of its mixture of nationalities had subsided. The foreign-born element represented 31 per cent of the town's population of 4,680. One out of three such persons was an Irishman. The largest nationality groups were the Irish, 571; German, 256; English, 130; Scottish and Scotch-Irish,

    [2] Edith W. Moore (comp.), MS Records of Natchez and Adams County Cemeteries; Francis A. Cook (ed.), *Cemetery and Bible Records: A Publication of the Mississippi Genealogical Society* (10 vols.; Jackson, 1954–63), II, III; *Biographical and Historical Memoirs of Mississippi*, II; U. S. Census (1820), MS population schedules; Mississippi Territorial Census, 1816.

64; and Italian, 63. At least seventeen nations were represented at Natchez in 1850. As for the American-born residents, 69 per cent were of Mississippi birth, 18 per cent were from the other southern states, 10 per cent from the Middle Atlantic and northwestern states, and 3 per cent from the New England states.[3]

Just as the aristocracy comprised commercial, professional, and agricultural subclasses, so the middle class had its divisions. Since the number of middle-class farmers who resided in town was small, the bourgeois element consisted mainly of commercial and professional groups. Whereas most wholesalers, commission merchants, and bankers were wealthy enough to be considered in the aristocracy, the middle-class commercial types were largely merchant capitalists of comfortable but not opulent means who owned their own establishments, ranging from firms dealing in plantation supplies to "variety stores" and small foundries. The group also included editors, accountants, tellers, small shippers, public ginners, keepers of respectable inns, and the like. The middle-class professionals were principally teachers and young attorneys and physicians, many of the last two vocations eventually attaining aristocratic status. The social distinctions of the time which separated the middle class from the elite are impossible to define. Any attempt to delineate the two economically must be arbitrary; but, judging by the approximate correlations between residential elegance, known social relations, and property valuations, the possession of twenty slaves and about $50,000 worth of real and personal property seems to roughly mark the line. There were numerous exceptions, of course. H. D. Gurney, for example, was a young photographer from Massachusetts whose total property valuation in 1860 was $100,000, but his name never appeared in accounts of aristocratic social activities nor did he acquire one of the finer homes. As earlier emphasized, the prerequisites for entry into the gentry class by the late antebellum era were "connections" as well as wealth.[4]

[3] U. S. Census (1850), MS population schedules.
[4] U. S. Census (1860), MS population and slave schedules.

The depression which followed the Panic of 1837 lasted until the mid-1840's in the Natchez region. Thereafter the town's economy began to recover slowly, and by the early 1850's an era of unprecedented business and agricultural prosperity had dawned. Some indication of the upswing is evident from the following typical cases of successful men who belonged to the middle class in 1850:[5]

	Slaves		Real Estate		
	1850	1860	1850	1860	Vocation
E. B. Baker	5	9	$ 3,200	$16,000	Merchant
Emile Profilet	10	12	6,000	7,000	Merchant
James Carradine	0	10	4,000	18,000	Merchant
Rhasa Parker	0	8	4,500	31,000	Carpenter
A. J. Postlethwaite	0	13	3,500	5,000	Merchant
Cyrus Marsh	0	14	15,000	61,000	Merchant
Giles M. Hillyer	1	5	3,000	40,000	Editor
Ralph North	6	12	4,000	8,000	Attorney
George W. Koontz	6	11	8,000	95,000	Banker
Jacob Eiler	2	5	7,500	12,000	Merchant

If the line separating the middle class from the upper class is difficult to draw, even harder to delineate is the distinction between the middle and lower white classes. Although a few owners of small mercantile establishments fell into the lower-class category, the bulk of this element consisted of wage earners, such as mechanics, craftsmen, and clerks. The strongest Democratic sympathies were manifested by this group, and the *Free Trader* often catered to wage earners in its editorials. In May, 1837, as news came of the financial panic that was spreading from the northeast, the *Free Trader* offered the following paean to the lowly mechanic:

His outlay of capital is the knowledge of his art, calling, craft, and the application of it, combined with his personal labor, to the great purposes of utility. He is dependent on himself, and is his own bank. Such is the positive need which society feels of the aid of the

[5] U. S. Censuses (1850–60), MS population and slave schedules.

mechanic, that his occupation, in the midst of a storm of failures, is among the last to fail. The bank may have the ague; the commission merchant may suspend payment; the lawyer may return himself *non inventus*, even on a bill filed in Sterne's chancery, (that of heaven) but the mechanic is always "at home" for a good, cash-paying job.

Who pays the coin for all his debts on Saturday night? The mechanic. Who comes to the store with a jolly, care-for-nought face, bringing his companions with him, asking for the shortest possible credits? The mechanic. Who rises earliest in the morning and makes the day the longest? The mechanic. Whose vote at the polls tells as loud as a bank director's? The mechanic's. Who has the prettiest wife and the smartest children? The mechanic.[6]

If barber William Johnson's diary is indicative, the Irish residents were probably the most vociferous and surely the most hilarious element of the lower-class whites. Although most of them were engaged in reputable trades and possessed some property, they sporadically burst forth with violence indistinguishable from that of the transients at the landing. Johnson described one of their episodes thus:

The Irish Turned Out prety strong to Day, or this Evening, after a Fellow by the name of McCabe who tis believed Killed a man Last night and threw him over the Bluff so as to make it appear that he had fallen over the Bluff Himself. The Irish threw over the House that he lived in and Let it fall Down the Bluff. The Guards and Fencibles [militia] had to turn Out To Keep them from Linching him.[7]

The Negro barber delighted in witnessing such Irish melees as the following:

Whilst Standing on the Bluff this Evening nearly dark, I Saw 8 or 10 wild Irishman fighting all among One another It was realy Laughable indeed—They Beat one man by the name of Rountree—a guard he is for the City. He Hallowd Like a Clever fellow—Then on the Hill at the 10 pin alley, McFarlands place, there was two moore fights Car-

[6] *Mississippi Free Trader and Natchez Gazette*, May 6, 1837.
[7] *Johnson's Diary*, 240.

dine, 1 of them, got whiped—Folies wife struck him with a Brick
Bat—Cut his head thrugh mistake &c. Just like such people.[8]

Included among the lower-class whites also was an unknown
but perhaps considerable number of apprentices and journeymen. A popular source of apprentices was the Adams County
Orphans Court's guardianship system. The court often designated responsible citizens as "guardians" for indigent children
who had lost their parents. Through indenture contracts the
guardians assumed responsibility for rearing and providing voca-
tional training for the youths until they reached maturity, then
considered to be the age of eighteen. A typical indenture bond
certified by the Orphans Court bound the guardian to "take care
of the persons, estates and education of said infants" and, upon
the legal maturing of the youths, to "render a just and true account of the rents, issues and profits of the real estate of the
said infants, and in the mean time improve the same to their use
and best advantage, and make no sale, nor commit any waste or
destruction thereof or therein." The youth was then released as
a journeyman, whereupon he was on his own to find employment. In actual practice, many masters made wage agreements
with their former ward-apprentices, employing them at salaries
that generally ranged from $150 to $500 per year. Most apprentices were bound to printers, weavers, tailors, keepers of
shops and inns, bricklayers, and blacksmiths. For the most part,
the indenture system seems to have worked well, partly because
the shortage of skilled labor, typical of most frontier communities, made the town's capitalists eager to garner potential
workers. Some free Negroes were indentured, but that practice
became infrequent after 1840 as white animosity toward free
persons of color increased.[9]

Besides the above-mentioned "respectable" lower-class whites,
there were also those of disrepute, such as slave traders and

---

[8] *Ibid.,* 352.
[9] *Ibid,* 27–28, 385, 394–95, 615; Adams County Orphans Court Minute Book,
I–III.

operators of houses of prostitution. Most of the disrespectable element, however, were transients, who were ever milling about the lower town. They included boatmen, wagoners, professional gamblers, trappers, fishermen, and that large group of irresponsible adventurers perennially wandering from one end of the frontier to the other. Without families or relations in Natchez and possessing no property there, the transient populace was largely responsible for the tainted reputation of Natchez-under-the-Hill since they were the first and only contacts most river travelers had with the community. By the 1830's many of the landing's brothels and tippling houses had given way to warehouses and commercial facilities, and the influence of this element became negligible, though never entirely disappearing. In 1808, when the boisterousness of Natchez-under-the-Hill was in full sway, traveler Henry Ker described it thus:

A small part of the town is under the hill, immediately on the river; it is well known to be the resort of dissipation. Here is the bold-faced strumpet, full of blasphemies, who looks upon the virtuous part of her sex with contempt and hatred; every house is a grocery, containing gambling, music, and dancing, fornicators, &c. This is the stopping place for all boatmen from Kentucky, Tennessee, &c.; yes, I have in that place seen 150 boats, loaded with produce, bound to New Orleans, delaying their time, and spending days in the lowest orders of dissipation.[10]

Even when the visitor moved from the shabby structures of Natchez-under-the-Hill to the upper town, he was not always impressed by great differences in housing. At that time middle-class businessmen commonly maintained their residences in the same building with their business establishments, living above or immediately to the rear. In 1808 Christian Schultz, a river traveler, found the buildings atop the bluff "neat" but saw "none within the town that can be considered as elegant." The next year Fortesque Cuming, another visitor, remarked: "I was much

[10] Henry Ker, *Travels Through the Western Interior of the United States, 1808–1816* (Elizabeth, N. J., 1816), 41.

struck with the similarity of Natchez to many of the smaller
West Indian towns. . . . Several of the houses are new and very
good, mostly of wood, and I am informed many (more than half)
have been added within the last four years." William Richardson
in 1815 found the houses to be decent but not elegant: "They
are generally low, full of windows and doors for the admission
of as much air as possible." Two years later Edouard de Montulé
commented: "It [Natchez] is still in its infancy, but new buildings are being erected on all sides. It is pretty." That same year
Samuel R. Brown thought the downtown houses had "an air of
neatness" but few were distinguished for elegance or size."[11]   In
1835 Charles A. Murray, another visitor, was pleased with the
physical appearance of the community: "The upper town of
Natchez is pleasantly situated . . . [with] several handsome
buildings & some streets well laid out. . . . There are many hand-
home, well-supplied shops." He also noted that "many of the
wealthier merchants reside at villas, prettily situated on the
undulating slopes by which the town is surrounded."[12]   Thus
visitors were impressed or unimpressed by the town's structures
in accordance with the quality of the ones they visited or hap-
pened to notice. Other than the lower-class housing beneath the
bluff, there was no marked distinction in residences through the
various neighborhoods—a mansion often being surrounded by the
unpretentious homes of commoners. The free Negroes likewise
were not located in a segregated area but were interspersed
throughout the town. William Johnson, for example, resided in
the midst of one of the better white neighborhoods.[13]

[11] Schultz, *Travels on an Inland Voyage*, 133; Fortescue Cuming, *Sketches of a
Tour to the Western Country* (Pittsburgh, 1810), 293–95; William Richardson,
*Journey from Boston to the Western Country and Mississippi Rivers to New
Orleans, 1815–1816*, ed. William B. Wait (New York, 1940), 34; Edouard de
Montulé, *Travels in America, 1816–1817*, trans. Edward D. Seeber (Bloomington,
1951), 94–95; Samuel R. Brown, *The Western Gazetteer; or Emigrant's Directory*
(Albany, 1817), 234.
[12] Charles A. Murray, *Travels in North America During the Years 1834, 1835,
& 1836* (2 vols.; London, 1839), 178–79.
[13] Edwin A. Davis and William Ransom Hogan, *The Barber of Natchez*
(Baton Rouge, 1954), 98–99.

Little is known about slavery within the city limits, and no primary materials were found that shed light on the use of slaves at Natchez for other than domestic and farm chores. As was true of slave society elsewhere, domestic servants, the most numerous category of town chattels, probably considered themselves superior to slaves used as field hands, wagon drivers, store janitors, port workers, and the like. The few available glimpses into slave life at Natchez conflict somewhat on the degree of harmony that existed in slave-white relations. Joseph H. Ingraham, who frequently visited Natchez while teaching at nearby Jefferson College in the 1830's, claimed that the incidence of slave misbehavior rose perceptibly on weekends when many slaves were granted passes. Sundays were especially boisterous times, at least until the city bell rang at 4 P.M. signaling the return to quarters:

Then commences a ludicrous scene of hurrying and scampering, from the four corners of the town; for woe be to the unlucky straggler, who is found after a limited period within the forbidden bounds! The penalty of 40 lashes, save one, is speedily inflicted, by way of a lesson in the science of discretion. After the bell, slaves were soon seen following their noses, with all commendable speed, along the diverging highways, keeping time to the tune of "over the hills and far away" to their respective plantations.[14]

The most detailed account of slave activities within the city limits is that of John B. Nevitt, a large planter and leading Roman Catholic layman who lived on the northern edge of town. His home was situated about six blocks from the downtown area, yet his plantation lands began at the rear of the "big house," stretching out northward along the bluff. Nevitt's record book chiefly mentions his agrarian laborers but does include some details on his slaves' behavior in town when there as hired hands, as recipients of passes, and as miscreants. Below are his complete entries for 1831 relating to slaves:

[14] Ingraham, *South-West*, II, 72–73.

Jan. 13: Jerry got his waggon and two Horses in the Bayou near Mr Turners House and Killed the Rock Horse.

Jan. 23: gave Jerry & Rubin permission to visit Wm J Minors plantation near Concordia Louisiana they returned next morning a little before day.

Feb. 4: Jerry and Albert runaway the latter last night the former this morning.

Feb. 5: Jerry and Albert came home in morning gave Albert a flogging and forgave Jerry and set them to work gave Bill permission to go to Judge Turners plantation to see his wife gave him a mule to ride.

Feb. 12: gave Jerry & Rubin permission to go and see their wives.

Feb. 20: Jerry runaway in morning wrote Mr Wm Minors overseer on the subject.

Feb. 27: Bill left plantation of his own accord all day came home drunk.

Feb. 28: Jerry came home gave him a whiping and set him to work.

Mar. 13: gave Bill Rubin (in Evening) Betts & Milly passes to go to Natchez the two first got drunk the two latter stayed out untill 8 at night made a determination to withold passes in future.

Mar. 19: gave Bill pass to see his wife.

Mar. 20: negroes unruly at quarters perticularly Betts & Delly who runaway at night.

Mar. 27: gave Jerry & Rubin a pass to go to see their wives and paid them 11—for work done.

Mar. 28: Jerry & Rubin delayed by high wind over the river until 12 oClock. . . . Found that Albert had been taken up and put in Jail paid his Jail fees $3.00 and took him out had an Iron collar put on his neck by Mr Williams Blacksmith paid for it 1.50 cash sent him home with his hands tied behind him by Frank Alexander who let him *escape* one of the punch bowls [dense wooded areas along the bluff]. . . . Little Betts came home this morning sent her to work did not whip her lest it should prevent Delly from coming home.

Apr. 8: Mr Mill his brother and Mr Rowan brought home Delly and Albert found in Campbells straw house gave them both a severe whipping and sent them to Quarters to work.

Apr. 26: sent the articles purchased out by Bill found on my return home he had been stealing the greater part of a demijohn of molasses gave him a good whiping and sent him to Jail with a determination to sell him.

May 2: Sold Bill to Edw Turner for $600. . . . Jerry went over the river yesterday to see his wife without a pass gave him a light flogging for it Rubin came home this morning after being runaway for five or six weeks done nothing with him yet.

June 12: *took the Iron* off Rubins leg . . . gave Jerry pass to go to his wife.

June 14: Milly runaway at night.

Sept. 25: gave Rubin pass to go over the river.

Oct. 4: hands employed repairing Bridge on Publick road and working the road.

Oct. 11: heard Jerry had been shot by Mr Minors overseer (Hiner).

Oct. 12: Jerry came home with note from Mr Minors overseer (Mr Hyner) who had not shot him as reported yesterday but shot at him and missed gave Jerry a severe whipping and put him to work.

Oct. 28: rode to Natchez found much excitement fearing negroes will be troublesome joined the corps exempts done nothing.

Dec. 25: gave all the people passes for the day with presents of dresses Handkfs. &c.[15]

Nevitt, who for many years headed the local Roman Catholic Society, probably enjoyed as satisfactory relations with his slaves as did most owners. Yet, when it is recalled that nearly one out of three inhabitants at Natchez was a slave, the enormity of the problem of maintaining law and order and of curtailing racial friction is obvious. The maintenance of slave discipline must have been far more difficult in the crowded conditions of town life than in the isolated, self-contained environment of the rural plantation. Fear of an impending slave insurrection led the editor of the *Southern Galaxy*, a Natchez newspaper, to pen several essays on the need to lessen the severity of slave punishments. In one such editorial he warned:

[15] Record Book of John B. Nevitt, entries of 1831, typescript of Barnes F. Lathrop, Austin, Texas. Sometimes, as in the case of Nevitt's slave Jerry, a slave owned by one man was married to a slave owned by another master. This probably accounted for Jerry's frequent escapes and returns.

We have resided some years among slaves, and from often repeated enquiries, aided by personal observations we are justified in the remark, that the slave, to be useful, must not be barbarously treated. He must be well fed, well clothed, and humanely treated when sick; the master must not tamper with him—correction should not be often repeated, not done in anger. That moment you lacerate his back, confine him with stocks and hand-cuffs, and thus put him to the torture, that moment you have lost him. It would be well if the effect were restricted to the slave thus treated; but it is not, you have driven him to desperation—the effect is contagious—entire plantations become affected—in fact our woods and bayous are already filled by its effects. It is time to pause, to reflect and determine upon some course by which the evil may be arrested before its magnitude shall bid us defiance.[16]

On the other hand, free Negro Johnson, himself owner of fifteen slaves, gave little indication in his diary of 1835–51 that slave-white relations were troubled or tense. His observations ranged from mischievous and felonious acts committed by slaves, mostly against each other, to "darkey parties," several of which were held under white sponsorship in the fashionable ballroom of William Parker's Mississippi Hotel. In those seventeen years Johnson cited only ten instances of criminal acts by slaves. Four of these involved theft; two were incidents of brawling with whites; and the others were singular cases of fighting between slaves, gambling, murdering a Negro hotel cook, and hurling brickbats at a white man's house. Not a single case of a slave raping or murdering a white was found in the Johnson diary and the local newspapers of that period. No lynchings of Negroes at Natchez are mentioned, but Johnson does note a case across the river in which a white posse caught a slave who had murdered a white man and "Burned Him up soon after he was taken." The effectiveness of slave patrols and the harshness of punishment were undoubtedly the main reasons for the town's relatively quiet racial situation.[17]

[16] Natchez *Southern Galaxy*, October 9, 1828.
[17] *Johnson's Diary*, 222, 253, 314, 337, 347, 363, 394, 446–47, 462, 469, 558, 571.

In 1831 the news of the Nat Turner insurrection in Virginia and the start of William Lloyd Garrison's abolitionist offensive produced fears, real or imagined, in whites at Natchez. That year a local editor claimed that he had found the solution to the slaves' "unrest." He said: "If the free coloured people were removed, the slaves could safely be treated with more indulgence. Less fear would be entertained, and greater latitude of course allowed. . . . In a word, it would make better masters and better slaves. From the same cause also results another evil: the check, or rather stop, which has been given to the emancipation of slaves, no matter how meritorious their conduct."[18]

About three months later, in June, a group of the area's wealthiest men organized the Mississippi Colonization Society, an organization dedicated to resettling free Negroes and manumitted slaves in Africa. Led by Stephen Duncan, who served as president from 1831–40, the officials included over the years several dozen of the region's most prominent attorneys, planters, merchants, and ministers. Most active at Natchez, the society's headquarters, were Duncan, Dr. John Ker, and Alvarez Fisk. Duncan and Ker later became vice presidents of the American Colonization Society. In its first three years the Mississippi organization received over $100,000 in donations. By 1840 Duncan had given $50,000, David Hunt, over $35,000, and James Green, $32,000. William Winans, who had earlier served as pastor of the Natchez Methodist flock, became the society's most active agent in collecting funds and making promotional speeches. At least 571 Negroes were sent to the colony of Liberia by the state organization. In the later 1830's, however, Mississippi became so defensive about slavery in the face of the rising abolitionist fever that any form of manumission was frowned upon by the majority of citizens. Robert Walker told the United States Senate in 1837 that the Mississippi society, which "had been extremely popular," was declining rapidly in popular favor and effectiveness.[19]

[18] *Natchez,* March 5, 1831.
[19] Sydnor, *Slavery in Mississippi,* 190, 206–18; U. S. Congress, *Debates and*

When planter Isaac Ross died in 1836, willing his slaves to freedom in Liberia, a major legal battle ensued, with prominent Natchez persons aligned on both sides. Some heirs tried to block the execution of the will, while Ker and Duncan, representing Mrs. Thomas B. Reed, Ross's daughter and principal heir, succeeded after a long court fight obtaining the removal of about 250 to 300 of the Ross Negroes to Africa. Both men lost favor locally during the battle. So intense was town feeling in 1844 over the manumission of 72 of Mrs. Reed's slaves that Duncan hid them at night in an isolated sector along the Mississippi to await the steamboat. As the ambitious "Mississippi in Africa" project received less and less public support, both Duncan and Ker became disillusioned, resigning from both the state and the national colonization societies.[20]

Quitman symbolized the changed attitude toward slavery. Whereas in his earlier years he had occasionally deprecated the institution as inhuman, he told the state legislature in 1836 that the proslavery forces must counterattack against the abolitionists, who had contaminated the "reviews, orations, tracts, and even school books." He argued that "the morality, the expediency, and the duration of the institution of slavery, are questions which belong exclusively to ourselves," and that the people of Mississippi "have chosen to adopt into our political system, and still choose to retain, the institution of domestic slavery."[21] Samuel A. Cartwright, a Natchez physician who became a college professor, was a vociferous publicist for the proslavery forces, writing articles and delivering lectures to show that the blacks, by their physiological structures, were unsuited for freedom.[22] Mean-

Proceedings in the Congress of the United States; with an Appendix, Containing State Papers and Public Documents . . . [First to Eighteenth Congresses] (42 vols.; Washington, 1834–56), XIII, 535.

[20] Franklin L. Riley, "A Contribution to the History of the Colonization Movement in Mississippi," PMHS, IX (1906), 347–80; Sydnor, Slavery in Mississippi, 219–31.

[21] Quoted in Dunbar Rowland, History of Mississippi: Heart of the South (2 vols.; Chicago, 1925), II, 643.

[22] For Samuel A. Cartwright's proslavery argument, see his Essays . . . (Vidalia, La., 1843).

while, far to the north, aging John Quincy Adams wrote in 1838 to a young Massachusetts abolitionist: "The youthful Champions of the rights of human nature, have buckled and are buckling on their armour, and the Scourging overseer, and the Lynching Lawyer, and the Servile Sophist, and faithless Scribe, and the priestly parasite will vanish before them like Satan, touched by the Spear of Thuriol."[23] Somewhere between these two battle lines Duncan's dream of "Mississippi in Africa" was lost.

Nevertheless, the free Negroes of Natchez continued their precarious existence, living under ever present pressures and anxieties. Their freedom of activity was more curtailed by mores than by law; there was relatively little of the legal segregation that characterized the "Jim Crow" era much later. Johnson found few restrictions in his business dealings and was able to accumulate considerable property, including several barber shops, a small farm, a comfortable home, slaves, and some cultural trappings—an estate worth about $25,000 in 1851. He occasionally participated in public raffles, placed bets at Pharsalia, fished and hunted with white friends, loaned cash to white associates, and infrequently ate with them at his home. His attorney was William T. Martin, owner of "Monteigne" and later a Confederate general; his physician was Dr. Luke P. Blackburn, later governor of Kentucky; and his closest white friend was Adam Bingaman, large planter and distinguished Whig politician. Though accepted with equanimity in most business and financial activities, Johnson shrewdly kept his place according to the unwritten code of social discrimination.[24] Occasionally his tactfulness was able to gain some lowering of the barriers, as in the following incident when he managed to get passage on a steamboat for his wife:

I Spoke to A. L. Willson the other day to procure me a passage on the Steam Boat, Maid of Arkensaw, which he promised to do and to

[23] John Quincy Adams to Edmund Quincy, July 28, 1838, Quitman Papers, Mississippi Archives.

[24] *Johnson's Diary*, 39–40; Davis and Hogan, *Barber of Natchez*, 227–40.

day when the Boat Came I went down to see about it and I saw him
and He told me that he had spoke to the Capt. and that he had Refused to Let a State Room, But that my wife Could have the whole of
the Ladies Cabbin to Herself but it was a Rule on his Boat not to Let
any Col[olored] persons have State Rooms on Her—I asked him to go
with me on Board—He went on Board and showd me the Capt. and I
asked him if could not spare a State Room and he told me that He
Could not spare one that it was against the Rules of His Boat and
that he had said it once and that was Enough and that he was a man
of his word and Spoke of Prejudice of the Southern people, it was
damd Foolish &c, and that he was a doing a Business for other people
and was Compelld to adopt those Rules—I did not prevail by no
means—He then said that I Could have a State Room on Conditions
which I told him would answer.[25]

    In their own world the free Negroes reflected the urge for
status and manifested as sharp a class distinction as did the
whites. By the 1830's there were at least a half-dozen families
of free Negroes at Natchez who owned five to twenty slaves as
well as some relatively valuable real estate. Some had obtained
their holdings as legacies from white sires, and others had risen
through their own skill and enterprise in such trades as cabinet-
making, bricklaying, and barbering. A rather close-knit coterie,
they rarely hobnobbed with the lower levels of free Negroes and
slaves. Johnson was one of the leaders of this group. A considerable distance beneath them socially and economically were
the free Negroes who had modest incomes but little prospect
for advancement, such as journeymen barbers, draymen, steamboat and port hands, and some semiskilled craftsmen. Another
group consisted of free Negroes who were attached to white
households as domestic servants. The majority of free colored
folk, however, were extremely poor, working as peddlers, prostitutes, unskilled laborers, fishermen, woodchoppers, and the like.[26]
    With a large portion of the state's free Negro populace living
in and near Natchez, the local representatives in the state legis-

[25] *Johnson's Diary*, 391.
[26] Davis and Hogan, *Barber of Natchez*, 91–93, 241–43.

Benjamin L. C. Wailes, planter, scientist, and scholar.

Lower landing at Natchez as sketched by Edouard de Montulé, 1817.

Natchez waterfront as sketched by Henry Lewis, 1847.

The city of Natchez as seen from the old fort, from the lithograph by Pifeo H. Browne, c. 1835.

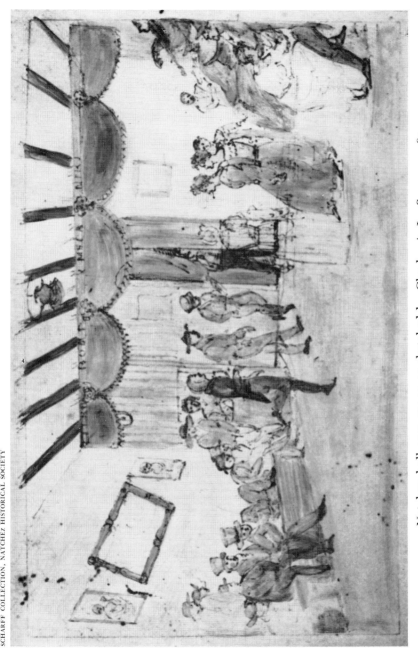

Natchez ballroom scene as sketched by Charles A. Le Sueur, c. 1830.

William Johnson,
Free Negro barber
and diarist.

Sunday morning scene at the Natchez post office, c. 1850.

Territorial Governor Winthrop
Sargent.

Senator Robert J. Walker.

General John A. Quitman.

lature in 1831 spearheaded a successful drive to require free Negroes to leave Mississippi within a stipulated period. A proviso allowed those in "good standing" to offer petitions with the signatures of reputable whites to the county board of police. The board, in turn, might approve requests to remain from free Negroes who were attested as "worthy characters." In 1837 and thereafter, however, demands grew for stricter regulations and enforcements to circumscribe the activities of free Negroes, who were stereotyped often as abolitionist in sympathy. By 1840 the main civil distinction between the free person of color and the slave was the former's right to possess property. Both were forbidden to testify against whites, vote, hold office, serve in the militia, or violate the unwritten social code of the community.[27]

In the summer of 1841 there began in Natchez a campaign against the free Negroes, which Johnson called the "Inquisition." A citizens' meeting, attended mostly by whites of the lower and middle classes, produced a vigilance committee whose job was to investigate the conduct of free Negroes, especially their conformity to the law of 1831, and to deport from the state any who had committed the slightest violation. The Democratic *Free Trader*, which heartily endorsed the movement, claimed that it was aimed "to strike a severe blow against the practices of the rogue, the incendiary, and the abolitionist." Johnson, whose own position was comparatively secure, wrote often in his diary of the "Horrows of the Inquisition." About ten days after the first public meeting he observed that "All Sorts of Tryals going on— The different offices have been full all day and they continue to arrest Still—The Lord knows how those things will terminate for I have no conception myself." Numbers of free Negroes were deported that summer and in ensuing years as their lot grew more insecure with the increasingly belligerent proslavery convictions of the white citizenry.[28]

[27] *Ibid.*, 151–53.
[28] Natchez *Mississippi Free Trader*, August 7, 1841; *Johnson's Diary*, 340–46.

The Inquisition seems to have been led by the middle-class municipal officials, while the nabobs appear to have cooperated with respectable free Negroes in obtaining tardy attestations of good character. Johnson frequently praised the men of wealth during the crisis that his people faced:

Lotts of F.P.C. [Free People of Color] are running arround Town with Petitions to have the Priveledge of rema[in]ing in the state, tis Laug[h]able almost, Wellington [West] was Out into the Country this Evening to have his Petition signed and He got the following Gentlemen on his Paper—Dr Steven Duncan & Col A L Bingaman, Dr Calhoun, Col. Wilkins, Mr R. C. Evans, Mr J Routh, Mr S. D. Elliotte —Those Names are Enough to make any Common man Proud—Those Names are an Ornament to Any Paper—Those are Gentlemen of the 1st Order of Talents and Standing.[29]

It is not clear why the aristocrats generally supported the free Negroes. It may have been sadistic vengeance since the town bourgeoisie had opposed the Mississippi Colonization Society and had long antagonized the nabobs by their municipal ordinances.

In the 1840's and early 1850's at Natchez the sectional controversy was rivaled as a paramount issue by the problem of the presence of free Negroes. The Inquisition continued sporadically. William Barland, Wilford Hoggatt, and other "respectable" whites emancipated more than one hundred mulattoes in the years 1824–40, but local manumission dropped to less than ten in the 1840's and even fewer in the next decade. The free Negro population showed a decline for the first time in 1850. But, as noted earlier, it suddenly and inexplicably rose again in the 1850's, reaching an all-time high of 208 in 1860. Local Democrats divided with Whigs as early as 1840 over the legality of free Negro testimony, with John D. Freeman sharply denounced by Whigs for his advocacy of free Negro court witnesses as he campaigned for the attorney generalship that year. Just as it seemed that opposition to free Negroes was subsiding somewhat,

[29] *Johnson's Diary*, 343.

the *Courier*, which had previously remained comparatively aloof from the issue, launched an attack in 1849 on free Negro rights and privileges. The editor warned that chaos would result unless officials immediately began to enforce the laws which made it illegal for free Negroes to keep "houses of entertainment" and "to vend any goods, wares, merchandise, or spirituous liquors."[30]

Feelings heightened two years later when Johnson, perhaps the most popular and prosperous barber in Natchez, was murdered by a small farmer, Baylor Winn, in the vicinity of Butler's Swamp south of town. Winn may have been provoked by a long-smoldering disagreement with Johnson over the line which separated their farms. After three mistrials Winn, whom many suspected was a mulatto, was freed through "proof" that he was white. Testimony by a Negro against a white was invalid, and the only witness was a black companion of Johnson. William T. Martin, therefore, had brilliantly argued the prosecution's case to no avail. The *Courier* eulogized Johnson as "an excellent and most inoffensive man" who held "a respectable position on account of his character, intelligence and deportment." But, as his his biographers put it, "his murder was avenged by law no more than if he had been a common slave."[31]

Such violence, however, was atypical of the community's mood and temper by the last decade before the Civil War. Antebellum Natchez society was unlike other Western municipalities in certain respects. Unlike New Orleans and Louisville, which had

[30] *Ibid.*, 11–13, 342, 352; Natchez *Courier*, November 30, 1849; Hutchinson, *Code of Mississippi*, 948–49; Charles S. Sydnor, "The Free Negro in Mississippi Before the Civil War," *AHR*, XXXII (October, 1927), 771–79.

[31] *Johnson's Diary*, 55–63; Natchez *Courier*, June 20, 1851. According to his biographers, Johnson's attitude toward the aristocrats had changed markedly by the late 1840's: "In his writings Johnson literally damned white men as 'infernal rascals' or 'scoundrels' for 'shaving' him in financial deals, but in public he walked and talked softly. The William Johnson of the 1830's was flattered by the chance attentions of the aristocracy, but after 1845 he recorded no such elation. As he grew older, as he gradually exhausted the scraps of privilege that he could catch from the abundance of the planter aristocrats, he may have become a trifle bitter. The Johnson of the earlier diaries was hardly the preoccupied, sometimes complaining Johnson of the last four or five years before his death in 1851." *Johnson's Diary*, 55.

developed more rapidly in population and trade, Natchez by the 1850's showed no signs of the urban impersonality typical of its larger competitors. Likewise, no trade unions developed, and no strikes by white mechanics against free Negro competition occurred. Also, unlike other southern and western urban centers, there was a sharp increase in the number of slaves and slave-holders. As elsewhere, however, social stratification and the quest for status had intensified greatly toward the end of the ante-bellum era. Despite some signs of restiveness and discontent, the various classes lived side-by-side in surprising harmony. The aristocrats viewed the middle-class domination of town politics with resignation and indifference, while the bourgeoisie accepted the socio-economic pre-eminence of the nabobs, even hoping to achieve that status themselves. The poor whites, except for periodic outbursts of violence and lawlessness, remained, like the slaves and free Negroes, inarticulate but colorful members of the town society. The potentiality of class struggle and racial up-heaval was not fulfilled, perhaps because the town did not be-come a city.

CHAPTER VIII

Realities and Illusions

of Prosperity

"KING COTTON" SO VITALLY AFFECTED THE town's economy that cycles of cotton prices offer a fair index to business trends in Natchez. Cotton prices averaged 44 cents per pound in 1801, bringing lucrative returns to growers and welcome money into the infant retail community. But prices dipped sharply in the 1809–15 period, reaching an ebb of 8 cents per pound in 1811 and precipitating depressed business conditions. In the following decades cotton prices and commercial prospects fluctuated sharply but correspondingly. In 1835, for instance, cotton sold at a relatively healthy 15 cents per pound, and local merchandise sales for the year exceeded $1,600,000. Four years later, with the depression in full sway, cotton sank to 7 cents and merchandise sales dropped to $695,000. By the 1850's cotton prices had again risen to profitable levels, ranging between 11 and 14 cents per pound, while merchandise sales were approaching the $2,000,000 mark annually.[1]

Charles Murray, an English nobleman who visited Natchez in 1835, was convinced that everybody in the town was somehow connected with buying, selling, or planting cotton. He was not far from being correct since the economic life of men of all walks of life, from banker and attorney to shopkeeper and drayman, was affected by the rise or fall of the region's key crop. The great planters, who conducted most of their export-import affairs

[1] *De Bow's Review*, V (1848), 381; Gray, *History of Agriculture in the Southern United States to 1860*, II, 1026–27; Alfred H. Conrad and John R. Meyer, "The Economics of Slavery in the Ante-Bellum South," *Journal of Political Economy*, LXVI (April, 1958), 440–43; Davis and Hogan, *Barber of Natchez*, 43.

through local commission houses owned by fellow nabobs or through factors in New Orleans, New York, and Great Britain, were few in number compared to the several thousand middle- and lower-class agrarians from Concordia to Claiborne who bought supplies in Natchez stores. From as far away as forty miles, farmers journeyed to the town on the bluff to purchase seeds, farm tools, whiskey, "Negro linseys," smoked herring, "segars," wagons, and countless other consumer items. Since many cotton growers were so obsessed with cultivation of the staple that they paid little heed to economic self-sufficiency, they perforce went into town also for mules, horses, corn, and salt meat, much of which was shipped from the Ohio Valley. Benjamin Wailes of Washington thought that his neighbors' readiness to enrich the pocketbooks of Natchez merchants and distant Ohio producers was "appalling."[2]

Rare was the bourgeois merchant or attorney at Natchez who did not dream of owning his own cotton domain. Most of the town's middle class accordingly invested their profits in cotton, slaves, and lands, further tightening the link between town and country economies. Many a merchant, moreover, obtained his entree into the plantation-slavery system through the liberal credit system of the times. From large wholesalers at Natchez or New Orleans the middle-class store owner procured his stock of goods on credit until crops were sold in late autumn and early winter. As much as 70 per cent of all merchandise bought by agrarians in Natchez may have been on credit, with store bills settled after crop harvests and sales. If unable to meet his debts because of drought, flood, or poor cotton prices, the farmer was often compelled to mortgage his holdings to the extent of his indebtedness. If the next year's crop was also insufficient to meet his obligations, foreclosure brought the merchant-creditor into possession of lands and slaves, which he, in turn, might manage himself or place on the auction block.[3]

[2] Murray, *Travels in North America*, II, 179; *Southern Cultivator*, I (1843), 92–93.
[3] See Natchez store bills and credit records in Lemuel P. Conner Papers, LSU;

More local farms probably changed hands during the depression following the Panic of 1837 than in any other period of Natchez-country history. In 1839 William Gwin wrote John Claiborne that conditions from Natchez to Vicksburg "are marvelous" and "will greatly benefit our speculation" in purchasing cotton crops, lands, and slaves from stricken owners. Gwin, an attorney by vocation, claimed that he was then "wielding a cash capital of near two million dollars" and added: "I can with this alone monopolize the *latter* part of the cotton season."[4] Writing thirteen years later, attorney Joseph G. Baldwin recalled the reaction of his legal colleagues at Natchez and Vicksburg to the multiplying litigations of the late 1830's: "It was a merry time for us craftsmen; and we brightened up mightily, and shook our quills joyously, like goslings in the midst of a shower." He concluded: "We look back to that good time, 'now past and gone,' with the pious gratitude and serene satisfaction with which the wreckers near the Florida keys contemplate the last fine storm."[5]

Soil exhaustion around Natchez had become a serious factor by the early 1830's. As intimately as the town's economy was tied to that of the surrounding area, it would seem that journalists and planters resident in the town would have been greatly concerned. Except for a plea by the *Southern Galaxy* editor in 1828 for silk culture to be undertaken as a start toward diversification, no evidence was found in any Natchez newspapers of the slightest interest in agricultural reform. Indeed, seldom did the town papers record activities of the enlightened group of scientific agriculturalists at Washington, Mississippi, who began the state's first agrarian reform movement. There in 1839 Benjamin Wailes, John C. Jenkins, Sr., Dr. John W. Monette, and other middle-

John C. Knight Papers and Absalom F. Dantzler Papers, Duke; Robert Cochran Papers, Nathan G. Howard Papers, Robert G. Hazard Papers, and Edward Dickinson Daybook, Mississippi Archives. The above men were Natchez merchants except Hazard, a Northern commission merchant who handled many orders from Natchez for goods.

[4] William Gwin to John Claiborne, October 9, 1839, Claiborne Papers, Library of Congress.

[5] Baldwin, *Flush Times of Alabama and Mississippi*, 175.

class planters organized the Agricultural, Horticultural, and Botanical Society of Jefferson College. With Wailes serving as president, they sponsored agricultural fairs, maintained a botanical museum, and inaugurated a short-lived journal, the *Southern Planter*, which well-educated but eccentric Samuel E. Bailey edited. In 1842 Thomas Affleck opened the state's largest nursery at Washington and, besides working with the society, published several works pleading for crop diversification, economic self-sufficiency, and progressive farming techniques. By 1843, however, the demise of the society was in the offing, caused by "a perfect greed after amusement" in Bailey's phraseology, which in translation means that the gentry were more absorbed in "horse shows" at the Pharsalia race track. Planters known to have been living in Natchez at the time had been conspicuously absent from the Washington society's activities from the start. By the mid-1840's Hinds County and Warren County agrarian organizations had assumed the helm of the agricultural reform movement in Mississippi. Nevertheless, a few planters of modest holdings in the Washington area, including Wailes, Monette, Charles Whitmore, and Eli F. Capell, continued to practice "scientific farming."[6]

Even the *Southern Telegraph*, which was published at the

[6] Ingraham, *South-West*, II, 288–91; Benjamin L. C. Wailes, *Address Delivered in the College Chapel before the Agricultural, Horticultural, and Botanical Society of Jefferson College* . . . (Natchez, 1841); *Southern Planter*, I (1842), 14; Jackson *Mississippian*, November 20, 1857. Since agricultural reform in the area around Natchez receives scant attention herein, the reader may wish to consult the following secondary accounts: John H. Moore, *Agriculture in Ante-Bellum Mississippi*, 36, 63, 87, 95, 101–102, 107, 137–38, 198–99; Albert G. Seal, "John Carmichael Jenkins: Scientific Planter of the Natchez District," *JMH*, I (January, 1939), 14–28; John W. Monette, "The Mississippi Floods," *PMHS*, VII (1903), 427–78; Mack B. Swearingen, "Thirty Years of a Mississippi Plantation: Charles Whitmore of 'Montpelier,'" *JSH*, I (May, 1935), 201–11; Wendell H. Stephenson, "A Quarter Century of a Mississippi Plantation: Eli F. Capell of 'Pleasant Hill,'" *MVHR*, XXIII (December, 1936), 355–74; Fred C. Cole, "The Early Life of Thomas Affleck, 1813–1842" (unpublished M.A. thesis, Louisiana State University, 1936); Louise Gladney, "History of Pleasant Hill Plantation, 1811–1867" (unpublished M.A. thesis, Louisiana State University, 1932); Albert G. Seal, "John Carmichael Jenkins: Scientific Planter of the Natchez District" (unpublished M.A. thesis, Louisiana State University, 1937).

tiny hamlet of Rodney, showed more concern for the long-range economic development of the region than did the Natchez newspapers. In the Gulf Hills area near Rodney Dr. Rush Nutt and other planters were actively engaged in seed and cross-breeding experiments in cotton cultivation. In 1833 Nutt developed the "Petit Gulf" strain, which became the leading variety of cotton used in the Southwest. For a number of years the seed business thrived at Rodney, its market outlets extending into the North Carolina Piedmont. Plantation-supply stores in Natchez offered for sale the hybrid seeds developed at Rodney as well as Affleck's successful strain of Bermuda grass, but that was the extent of the town's interest in the flurry of agricultural reform at Rodney and Washington.[7]

Although Natchez was the southern terminus of one of the best-known roads of the nation, the Natchez Trace, neither that route nor the other roads into the town were improved much during the long span from 1810 to 1860. No new overland route of any considerable length was constructed to Natchez after the completion of the "Three Chopped Way" (also known as the "Three Notched Way") from the Tombigbee Valley in 1807. For many years the only stage line was the six-mile run from Natchez to Washington. After 1815 roads bore little of the long-distance traffic, and the declining number of travelers who tried them usually wished afterward that they had chosen a water route. "Walking" Johnson, an expert hiker, beat the horse rider who carried the mail to Nashville on three occasions; Johnson's secret was that he avoided the Trace and took to the woods for much easier traveling. Besides the sorry condition of the roads, travelers were also liable to confront roving bands of white outlaws, escaping slaves, and thieving Indians.[8]

[7] Rodney *Southern Telegraph*, September 12, 1838; Claiborne, *Mississippi*, 141; Fulkerson, *Random Recollections*, 12–14.

[8] *The Louisiana and Mississippi Alamanac, 1815* (Natchez, 1815), 35–36; William Darby, *The Emigrant's Guide to the Western and Southwestern States and Territories* (New York, 1818), 149–50; Cuming, *Sketches of a Tour*, 292; *American State Papers, Indian Affairs*, I, 658; Toulmin, *Statutes of the Mississippi Territory*, 397–98; *Mississippi Herald and Natchez Gazette*, November 25,

That the Trace carried most of the road traffic is evident from the number of taverns strung along it. The most thriving inns of Natchez before the War of 1812 were those located on the narrow, meandering road to Nashville. They included Connelly's Tavern, King's Tavern, and the White Horse Tavern. Most tavern keepers dwelt at the rear of their inns, but George Overaker, who owned the White Horse Tavern, grew wealthy enough to purchase "Hope Farm" as a town house and "Hawthorne" in the countryside nearby. The only sizable inn of territorial Natchez that was not located on the Trace was Michie's Tavern, which was situated on Main Street. Although affluent enough to be able to buy "Cherokee" mansion, David Michie did not achieve the fine reputation that his father and brothers gained in Virginia as tavern keepers. Possibly the oldest tavern on the south end of the Trace was "Mount Locust," built about 1780 by British rebel John Blommart and operated later by James Chamberlain. Washington's principal inn was the Washington Hotel, formerly the home of Cowles Mead which Moses Richardson converted in 1813 into a successful hostelry, advertising it as "the large and commodious house under the sign of the spread eagle." Some Trace innkeepers as far as a hundred miles to the north advertised in Natchez papers, such as Turner Brashears, who in 1806 announced the opening of his "house of entertainment" in "the Wilderness . . . about 40 miles from William Smith's at the Indian line."[9]

The flourishing inns along the south end of the Trace suffered seriously from the advent of upriver steamboating, and by the 1830's the most successful and spacious Natchez hotels were those which catered to river travelers. The better inns were clustered

1806; Washington *Republican*, April 6, 1813. On roads, see also George J. Leftwich, "Some Main Travelled Roads," *PMHS Centenary*, I (1916), 463–76; Robert S. Cotterill, "The Natchez Trace," *Tennessee Historical Magazine*, VII (January, 1921), 29–36; and the articles by Cotterill, Jamison, and Phelps cited in footnote 30 of Chapter II.

[9] See Dawson A. Phelps, "Stands and Travel Accommodations on the Natchez Trace," *JMH*, XI (January, 1949), 1–54; Samuel B. Olden, Jr., "Hotels, Inns, and Taverns in Mississippi, 1830–1860," *ibid.*, V (July, 1943), 171–84.

in the western section of the upper town, usually one to three blocks from the bluff, so that travelers reaching the top of the landing-road could readily locate them. William Parker's three-story Mississippi Hotel, according to one authority, offered "probably the best accommodations to be had" in Mississippi in the 1830's. But the structure was damaged by fire in 1839 and was completely destroyed the next year by a tornado. When the City Hotel was constructed in 1837 on the site of a previous inn that had been gutted by fire, a local journalist boasted that the 120-room building "may vie with the Astor House, New York."

If its record of distinguished guests and extravagant festivities is indicative, Elijah Bell's Mansion House succeeded the City Hotel as the town's best. For instance, when the town feted Henry Clay with a grand ball in 1844, it was staged at the Mansion House. Like its rivals, the Bell hostelry was damaged by fire, barely escaping total ruin when a conflagration swept away the other buildings on the block. It was quickly repaired and reputedly looked "finer than ever." In addition to the main hotels, there were numerous other cheaper accommodations, including several at the landing that offered services other than merely room, board, and bar.[10] In the late 1830's James S. Buck-

[10] Natchez *Mississippi Free Trader*, January 8, March 11, and April 15, 1836; *Johnson's Diary*, 74, 89, 133, 372, 476. The following entries of December 31, 1837, in the Mansion House Daybook, Mississippi Archives, indicate charges for various inn services at Natchez:

Thos. J. Johnston
To Board fro. 19th July to 31st Dec. @ 50¢	270.00
To Board for Horse fro. 3 Oct. to 31st Dec. @ 20¢	58.00
	328.00

Doctr. Lawrence
To 6 mos. Board Self, Lady & Servt. fro. 1 July to 31st Dec. @ 112$	672.00
To Fuel 2 mos. @ 15$	30.00
Deduct for lost time 3 mos. by Lady & Servt. @ 62$	186.00
To Horse to Livery 12 mos. @ 20$	240.00
	756.00

ingham, an English aristocrat, visited the town and noted in his journal:

There are no less than twelve hotels, the principal of which are the Mansion House, the City Hotel, and the Mississippi Hotel; but so many of the population are in constant motion, and so many of the permanent residents live at hotels and boarding-houses, that even this large number, accommodating upon the average about 100 persons each, besides many private establishments capable of receiving fifty persons each, are insufficient to supply the demand. It is, therefore, often difficult to get a sleeping-room at all, and very rarely a sitting-room; while the table is ill attended to, the slaves who act as servants are careless, and the charges are exorbitant.[11]

When railroad construction began in Mississippi in the early 1830's, Natchez lagged behind Vicksburg and Woodville from the start. Edward McGehee, a large planter and pioneer textile manufacturer at Woodville, obtained a charter in 1831 for the West Feliciana Rail Road Company, while later that year a line from Vicksburg to Clinton was chartered. When the Vicksburg company later received banking privileges in an amendment to its charter, the Natchez *Courier* warned its readers that "in self defense" Natchez must rise to the occasion and obtain a rail line also. But the challenge brought no response in Natchez. When the Vicksburg-Clinton railroad was completed in the mid-1830's, Vicksburg quickly became the main cotton export center for the growing production of the Yazoo-Mississippi Delta, eventually passing Natchez in cotton trading. After a rail line linking Grand Gulf and Port Gibson was begun, Natchez leaders talked of a possible line from Natchez to tap the Pearl River Valley. If such a line were built, a Vicksburg editorialist direly predicted, it would mean for Vicksburg that "our roads will become bridle paths and our city will become a hamlet." As it turned out, Vicksburg had little to fear from Natchez enterprise in railroading. Both river towns, however, had grounds for anxiety

[11] James S. Buckingham, *The Slave States of America* . . . (2 vols.; London, 1842), I, 450–51.

when construction of the New Orleans and Nashville Railroad began in 1835, with its projected line to run through the center of Mississippi. Later to become the New Orleans, Jackson, and Great Northern Railroad (ultimately absorbed in the Illinois Central system), this line would prove to be the major carrier of rail traffic in the Lower Mississippi Valley. The decision by its officials to bypass Natchez may have been one of the most significant factors in the town's relative decline as a commercial center.[12]

Anticipating handsome profits by tapping this central north-south railroad with a branch to Natchez, Quitman and some Natchez associates organized the Mississippi Rail Road Company in 1835, obtaining a state charter the next year while Quitman was senate president. The tracks were to be laid in a northeasterly direction, running from Natchez to Canton where they would join the main line from New Orleans to the Upper Mississippi Valley. In 1837 the charter was amended to grant banking privileges, and two years later bank branches were opened at Canton, Raymond, and Gallatin, which lay along the projected route. As many as eight hundred hands were employed by the end of 1837, with $35,000 worth of property at its depot and shop in Natchez, and fourteen miles of track completed from the town. Quitman, who served as president of both rail company and bank, persuaded the legislature in 1839 to transfer $2 million it had invested in the stock of the Planter's Bank of Natchez into Mississippi Rail Road Bank securities.[13]

Nevertheless, the financial stringency of the depression was beginning to tell, and the railroad was in need of more funds. In mid-1839 Quitman decided to go to Europe in a frantic attempt to float a loan. In Westphalia he tried in vain to influence the Rothschild financiers through an old friend, William Brune, who had once been a Natchez merchant and had later taken a small fortune back to his native Soest where he had purchased a

---

[12] Natchez *Courier*, December 20, 1833; Vicksburg *Register*, quoted in Woodville *Republican*, October 18, 1834.

[13] Woodville *Republican*, January 7, 1837; McLendon, "John A. Quitman," 145–49.

barony. Brune tried to prepare Quitman for failure even before the latter's arrival: "Mr. Rothschild is, I believe, the only Banker in Germany who has loaned to New York, but even he, a very smart man, is not willing to make loans to the South. . . . I presume, he thought a Slave holding State not safe enough."[14] As Brune predicted, Quitman returned to Natchez empty-handed, having also failed to persuade the financiers of London and Paris. By early 1840 the tracks of the Mississippi Rail Road Company extended twenty-five miles out of Natchez, but the company's stock had fallen to 25 per cent of its par value. In May the tornado that wrought terrible destruction to large segments of the town also completely destroyed the depot and machine shop on the west end of Main Street. Since he personally owed $95,000, "over $40,000 of which I have had to assume for others," Quitman resigned as president and returned to his law partnership with John T. McMurran. The railroad and its bank were soon bankrupt and in receivership.[15] So ended the only attempt before the Civil War to tie Natchez into a major rail network. Its isolation from this "modern" mode of conveying freight and passengers would be sorely felt as the decades passed.

On the other hand, the town's river trade steadily increased throughout the antebellum era. As early as 1801 a traveler observed 450 flatboats, 26 keelboats, 7 pirogues, 2 schooners, and a brig docked at the same time at Natchez under-the-Hill. Several years later Schultz counted 83 vessels at the landing, "all loaded with the produce of the upper country." Another visitor was as impressed by the variety of river craft as by their number: "the singular, whimsical, and amusing spectacle" of bateaux, "broadhorns" (flatboats), keelboats, "Alleghany skiffs," and "monstrous anomalies, reducible to no specific class of boats."[16]

[14] William Brune to Quitman, July 17, 1839, John F. H. Claiborne Papers, UNC.
[15] Claiborne, *Quitman*, I, 186–87.
[16] Schultz, *Travels on an Inland Voyage*, 135–36; Timothy Flint, *Recollections of the Last Ten Years* (Boston, 1826), 171–73; Edward Quick and Herbert Quick, *Mississippi Steamboatin': A History of Steamboating on the Mississippi and Its Tributaries* (New York, 1926), 23–24. In the pre-steamboat era Bernard Lintot

A new epoch in Mississippi navigation dawned in late 1811 with the arrival of the *New Orleans*, the river's first steamboat. Joseph D. Shields has left an amusing description of the occasion:

I was dozing quietly on my hill when I was somewhat startled by a loud, hoarse cough, apparently from the lungs of a Mastodon. . . . I looked up and saw the most extraordinary monster that ever met my vision; the smoke fumed from its nostrils and it coughed at every step; it moved like a thing of life and literally walked upon the water. . . . The thing was of the bell cattle kind, for when she got opposite she rung her bell.[17]

From 1811 to 1814 steamboats operated only on the Natchez–New Orleans stretch of the river where the current was sluggish. But by 1815 several steamboats with more powerful engines, pioneered by those of Henry Shreve, had ascended to Louisville. Any doubts about the steamboat's conquest of the Mississippi vanished in 1816 when Shreve's *Washington* made the round trip between Louisville and New Orleans in the unheard-of time of only forty-five days. The upstream trip from New Orleans to Natchez required less than ninety-six hours by 1817. Rapidly mounting incidents of steamboat explosions did not seem to affect the expanding volume of traffic. Despite the rise of the steamboat, however, the bulk of the growing river trade continued to be borne by flatboats and keelboats until the 1850's. In 1815 merchant Samuel Postlethwaite, I, postmaster John Hankinson, and five other businessmen organized the Natchez Steamboat Company. They were unable to get a charter until 1819, at which time the company was capitalized at $500,000. Unfortunately nothing is known of their success in exploiting the new trade opportunities on the river.[18]

---

attempted to use horses to tread on the steps of a stern wheel on his boat, but the wheel quickly split and the boat was wrecked. Shields, *Natchez*, 82.

[17] Shields, *Natchez*, 84.

[18] E. W. Gould, *Fifty Years on the Mississippi; or, Gould's History of River Navigation* (St. Louis, 1889), 190–91, 201–202; James T. Lloyd, *Lloyd's Steamboat Directory and Railroad Directory, and Disasters on Western Waters* (Cincinnati, 1856), 55–57, 279; Poindexter, *Revised Code of the Laws of Mississippi,*

The surge of trade that came to the landing partly as a result of steamboating marked the beginning of the end for Natchez under-the-Hill's reputation solely on the basis of notoriety. As early as 1813 the landing's bustling, cosmopolitan atmosphere had its attractiveness to editor Andrew Marschalk:

Natchez, from January to June, is among the most interesting places in the United States. The constant descent and landing of the boats, frequently a dozen a day, these loaded with everything a rich and fertile country of two thousand miles in extent can produce, dead and living, vegetable and animal;—the crowd of multifarious people, of different nations, colours and language—the traffic of various kinds, from an apple to a bale of cotton, and from a chicken to a fine horse— from the pint to the boat load of whiskey—the Irish potatoes and sweet oranges.—These with the New Orleans barges, rafts of logs, boards, pickets, etc. and then again, the arrival and departure of the steam boat, with hundreds of gazing admirers lining the bluff's edge, and crowding the landing—altogether exhibit a scene uncommonly interesting, either to the speculator or the philosopher.[19]

In 1820 Englishman Adam Hodgson found the place "a perfect Wapping, crowded with Kentucky boats."[20] Quitman wrote soon after his arrival in the early 1820's: "The streets are lined with carriages, drays, and wagons. The rush to the river is incessant. Every hour we hear the roar of cannon, announcing the arrival and departure of steamers. Hundreds of arks, or flat-boats, loaded with the produce of the Western States, even from the interior of Pennsylvania, here line the landing for half a mile, often lying five tier deep!"[21]

Although 229 steamboats and 542 flatboats, besides sundry other craft, docked at Natchez under-the-Hill in 1824, there were days when the landing had no vessels. This was because river

644; Natchez Steamboat Company stock certificate book, entries of 1815–1820, Mississippi Archives; Louis D. Hunter, *Steamboats on the Western Rivers: An Economic and Technological History* (Cambridge, Mass., 1949), 10–12.

[19] *The Louisiana and Mississippi Almanac, 1813* (Natchez, 1813), 49.
[20] Adam Hodgson, *Letters from North America, Written During a Tour in the United States and Canada* . . . (2 vols.; London, 1824), I, 168.
[21] Quoted in Claiborne, *Quitman*, I, 70–71.

traffic was in great measure seasonal, dependent upon the time of harvests and ginning. For example, an average of two steamboats per week visited the landing in June, 1828, five per week in August, seven per week in October, and ten weekly from December through January. By 1832 the figures had nearly doubled but continued to exhibit the same seasonal pattern.[22]

Travel by steamboat was exciting and precarious. On a journey in 1829 Benjamin Wailes was forced to endure a maddening four-hour race against another steamboat that resulted in boiler damage to his craft and delayed his arrival in Memphis nearly a half day. One spring night in 1837 the boilers of the steamboat *Ben Sherrod* burst during a race just below Natchez; it sank with a loss of 150 lives. Two nights after Christmas that year the *Blackhawk* exploded in a race near the Natchez landing, killing 50 persons. Julius Reed, traveling to Illinois by steamboat in 1833, experienced a wreck on a sand bar, a collision with a snag that filled the hold with three feet of water before repairs were made, and a cholera epidemic that threatened to decimate the passengers and crew—all occurring on that one voyage.[23]

Despite the fact that Natchez showed little initiative in railroad enterprises, its commercial leaders did attempt a bold experiment in promoting direct trade with Europe. The town was declared an official port of entry in 1833, and later that year the Mississippi Shipping Company was chartered. Its officials included John P. Walworth, Jefferson Beaumont, and three other Natchez merchants. The company managed to get a few Atlantic sailing vessels towed by steam tugs over four hundred miles up the Mississippi to load cargoes of cotton at the Natchez landing. The project was soon defunct, however, because of poor management and lack of capital. In 1839 the company was revived and

---

[22] Natchez *Mississippi State Gazette*, September 24, 1824; Natchez *Southern Galaxy*, August, 1828–January, 1829; *Mississippi Journal and Natchez Advertiser*, November 16, 1832.

[23] Wailes diary, entry of December 3, 1829, Wailes Papers, Mississippi Archives; Natchez *Mississippi Free Trader*, May 12 and December 27, 1837; Reed to Watson, May 10, 1833, Watson Papers, Duke.

rechartered, with innkeeper David Michie as president and with the financial backing of some large merchants.

Meanwhile in 1838 a group of Natchez nabobs organized the Mississippi Towboat Company and the Natchez Steam Packet Company to finance and operate their own tugs and sailing ships. The officers of the latter company included Stephen Duncan, James Wilkins, Levin Marshall, Alvarez Fisk, John Routh, Adam Bingaman, and William Minor. An ocean-going vessel was built for them at a Brooklyn shipyard, christened the *Natchez*, and hailed with public enthusiasm when it arrived for its first cargo in late 1838. About 41,500 bales of cotton were shipped from Natchez in direct trade during the next year. Moreover, steam cotton compresses to repack bales for oceanic travel were set up in Natchez and Grand Gulf. When James Buckingham was at the landing in 1839 he observed the departure of two large vessels bound for Liverpool, the *Talleyrand* with $1,296,000 worth of cotton aboard and the *Franklin* with a cotton cargo valued at $1,111,998.[24]

By the early 1840's, however, disappointing prices received in the direct trade and the lingering depression dispelled enthusiasm for the oceanic enterprises at Natchez. Cotton prices were about the same as at New Orleans. Also the savings in freight, commissions, and other middlemen's charges by bypassing the Louisiana port amounted to very little, particularly in view of the heavy expenses entailed in the operation of tugs and steam compresses. By the middle of the decade the cotton of the Natchez country was again flowing through the commission houses of the Crescent City for sale and transshipment, and the direct-trade dream had disappeared.[25]

The tremendous expansion of the cotton empire in the South-

[24] Natchez *Courier*, September 11, 1835; *Mississippi Free Trader and Natchez Gazette*, November 5, 1839; John C. Knight to his wife, August 21, 1839, Knight Papers, Duke; Buckingham, *Slave States of America*, I, 447. In 1801 a brief attempt to lure oceanic vessels to Natchez proved unsuccessful. Carter, *Territorial Papers*, V, 138–39.

[25] *Grand Gulf Advertiser*, February 8, 1839; Ingraham, *South-West*, II, 160; Thomas Reber, *Proud Old Natchez* (Natchez, 1909), 7.

west after the War of 1812 made the slave markets at Natchez and Algiers (across the river from New Orleans) the busiest ones in the entire South. The "Forks of the Road" mart handled the largest volume of business in Natchez, but slave auctions were also held at other places around town, sometimes even on the front steps of the Mansion House. Moreover, numerous slave transactions were negotiated at the landing, as attested by traveler Henry Fearon, who saw fourteen flatboats loaded with Negroes for sale there in 1817. Slave traders with permanent residence in Natchez did most of the local business and were exempt from the state tax of 1 per cent on gross sales of slaves, which auctioneers and transient traders had to pay. The extent of the slave trade is suggested by the fact that for an unknown "part of the year 1833" the Natchez sales of thirty-two non-resident slave merchants were $238,879.[26]

Franklin, Armfield and Company of Alexandria, Virginia, the main firm engaged in the interstate slave trade, maintained its headquarters in the Southwest at the "Forks of the Road" on the northeast edge of Natchez. Isaac Franklin, probably the richest slave trader in the Old South, personally managed his company's affairs at Natchez during much of the period 1819–36. According to Joseph H. Ingraham, the Jefferson College instructor, Franklin "supplied this country with two-thirds of the slaves brought into it" and "amassed a fortune of more than a million of dollars by this traffic alone." Yet, Ingraham continued, even the most opulent slave traders were never accepted into the genteel society of the town: "Planters associate with them freely enough, in the way of business, but notice them no farther."[27]

As for slave prices at Natchez, they approximately quadrupled

[26] Henry Fearon, *Sketches of America: A Narrative of a Journey of Five Thousand Miles Through the Eastern and Western States of America* . . . (London, 1818), 267–68; George W. Featherstonhaugh, *Excursion Through the Slave States, from Washington on the Potomac to the Frontier of Mexico* . . . (2 vols.; London, 1844), I, 119–30, 151–71.

[27] Ingraham, *South-West*, II, 245. See also Wendell H. Stephenson, *Isaac Franklin, Slave Trader and Planter of the Old South* (Baton Rouge, 1938), 53–67; Ulrich B. Phillips, *American Negro Slavery* (New York, 1918), 187–97.

during the years 1798–1860, with prime field hands selling at
$1,400 to $1,800 by the latter year. A comparison of local prices
with those of the New Orleans mart indicates that they were
similar, the average running slightly higher at Natchez. In both
markets one of the main reasons for the high cost of slaves by the
1850's was the increasing significance of chattel ownership as a
symbol in the frenzied quest for status among the middle and
upper classes of whites.[28]

Ranking with the slave mart as one of the busiest establishments in town until 1830 was the Bank of Mississippi. Chartered
in 1809 with a capital stock of $500,000, the bank did much to
bring financial stability to the area and to relieve the stringent
specie situation that had compelled the legislature to recognize
Spanish coins and cotton-gin certificates as negotiable currency.
With the coming of statehood the institution was renamed the
Bank of the State of Missisippi and was granted a monopoly of
state banking for twenty years. Under the able presidencies of
Samuel Postlethwaite and Stephen Duncan the bank continued to
prosper during the 1820's despite growing piney-woods opposition to its monopoly.[29] With its capitalization enlarged to $3
million, the bank in 1824 made the following report:[30]

	Principal Bank [Natchez]	Woodville Office	Port Gibson Office
Deposits	$ 232,267	$ 25,273	$ 21,363
Notes in circ.	300,292	94,790	5,610
Bills receivable	449,323	248,120	245,557
Total assets	$1,612,595		

[28] Sundry notices of slave sales in Natchez newspapers, particularly the
Courier and the *Mississippi Free Trader;* Adams County Inventories and Appraisements, I–II, Chancery Clerk's Records; Phillips, *Life and Labor in the Old South,*
177; Sydnor, *Slavery in Mississippi,* 150–57.

[29] On the Bank of Mississippi, see Douglas C. McMurtrie (ed.), *Mississippi
Banking Act of 1809* (Chicago, 1936); William D. McCain (ed.), "The Charter
of Mississippi's First Bank," *JMH,* I (October, 1939), 251–63; Robert C. Weems,
Jr., "The Bank of Mississippi: A Pioneer Bank of the Old Southwest, 1809–1844"
(unpublished Ph.D. dissertation, Columbia University, 1951); Weems, "The
Makers of the Bank of Mississippi," *JMH,* XV (April, 1953), 137–54.

[30] Financial statement of December 20, 1824, Bank of the State of Mississippi
Papers, Box 66, Mississippi Archives.

But in 1830 the eastern Mississippi legislators succesfully maneu-vered the passage of a bill which annulled the bank's charter. Though it ceased operations in 1831, Duncan and some of its former officials two years later obtained another charter, this one being without monopolistic privileges, and reopened as the Agri-cultural Bank of Natchez.[31]

With the curtailment of the banking monopoly, James Wilkins in 1830 spearheaded a movement which, despite intense eastern opposition, culminated in the chartering of the Planter's Bank of Natchez. Capitalized at $3 million and with branches ultimately in six towns, the Planter's Bank became the largest banking insti-tution in the state. The Mississippi government had a large stake in its future by virtue of the fact that two-thirds of its capital was subscribed by the state. Furthermore, the governor and the senate were empowered to appoint seven of the bank's thirteen directors. The Planter's Bank also gained an affinity with the federal government in 1832 when Secretary of the Treasury Roger B. Taney designated it and the Agricultural Bank as depositories of federal funds under the so-called "pet-bank" scheme.[32] But in Natchez, Wilkins' bank faced strong animosity from the Duncan faction. Felix Huston, a lawyer and director of the Planter's Bank, commented:

When I first took an active part in behalf of this Bank, I knew that I would create many and violent enemies, I knew that men who had had the entire & complete control of all the money transactions of a whole state, *would die hard* and would never forgive those who had contributed to drive them from their triumphant ascendancy. . . . It was verry [sic] common amongst them to laugh at our *Plebeian Bank* until 4½ pr ct dividends for 6 months, changed their tune. You can hardly conceive how the whole aristocratic pack ridiculed the notion of any body but Dr. Duncan and Gab. Tichenor [cashier under Dun-can] knowing anything about Banking, or even being able to put their feet in a Bank except as petitioners, until we rejoiced to declare

[31] *Mississippi House Journal* (1830), 212–13; *ibid.* (1831), 163; Weems, "Makers of the Bank of Mississippi," 150–54.
[32] Hutchinson, *Code of Mississippi*, 310–13; Miles, *Jacksonian Democracy in Mississippi*, 73–74.

dividends nearly as high as they ever had and we being under a re-
markably heavy expense in starting and locating at Natchez—in 14
months from our commencement our dividend was 11 pr ct.[33]

In turn, Planter's Bank officials, led by Wilkins, president, and
directors Huston and Bingaman, offered the staunchest opposition to "the rechartering of the old Bank" as the Agricultural
Bank.[34] Divisive feuding among themselves thus characterized
not only the politics of the nabobs but also their financial relations.

When Nicholas Biddle, president of the Second Bank of the
United States, forced a brief financial crisis in the winter of
1833–34 in a counteroffensive against President Jackson, Taney
transferred $500,000 from the Planter's Bank to the Union Bank
of New Orleans to strengthen the latter institution. Faced with
$682,000 worth of notes on which payments were due, Wilkins'
bank was temporarily in danger of insolvency, but, as the national economy again began to surge by the spring of 1834, the
pressure lessened.[35] This near fiasco had important political consequences. John Claiborne says that Wilkins, "the most influential Democrat in the river counties," and Charles Lynch,
"who held the same rank in the East," thereupon "publicly
abandoned the administration, carrying with them a host of followers." On Wilkins he adds with some exaggeration: "He and
his connections controlled virtually, the whole banking capital
of the state, and at that era of expansion and speculation, this was
a prodigious power, especially when exerted by men of ability
and of high social position."[36]

In the late 1820's southwestern members of the state legislature had submitted bills three times to authorize a branch of the
United States Bank for Natchez, but they were beaten on each
occasion by determined eastern opposition. In 1828 the *Southern*

[33] Felix Huston to Nathan G. Howard, January 24, 1833, Howard Papers,
Mississippi Archives.
[34] Huston to Howard, February 21, 1833, *ibid.*
[35] Miles, *Jacksonian Democracy in Mississippi*, 75–77.
[36] Claiborne, *Mississippi*, 411.

Galaxy, a pro-Adams Natchez organ, championed the branch-bank proposal while attacking the monopoly then held by the Bank of the State of Mississippi. By conducting foreign exchanges at a lower rate than the state bank, the newspaper said, the United States Bank branch "would tend to restrict the operations of the State Bank within the limits for which it was intended." Furthermore, the branch would promote "a liberal system of Internal Improvements" by bringing "to its aid the credit of a monied capital."[37]

With the plantation system expanding into the upper Pearl River Valley and the need for credit increasing, the Mississippi legislature voted in 1830 to authorize a United States Bank branch at Natchez. It opened the next year with surprisingly strong support from both the Duncan and Wilkins banking factions. But the Natchez branch quickly became a sectional political issue. Franklin E. Plummer and other Jacksonians of eastern Mississippi lambasted it as a citadel of invested interests and privileged nabobery. After Jackson's veto of the recharter of the United States Bank in 1832 and the eventual removal of federal deposits, the Natchez branch of "Biddle's Bank" was left impotent and soon closed its doors. Arguments over Jackson's "war" against the United States Bank continued to echo in Natchez for many months, precipitating a growing migration of conservative, moneyed men into the ranks of the new Whig party. In 1834 differences over the bank issue during a session of the United States District Court in Natchez led to a wild brawl on the floor of the courtroom. John Claiborne, Thomas Hinds, and Joseph Dunbar were the principal Jacksonian pugilists against Huston, Spence Grayson, and several other Whigs. Claiborne finally halted the melee by brandishing a double-barreled shotgun. Four years later, however, he reopened the controversy by writing a strongly-worded article in the *Courier* attacking Whig plans for another United States Bank.[38]

[37] Natchez *Southern Galaxy*, July 15, 1828.
[38] Natchez *Courier and Journal*, January 5, 1838; Claiborne, *Mississippi*, 410–11.

As Mississippi passed into an era of flush times and "wild-cat" banking in the mid-1830's, the legislature bestowed state banking charters with reckless abandon. The total capitalization of state banking increased five-fold in four years. Among the banks created on the eve of the Panic of 1837 was the Commercial Bank of Natchez. It was capitalized at $2 million, and, like the other state banks of that era, it began issuing notes in wild profusion. Its four branch offices extended as far north as Canton. Levin Marshall served as president, and the directors included Henry Chotard, John McMurran, and Aylette Buckner, each of whom possessed considerable wealth.[39]

Because of their reckless overexpansion and loose banking practices, the Natchez banks collapsed as quickly after the Panic of 1837 as any of the lesser banking institutions in the state. In fact, among the very first to close their doors in 1837 were the Agricultural Bank and the Planter's Bank. The two-year-old Commercial Bank suddenly suspended specie payments in 1839, and liquidation began. Within a year the Mississippi Rail Road Bank was bankrupt. Seargent Prentiss complained in 1839: "The general state of things is very bad, money continues scarce, more so I think than I have ever known it—The banks are all broke and a large part of the people." Forced to borrow $50,000 to meet pressing creditors that year, John Claiborne moaned: "The loss of almost every thing, the publicity attached to it, the want of sympathy in the community affect me—for my politics have long made me odious" to the Whig bankers of Natchez.[40]

During the 1840's the state repudiated the bonds it had issued to support the Planter's Bank of Natchez and the Union Bank of Jackson, seriously undermining Mississippi's credit for many years as far as Northern and European investors were concerned. As one bank after another had shut its doors during the depres-

---

[39] *Mississippi Free Trader and Natchez Gazette,* November 5, 1839; *Mississippi House Journal* (1835), 231–32; entries of 1836–39, Ledger I, Commercial Bank of Natchez Papers, LSU.

[40] Prentiss, *Memoir of S. S. Prentiss,* II, 147; Gwin to John Claiborne, October 14, 1839, Clairborne Papers, Library of Congress; Claiborne to Gwin, January 14, 1839, *ibid.*

sion, the faith of many persons regarding banking institutions was so shaken that they preferred to borrow from personal creditors at much higher rates of interest. Such, for instance, was the case of planter William Smith of Natchez, who chose to borrow $46,351 from David Hunt at 11 per cent in 1838–39 rather than trust any bank with his credits or debits. The people of Natchez were so loath to deal with banks that W. A. Britton and Company, a lottery and exchange brokerage, served as the town's chief financial institution for the final two antebellum decades. Britton's concern had obtained state banking privileges in 1835 and had been the only Natchez institution engaged in banking to survive the depression. In the 1850's George Koontz became a partner in the multi-purpose Britton company. Eventually banking became its only business, and it is still in operation under the name of the Britton and Koontz Bank.[41]

From territorial times through the 1840's Natchez was the undisputed manufacturing and commercial center of Mississippi. The value of manufactures in the Mississippi Territory in 1810 was only $314,305 (compared to over $32 million in Pennsylvania), but Natchez virtually dominated what there was. Over 87 per cent of the territory's production of 7,898 yards of woolen goods was made in Natchez. Six cotton manufacturing establishments in the town utilized 343 spindles and turned out 58,794 yards of finished cotton goods. The yardage represented about a fifth of the territory's output, but no single town or county's production was nearly as large. Though the tin manufactory at Natchez only turned out $7,200 worth of products in 1810, it was the only one in the territory. The two tanneries in the town produced goods valued at $16,500, or nearly half of the total valuation of leather items made in the territory that year.[42] In

[41] Notes of William S. Smith, 1838–39, Merrill Papers, LSU; *Johnson's Diary,* 470, 489, 694, 711; W. A. Britton and Company's advertisements in *Courier* and *Free Trader*, 1839–60; J. A. C. Campbell, "Repudiation of the Union and Planters Bank Bonds," *PMHS*, IV (1901), 493–97.

[42] Dunbar Rowland, *Official and Statistical Register*, 1917, 740; J. L. Bishop, *History of American Manufactures from 1608 to 1860* (3 vols.; Philadelphia, 1861–68), II, 163.

1812 the business and professional community of Natchez contained the following:

4 Tailor shops, 5 Blacksmith shops, 4 Saddler shops, 6 Carpenter make shops, 1 Coach and sign painter, 2 House painters, 3 Hatter shops, 2 Tinner shops, 4 Boot and shoemaker shops, 1 Trunk maker, 1 Bookbinder, 1 Wagon maker, 1 Chair maker, 1 Nail manufactury, 3 Barbers, 4 Brickyards, 1 Butcher, 4 Magistrates, 3 Printing offices, 2 Porter houses, 6 Publick inns, 6 Ware houses, 1 Brush maker, 3 Gold and silversmiths, 1 Confectioner and distiller, 4 Bricklayers, 1 Horse mill to grind corn, 1 Plasterer, 12 Water carts, 8 Practising physicians, 7 Lawyers, 3 English schools, 1 Incorporated mechanical society, 1 Free mason lodge, 1 Reading room and coffee house, 24 Mercantile houses (or Dry good stores), 4 Grocery stores, 2 Wholesale commission stores, 17 Catalene shops (or small stores, where a little of everything is sold), 1 Vendue and commission store, 1 Bank (called the "Bank of the Mississippi"). Under the hill or [at the] landing place, there are 1 Tavern, the "Kentucky," 2 Blacksmith shops, 13 Catalene shops, Porter houses, &c. On the road up the hill, are 3 Catalene shops, in which are a tinner and shoemaker.[43]

The first textile mill in Mississippi was erected on the outskirts of Natchez in 1842 by John Robinson, a Scot with considerable experience in textile manufacturing. Robinson intended to supply the Lower Mississippi Valley with coarse cotton and woolen fabrics, yarns, bagging, rope, twine, and sacks. Within two years, however, he found certain problems insurmountable, including insufficient capital, inadequate machinery, shortage of skilled white laborers, high cost of importing Indiana coal for fuel, and ruthless competition from New England textile producers. In 1844 a Boston textile firm purchased his factory, imported some experienced New England workers, and installed more powerful steam-powered machinery. Soon the operation was turning out

[43] *The Louisiana and Mississippi Almanac, 1812* (Natchez, 1812), 28–29. The water carts delivered "about six barrels [each] per day, at 18¾ cents per barrel." The "Catalene shops" were named for the Catalonians who first established them in Natchez. See also George H. Gibson (ed.), "The Mississippi Market for Woolen Goods: An 1822 Analysis," *JSH*, XXXI (February, 1965), 80–90.

550 yards of cotton goods and 300 yards of woolens per day. Before the year ended Samuel T. McAlister, a local commission merchant, bought the mill. He then hired a Lowell-trained superintendent who, in turn, worked seventeen slaves as well as several white persons. McAlister tried hard to market his goods from Vicksburg to New Orleans but met with little success. Three years after taking title to the property McAlister relinquished it to two Natchez mechanics, Henry Wood and Alexander Clarkson. They also were unsuccesful in making the mill a profitable enterprise. By 1848 the textile mill had closed and was not reopened.[44]

One of the most successful operations of James Wilkins in his later years was the large foundry he established with several associates. In 1848 it was described thus:

The foundry of Wilkins, Humason & Co. gives employ to 28 to 30 engineers, artificers, blacksmiths, moulders and hands, and we are informed by one of the proprietors that a much larger amount of capital might profitably be invested in opening other branches of the business, such as the manufacture of plows, harrows, and other implements for plantation use. Wilkins, Humason & Co. have orders for their gin house, sugar house, steam mill and steam boat machinery from Baton Rouge and Donaldson on the Mississippi to Memphis, including all the plantations on the river bayous of western and northern Louisiana. In these orders they are able to compete in price and in the perfection of their work with the best foundrys of Cincinnati and Pittsburgh—having besides the advantage of being able to send their own

[44] *Southwestern Farmer*, I (1842), 117; Natchez *Courier and Journal*, June 23, 1847, and July 5, 1848; John H. Moore, "Mississippi's Ante-Bellum Textile Industry," *JMH*, XVI 1954), 83–85. The *Free Trader*, quoted in *De Bow's Review*, V (1848), 381, gave an over–optimistic report on the mill's potentiality: "The cotton factory in Natchez, against Lowell, has only to contend with the higher price of fuel in the propulsion of the steam engines; against which we can offset the transportation of the raw material three thousand miles, with the transit charges of brokerage, storage, factorage; the transportation of the wrought fabrics back again, to which the merchant's profits are to be added. All these added will make fifteen per cent, in favor of Natchez manufactures, especially since it has been conclusively proved by experiments in the States of Georgia and Alabama, that young negroes, of both sexes, can be as readily learned the business and as profitably employed in this as in any other department of labor." But a few months later the Natchez mill was again closed.

engineers to put the machinery in action, or to make the necessary repairs. They have on hand orders for five new engines.[45]

Other manufacturing establishments in Natchez at that time included Maurice Lisle's Natchez Brass and Iron Foundry, which employed twenty-five to thirty laborers and was considered to be "one of the most complete establishments in the Southwest." Nearby was Amasa Davis' Gin Stand Manufactory, which employed five workers and did about $10,000 worth of business per year. Three firms were engaged in the "coach-making and repairing business." The "wagon-making and wheelright business" was handled on a part-time basis by three smitheries, "yet by no means to that extent as to supply the demand and supercede [sic] exportation from Pittsburgh and Cincinnati." According to De Bow's Review of New Orleans, wherein this account of Natchez manufactures is found, "almost a fortune could be made yearly in a wagon and wheel manufactory in Natchez." There were "two great saddle and harness making establishments" in the town, one headed by George Dicks, who served several terms as mayor. Each employed about thirty hands. And each turned out "work of such excellence, splendor, and cheapness, that no foreign competition is either feared by these gentlemen, or attempted by others—articles of Northern manufacture not even brought into Natchez as merchandise." Three firms were engaged in 1848 in "tin, copper and sheet iron manufactory." They were reported to be doing "a profitable business" in providing "cisterns with tin pipes and conductors to all the edifices in Mississippi and Louisiana." Three firms handled the "gun making business," chief of which was the one owned by Stephen Odell.

Some of the other manufacturing activities at Natchez in 1848 included five jewel-cutting establishments; a "bindery and blank book" firm; four "blacksmithing establishments," each employing about five hands; four "boot and shoe makers," of which the claim was made that "there are none more celebrated in any city"; several firms engaged in the "manufacture of gentlemen's cloth-

[45] De Bow's Review, V (1848), 379.

ing"; three "extensive" brick yards, each of which had eight to fifteen workers; a "plough making business" with eight to ten employees; a "pottery establishment at the Upper Landing," which employed "several hands"; and several concerns engaged in "the shingle making and wood business along shore, at and near the various landings," employing a total of fifty to sixty laborers.[46]

By the late 1840's the largest sawmill operation in Mississippi was that belonging to Andrew Brown at Natchez under-the-Hill. In the 1820's he had purchased Peter Little's pioneer sawmill at the landing, developing it into a highly profitable business that has been in continuous operation ever since. At one time the town's leading slaveholder, Brown was the only nabob to reside beneath the bluff. He built a mansion (later called "Magnolia Vale") at the north end of the landing area and cultivated a fifteen-acre flower garden that was admired by many a steamboat passenger.[47] In 1848 Brown was operating two sawmills, one at each end of the narrow region beneath the bluff. The smaller establishment employed ten hands and produced "a little over eleven hundred thousand feet of boards and sawed lumber of all kinds, averaging in price eighteen dollars per thousand—making a total of $19,800 worth of work in a year." The larger mill was described as follows:

The engine of Andrew Brown's splendid mill is in action fourteen hours each day, and its various operations employ from forty to fifty hands, producing a daily average of 15,000 feet of all kinds of lumber, or four millions, five hundred thousand feet in a year. The lumber turned out at this mill is of such value that its average price is twenty-five dollars per thousand, amounting by actual sales, during the year 1847, to *fifty-six thousand dollars*, with an increase of stock on hand of

[46] *Ibid.*, 379–81. On Natchez businesses in the 1850's, see George W. Fox (ed.), *The Natchez Almanac for the Year 1853* (Natchez, 1853); W. H. Rainey (comp.), *New Orleans Business Directory . . . Also a Business Directory of Algiers, Baton Rouge, Natchez, Vicksburg, Bayou Sara, Port Hudson, Woodville, Clinton* (New Orleans, 1858).

[47] Kane, *Natchez*, 133–40. After Brown's death his stepson, Rufus F. Learned, took over the sawmill operations. See R. F. Learned Papers, Lumber Archives, University of Mississippi. See also John Hebron Moore, *Andrew Brown and Cypress Lumbering in the Old Southwest* (Baton Rouge, 1967).

half a million feet of sawed lumber. One half of the above sum, or $28,000, was a clear profit over and above all expenses—a sum larger than that produced by any two of the best Plantations in the State.[48]

An impression of the retail community of Natchez and its offerings may be obtained from newspaper advertisements. Most retail businesses did not specialize in certain categories of consumer items. A typical advertisement was that of Louis Miller and Company in 1825, wherein the firm offered to buy and sell cotton, and to sell Negroes, smoked mackerel, whiskey, flour, bacon, lard, butter, candles, soap, and dry goods. J. and C. Broadwell and Company purported to be a grocery store, offered in 1829 "pork, bacon, ham, common and old Whiskey, Louisiana sugar, Havana coffee, Malaga and Madeira wines, gin, brandy, sugars, linen, flour, tobacco, mackerel, molasses, butter, cheese, dry goods, and a general stock of up-country produce." It was not uncommon for a customer to be able to purchase in one store all of his needs in clothing, food, farm tools, medicines, crockery, whiskey, books, saddles, soap, nails, candles, and seed. One of the earliest specialty shops in Natchez was that opened by Miss L. Dowell in 1833, which was exclusively devoted to "glassware, china, and crockery." In 1852 Emile Profilet, a former blacksmith, opened a shop that dealt in jewelry and watches only. But such shops were the exception; even in the late 1850's the most successful establishments still were the "plantation-supply" firms that stocked almost everything the consumer might wish.

Some retailers kept on hand surprisingly large stocks, prompting one to wonder about the quality of the final items sold in depleting the supply. For instance, the firm of J. H. Sturgess and William A. Baughan announced in 1825 that they had for sale two thousand barrels of pork, six thousand pounds of bacon, twenty barrels of mackerel, and thirty barrels of whiskey, in addition to large quantities of lard, flour, and butter. John Walsh advertised the next year that he had just received a shipment of 150 barrels of whiskey, 20 barrels of gin, 20 barrels of smoked mackerel, 10

[48] *De Bow's Review*, V (1848), 380.

barrels of molasses, as well as a considerable stock of dry goods, ready-made clothing, shoes, boots, hats, and "tallow, wax, or sperm candles." Occasionally merchants resorted to quite modern phraseology in advertising their wares, as in 1854 when S. D. Boyd and Company proclaimed: "THE EXCITEMENT STILL CONTINUES! REDUCED PRICES on French linens, embroideries, organdies, and other summer goods."[49]

Generally prices at Natchez were less than those at New Orleans on items shipped from the Upper Mississippi Valley. On the other hand, Natchez prices were higher on commodities shipped upriver, with freight and handling charges spelling the difference. In 1825, for example, some of the current produce prices at the two locations were:[50]

	Natchez	New Orleans
Molasses (gal.)	35¢	31¢
Sugar (lb.)	11¢	8¢
Ham (lb.)	12¢	15¢
Butter (lb.)	15¢	15¢
Whiskey (gal.)	30¢	30¢
Flour (bbl.)	$ 5.00	$ 9.00
Pork (bbl.)	$14.00	$15.00

Contingent upon supply and demand, prices on consumer items, especially food, tended to vary rather widely over the years. Bacon, for example, sold at Natchez for 9 cents per pound in 1825, 10 cents in 1837, 2 cents in 1849, and 7 cents in 1851. A barrel of corn cost 75 cents in 1825, $1.25 in 1837. $1.00 in 1847, and 90 cents in 1855. "Havana green coffee" sold at 22 cents per pound in 1825, 15 cents in 1832, and 11 cents in 1849. Sugar sold at 11 cents per pound in 1825, 5 cents in 1832, 17 cents in 1836,

[49] Based on commercial advertisements in various issues of the following Natchez newspapers and years: *Mississippi Messenger*, 1805; *Mississippi Herald and Natchez Gazette*, 1806; *Mississippi Republican*, 1817, 1823; *Mississippi State Gazette*, 1818; *Ariel*, 1825, 1828; Natchez *Gazette*, 1826; *Mississippi Statesman and Natchez Gazette*, 1827; *Southern Galaxy*, 1829; *Natchez Courier, and Adams, Jefferson and Franklin Advertiser*, 1833; *Courier and Journal*, 1838, 1846, 1847; *Courier*, 1850–54, 1858–60; *Mississippi Free Trader*, 1849, 1857–60.
[50] Natchez *Ariel*, July 20, 1825.

and 7 cents in 1855. Butter prices went up rather steadily from 15 cents per pound in 1825 to 50 cents in 1851. A study of prices, 1825–55, on thirty-seven selected consumer items shows that twenty-four appreciably declined over the period. The selected items ranged from prime pork and corn meal to curry combs and spades. Since many of them were imported from the Upper Mississippi Valley, the steady reduction in freight rates on river navigation must have been partly responsible for the price declines.[51]

A perusal of newspaper advertisement also reveals a characteristic common to all commercial communities, namely, frequent mobility by individuals from one type of capitalistic enterprise to another. For instance, one of the most persistent advertisers from 1820 to the 1850's was James Foster. First appearing as a saddler, in 1826 he announced the opening of his boot and shoe factory. Yet the next year he was in the grocery business, offering among other things, "600 bbls. of fresh pork" for sale. He and John Steele formed a tannery firm three years later. By 1838 Foster was in a partnership with David Greenleaf, selling "russet brogans, shirting, sheeting, and boots" at their mercantile establishment. In the early 1850's Foster entered the cotton-commission business. In 1860 he is listed in the federal census returns as a farmer, producing for export five hundred bushels of corn but no cotton.[52]

Another interesting gleaning from advertisements is the habit of dentists, unlike attorneys and physicians, of vying with each other in attracting customers. Dr. L. S. Farmley, for example,

[51] Compiled from Natchez newspapers, 1825–60, especially the *Ariel, Southern Galaxy, Courier,* and *Mississippi Free Trader;* J. Falmor to Nathaniel Ware, January 8, 1842, Nathaniel A. Ware Papers, Mississippi Archives; Entries of 1847, journal of Lemuel P. Conner, I, Conner Papers, LSU; Sundry entries of 1827–32, Nevitt Record Book; Purchases of January 28–September 30, 1851, daybook of William T. Johnson, XIV, William T. Johnson Papers, LSU; *Johnson's Diary, passim.*

[52] Natchez *Mississippi Republican,* October 3, 1820; Natchez *Gazette,* October 21, 1826; *Mississippi Statesman and Natchez Gazette,* February 22, 1827; Natchez *Southern Galaxy,* July 30, 1829; Natchez *Courier and Journal,* January 5, 1838; Natchez *Courier,* September 28, 1852; U. S. Census (1860), MS population and slave schedules.

boasted in 1825 that he pulled teeth at the lowest rates in the area, charging nine dollars for a "front tooth" and only five dollars for a "back tooth." Moreover, he assured his customers that they could freely borrow copies of famous paintings that he kept in his office. Dr. Henry Clagett in 1850 boasted that he possessed "the exclusive right in Adams County to use Dr. Levett's Patent Enamel."[53]

Certainly among the most fascinating of businessmen in antebellum Natchez was William Johnson, the free-Negro barber. In addition to his busy shop on Main Street, he had two smaller barber shops and a four-tub public bath house. Charging 25 cents for a haircut and one bit (12½ cents) for a shave, Johnson built up a large and profitable clientele, which included the elite of the town whites. By 1840 he was respected widely as one of the most popular and successful small-businessmen in the community.[54]

Perhaps the largest tailoring and retail clothing firm in Mississippi was that of Edward Dickinson, who maintained shops in Natchez and Washington. His business records show tailoring jobs performed for persons living from Woodville to Columbus. His entries seem like a roll call of the state's best-known figures, including David Holmes, Albert Gallatin Brown, Seargent S. Prentiss, Gerard Brandon, and Charles Lynch. For a Dickinson-made merino coat these men paid $14, and for one of his tailored velvet vests the price was $4.50, which at the time (1833) were very reasonable charges. In addition to his tailoring, Dickinson also sold the "latest Eastern fashions" in men's wear.[55]

The state's principal insurance firm also was located at Natchez. The Natchez Protection Insurance Company was chartered in 1829 and engaged mainly in the business of insuring cotton crops from the time of ginning to the time of sale in New Orleans or elsewhere. The firm's president for many years was wealthy planter William St. John Elliott, who resided at "D'Evereux."

[53] Natchez *Ariel*, December 5, 1825; Natchez *Courier*, August 3, 1850.
[54] *Johnson's Diary*, 24–26.
[55] Entries of July, 1833, Edward Dickinson Daybook, Mississippi Archives.

Leading stockholders included Levin Marshall, John Hutchins, Oren Metcalfe, and other prominent planters of the Natchez vicinity.[56]

Perhaps unique for the antebellum era was the Natchez Building Association, which was chartered in 1852. An early form of the savings and loan firm, its purpose was "to accumulate savings funds and award loans for the building or buying of houses." The charter stipulated that interest in excess of 6 per cent could not be charged on its loans. The association was capitalized at $60,000 and was authorized to sell shares at $200 each. Its main officials were attorney Ralph North and editor Giles M. Hillyer.[57]

Business cycles at Natchez seem to have corresponded roughly to those of Memphis, New Orleans, and other cities of the South and Southwest. The worst depression periods were the five to seven years following the panics of 1819 and, especially, 1837. The state of Johnson's barber business illustrates the sharp downward swing of Natchez business conditions after the great crisis of 1837. In the previous two years Johnson's daily receipts had often totalled $15 to $20 and sometimes as much as $30. But in September, 1837, he commented: "There is nothing doing here— 1.50 is a big days work here now—I never heard of such times in my life." His business revived temporarily but by 1843–44 Johnson was contemplating a change of occupation. In early 1844 an income of $5 to $10 a day was judged by him as "tolerable fair" and $12 as "exceptional." By the time of his death seven years later, however, his business, like that of most Natchez entrepreneurs, was again booming.[58]

In the spring of 1860 the *Free Trader* carried an editorial entitled "Our City Flourishes." The writer began by noting the impressive new buildings and additions that were under construction, mentioning, among others, Stanton and Stockman's new "Plantation Supplies and Family Grocery Store," Robinson

[56] Sundry entries of February-April, 1834, Natchez Protection Insurance Company Papers, Mississippi Archives.
[57] *Laws of the State of Mississippi, 1852*, 122–24.
[58] *Johnson's Diary*, 26–27.

Walker's "wagon and plow manufactory," and Andrew Boyer's "wagon and plow making" firm. Then he turned to an analysis of the comparative growth of Natchez commerce:

Notwithstanding those great drawbacks, the apathy of the people and the hoarding of treasure by those who have it, and the consequent delay in perfecting the New Hotel arrangements and in beginning those Railroads—we say "delay," for in time all we have suggested as necessary will be accomplished—yet our city flourishes. New buildings spring up in every direction constantly, and still the cry is "more room," "more stores," "more houses." The wages of laborers and servants are high, rents are high, provisions are high, and the money market is wonderfully depressed and tight, yet our city flourishes. . . .

Those of our quiet, staid, reserved, non-enterprising, stay-at-home citizens, who seem to think Natchez is doing well enough and is large enough, great enough, and sufficiently enterprising and prosperous, would do well to take drives, rides or strolls around the city and suburbs, and note what marked improvements have been and are being made—without their aid—then travel abroad and observe what enterprize [*sic*] and public spirit have done for other places and how far they have outstripped Natchez in wealth and consequence, when their advantages were in no respect a tithe as great as ours, and then return home and contemplate the picture presented. Natchez flourishes as the good ship with bare poles rides the waves; but with all sails set how gloriously she would skim over the ocean and reach the great haven.[59]

How correctly the editorialist judged the relative status of Natchez with other towns is attested by the following figures on manufactures in 1860 (the percentiles showing increases since 1850):[60]

	Natchez	Vicksburg	Woodville	Port Gibson
Capital invested in manufactures	$161,000 (68%)	$643,550 (232%)	$135,500 (1,033%)	$108,100 (172%)
Total value of manufactures	$214,900 (3%)	$643,700 (128%)	$151,735 (347%)	$180,390 (169%)

[59] Natchez *Mississippi Free Trader*, May 10, 1860.
[60] Dunbar Rowland, *Official and Statistical Register, 1917*, 731–35.

A comparison with Memphis is even more striking. With several
dozen persons and no manufactures in 1820, Memphis, by 1860,
was over three times the size of Natchez, had $1,551,250 invested
in manufactures, and produced $4,237,471 worth of manufactured
goods.[61]

On two occasions after 1840 Natchez leaders made bids to
revive the town's stake in the growing economy of the Lower
Mississippi Valley. In 1843 the town officials petitioned Congress
to designate Natchez as the location for the Navy Yard on
Western Waters which the national legislators were then considering. Matthew F. Maury and other influential naval and
political figures supported Memphis instead, and in 1844 Congress appropriated funds for the construction of a navy yard at
Memphis.[62]

Sixteen years later Natchez commercial and agricultural
leaders eagerly anticipated the opening of the Southern Commercial Convention at Vicksburg, which was expected to work
toward solutions to some of the South's economic problems.
Natchez men hoped that somehow the convention's deliberations
might result in a reopening of direct trade with Europe and other
actions considered beneficial to the river towns of the Southwest.
But radical Democrats from upstate took control of the selection
of the Mississippi delegation, and not a single Natchez man was
invited. Meeting in May, 1859, the convention soon turned into
a sectional and political sounding board, as had other southern
commercial conventions of the past. The *Free Trader* entered the
fray, heartily endorsing the convention's main resolution, which
called for reopening of the African slave trade. The *Courier*
just as strongly opposed the resolution and urged the delegates
to turn to the genuine commercial needs of the region. The *Free
Trader* retorted that withdrawal from the Union would enable
the South to revive the oceanic slave trade, which, in turn, would
greatly benefit Natchez. The prosperity of Natchez, said the

[61] Capers, *Biography of a River Town*, 83, 101–03, 185.
[62] Natchez *Courier*, May 22, 1843; Russel, *Economic Aspects of Southern Sectionalism*, 226–29.

Democratic organ, had always followed that of New Orleans, and "a dissolution of the present union would make New Orleans in five years what New York is now."[63] Of course, secession did not lead to a reopening of the African slave trade but did accentuate the economic decline of Natchez.

Another illusion fondly held by many Natchez citizens was that of the mounting economic significance of the Mississippi River. The notion stemmed quite naturally from the ever-increasing numbers of vessels that docked at the landing, especially in the final antebellum decade. The interior-trade receipts for Natchez are not available, but those for New Orleans, which probably paralleled Natchez though on a much greater scale, showed a growth from $12,637,000 in 1820, to $49,764,000 in 1840, to $185,211,000 in 1860. It is little wonder that Natchez residents felt optimistic about their community's future, with the cannon on the bluff booming with unprecedented frequency in the 1850's to herald the arrivals of steamboats. But in the upper reaches of the Mississipi Valley the eastern railroads and canals that tapped the Northwest by 1860 were carrying 62 per cent of the Northwest's flour exports, 61 per cent of its salt meat, 80 per cent of its corn, and nearly 100 per cent of its wheat—much of which produce had formerly been floated down the Mississippi. In 1855 alone the Erie Canal carried over $204 million worth of trade products, much of it drawn from the Northwest via the Great Lakes and the connecting rail grid.[64] Thus the prosperity of Natchez and other ports on the Lower Mississippi may have been at all-time peaks as far as their prior records were concerned, but proportionately more and more of the Upper Mississippi Valley's produce was being channeled eastward by rail and canal each year.

Indeed, as the *Free Trader* pointed out, the citizens of Natchez

[63] Natchez *Mississippi Free Trader*, April 13, 1858, May 18 and June 12, 1859; Natchez *Courier*, May 17 and June 13, 1859. See also Herbert Wender, *Southern Commercial Conventions, 1837–1859* (Baltimore, 1930), 230–35.

[64] George R. Taylor, *The Transportation Revolution, 1815–1860* (New York, 1951), 163–64; Avery O. Craven, *The Coming of the Civil War* (Chicago, 1942), 317.

in 1860 might easily be deluded into thinking that "our city flourishes." Commerce and manufactures were "doing well enough" in the eyes of many local persons. But the farm lands of the vicinity were declining in productivity as soil exhaustion and erosion exacted their tolls. The great men of wealth showed no sign of diverting capital from cotton and slaves into manufactures. Furthermore, the town was isolated from the Southwest's major rail lines—the transportation arteries of the future that would make cities and turn other municipalities into sleepy towns that "might have been." No better description of the economic plight of Natchez by 1860 has been penned than the words of the editorialist: "Natchez flourishes as the good ship with bare poles rides the waves."[65]

[65] Natchez *Mississippi Free Trader*, May 10, 1860.

CHAPTER IX

The Molding of Ideas, Tastes, and Beliefs

DESPITE THE FACT THAT POSSIBLY ONE-fifth of the white adults in antebellum Natchez were illiterate, there were reasonably good educational opportunities for children of well-to-do parents. Although the tutorial system had declined rapidly in the upper South before 1800, the Natchez aristocrats utilized it actively until the Civil War. In 1832 Julius Reed, for instance, met at least four other young northerners who were also serving as tutors to rich families in the same neighborhood. One of the system's drawbacks was the dubious character of many of the tutors who came to the Old Southwest. Joseph A. Lloyd, a tutor in the Surget, Sargent, and Bingaman households (and a confirmed drunkard), describes in his diary a wild frolic in a planter's drawing-room involving himself, a dancing instructor, and a music teacher, each thoroughly inebriated. Vociferous Methodist preacher Thomas Griffin sarcastically charged that the typical Natchez tutor was a deist, "a hog stealer who was whipped out of North Carolina," and "a student of natural philosophy at the University of Natchez-under-the-Hill." Most antagonistic to Natchez employers after 1830, however, was probably the type epitomized by Reed, the pious young Yankee college graduate whose abolitionist sentiments made it impossible for him to adjust to life in a slave-served household.[1]

Families of means who could not tolerate tutors could either send their children to northern or European schools or enroll

[1] Reed to Watson, February 11, 1832, Watson Papers, Duke; Diary of Joseph A. Lloyd, entry of March 25, 1808, Wailes Papers, Mississippi Archives; Charles B. Galloway, "Thomas Griffin: A Boanerges of the Early Southwest," *PMHS*, VII (1903), 161.

them in the local private schools. About half of the known families of aristocracy enrolled their children in educational institutions outside the South, particularly for their college training. At least sixteen private schools were opened for the lower-level grades in Natchez from 1801 to 1817. Most of these, however, were of brief duration. A majority met at inns, catered to either young men or young ladies, and offered basic curricula in reading, writing, and arithmetic plus an introduction to classical learning. At least one dancing school, one singing school, and two fencing schools were founded before 1817.

Presbyterian leadership was prominent in the few private schools that lasted more than a year or two. Presbyterian minister David Ker and his wife established a girls' school in 1801. James Smylie and Jacob Rickhow, also Presbyterian clergymen, founded boys' academies in 1808 at Washington and Natchez, respectively. Two Presbyterian elders, Richard Pearce and Israel Spencer, conducted a private high school at Natchez, beginning in 1815. Scotsman John Henderson, another Presbyterian officer, was one of the chief financiers of these schools. In 1829 the Natchez Academy opened on a high-tuition basis, but it had only twenty-six students a decade later. By 1856 the private schools of Natchez consisted of one with an enrollment of 18 boys and 27 girls, three for girls with an aggregate enrollment of 137, and one for boys with 36 enrolled. All charged relatively high fees and therefore attracted students mainly from the upper middle class and aristocracy.[2]

With the establishment of a bishopric at Natchez in 1841, local Roman Catholicism underwent a revival of activity in the next twenty years which included the development of several

[2] Eron Rowland (ed.), *Life, Letters and Papers of William Dunbar of Elgin, Morayshire, Scotland and Natchez, Mississippi: Pioneer Scientist of the Southern United States* (Jackson, 1930), 361, 399; Natchez *Ariel*, December 5, 1825; Natchez *Southern Galaxy*, September 26, 1829; Natchez *Courier*, April 7, 1838; Natchez *Mississippi Free Trader*, January 30, 1856; *Constitution and Bye-Laws of the Natchez Academy* (Natchez, 1829); Margaret D. Moore (ed.), "Early Schools and Churches in Natchez," *JMH*, XXIV (October, 1962), 254–55. See also various schools' advertisements in Natchez *Mississippi Messenger, Mississippi Herald and Natchez Gazette,* and Natchez *Chronicle.*

parochial schools. Marcilly Academy, a fashionable school for girls, was founded in 1847 by two Catholic ladies. That same year the Daughters of Charity of St. Vincent de Paul founded St. Mary's Orphan Asylum for girls. With John Nevitt as board president and six nuns as teachers, the orphanage was soon operating a day school for girls which in 1852 enrolled seventy day students and thirty orphans. The asylum structure, which was near the downtown area, was enlarged in 1858, but the institution's debts were heavy, compelling the bishop to plead frequently for donations. A Catholic boys' orphanage, D'Evereux Hall, took its name from the home of William St. John Elliott, who in 1855 bequeathed a large pasture on the northeast edge of town to the church as the site of a male orphanage. Because of lack of funds and staff, the institution did not open until 1860 when Father Frederick Muller began operations in a small temporary structure on the Elliott tract. No Catholic boys' school existed until 1857 when a class of fifteen was organized by the bishop in the basement of the cathedral. Enrollment in the Catholic schools, as was typical of Catholic church membership, was usually drawn from the lower-income immigrant element.[3]

In the spring of 1816 the Female Charitable Society was founded by a group of well-to-do Protestant ladies, including the wives of Winthrop Sargent, William Dunbar, and George Overaker, as well as Miss Elizabeth Tichenor. At their first meeting the ladies drew up a statement of purpose and aims: "The primary object . . . shall be to give instruction to poor children, The surplus fund may be applied to the relief of orphan children and poor widows, according to the discretion of the managers." The managers' duties were "to search out needy children; to provide a school room; to superintend their education; and to make such regulations for the government of the school as they may deem necessary." By fall the society had raised over twelve hundred dollars, including the proceeds from "Dr. King's Electricity and Galvanized Exhibition." In November, 1816, the

[3] Gerow, *Cradle Days of St. Mary's*, 205–207, 233–38, 245–53.

school, known as the Lancastrian Academy, opened with Benjamin Davis as the first headmaster at a salary of five hundred dollars per year. When a committee of the society inspected the school several months later, they found that the children had "progressed very rapidly."[4]

The most ambitious undertaking of the city government and one of the most successful public schools in the Old South was the Natchez Institute, which began operations in 1845. It opened in a building donated by the Natchez Mechanical Society; the lot was the gift of wealthy merchant Alvarez Fisk, who also gave the money for a new brick structure in the early 1850's. The city magistrates passed an ordinance levying a special city tax to operate the school and sent examining committees annually to assess the quality of education at the Institute. As the school was preparing to open in 1845, Presbyterian minister Joseph B. Stratton rallied support at a public gathering by preaching a stirring message from a text in Hosea, "My people are destroyed for lack of knowledge." The clergyman, who was chairman of the Institute examining committee for eight of the next fifteen years, stated that the school's early development was menaced by "much distrust and opposition" from obstructionist-minded "wealthy persons," who resented tax funds being used in that manner. A state public-school act of 1846 helped the Institute's fiscal situation by providing for a special state tax to support public education. In 1847 the Institute's May Day picnic at "Minor's Grove" drew 700 pupils and "joyous thousands" of parents and friends. From then until the end of the antebellum era the enrollment ranged from 600 to 750 pupils.[5]

Considering the facts that epidemics and rumors of contagions

[4] Natchez Female Charitable Society Minute Book, entry of March 12, 1816, also sundry entries of November, 1816-March, 1817, in archives of Protestant Children's Home, Natchez; *Annual Report of the Managers and Officers with the Annual Address Before the Natchez Orphan Asylum, Delivered at the Asylum by Rev. Jos. B. Stratton* . . . (Natchez, 1855), 5–26.

[5] Stratton, *Memorial of a Quarter–Century's Pastorate*, 50–52; Natchez *Courier*, April 30, 1847; Natchez *Mississippi Free Trader*, January 30, 1856; *Second Report of the Board of Visitors of the Natchez Institute to the President and Selectmen of the City of Natchez* (Natchez, 1846), 3–5.

were frequent and that most of the pupils were of young ages, attendance at the Institute was surprisingly good. For the school year 1853–54 there were 603 students, consisting of 344 males and 259 females. The average daily attendance that session was 525, or 87 per cent. The age breakdown of Institute pupils was as follows: 353 were six to ten years old; 217 were eleven to fourteen; and 33 were fifteen to eighteen. The average was ten years. The opening of school for the next year's session, however, had to be postponed four months because of a yellow fever epidemic, which left 209 pupils stricken.

Institute expenditures, as mentioned earlier, comprised a large proportion of the annual municipal budget, sometimes amounting to nearly one half. For the school year 1853–54 Institute expenses totaled $9,269, including $8,400 for instructors' salaries, $300 for janitorial services, and $569 for "repairs, insurance, rent, coal, &c."[6]

Sixteen teachers were employed in thirteen "departments," which may have been similar in gradation to the present public-school system of kindergarten through the twelfth grade. As is typical in today's schools, female teachers outnumbered the male. The men handled classes in Departments Seven, Five, Three, and One (the highest level of instruction), leaving the equivalents of kindergarten and the first five elementary grades wholly under the supervision of the ladies. The basic rudiments of "reading, spelling, and mental arithmetic" were supposedly taught in Department Thirteen, the beginners' class. If the pupils were six-year-olds, however, more energy undoubtedly went into "teaching" than into "learning" such subjects. In Departments Twelve through Nine the same subjects plus geography were offered. In Department Eight, perhaps similar to the present fifth grade, the pupils studied "mental arithmetic, geography, reading, Davies' Arithmetic, spelling," or the same curriculum as earlier except, of course, at more advanced levels. Departments Seven and Six continued the same subjects, with

[6] *Annual Reports of the Board of Visitors and the Board of Examiners of the Natchez Institute, 1854* (Natchez, 1854), 8–11.

the addition of history in the latter. In Department Five grammar was added to the previous curriculum. The subjects taught in Department Four were "Mitchell's Geography, parsing and grammar, United States history, English history, algebra, composition." Beginning with Department Three, probably the equivalent of the tenth grade, boys and girls went into separate classes. The curriculum was about the same as for the previous department except for the addition of Latin. In Department Two the students learned "French history, algebra, chemistry, astronomy, physiology, geometry," with the girls required to take singing lessons also. In Department One, or the most advanced level, the pupils studied "natural philosophy, astronomy, geometry and trigonometry, algebra, Latin, physiology, chemistry, and bookkeeping."[7]

The Institute examining committee in 1854, composed largely of middle-class merchants and attorneys, visited each department and reported in detail to the Board of Selectmen. In their conclusion the examiners assured the city fathers:

> The Institute has fully answered the purpose for which it was intended. The expectations of the most sanguine friends have been more than realized. The Schools [departments] are now permanently established. With commodious, and well appointed rooms for teaching, a superior Hall for exhibitions, and exercises of all the pupils; with an internal policy which the experience of nine years has elaborated and settled, nothing remains to be done but to use ordinary care in the selection of competent teachers, and faithfully to execute the rules already proved efficacious by experience. Patient industry to keep up the efficiency, and prevent the system from falling into a dull routine, is all that is required. . . . No Southern city has tried this means of general education with better results.[8]

Undoubtedly the examiners had not compared the Natchez puplic school with others across the South and had based their evaluation simply on local pride, but they were close to the

[7] *Ibid.*, 16–21.
[8] *Ibid.*, 11–12.

truth. When a comprehensive comparative study of antebellum southern schools is made, the Natchez Institute may stand out as the most eminently successful operation undertaken by a small town. So far most attention and praise have gone to Calvin Wiley's public-school system in North Carolina. The average public school of that state in 1860 had 50 pupils, operated on a four-month term, and paid a teacher $336 for the session. On the other hand, the Institute enrolled an average of 641 pupils during the period 1845–60, had a normal term of six months, and paid an average instructional salary of $525 per session. Succeeding in spite of opposition or indifference on the part of many influential citizens, the Institute was the proudest achievement of the bourgeois leaders who guided the municipal affairs of Natchez.[9]

Charles L. Dubuisson, a lawyer who wrote the Institute committee's report to the selectmen in 1854, included his group's recommendation that "a University of Natchez" be created. Such an institution was "urgently needed now," the report stated, but it should be "free of denomination influence" from the start. The Institute "can furnish twenty students a year and as many from private schools" can be obtained. Noting that an institution of higher learning at Natchez was long the dream of the late Alvarez Fisk, "emphatically the founder of the Institute," Dubuisson's report called for immediate plans to be laid for a liberal arts college, a college of law, and one of medicine. The university would be financed by "wealthy and small donors." The proposal concluded: "There is no town in the Southwest in which the facilities for the establishment of a University are greater than here."[10] Nothing came of the recommendation although popular resentment at Natchez over the distant location of the University of Mississippi remained strong.

The only college in the Natchez vicinity, Jefferson College at

[9] *Ibid.*, 10; Clement Eaton, *A History of the Old South* (2nd ed., New York, 1966), 420–21.

[10] *Annual Reports of the Board of Visitors and the Board of Examiners of the Natchez Institute, 1854,* 13–15.

Washington, was engaged in a continuous struggle for survival from its founding in 1811 to the Civil War. Seven years after its opening it had four teachers, led by principal James McAlister, who was advertised as "eminently qualified to teach every branch of learning." The school offered courses in reading, history, belles lettres, writing, moral and natural philosophy, grammar, French, Greek, Latin, bookkeeping, arithmetic, advanced mathematics, and astronomy. At best, the institution amounted to no more than a preparatory school, however, and no college work was offered during its first three decades. In fact, enrollment was so poor in the late 1820's that the school was temporarily closed. The board of trustees, numbering as many as forty, sometimes was larger than the student body.[11]

In 1840 a committee headed by Dr. John Monette presented a plan to the board for a higher-education program "as thorough as in most colleges of the United States, with every facility afforded by a choice classical and scientific library." The board approved the proposal, set the tuition "much below" that of other colleges as "an additional inducement," and decreed that prerequisites for entrance into the college program were to be a reading knowledge of Virgil and Sallust, and a thorough understanding of geography and "Arithmetic to the Rule of Three." In the next few months the board hired, at competitive salaries of two to three thousand dollars a year, four college professors, drawing them from the faculties of the University of Nashville, the United States Military Academy, New York University, and a Prussian university. They were to offer courses at the college level in intellectual philosophy, belles lettres, mathematics, geology, modern languages, civil engineering, Greek, Latin, natural philosophy, and chemistry. The "Primary Department," or pre-college division, was to be continued under the guidance of two instructors. In 1844 Jefferson College awarded its first

[11] Journal of the Board of Trustees of Jefferson College, III, entry of November 11, 1830, Jefferson College Papers; Natchez *Mississippi State Gazette,* January 24, 1818; William B. Hamilton, "Jefferson College and Education in Mississippi, 1798–1817," *JMH,* III (October, 1949), 259–76.

baccalaureates and also bestowed a doctor of laws degree upon Frederick A. P. Barnard, future chancellor of the University of Mississippi and president of Columbia University.[12]

Despite able leadership and an expanded curriculum, the institution encountered serious obstacles in the period from 1840 to 1860. Though its board was packed with wealthy planters, the school received no large donations; none of its gifts exceeded $700. Hostility of legislators from the northern counties led to a suit by the state in the late 1850's to recover a pre-1820 state loan to the school of $10,000 plus back interest. Persistent lobbying by Benjamin Wailes, perhaps the most dedicated of the trustees, influenced the legislature to drop the suit after a three-year legal hassle. Enrollment was an ever-present problem; the student body rarely exceeded ninety, of which three-fourths were usually in the pre-college division. An offer of free tuition to one deserving student from each county was ignored by the counties outside the Natchez area. Most students as well as trustees came from the aristocratic families of Adams County, with few representing Natchez itself. Morale, as well as enrollment, sank to a new ebb in 1859. During the absence of Superintendent E. J. Cornish heavy drinking and fighting with instructors broke out among the students. Amidst "wild outbursts of horrid sounds" the board met on campus and persuaded the iron-willed wife of the superintendent to take over the school long enough to restore order and oust the miscreants. By the end of the year enrollment was down to thirty.[13]

Two incidents of the late 1850's demonstrate that the old jealousies between Natchez and Washington were not dead. In 1857 John A. Quitman, once head of the college trustees, maneuvered a transaction in the national capital whereby the Natchez Institute was made the depository for federal government docu-

---

[12] Journal of the Board of Trustees, IV, entry of June 4, 1840, Jefferson College Papers; Ferdinand L. Claiborne to Levin Wailes, July 21, 1840, Ferdinand L. Claiborne Papers, Mississippi Archives. See also *Charter and Statutes of Jefferson College* . . . (Natchez, 1840).

[13] Benjamin Wailes to William McWillie, November 11, 1858, Jefferson College Papers; Wailes diary, entry of May 9, 1859, Wailes Papers, Duke.

ments in southwestern Mississippi, an "honor" long held by
Jefferson College. Largely through Wailes' efforts, the document
service was restored to the college in 1859. The next year Jefferson College trustees James Carson and Alexander Farrar, on
behalf of some of their wealthy Natchez friends who despised
the Institute, tried to get the college moved to Natchez. Calling
the proposal "a preposterous and impracticable scheme," Wailes
persuaded the board to defeat the move.[14]

The radical-controlled state legislature in 1860 passed an act
transforming Jefferson College from a liberal arts institution into
a combination of military academy and normal school. Henceforth the state would pay staff salaries, determine school policies
through a "Board of Visitors," and select annually twenty gratis
students. Thus by the eve of the Civil War the financial problems
of the college were solved but at the sacrifice of complete control by the upstate Democracy.[15]

Reputed to be the first female college in the nation, Elizabeth
Female Academy opened in 1818 on the edge of Washington.
The school was under Methodist sponsorship, and the tract was
donated by Mrs. Elizabeth Roach, a leader in the nearby Methodist church. Like Jefferson College, it offered mainly college
preparatory work, including courses in Latin, French, English,
history, composition, chemistry, geography, astronomy, and arithmetic. The school advertised that its teaching was based on
"the improved education methods of Pestalozzi and Condillac
of addressing the understanding without oppressing the
memory." Most of the presidents were Methodist ministers,
outstanding among whom was the Reverend Benjamin M. Drake
(1829–33). Though it received some church support, the acad-

[14] Wailes diary, entry of November 2, 1860, Wailes Papers, Duke; sundry
letters of William Whitehurst relating to the college, 1859–1860, William N.
Whitehurst Papers, Mississippi Archives. Whitehurst, the Washington land
registrar, often joined Wailes in crusading for Jefferson College against upstate
interests.

[15] Wailes to Lieutenant Thomas C. Sullivan, November 7, 1859, Jefferson College Papers; An Act to Establish a Military Organization and a Normal School in
Jefferson College, January, 1860, ibid.; Natchez Mississippi Free Trader, February
2, 1860.

emy seems to have operated mainly on private donations, with Beverly R. Grayson of Washington the main financial supporter. By 1844, however, dire financial straits forced the school to close its doors for one session, and three years later it terminated operations permanently. During its final decade the school had a limited college program and supposedly conferred several baccalaureates.[16]

One reason why Jefferson College and Elizabeth Female Academy received scanty financial support was the strong backing given by Natchez aristocrats to Oakland College, a Presbyterian school south of Port Gibson. David Hunt gave the college over $50,000; Dr. John Ker donated $20,000; and at least eight other Natchez donors contributed amounts in excess of $5,000 each. Opening in 1830, Oakland in the next fifteen years, graduated fifty-six young men, many of whom were from Natchez. As the only strong college in the Natchez country and possessing a highly-regarded faculty, a 6,000-volume library, and a large endowment, Oakland attracted non-Presbyterians as well as Presbyterians and easily overshadowed the two Washington schools. Indeed, its ability to lure the money and offspring of Natchez aristocrats probably helped to discourage efforts to establish a higher-education institution in the town.[17]

A molder of ideas and tastes as well as a form of amusement, the theater played a significant and colorful role in Natchez cultural life from the early territorial days onward. The first professional theatrical performance there, and perhaps the earliest given in English west of the Alleghenies, was Mr. Rannie's

[16] Natchez *Mississippi State Gazette*, October 24, 1818; Natchez *Ariel*, December 19, 1825; Charles B. Galloway, "Elizabeth Female Academy: The Mother of Female Colleges," *PMHS*, II (1899), 170–78; Henry G. Hawkins, *Methodism in Natchez; Including "A Centennial Retrospect or Methodism in Natchez, Miss., from 1799 to 1884," by W. C. Black* (Jackson, 1937), 208.

[17] MS history of Oakland College, 1829–1845, by Henry Hughes, Henry Hughes Papers, Mississippi Archives; John W. Buie to Joseph A. Montgomery, April 11, 1840, Joseph A. Montgomery and Family Papers, Mississippi Archives; Robert L. Stanton to the Rev. David Legburn, June 15, 1854, Robert L. Stanton Papers, Mississippi Archives. Most of the Oakland College records are located at Chamberlain-Hunt Academy, Port Gibson.

production of an English comedy, *The Provoked Husband*, staged at the City Tavern in 1806. The same program featured "magical experiments," "mimicking of various birds and beasts," and ventriloquism. The townsfolk also supported the Natchez Theatrical Association's performances. Between 1808 and 1817 this amateur group presented twenty-eight programs, each usually consisting of an English drama and an Irish farce. James Wilkins, Lewis Evans, John Taylor, and Frank Surget were among the association's wealthy supporters. Its plays were staged first at the old Spanish hospital and later at a five-hundred-seat wooden theater, which was gutted by fire; in 1828 a seven-hundred-seat brick theater was built with members' donations. By the time of statehood theatrical activity was lively. Between 1817 and 1821 the amateurs presented an average of three plays a year, and touring professionals staged plays for a total of seventy weeks of the period. The acting of both amateurs and professionals was mediocre; scenery and costumes were cheap and worn, and sperm-oil lighting was inadequate.[18] But in a river town far from large-city entertainments the theatricals' shortcomings were overlooked by the appreciative audiences.

Gradually Natchez began to attract superior performers such as Edwin Forrest, one of the finest actors in antebellum America, who performed in *Hamlet* at the theater in 1829. Six years later the celebrated Irish actor Tyrone Power attracted large crowds there. According to Power, his audiences consisted mainly of "the planters of the neighboring country, many of whom came nightly to the theatre from considerable distances, forming such an audience as cannot be seen elsewhere." Some performances,

[18] Natchez *Mississippi Herald*, February 4, 1806; Natchez *Mississippi Republican*, April 13, 1814; *Washington Republican and Natchez Intelligencer*, May 26, 1817; Natchez *Southern Galaxy*, October 9, 1828; Noah M. Ludlow, *Dramatic Life as I Found It* (St. Louis, 1880), 134; Journal of James Scott, entries of 1817–21, Natchez and Vicksburg Theatrical Papers, Mississippi Archives. On the Natchez theater, see also Joseph M. Free, "The Ante–Bellum Theatre of the Old Natchez Region," *JMH*, V (January, 1943), 14–27; William B. Gates, "The Theatre in Natchez," *ibid.*, III (April, 1941), 71–129; William B. Hamilton, "The Theatre of the Old Southwest: The First Decade at Natchez," *American Literature*, XII (January, 1941), 471–85.

however, were not so well received. In 1831 John Nevitt called Sol Smith's *My Old Woman* "a good play rather Vulgar," but indignant church leaders, headed by Dr. Henry Tooley, forced Smith to leave town.[19]

From 1828 onward the association employed a full-time manager, usually a former professional actor. Receipts must have been good, if judged by the theater's continued operation with relatively heavy expenses. In 1838 co-managers James Scott and James Thorne paid a family of pantomimists $1,170 for six performances, and a year later actor Edwin Booth received $1,229 for nine performances. Between January and May, 1839, theater expenses were $10,333, which included salaries, sperm oil for lighting, maintenance, scenery materials, and freight charges.

On May 7, 1840, the theater was destroyed by the great tornado, but nine months later a new theatrical season opened to a capacity audience in a large warehouse that Scott had rented. Actor G. V. H. Forbes addressed the opening-night crowd, beginning with these lines:

> As when the battle scathe hath bronzed the plain
> > Green springs the grass and flowers bloom again,
> So Natchez rises o'er the storms of fate,
> > Bursts through the clouds, throws off misfortune's weight.[20]

Over the years a great variety of programs was presented by touring artists and experts to uplift the cultural level of the townsfolk and to enrich the purses of the sponsors. One of the highlights was a P. T. Barnum-sponsored concert by soprano Jenny Lind in 1851. An enthusiastic audience of nearly eight hundred packed the Methodist church to hear the "Swedish Nightingale," and the performance grossed $6,643. But the *Courier* editor sourly noted that the Barnum troupe "did not give or spend a cent in this city." A number of lecture series were

[19] Nevitt Record Book, entries of March 21 and June 5, 1829, April 5 and 8, 1831; Scott journal, entries of 1829–36, Natchez and Vicksburg Theatrical Papers; Tyrone Power, *Impressions of America, During the Years 1833, 1834, and 1835* . . . (2 vols.; London, 1836), II, 119–31.

[20] Scott journal, entries of 1838–40, Natchez and Vicksburg Theatrical Papers.

offered, usually at the theater or the Institute building. The programs varied as much as did the lyceums of the North, ranging from talks on "Laughing Gas" and "polite Magic" to learned geological discourses by Yale's distinguished Benjamin Silliman. Concerts by local groups, such as the Natchez City Band and Charles Gaita's Philharmonic Club, were common after 1840. Among touring art exhibitions were "truly moral and celebrated" paintings of Adam and Eve, huge panoramic paintings fifty feet or more in length, and also original works by Benjamin West.[21]

Natchez citizens were apparently avid newspaper readers, as evidenced by the fact that the community was never without at least two local journals. During the years 1802–17 nineteen newspapers were printed in Natchez and Washington, most of which lasted only a year or two, the longest being five years. By the 1840's the town had only two regular newspapers, the *Courier* and the *Mississippi Free Trader*, although other brief-lived journals tried to compete. The *Courier* became one of the best written and most accurate small newspapers of the South, despite the Whig bias of its editorials. Like other papers of its time, however, the *Courier* was weak in its coverage of local events. The typical editor's attitude seemed to be that local happenings did not really constitute news since most subscribers were well aware of the events before the next issue of the paper was published. Except for the *Courier* and *Free Trader*, which published daily and weekly issues, Natchez newspapers were weekly, triweekly, or biweekly publications. Even the dailies, however, tended to keep the reader better informed on happenings in New York and London than on occurrences in Natchez.

Outstanding among the pre-1830 editors was Andrew Marschalk, the fiery political-minded journalist who once was beaten with a cane by George Poindexter for his libelous editorials. Besides introducing printing to the Mississippi area and serving

[21] *Johnson's Diary*, 779–80; Natchez *Courier*, April 9, 1851; Davis and Hogan, *Barber of Natchez*, 188–201. See also Charles G. Rosenberg, *Jenny Lind in America* (New York, 1851).

at various times as city, territorial, and state printer, Marschalk edited at least five newspapers in Natchez and nearby towns. His chief publications were the *Mississippi Herald and Natchez Gazette* (1802–1807) and the *Washington Republican and Natchez Intelligencer* (1813–17). Another colorful and competent journalist was Lorenzo A. Besancon, editor of the Democratic *Mississippi Free Trader* in the 1830's. Besancon also won fame as a duelist, state legislator, bank commissioner, Mexican War soldier, and California gold seeker. His later years were spent as a newspaperman in New Orleans.

Best known of the *Courier* editors was Giles M. Hillyer, who operated the paper in the 1840's and 1850's. A staunch opponent of "Brownism," he first attracted widespread notice by his courageous Unionist editorials during the secessionist movement of 1849–51. When his idol, Henry S. Foote, became disgusted at the resurgence of the "fire-eaters" and left the state at the end of his governorship in 1854, Hillyer joined many local Whigs in a temporary flight into nativism, winning a legislative seat as a Know-Nothing candidate. As the secessionist furor continued to its ultimate climax, Hillyer stood as firmly as ever on the side of Unionism.[22]

The Natchez-Washington area had a number of societies dedicated to cultural and scientific pursuits. Earliest to be organized was the Mississippi Society for the Acquirement and Dissemination of Useful Knowledge, founded in 1803. Its nineteen charter members included most of the territorial officials as well as such influential, well-educated local leaders as William Dunbar, John

[22] Clarence C. Brigham (comp.), *History and Bibliography of American Newspapers, 1620–1820* (2 vols.; Worcester, Mass., 1947), I, 423–30; Winifred Gregory (comp.), *American Newspapers, 1821–1936: A Union List of Files Available in the United States and Canada* (New York, 1936), 347; *Mississippi Newspapers, 1805–1840: A Preliminary Checklist of Mississippi Newspaper Files Available in the Mississippi Department of Archives and History* (Jackson, 1942); *Biographical and Historical Memoirs of Mississippi*, II, 242–43; Charles S. Sydnor, "The Beginning of Printing in Mississippi," *JSH*, I (February, 1935), 49–55; Madel J. Morgan, "Andrew Marschalk's Account of Mississippi's First Press," *JMH*, VIII (July, 1946), 146–48; Edwin A. Miles, "The Mississippi Press in the Jackson Era, 1824–1841," *ibid.*, XIX (January, 1957), 1–20; Natchez *Courier*, especially issues of 1850, 1854, and 1860.

Girault, Samuel Brooks, John Ellis, and William Shields. Meetings were usually held either in Natchez or in Washington. Dunbar, the group's leader, ordered from London a number of scholarly volumes and scientific instruments for the society. The organization was still active in 1813, but nothing is known of it after that time. Over half of its charter members were among the first trustees of Jefferson College. The only other known cultural group of the territorial era was the Natchez Debating Club, which met in the City Hall.[23]

The Adams Atheneum held its first meeting in March, 1825, at which time Benjamin Wailes, its first and only president, expressed the hope that the society would surpass "the few abortive attempts at the formation of literary organizations" in previous years. Within a month the Atheneum opened a reading room at Washington and began a library under Dr. Monette's supervision. Complete files of back issues and subscriptions to ten periodicals were ordered, such as the *North American Review, London Quarterly Review,* and *Edinburgh Philosophical Journal.* In April, Wailes addressed the group on "The Jumping Plough," a new implement superior to those in use. At the May meeting John McDowell, an instructor at Jefferson College, delivered "an experimental philosophical lecture." Levin Covington served as Atheneum secretary, and Andrew Marschalk was a leading donor. Unfortunately and inexplicably, the Atheneum was defunct after nineteen months of promising activity.[24]

The Washington Lyceum was founded in 1835, with Charles Dubuisson, then Jefferson College superintendent, serving as first president. He was followed in 1837 by Monette. The mem-

[23] William D. McCain (ed.), *Journal of the House of Representatives, Second General Assembly, Second Session, October 3-November 19, 1803* (Hattiesburg, 1940), 17, 54–55; Monette, *Valley of the Mississippi,* II, 350; *Mississippi Herald and Natchez Gazette,* October 19, 1804; Dunbar to Jefferson, December 17, 1805, Dunbar Papers, Mississippi Archives; *Washington Republican,* June 16, 1813; Selectmen Minute Book, II, entry of March 29, 1817, City Clerk's Records; William B. Hamilton, "The Southwestern Frontier, 1795–1817: An Essay in Social History," *JSH,* X (November, 1944), 396–97.

[24] Minutes of Adams Atheneum, March 15, 1825–October 12, 1826, in Daybook of Levin Covington, Mississippi Archives.

bers, numbering twenty-one by 1838, were mostly teachers and trustees of the college. Among the instructors were Leonard D. Gale, Joseph H. Ingraham, and Caleb G. Forshey. Other active members were Wailes, Dr. Henry Tooley, Dr. Samuel Cartwright, and John Claiborne. Papers read at Lyceum meetings varied widely in topics, such as one by Dubuisson on "Eloquence"; the Reverend Benjamin M. Drake on "The Effects of Religion on the Political, Intellectual, Moral, and Social State of Man"; Judge Joseph S. B. Thacher on "The Philosophy of Law"; editor Lorenzo Besancon on "The Periodical and Newspaper Press of the United States"; and Monette on "The Epidemic Yellow Fevers of Natchez." A few formal debates were staged, for instance, when Forshey opposed Drake on the question of required military training for the Jefferson students. A report by Monette on the Lyceum's excavations of Indian mounds near Selsertown was published in Volume I of the *Proceedings* of the American Philosophical Society. The Lyceum's principal undertaking was a literary periodical, the *South-Western Journal*, which was "devoted to the scientific and literary interests of the Southern section of the great vale of the Mississippi." Well printed and carefully edited, the *Journal* carried Lyceum papers, book reviews, literary news, quotations from the *Southern Literary Messenger* and other leading literary periodicals, and even meteorological data. The Lyceum and the *Journal* died in 1838, possibly as a result of an ebb in Jefferson College's program when several instructors departed. Nevertheless, the Lyceum did provide the stimulus for the establishment of similar societies at Woodville, Grand Gulf, Clinton, and Columbus.[25]

Estate inventories indicate that many of the Natchez gentry were well-read, or at least owned impressive personal libraries. Abijah Hunt's library may have been typical of the private collections of the aristocrats. In 1811 it consisted of nearly two hundred volumes valued at $658. The collection included ten volumes of Robert Burns' writings, sixteen volumes of David

[25] *South–Western Journal*, I, Nos. 1–16 (December, 1837–July, 1838). Apparently these were the *Journal's* only issues.

Hume's history of England, and twenty-four volumes of Jonathan Swift's works.[26]

How deep cultural interests penetrated beyond a coterie of aristocrats who could afford books and works of art is not known. It would be encouraging if one could believe that Everard G. Baker was typical of the small planter's cultural inclinations. In his diary Baker mentions his study of such authors as Samuel Johnson, Alexander Pope, Joseph Addison and Thomas Macaulay. He also enjoyed exploring Indian mounds, often going considerable distances to collect relics.[27]

Excluded though he was from most of the town's cultural activities, William Johnson exhibited what his biographers termed "the impulse toward civilized gesture and aspiration, the impulse to give the life of every day a certain purpose and dignity." His home was furnished with handsome furniture and carpets. He owned a number of paintings, a piano, a guitar, a flute, several violins, and a thirty-dollar music box. Johnson's liquor cabinet usually contained a wide selection of domestic and imported whiskey, ale, gin, and wine. Among the books he purchased were numerous novels, French and Spanish grammars, historical works, and Shakespearean dramas. His subscriptions included the *Saturday Evening Post,* the *New Yorker,* the New York *Mirror,* the *Spirit of the Times* (a turf journal), and a half dozen newspapers of Mississippi and Louisiana.[28]

Although there were aristocrats and commoners as well who enjoyed serious reading, Natchez produced little literary creativity. Besides some verses by merchant John Henderson and printer John Shaw which appeared in the local newspapers, the principal writings of Natchez men before the statehood era concerned scientific and quasi-scientific subjects. Garrett E.

[26] Estate of Abijah Hunt, 1811, Inventories and Appraisements, I, Chancery Clerk's Office.

[27] Diary of Everard G. Baker, entries of August 12 and September 29, 1849, February 8, 1850, Ramsdell Microfilms, University of Texas. Besides several local papers, Baker subscribed to the *Genesee Farmer,* *Graham's Magazine,* and the New Orleans *Delta.*

[28] *Johnson's Diary,* 48–49.

Pendergrast, a physician educated at the University of Pennsylvania, published a book in 1803 on the geography and topography of the Lower Mississippi Valley. Governor Sargent, a Harvard graduate, contributed an article on a local Indian mound to the *Transactions* (the predecessor of the *Proceedings*) of the American Philosophical Society. A total of fifteen articles by William Dunbar appeared in the *Transactions,* ranging in subject matter from surveying to archaeology. Dunbar was elected to membership in the American Philosophical Society in 1800 upon nomination of Thomas Jefferson, with whom he frequently corresponded on topics of common interest, such as meteorology and Indian sign languages. In 1804–1805 Dunbar, commissioned by Jefferson, led an expedition to explore the Ouachita Valley and made the first scientific analysis of the Hot Springs of Arkansas. The President then appointed him to explore the sources of the Arkansas and Red rivers, but Congress withheld the necessary appropriations. In 1806 Dunbar published a book on his and other explorations of the Louisiana Purchase.[29]

Several instructors at Jefferson College were active scholars. Leonard Gale, who held degrees in medicine and chemistry, published two college textbooks in chemistry and later assisted Samuel F. B. Morse in perfecting the telegraph. Caleb Forshey produced articles on geology, mathematics, and civil engineering. Joseph Ingraham's *The South-West, by a Yankee,* an extremely valuable social study of the Natchez area, was published in two volumes in 1835. A language teacher at the college, Ingraham

[29] Swearingen, *Early Life of George Poindexter,* 58; Sydnor, *Wailes,* 122–24; American Philosophical Society *Transactions,* IV–VI (1802–1804); *DAB,* III, 507–508; Franklin L. Riley, "Sir William Dunbar, the Pioneer Scientist of Mississippi," *PMHS,* II (1899), 85–111; Arthur H. DeRozier, Jr., "William Dunbar, Explorer," *JMH,* XXV (July, 1963), 165–85; Dungan, "'Sir' William Dunbar of Natchez," 221–34. Over thirty letters exchanged between Dunbar and Jefferson, 1801–1809, can be found in Eron Rowland, *William Dunbar,* e.g., 174–77, 192–95, 207–208. Dunbar's book was entitled *Discoveries Made in Exploring the Missouri, Red River and Washita, by Captains Lewis and Clark, Doctor Sibley, and William Dunbar, Esq.; with a Statistical Account of the Countries Adjacent; with an Appendix by Mr. Dunbar* (Natchez, 1806). Garrett E. Pendergrast's work was *A Physical and Topographical Sketch of the Mississippi Territory, Lower Louisiana, and a Part of West Florida* (Philadelphia, 1803).

236 A N T E B E L L U M   N A T C H E Z

later became a prolific novelist and an Episcopalian minister.[30] Nathaniel A. Ware, a territorial official and rich land specu- lator, became in his later years an ardent economic nationalist and belligerent Whig. In the 1840's he published three books— an insignificant novel, a jeremiad against Jacksonian Democracy, and an economic treatise which may be one of the most care- fully reasoned expositions of the economic theory of national Whiggery that has been penned. In this work, *Notes on Political Economy as Applicable to the United States* (1844), Ware sound- ly argued the case for protective tariffs, increased manufactures, and federal support of internal improvements and education.[31]

Henry Tooley, a physican and later a Methodist minister, pub- lished a competent study of yellow fever in 1823 and also kept detailed meteorological tables which Wailes incorporated in his work on the state's agriculture and geology. Henry Vose, an eccentric journalist, published in over thirty newspapers many thousands of lines of poetry and over a hundred essays on sundry topics. With Marschalk he edited a literary paper at Natchez in the late 1820's called *The Tablet*. Vose also compiled a Choc- taw dictionary, and in 1835 published a topographical study of the state. He died of smallpox at the age of thirty-five, leaving over two thousand manuscript pages of an unfinished history ot Mississippi.[32]

[30] *DAB*, V, 479–80, IX, 480, XIII, 247–51; Sydnor, *Wailes*, 128–33, 141–42; Warren G. French, "A Sketch of the Life of Joseph Holt Ingraham," *JMH*, XI (July, 1949), 155–71; French, "Joseph Holt Ingraham: Southern Romancer, 1809–1860" (unpublished M.A. thesis, University of Texas, 1948). While pre- paring paintings for his monumental *Birds of America* John James Audubon taught French and art at Jefferson College in 1822–23 where he became a close companion of Levin and Benjamin Wailes. Stanley C. Arthur, *Audubon: An Intimate Life of the American Woodsman* (New Orleans, 1937), 224–25. On an earlier visit by Audubon to Natchez, see John J. Audubon, *Journal of John James Audubon Made During His Trip to New Orleans in 1820–1821*, ed. Howard Corning (Cambridge, Mass., 1929), 88–95.

[31] William Diamond, "Nathaniel A. Ware, National Economist," *JSH*, V (November, 1939), 501–26. Besides his *Notes on Political Economy*, Ware also wrote *An Exposition of the Weakness and Inefficiency of the Government of the United States of North America* (1845) and a novel entitled *Harvey Belden; or a True Narrative of Strange Adventures* (1848).

[32] Sydnor, *Wailes*, 134–35, 142–43.

Charles S. Sydnor, foremost authority on the antebellum Natchez region, said of the area's intellectual trend by the 1830's:

These two New Englanders [Ingraham and Vose], especially Ingraham, added to the early intellectual interests of the Natchez region what may be called self-consciousness. Furthermore, the rise of the abolition movement, the lectures of Robert Owen at Natchez [1828], and the decline of the power of the Natchez region in state politics, all implied a criticism of the established order in that part of Mississippi. Undoubtedly, the former frontier civilization of this region had evolved by the 1830's into a different kind of society—the plantation regime. The West had become the South. But citizens of the region seemed unaware of this change until others called it to their attention. . . . After Ingraham and Vose touched the mind of this region, its intellectual current broadened to include the study of its history as well as its natural phenomenon. . . . Although it was conscious of being a distinct section of the United States after the 1830's its history more than its present attracted self-study.[33]

Wailes, Monette, and Claiborne, who were active in the Atheneum, Lyceum, and Jefferson College intellectual endeavors of the 1820's and 1830's, became the vanguard of the post–1840 escape into the past through historical writings. The first 116 pages of Wailes' *Report on the Agriculture and Geology of Mississippi* (1854) constitute the best historical study of the pre-1800 Mississippi area that was written before the Civil War. An avid collector of manuscripts for many years, Wailes was an able historian and might have achieved national renown in the field if his versatile interests had permitted him to undertake a major historical work. As it was, his only book strictly in the historical field was a life-and-times biography of his father-in-law, General Leonard Covington, which he finished in 1862. When the Mississippi Historical Society was organized in 1858, Wailes was elected its first president. His thirty-six-volume diary, spanning the years 1852–62, ranks with William Johnson's diary as the most valuable source on the antebellum Natchez area. Wailes'

[33] *Ibid.*, 135–36.

many roles, besides small planter and historian, included those as curator of an archaeological and geological museum at Washington, trustee of Jefferson College, charter member of the American Association for the Advancement of Science, and professor at the University of Mississippi. He also carried on an active correspondence with Louis Agassiz, Joseph Henry, and other well known scientists of the time. He contributed hundreds of valuable zoological and geological specimens to Harvard, the Smithsonian Institution, and the Academy of Natural Science. Unfortunately for the field of history, this talented man's devotion to natural science surpassed his love for the human past.[34]

John F. H. Claiborne, who was one of the area's most active Democratic politicians, was an eyewitness to many events recorded in his historical writings. His collection of manuscripts was undoubtedly the most extensive in Mississippi. They comprised, besides the family papers of many political colleagues, the papers of his own influential family, including those of his father, General Ferdinand Claiborne; his grandfather, Anthony Hutchins; his uncle, William C. C. Claiborne; and his father-in-law, William Dunbar. From these he published in 1860 biographies of John Quitman and Indian fighter Sam Dale. Two decades later he produced *Mississippi, as a Province, Territory and State*, which is probably the most important printed source of pre-1840 Mississippi history, though the second volume on the post-1840 era was destroyed by fire before publication. Claiborne's intimate knowledge of persons and manuscripts makes his works indispensable for the Mississippi historian, but his sometimes savage political encounters left him more biased toward certain state figures than was the more retiring Wailes. As might be expected, too, Claiborne's writing is much more heavily political in emphasis than Wailes'.[35]

[34] *Ibid.*, 170–71, 203, 234–36, 250–58; *DAB*, X, 315–16; Charles S. Sydnor, "Historical Activities in Mississippi in the Nineteenth Century," *JSH*, III (May, 1937), 142–55; Z. T. Leavell, "The Ante-Bellum Historical Society of Mississippi," *PMHS*, VIII (1904), 227–37.

[35] Sydnor, "Historical Activities in Mississippi," 155–59; *DAB*, II, 112–13;

The other member of the Natchez–Washington triumvirate of late antebellum historians was Dr. John W. Monette. In addition to numerous articles on yellow fever and agricultural reform, he wrote a six-volume study of the geology of the Mississippi Valley which, for unknown reasons, was not published. While doing the research for this work, he also compiled historical data which resulted in his excellent two-volume *History of the Discovery and Settlement of the Valley of the Mississippi*, published in 1846. At first he discounted his historical endeavors as a mere by-product of his geological studies, but as he neared completion of his history he wrote the publisher: "I feel assured it will meet a ready circulation throughout the valley—& also east of the Mountains, if not in Europe—for it is not a loosely gotten up M.S." Today his history is generally accepted as a careful, critical regional study based on the thesis that the Mississippi Valley represents "the heart, strength, and future of the nation."[36]

The only other area of the arts and sciences wherein local contributions were noteworthy was architecture. Unfortunately, the names of some of the architects of the great Natchez mansions have been forgotten. One of the earliest known architects was John Scott, a Scotsman who is variously referred to in the Spanish archives as a shipwright, markethouse operator, carpenter, and physician, as well as architect. He probably designed "Connelly's Tavern" (1794) and the original sections of "Holly Hedges" (1795), "The Elms" (1783), "Linden" (1789), "Cottage Gardens" (1793), and "Gloucester" (1800). Levi G. Weeks, an immigrant from Boston, specialized in Greek Revival styling,

Riley, "Life of Col. J. F. H. Claiborne," 217–44; Hamilton and Nuermberger, "An Appraisal of J. F. H. Claiborne," 155–62.

[36] Monette to Harper and Brothers, September 27, 1845, Monette Papers, Mississippi Archives; Herbert H. Lang, "Nineteenth Century Historians of the Gulf States" (unpublished Ph.D. dissertation, University of Texas, 1954), 139–40; Franklin L. Riley, "Life and Literary Services of Dr. John W. Monette," *PMHS*, IX (1906), 199–237; *DAB*, VII, 85; David D. Van Tassel, *Recording America's Past: An Interpretation of the Development of Historical Studies in America, 1607–1884* (Chicago, 1960), 127.

which had become a fad in Natchez by 1808. He designed, among other buildings, the Bank of Mississippi structure (1809) and "The Briers" (1812) and added a Greek-Revival front to "Gloucester" (1808) and "Cherokee" (1811). He is also believed to have designed the Georgian mansion "Auburn" (1812), which some modern architects regard as one of the best examples of English Georgian architecture in America. James S. Griffin, who came to Natchez from Baltimore, also designed along Georgian lines; his only known work in the town was "Rosalie" (1820). James Hardy designed several of the later Greek-Revival homes, including "D'Evereux" (1840). George Swainey, who was the architect for a number of Louisiana mansions, may have designed "Dunleith" (1849), one of the most impressive Greek-Revival structures at Natchez.[37]

Six main architectural styles are found in the large houses of the town: French, British, and Spanish Provincial; Southern Plantation; Georgian; and Greek Revival. Most prevalent by far is what is locally known along the Lower Mississippi as Spanish Provincial. About one third of the surviving pre-1861 houses are of this design. It little resembles the "Spanish Colonial" architecture with its Moorish arches, tile-work patios, and thick plastered-brick or adobe construction found from South Texas westward to the Pacific Coast.

Spanish Provincial in Natchez actually encompasses several differing designs. One type has a brick first level and a wooden second story, with the lower level used for storage, livery, offices, or servants' quarters, as at "Concord" (1794), which also has a wide carriage-way through the middle of the bottom level. Another variation is a plain box-like design, such as is found in

[37] Interview with A. Herbert Rodgers, Nashville architect, July 21, 1937, in Mary C. Cunningham, "The Development and Appreciation of Historic Architecture at Natchez, Mississippi" (unpublished M.A. thesis, George Peabody College for Teachers, 1937), 70–71; Edith W. Moore's articles on Natchez homes in Natchez *Democrat* and Natchez *Times*, 1959 Pilgrimage editions. Mrs. Moore's articles are the results of painstaking research in the Spanish and county archives at Natchez. Confused wording in these records makes the dating of some homes approximate.

"Texada Tavern" (1792), which has thick walls of brick and is two stories high, with no porticoes or porches. A third variation resembles the later Southern-Plantation style. An example is "The Gardens" (1786), which has wide, colonnaded galleries, low ceilings, small rooms, massive walls, and heavy shutters. Hand-hewn timbers, fitted with wooden pegs, were used here as in most of the early homes. Over half of the houses now displayed on the Natchez Pilgrimage are of pre-1817 construction, but those built after the territorial period are generally more spacious and grand.

Certain characteristics were common to most of the "big houses" of Natchez irrespective of style. They were located with care so that the settings of moss-hung oaks would best enhance the beauty of the houses. The sites also were usually chosen on elevations, perhaps to minimize the mosquito problem and sometimes to enable the owners to observe their slaves and overseers from the upper windows. In order to provide relief from the semitropical climate, there were high ceilings, large rooms, wide porches, and central halls. The materials used in construction were almost always wood or clay, rarely stone. The timbers and bricks were purchased locally or made by slaves on the place. Furnishings were frequently imported from England or France. The front doors were ornate and thick, with fanlights and sidelights of intricate design, flanked by built-in Corinthian or Doric pilasters. Graceful stairways in the main halls, some in unsupported spiral patterns, were often the most striking interior-design features. Auxiliary wings or separate buildings in the rear provided areas for the kitchen, servants' quarters, planter's office, laundry, and billiard room. Like the ancient Egyptians, the proud nabobs of antebellum Natchez seemed to build for eternity. The solidity and permanence of their dwellings, many of which still stand, have contributed greatly to the popular and scholarly neglect of the commoners' Natchez, which lay beyond the shadow of the white pillars.[38]

[38] Based on U. S. Department of the Interior, *Historic American Buildings*

The most distinctive fact about religion in Natchez is that it was not the influential molder of character and faith that it was in most regions of the Old South. Whereas much of the spiritual apathy that had characterized the southern frontier before 1800 vanished with the onset of the "Great Revival," or "Second Awakening," during the first decade of the 19th century, the revival movement appears to have made very little impact upon the Natchez populace. A study of local church memberships in 1817 indicates that less than 15 per cent of the white adults of Natchez professed any denominational affiliation. On the eve of the Civil War the figure had risen to only 28 per cent.[39] Sparsity of population and isolation from the organized governing bodies of the various denominations undoubtedly were deterrents. But the principal reason for the citizens' indifference to religion seems to have been the fever of materialism that gripped the town from the introduction of the saw gin to the end of the antebellum period. The attitude of the majority was definitely Epicurean, and only a conspicuous few had time for such depressing notions as guilt and sin. Traveler Christian Schultz probably described the hedonistic spirit of the majority quite accurately when he quipped: "All make love; most of them play; and a few make money. With Religion they have nothing to do."[40]

For the first four decades of American control, Natchez Catholics found themselves in a neglected position, owing in part to their isolated position in the Diocese of Baltimore. In 1802 the

Survey No. 17: Outline of the Development of Early American Architecture in Mississippi (Jackson, 1936); Pishel, Natchez; Cooper, Natchez, passim. Studies of antebellum architecture which include data on Natchez are Henry C. Forman, The Architecture of the Old South: The Medieval Style, 1585–1850 (Cambridge, Mass., 1948); T. F. Hamlin, Greek Revival Architecture in America (New York, 1944); James C. Bonner, "Plantation Architecture of the Lower South on the Eve of the Civil War," JSH, XI (August, 1945), 370–88.

[39] Compiled from Session Minute Book, I (1817–72), First Presbyterian Church, Natchez; Trinity Episcopal Church Records, 1826–1852, microfilms, Mississippi Archives (originals at Trinity); Z. T. Leavell and T. J. Bailey, A Complete History of Mississippi Baptists (2 vols.; Jackson, 1904), I, 97–99; Gerow, Cradle Days of St. Mary's, 108, 121; Hawkins, Methodism in Natchez, 73–74, 170–71.

[40] Schultz, Travels on an Inland Voyage, II, 234.

dozen or so remaining Catholic families formed a legal society and bought back part of their church property, which had been confiscated by the American government along with other properties formerly held by the Spanish crown. Petitions were sent by the laity to their bishop requesting that a resident pastor be sent, but for several decades none came to stay and few to visit. In 1815 the dejected Catholics leased their unused church to the city as a public hall, the annual rental being "one Pepper Corn." Two years later tavern keeper Manuel Garcia de Texada bequeathed $1,500 to the church on condition that it be formally organized with a resident priest within two years, but the prerequisite was not met. Other such bequests also went unclaimed.[41]

Renewed hope came with the transfer of their congregation from the supervision of the Diocese of Baltimore to that of the Diocese of New Orleans in 1825. John Nevitt, president of the struggling Roman Catholic Society of Natchez, often communicated with Bishop Nechere in New Orleans, held meetings of the local trustees, and occasionally hosted visiting priests. Nevitt also helped his group to get a satisfactory settlement in 1831 to a legal dispute of long standing with the heirs of William Rutherford over part of the church's downtown property. After long years of patient waiting the local parishioners were informed in 1837 that Pope Gregory XVI had issued "a special brief" establishing a Diocese of Natchez, with a bishop and cathedral to be located in the town. Nevitt, William St. John Elliott, Henry Chotard, and other lay leaders who had worked hard to keep the members faithful over the years rejoiced in anticipation of the new era. Again, however, they had a lengthy wait—it was four more years before a priest could be found who was qualified and interested in the post.

The first bishop was Father John M. J. Chanche, who came in

[41] Richard O. Gerow, *Catholicity in Mississippi* (Natchez, 1939), 32; Gerow, *Cradle Days of St. Mary's,* 8–13; wills of Elizabeth Brooks, 1812, and Manuel Garcia de Texada, 1817, Adams County Records of Wills, I, Chancery Clerk's Records.

1841 and soon won widespread respect. Under him the beautiful cathedral was begun in 1843, but Bishop Chanche was stricken fatally by cholera in 1853, a year before the structure's completion. His successor, the Right Reverend James O. Van de Velde, soon found that "this unhappy Catherdral" had serious problems, "whose difficulties discouraged Mons. Chanche. . . . Our Catholics are almost all very poor . . . a very sad state of affairs." In 1856 Bishop Van de Velde died during an epidemic of yellow fever. Under Father William H. Elder, the next bishop, the church enjoyed some progress, but financial worries continued to plague it. The adult communicants by 1860 may have exceeded 225, but a large proportion of them were Irish and Italian immigrants of great emotional zeal and little financial means.[42]

In 1800 the Presbyterian Synod of the Carolinas sent three missionaries—James Hall, James Bowman, and William Montgomery —to Natchez on a brief evangelical crusade. As the ministers completed their mission and prepared to leave, territorial secretary John Steele and thirty other citizens sent a letter to their Synod superiors praising the missionaries' preaching as "equally interesting, equally engaging" and expressing gratitude for their informative course in "natural philosophy." Hall later wrote the first history of the Mississippi Territory, and Montgomery returned as president of Jefferson College in 1812–13 and pastor of the Pine Ridge church.[43]

Presbyterian churches were established in the years from 1805 to 1807 at Pine Ridge, Church Hill, and Union Church where numbers of Scottish and Scotch-Irish families were settling. Ministers David Ker, James Smylie, and Jacob Rickhow undertook educational work at Natchez and Washington, but no Pres-

---

[42] Gerow, Catholicity in Mississippi, 36–37 Gerow, Cradle Days of St. Mary's, 64, 87, 108–37; James J. Pillar, The Catholic Church in Mississippi, 1837–1865 (New Orleans, 1964), 21–29; Nevitt Record Book, entries of March 26, 1829, May 4, 1830, September 18 and October 20, 1831. Before the Catholic church's reactivation Nevitt sometimes worshipped at the Presbyterian church and pledged funds for the building program of the Washington Methodist church.

[43] James Hall, A Brief History of the Mississippi Territory (Salisbury, N.C., 1801), 32–35; Natchez Mississippi Republican, October 27, 1813.

byterian church was established in Natchez until 1815. In that year "a substantial brick church of good size" was erected on a lot opposite the public square. The First Presbyterian Church was formally organized in 1817 when eight members "in full communion of the Presbyterian and Congregational churches" met at John Henderson's house. Joseph Forman was later chosen as moderator. By early 1818 the church had twenty-one members. New England minister Daniel Smith served as "stated supply" until Irishman William Weier was installed in 1819 as the church's first resident pastor.[44]

The Natchez Presbyterian church grew steadily in numbers, with 49 members on the roll in 1824, 135 in 1837, and 250 in 1860. It attracted many families of the upper-middle-class and aristocracy; and in the students and donations it sent, it became one of the chief supporters of Oakland College. The wealth and optimism of the church is suggested by its construction in 1829 of a sanctuary that could seat 700 persons and an annual salary of four thousand dollars for its minister by 1837. A large manse, still in use, was purchased in 1838 for sixteen thousand dollars. Its ministers often fared well in respects other than salaries. For instance, the Reverend George Potts, who served from 1823 to 1835, acquired "The Elms" and considerable other landed wealth by marrying a daughter of Samuel Postlethwaite, I. The Reverend Joseph B. Stratton, who came to the church in 1843 and remained for sixty years, owned $23,000 worth of real and personal property in 1860, including several slaves. He also became a well-known religious writer, publishing three books.[45]

[44] Session Minute Book, I, entries of March 20–August 30, 1817, First Presbyterian Church, Natchez; Walter B. Posey (ed.), "The First Session Book of the Oldest Presbyterian Church in Mississippi," *JMH*, X (April, 1948), 132–49; Thomas Grafton, "The Scotch at Union Church," *PMHS*, IX (1908), 263–64; Haman, "Beginnings of Presbyterianism in Mississippi," 214–15. The Presbyterian and Congregationalist churches had operated since 1801 under a "Plan of Union" whereby members of both churches might form a single congregation and call a minister of either denomination. The aim was to enable the two churches, both requiring rather highly trained clergy, to compete better with the Baptists and Methodists on the frontier. William W. Sweet, *The Story of Religion in America* (New York, 1950), 211–12.

[45] Session Minute Book, I, various entries of 1829–38, First Presbyterian

Like the Presbyterians, the Natchez Methodists lagged behind their country brethren in church organization. By the time the Reverend Caleb Cloud induced the Natchez laymen to erect the small Cokesbury Chapel in the downtown area in 1807, there were already numerous Methodist churches in Adams, Wilkinson, Claiborne, and Amite counties, usually served by circuit riders. During the territorial era the tiny Natchez congregation could not afford a full-time pastor and therefore shared one with the rural churches nearby.[46]

One of the earliest Methodist preachers on the Natchez circuit was fiery, eccentric Lorenzo Dow. His journal provides a fascinating account of the frontier clergyman's many trials and tribulations. Besides the frequent hostility he encountered at meetings "where some were offended" by his accusations of sinfulness, Dow often made personal pecuniary sacrifices to promote Methodism in the Natchez area. In 1803 he sold his gold watch to buy the lot for the Kingston church, and on several occasions he paid Negro boys to perch in trees and scream at dramatic moments during his Judgment Day sermons. As for Natchez, Dow confessed: "I found it almost impossible to get the people out to meeting any way, and had my scruples whether there were three Christians in town, either black or white."[47]

Supporting Dow's contention in 1811 was the Reverend John Johnson, who found the Natchez whites "very rich, very proud and very polite—exceeding all for compliments," but possessing

Church, Natchez; J. Walton Stewart, Jr., *History of First Presbyterian Church* Natchez, 1955), Francis A. Cabaniss and James A. Cabaniss, "Religion in Ante-Bellum Mississippi," *JMH*, VI (October, 1944), 215–16; Stratton, *Memorial of a Quarter-Century's Pastorate*, 15–57; U. S. Census (1860), MS population and slave schedules. Besides his *Memorial*, Stratton wrote *Confessing Christ: A Manual for Inquirers in Religion* (Philadelphia, 1880) and *A Pastor's Valedictory: A Selection of Early Sermons* (Natchez, 1899). Outside of Natchez proper Presbyterian ministers fared salary-wise about like other Protestant clergymen. Chase to James Smylie, January 19, 1822, Montgomery Papers.

[46] Hawkins, *Methodism in Natchez*, 29–44; Charles B. Galloway, "Lorenzo Dow in Mississippi," *PMHS*, IV (1901), 236–37.

[47] Lorenzo Dow, *History of Cosmopolite: Lorenzo's Journal, Containing His Experience and Travels from Childhood to 1815* . . . (Philadelphia, 1815), 160–61, 212.

"little humility, little religion, and little piety." He added that his year's pay on the Natchez Circuit was $74.50, "and of that the Natchez Church paid not one cent." Other Methodist ministers to serve the Natchez pulpit included William Winans, who became better known as a leader of the movement to promote "Misissippi in Africa"; Thomas Griffin, who won the nickname of "Boanerges," which means "Son of Thunder," for his passionate preaching that resembled the Old Testament's picture of God's wrath against Sodom; and John N. Maffitt, who converted Robert J. Walker, considered to be "an impossible feat" by some members. At least three of the Natchez Methodist ministers left the pulpit to pursue callings as cotton farmers, another became an affluent commission merchant, and one was a drunkard killed in a brawl. Moral standards of laymen, however, were rigidly watched, several being excommunicated in the 1830's for such offenses as quarreling with neighbors or wearing "costly apparel." Among the most competent preachers to serve the Natchez church were William H. Watkins, who led in the formation of the Methodist Episcopal Church, South, in 1845 and later became president of Centenary College in Louisiana; and John G. Jones, who became the chief clerical historian of Methodism in the Old Southwest.

Besides its claim to the most colorful line of ministers of any local church, the Natchez Methodist church could boast of more worthy distinctions. Its mission society, founded in 1835, was the oldest such body in Protestantism in the South. Its Sunday school, which began in 1829, was reputedly the first "in the United States south of Philadelphia." Maffitt's *Mississippi Christian Herald*, established in 1835, became the state's largest church weekly in terms of circulation. Furthermore, probably the most effective evangelical program among Negroes in Mississippi was that of the Natchez Methodist church. By 1840, when it had 160 members, the local Methodist church had already pulled ahead of the other Natchez churches in numbers. With 400 communicants in 1860, it was well ahead of the rest in town.

Most members were drawn from the middle-class merchant element, the key lay leaders including George Dicks, William Mellen, and Isaac Lum.[48]

Although the Mississippi Baptist Association was organized in 1807 and soon had seventeen churches, no Baptist church was founded at Natchez until 1837. The fifty charter members consisted of lower-middle-class families for the most part; merchants John Snodgrass and John Richards were among the most active laymen. The Reverend Ashley Vaughan, a Northerner who "came south in search of health," became the first pastor of the Baptist flock in Natchez. The congregation suffered early from dissension provoked by a "Hardshell" element which opposed aid to foreign missions. Nevertheless, the membership grew rapidly, and by 1860 its 275 members comprised the second largest church body in the town. The spacious First Baptist Church building was constructed in 1851 and had to be enlarged six years later to accommodate the growing congregation.[49]

The idea of Trinity Episcopal Church was born one evening in 1822 when a group of aristocrats at Dr. Duncan's "Auburn" were planning a wedding and discussing the need for a building and minister appropriate for the occasion. By 1823 the well-to-do interested people had raised adequate funds to erect the edifice still in use and had called a minister. The list of early vestrymen

[48] Hawkins, *Methodism in Natchez*, 38–67; John G. Jones, *A Complete History of Methodism as Connected with the Mississippi Conference of the Methodist Episcopal Church, South* (2 vols.; Nashville, 1887), I, 220–23, II, 322, 345–48, 390–92; sundry letters of William Winans, 1813–1815, William Winans Papers, Mississippi Archives; Walter B. Posey, "The Advance of Methodism into the Lower Southwest," *JSH*, II (November, 1936), 450; John B. Cain, *Methodism in the Mississippi Conference, 1846–1870* (Jackson, 1939), 9–87; T. L. Mellen, *Life and Labors of William H. Watkins* (Nashville, 1886), 35–39.

[49] Z. T. Leavell, "Early Beginnings of Baptists in Mississippi," *PMHS*, IV (1901), 248–52; Leavell and Bailey, *Mississippi Baptists*, I, 21–40; Steve Power, *The Memento: Old and New Natchez, 1700 to 1897* (Natchez, 1897), 83; Shields, *Natchez*, 248. Much material relevant to the development of Natchez Protestantism can be found in the following works by Walter B. Posey: *The Development of Methodism in the Old Southwest, 1783–1824* (Tuscaloosa, 1933); *The Presbyterian Church in the Old Southwest, 1778–1838* (Richmond, 1952); *The Baptist Church in the Lower Mississippi Valley, 1776–1845* (Lexington, 1959).

resembled a roll call of the elite: Benjamin Farrar, Richard Ellis, William Minor, Stephen Duncan, William Mercer, Edward Turner, George Winchester, Seargent Prentiss, Joseph Davis (Jefferson's elder brother), Ayres Merrill, Bela Metcalfe, and John Quitman. The best-known Episcopal minister was David C. Page, who, besides his excellent pastoral leadership, was an official in the Mississippi Colonization Society. He is also remembered as the clergyman who performed the marriage ceremony of Jefferson Davis and Varina Howell. A convention was held at Trinity Church in 1826 to establish a Mississippi diocese with Natchez as the diocesan seat, but this was not accomplished until twenty-four years later when the Right Reverend William M. Green was consecrated as the diocese's first bishop. As was generally true elsewhere, the Episcopalian church attracted a large proportion of the religiously inclined aristocrats, but the size of Trinity's membership by 1860 was not impressive.[50]

Little is known about Negro religious life at Natchez before 1817. Daniel Smith, the Presbyterian supply pastor, commented that "when the church was opened last March [1815] I observed no place was assigned to the blacks. The poor creatures were hanging about the doors, afraid to enter." Some house servants probably were allowed to accompany their masters to church but were assigned seats in the rear. The Methodist society which Tobias Gibson organized shortly after 1800 claimed two slaves among its eight charter members. If their owners were active laymen, field hands presumably received some spiritual instruction in the quarters. Until the closing of the African slave trade in 1808 a considerable number of slaves must have been directly imported from the "Black Continent"; many others were no more than one generation removed from Africa. Therefore many animistic practices and superstitions undoubtedly prevailed among

[50] Charles Stietenroth, *One Hundred Years with "Old Trinity" Church, Natchez, Mississippi* (Natchez, 1922), 12–39; Various entries of 1826–35, Trinity Episcopal Church Records; Burger and Capers, "Episcopal Clergy of Mississippi," 59–60; Burger, "Adam Cloud," 95–97; *Journal of the Proceedings of a Convention of the Protestant Episcopal Church in the Diocese of Mississippi Held in Natchez* (Natchez, 1826).

the Negroes. Animism persisted later in that mixture of magic and witchcraft called voodooism which Negroes practiced secretly in the swamps near the town. In religion, music, and dance Africanism remained a powerful influence among many of the local Negroes long after the territorial era.[51]

Joseph Ingraham found that among the slaves who professed Christianity few understood its basic doctrines: "They are apt to consider the name as the thing." The main attraction of religion for most slaves, he believed, was the emotional outlet:

"The religion of most of them is made up of shouting, which is an incontrovertible argument of proof, with them, of conversion. This shouting is not produced generally by the sermon, for few are able to understand a very plain discourse, of which every sentence will contain words wholly incomprehensible to them. But they always listen with great attention, and so they would do were the sermon delivered in any other tongue. A few of the more intelligent and pious negroes, who can understand most of the sermon, perhaps become affected, and unable, like their better disciplined masters, to controll [sic] their feelings, give vent to them in groans and shouts. Those about them catch the infection, and spread it, till the whole Negro portion of the audience in the gallery, becomes affected ostensibly by religious feeling, but really by a kind of animal magnetism, inexplicable and uncontrollable."

Yet Ingraham could not resist balancing this opinion with an illustration of their sincerity: "One of the most touching and eloquent prayers I have ever heard, I recently listened to from the lips of an old negro (who sometimes preached to his fellows), as he kneeled by the pallet of a dying African, and commended in an appeal—which for beautiful simplicity and pathos, is seldom equalled—his departing spirit to God."[52]

No separate Negro denomination existed in Natchez before

---

[51] V. Alton Moody, "Early Religious Efforts in the Lower Mississippi Valley," *MVHR*, XXII (September, 1935), 176; Jones, *Complete History of Methodism*, II, 239. On the survival of Africanisms, see Melville J. Herskovits, *The Myth of the Negro Past* (New York, 1941).
[52] Ingraham, *South-West*, II, 263–64.

1861, but Negro members of the Wall Street Baptist Church had a separate building of their own called the Rose Hill Baptist Church, whose services were attended by a few whites to make the assemblies legal. Ingraham claimed in the 1830's that a majority of the religious slaves of Natchez were Methodists. Bishop Chanche had from 150 to 200 Negroes in his weekly catechismal classes in the 1840's. The Presbyterians added large galleries on each side of their house of worship for the purpose of accommodating slaves. Whether the slaves were given full membership rights, such as voting, is doubtful.[53]

As for religion among the free Negroes, neither Johnson's diary nor other sources shed much light. Johnson gave a small sum to the Catholic church and had his children baptized as Roman Catholics, probably not because he was a Catholic but because he wanted their legitimacy and free status recorded. The free Negro barber subscribed to a Methodist periodical and was buried by a Methodist minister, but there is no evidence of his membership or activity in any church.[54] Johnson's rare mention of churches and preachers may suggest merely his own indifference, or it may indicate that the free persons of color—ever relegated to a twilight zone of existence in white society—refused to be seated in the slave sections of the town's churches.

Unlike many clergymen of the Deep South, the ministers of Natchez generally did not become involved in the proslavery defense and the crusade for secession. It is true that James Smylie, who once preached in the Natchez vicinity, became a vehement champion of the Scriptural defense of slavery, but this wrath was not kindled until the 1830's, after he had become

[53] *Ibid.*, 264; Natchez *Democrat*, February 15, 1959; Gerow, *Cradle Days of St. Mary's*, 265–67; Patrick Thompson, *The History of Negro Baptists in Mississippi* (Jackson, 1898), 25. In predominantly slave-populated Concordia it was reported in 1851 that "religion here is only talked of as one of the by-gones. . . . There are very few people who make any pretensions of religion. . . . There is but one church edifice in the parish [a Methodist church]." *De Bow's Review*, XI (1851), 62.

[54] *Johnson's Diary*, 49–50.

pastor at the nearby town of Fayette.[55] Joseph Stratton, a friend and admirer of New Orleans Presbyterian minister Benjamin M. Palmer, ignored his distinguished colleague's fiery secessionist preaching. Even Palmer's famous Thanksgiving Day sermon in 1860, a fire-eating tirade which the *Free Trader* said "ought to be printed in letters of gold and spread wide-cast among the people," was studiously disregarded by Stratton. When the Charleston shore batteries opened fire the next April, Stratton entered the following simple remarks in his diary:

Apr. 13: News of *takg. Fort Sumter today*—"Quo tendimus?" Apr. 14: Sabbath—Preached in the morng. on the crime of takg. human life—fr. *Ex. 20:13*—in the afternoon at 4—fr. *Rom. 1:20*—The town has been disturbed—by a military parade on the occasn. of the departure of an artillery company to Pensacola.[56]

Just prior to South Carolina's secession, Catholic Bishop Elder had issued a diocesan circular which ignored political issues and called for prayer and fasting, beseeching "the merciful guidance and protection" of Almighty God. Ironically, though most local Episcopalians deplored secession, Bishop Green felt that "our differences are irreconcilable" and joined the fire-eaters' camp.[57] The pastors of the Methodist and Baptist churches, which generally drew more commoners than did the more class-conscious Presbyterian and Episcopalian churches, may have joined the secessionist chant, but no evidence has been found to support such an assertion.

Although the accomplishments in the fields of education, culture, and religion were largely through the efforts of a minority

[55] Smylie to Joseph Montgomery, July 27, 1833, Montgomery Papers, Mississippi Archives.

[56] Diary of Joseph B. Stratton, entries of April 13–14, 1861, LSU; Natchez *Mississippi Free Trader*, December 4, 1860.

[57] Natchez *Mississippi Free Trader*, December 8, 1860; Vicksburg *Whig*, December 29, 1860; John K. Bettersworth, *Confederate Mississippi* (Baton Rouge, 1943), 285–86. On slavery and church attitudes, see also Walter B. Posey "The Slavery Question in the Presbyterian Church in the Old Southwest," *JSH*, XV (August, 1949), 311–24; Posey, "Influence of Slavery upon the Methodist Church in the Early South and Southwest," *MVHR*, XVII (March, 1931), 530–42.

of middle-class leaders, it is true that several Natchez aristocrats were active in such endeavors. Their participation, however, was usually limited to monetary contributions. Churches, like literary societies, found it virtually impossible to turn the heads of most citizens from material pursuits. If Mississippi had a cultural center, the honor goes to Washington rather than to Natchez. Noting that Natchez was heavily sprinkled with men trained at northern universities who had forsaken their professions as doctors and lawyers in the mad chase for cotton fortunes, the *Southern Galaxy* editor lamented and exhorted:

> Our merchants may be enterprising—our professional men may be ambitious and aspiring—beauty, wit and intelligent refinement may adorn our community—but where shall we look for the spirit of science and literature? Almost every city of the Union, of consequence, teems with periodicals, embellished, in a greater or less degree with genius, and extensive research, while Natchez loiters behind—This will not do. . . . We have men who have drunk deeply at the "Pierian spring"— we have females of richly cultivated intellect, and correct taste; let them climb Pindus and Parnassus, and tell us what they see—let them divide among them all the daughters of Jupiter if they will—say, consult Apollo himself, and tell us what they hear.[58]

But Parnassus was not scaled and Apollo was not consulted by the Natchez aristocrats, who found it much easier to purchase beauty than to create it.

[58] Natchez *Southern Galaxy,* October 9, 1828.

CHAPTER X

Amusements, Vices,

and Disasters

RECREATIONAL ACTIVITIES, PASTIMES, AND amusements in antebellum Natchez were limited to some extent for all the people, but less so, of course, for persons of means. From the territorial years onward the most talked-about sporting attraction was horse racing at the well-kept Pharsalia Course, which lay just outside the town near St. Catherine's Creek. The track was owned by the aristocratic Mississippi Jockey Club, in which the Bingamans, Surgets, Minors, and Duncans were key families. David Burney, one of its charter members, is said to have been "the first breeder of fast horses and game cocks in the Territory and a great patron of the turf." Club members often imported horses from abroad, and private race tracks were maintained on several plantations. A visitor in 1817 commented: "The horsemen appeared to me more skillful than those at New Orleans and in [other] parts of America I have seen." Besides Pharsalia and the planters' private tracks, quarter races were held at Natchez under-the-Hill, presumably for those who did not have the wealth or influence to join the Jockey Club.[1]

William Minor and Adam Bingaman took the lead in the 1820's not only in heading the Mississippi Association for Improving the Breed of Horses but also in sponsoring some of the finest race horses in the South. For over two decades the Minor and Bingaman stables, stocked with expensive thoroughbreds, dominated the tracks at Natchez, St. Francisville, and Metairie

[1] Montulé, *Travels in America*, 96; Sparks, *Memories of Fifty Years*, 149; Harrell, "Horse Racing in the Old Natchez District, 1783–1830," 123–29. For activities of Natchez turfmen at other tracks in the Old Southwest, see Arvilla Taylor, "Horse Racing in the Lower Mississippi Valley to 1860" (unpublished M.A. thesis, University of Texas, 1953).

(near New Orleans). Bingaman, a staunch anti-Jackson politi-cian-planter, must have been delighted when his "Henry Clay" defeated Thomas M. Green's "Jackson" in a featured mile race at Pharsalia in 1832. In the early 1840's Bingaman's "Sarah Bladen" won so many races that the nation's principal turf magazine designated her "Champion of the Southwest." Other wealthy Natchez men whose horses vied for honors at Pharsalia were John Perkins, Dr. Lemuel Gustine, and James Hoggatt.[2]

In the 1850's Minor's horses became the most highly regarded on the southwestern tracks after Bingaman moved to New Orleans and withdrew from the sport. By that time the Metairie course was the main drawing card for turfmen of the Lower Mississippi Valley, and Pharsalia was patronized mainly by local people with undistinguished horses. In 1857 Minor said of Pharsalia: "I consider that the 'Pharsalia Course' has been *desecrated* by this mule race. If the Club . . . [survives] it is immortal." His reference was to the practice, begun in the late 1840's, of permitting commoners and even free Negroes to race their horses and mules after the featured events at Pharsalia. Disgusted with the situation, Minor moved his thoroughbreds to a plantation he owned in Ascension Parish, Louisiana. With the departure of Bingaman and Minor, the reputation of Natchez as a horse racing mecca declined rapidly.[3]

The spa at Washington was another local attraction which seems to have suffered as the years passed. In 1809 Fortescue Cuming went to the "delightful spring" which was the nucleus for "a fashionable resort of the neighboring country for miles around." There one could get hot or cold baths for "three eights of a dollar." "Wine, liquors, and spirits are sold," said Cuming, "and I found three or four companies of males and females, seated in the shade of some spreading forest trees enjoying the cool

[2] Natchez *Ariel*, December 1, 1826; Nevitt Record Book, entries of December 4 and 12, 1828, February 18, December 13 and 15, 1832; *Johnson's Diary*, 104–105, 306.
[3] Diary of William J. Minor, entries of April 1, 1849, and March 22, 1857, Minor Papers, LSU; Sitterson, *Sugar Country*, 80.

transparent water either pure or mixed to their taste."[4] However, the spa lost so much business after Washington ceased to be the territorial capitol that it was forced to close. The local aristocrats preferred the more luxurious spas around Nashville and White Sulphur Springs, Virginia.

Fraternal societies at Natchez served a variety of functions, particularly social and recreational, and were largely made up of aristocrats. Before the War of 1812 two local militia units were organized, and they served in minor capacities under General Jackson at New Orleans. They were the Natchez Rifle Corps, led by James Wilkins, and the Adams County Dragoons, led by planters Abram Ellis, Richard King, and Benjamin Farrar. Both continued to drill long after the war. Their main purpose seems to have been to sponsor celebrations on patriotic holidays, affording the men of wealth excuses for large banquets, and to justify the continuation of honorary military titles. It would be difficult to find an antebellum newspaper reference to a Natchez nabob without a title such as "Colonel" or "Major." John A. Quitman, who organized the Natchez Fencibles in the late 1820's and later became the commander of the state militia, was one of several shrewd politicians who found his militia experience socially and politically rewarding. Another form of fraternal society very popular among the upper-class men was the Masonic lodge, the first in Mississippi being founded at Natchez in 1801 (Harmony No. 7); in 1816 a second, Andrew Jackson Lodge, was organized in the town. It will be recalled that Quitman also rose to the top of the state Masonic organization just prior to launching his political career. Fraternal societies that attracted men below the aristocratic level included the Hibernian Society and the Natchez Mechanical Society.[5]

[4] Cuming, Sketches of a Tour, 292–93.
[5] Mississippi Herald and Natchez Gazette, January 6 and June 3, 1806; David Holmes to Ferdinand Claiborne, July 22, 1813, Ferdinand Claiborne Papers, Mississippi Archives; Natchez Mississippi Free Trader, April 1 and 8, 1836; Dunbar Rowland, History of Mississippi, I, 113. Another local militia unit by the 1830's was the Natchez Guards. Other town or county militia companies that

Surely the most popular and time-consuming pastime of the well-to-do was visiting. John Nevitt of "Clermont" dined out several evenings a week and sometimes had as many as fifty guests in his home for supper and all-night card-playing sessions. Richard H. Eggleston of "Learmont" was only a planter of medium-size holdings, but a look at his diary indicates great amounts of time spent in socializing. Three typical days in 1830 will show the round of activities. On January 28 his wife dined at a neighboring plantation, while he dined with another neighbor and visited Poindexter's home still later that evening. On the following day he spent the afternoon visiting with a neighbor and dined at still another home, while his daughter visited in town, returning with three overnight guests. On January 30 Eggleston visited Poindexter in the afternoon and had four adult guests for dinner that evening.[6] Quitman described a normal day's activities at Ferdinand L. Claiborne's home, "Soldier's Retreat," in 1823:

Mint-juleps in the morning are sent to our rooms, and then follows a delightful breakfast in the open veranda. We hunt, ride, fish, pay morning visits, play chess, read or lounge until dinner, which is served at two P.M. in great variety, and most delicately cooked in what is here called the Creole style—very rich, and many made or mixed dishes. In two hours afterward every body—white and black—has disappeared. The whole household is asleep—the *siesta* of the Italians. The ladies retire to their apartments, and the gentlemen on sofas, settees, benches, hammocks, and often, gipsy fashion, on the grass under the spreading oaks. Here, too, in fine weather, the tea-table is always set before sunset, and then, until bed-time, we stroll, sing, play whist, or croquet. It is an indolent, yet charming life, and one quits thinking and takes to dreaming.[7]

existed for short spans were the Hussars and the Adams Light Guards.

[6] Nevitt Record Book, entries of December 16, 1827, and April 17, 1828; diary of Richard H. Eggleston, entries of January 28–30, 1830, Eggleston-Roach Papers, LSU.

[7] Quitman to Colonel Platt Brush, August 23, 1823, in Claiborne, *Quitman*, I, 83–84.

It must be remembered that the above description is of the guests and the ladies. The planters themselves, as many plantation journals attest, were men whose days were often packed with worrisome responsibilities and hard work.

The chief public amusements for commoners were the occasional traveling shows that came to town. A lion, an elephant, and a dromedary offered the principal excitements of the several exhibitions that came to the landing before 1810. A one-man Canadian show was staged at Texada's Tavern in 1808 that consisted of wax figures, bird imitations, and "Herculean balancing and slack wire." Two trained bears were the attraction at the Mississippi Hotel in 1835. A high point in public amusements was the performance in 1836 of a "bold Aeronaut" whose balloon, "Star of the West," ascended at Natchez amidst loud cheers and came to earth in a field fifteen miles away.[8]

Circuses appeared with increasing frequency in the late antebellum years. Most came to Natchez after appearing in New Orleans. The Rockwell Circus entertained in 1848 with a brass band, dog and horse acts, clowns, acrobats, and even a "Spanish Bull Fight." The main excitement, however, was the collapse of Rockwell's large tent. Of a "Mammoth Double Circus" two years later William Johnson commented: "Tis the best Performance of the Kind that I have seen for a Long time if Ever." Tom Thumb, the famous twenty-five-inch-high dwarf who visited the town in 1847, 1848, and 1850, won widespread adulation among the populace.[9]

Johnson, who boasted that he was "always ready for Anything," indulged in pastimes that were probably typical of most young men of the lower classes. In his diary he mentions his skill at

[8] *Mississippi Herald and Natchez Gazette*, February 11, 1806; Natchez *Mississippi Messenger*, January 21, 1808; Woodville *Republican*, December 19, 1835; *Johnson's Diary*, 105; Andrew Oehler, *The Life, Adventures, and Unparalleled Sufferings of Andrew Oehler, Containing an Account of His Travels* . . . (Princeton, 1811), 110–11, 180–81; Treasurer's Reports, I, entry of January 19, 1810, City Clerk's Records.

[9] *Johnson's Diary*, 612, 635–37, 707; Davis and Hogan, *Barber of Natchez*, 195.

shuffleboard, checkers, quoits, marbles, cards, target shooting, broad jumping, high jumping, toy boat races, hiking, raffles, horse racing, fishing, and hunting. Occasionally Johnson found his pleasures in more novel ways: "Nothing new that I know of Except that I won 5 Cegars from Mc[Cary] a shooting with a Blow-Gun this Evening." Since game in the woods and fish in the streams nearby were plentiful, fishing and hunting, which provided both recreation and food, were undoubtedly the most popular pastimes among the lower classes.[10] Much of the unrest and rowdiness among the commoners probably arose from boredom in the absence of a greater variety of innocent diversions.

Organized gambling had been forbidden by municipal ordinances since the territorial period, but it continued to exist. An alarmed journalist reported in 1832 that "in Natchez under-the-Hill the Sabbath as a day of worship is not observed; stores open and gambling dens seethe with negroes and boatmen."[11] When irate Vicksburg citizens hung five professional gamblers for murder in 1835, most of that town's organized-gambling fraternity fled to Natchez. Quitman thereupon hastily organized an Adams County Anti-Gambling Society. Its Committee of Vigilance rounded up a number of gamblers, whipped them severely, and ordered them to leave town. For the next few years little was heard of professional gamblers in Natchez, but in 1840 their renewed activity provoked a citizens' meeting at the courthouse which resolved that "the pickpockets, gamblers & loafers who have no ostensible mode of making a living be allowed forty-eight hours to leave the city, & all those remaining after that time may expect to receive their just dues." Organized gambling does not appear to have made much headway at Natchez after 1840.[12]

[10] Davis and Hogan, *Barber of Natchez*, 69, 74.

[11] Unidentified Natchez newspaper quoted in Nola N. Oliver, *This Too Is Natchez* (New York, 1953), 9.

[12] Murray, *Travels in North America*, 107–108, 175; François Marryat, *A Diary in America* (2 vols.; Philadelphia, 1839), II, 196–201; Fulkerson, *Random Recollections*, 95–97; Natchez *Mississippi Free Trader*, March 12, 1840; Robert M. Coates, *The Outlaw Years: The History of the Land Pirates of the Natchez Trace* (New York, 1930), 276–301. In the summer of 1835 Vicksburg citizens also

The stigma attached to professional gambling had no inhibit-
ing effect upon the widespread practice of informal betting on
card games, billiards, ten pins, horse races, and other activities
with problematical outcomes. John Nevitt, planter and Catholic
leader, often spent his evenings wagering on card games and billiards until the early morning hours. In the years from 1827 to
1832 he won $306 and lost $207 in 24 evenings of billiards. During the same period he won $2,748 and lost $3,306 in 108
evenings of card playing. The most frequent occasions for his
card-playing sprees were after "Mrs. Terrell's oyster supper" each
Saturday night. His companions at "eucre," "brag," "loo," and
"vingt et une" were usually adventurer James Bowie, politician
Seargent Prentiss, attorney Charles Griffin, merchant Phineas
Merrick, former territorial secretary John Steele, attorney Felix
Huston, and Drs. Lemuel Gustine and J. A. Denny. In the same
period Nevitt made twenty-five trips to Pharsalia races, winning
$209 and two hats while losing $245. His wagers were modest
compared to the sums, up to $10,000, gambled by the Minors and
Bingamans at the race track.[13]

Apparently no city ordinance against prostitution was ever
passed, and no citizens' protest movement against the practice
was organized. Prostitution, of course, was well entrenched at
an early stage in the town's history. In 1808 traveler Christian
Schultz found it difficult to make his way to the upper town without being stopped repeatedly by solicitors. When he reboarded
his vessel, he was "so unfortunate as to disturbe [sic] the morning
slumbers of exactly one quarter of a dozen of the copper-coloured
votaries of the Cyprian queen, who it seems had undertaken to
enliven the idle hours of our Canadian crew." Apparently the
city fathers were able to contain the houses of prostitution at the
landing. Planters and merchants, who were often at Natchez
under-the-Hill to conduct business, not infrequently remained
for an evening of assorted pleasures. Of course, with the presence

lynched "ten or a dozen wretches called steam doctors" who were accused of
plotting with outlaw John Murrell to incite a Negro insurrection.
   [13] Compiled from Nevitt Record Book, sundry entries of 1827–32.

of so large a slave population miscegenation was common and may have contributed to less organized prostitution than in river towns farther north.[14]

Excessive drinking was a major contributor to crime and disorder despite the earnest efforts of a small group of temperance crusaders. In 1828 Mrs. White Turpin, wife of a state senator and Jefferson College trustee, organized the Natchez Temperance Society, "comprised of three score and fifteen persons, most of whom are bachelors." Members promised to "refuse to put an enemy in their mouths to steal away their brains." Shortly thereafter a critic using the pseudonym of "Cousin Tabitha" claimed that, while sincere Mrs. Turpin "gathereth them as a hen gathereth her brood under her wings," drinking was common "with at least one half" of the temperance society. Pointing to the example set by their son, a student in a Northern college, the Turpins boasted that he was "determined to show that all the Southern youths that have been to the North shall not return home and enter all kinds of dissipations and extravagances." In 1837 the society founded a temperance journal, *The Cold Water Man,* but it was bankrupt within two years. Some help for the temperance cause came in 1839 when a state law was passed forbidding the sale of liquors in quantities under a gallon and prohibiting the sale of any alcoholic beverages to Negroes, free or slave. Enforcement may perhaps be judged from a statement in the *Courier* the next year: "Hundreds of negroes are nightly drunk in consequence of the attention paid to them by the grog-shops on the roads leading out of Natchez."[15] The local papers do not mention the temperance organization after the early 1840's. Like similar societies in other river towns, the Natchez group probably gave up in despair.

[14] Schultz, *Travels on an Inland Voyage,* 136, 140–41; Ker, *Travels through the Western Interior,* 41; Ideson and Higginbotham (eds.), "A Trading Trip to Natchez and New Orleans, 1822," 388–89; Edith W. Moore, *Natchez Under-the-Hill,* 44–52.

[15] Natchez *Southern Galaxy,* July 15, 1828; Natchez *Courier,* August 13, 1840; White Turpin to Joseph Turpin, October 19, 1835, Drake-Satterfield Papers, Mississippi Archives; *Johnson's Diary,* 309.

Ranking with gambling, prostitution, and drinking as the most popular vices of the town was street fighting, at which boatmen Mike Fink and James Girty became renowned. Schultz witnessed two drunken rivermen vying for the attention of a "Choctaw lady":

> One man said, "I am a man; I am a horse; I am a team. I can whip any man *in all Kentucky*, by G——d." The other replied, "I am an alligator; half man, half horse; can whip any *on the Mississippi*, by G——d." The first one again, "I am a man; have the best horse, best dog, best gun, and handsomest wife in all Kentucky, by G——d." The other, "I am a Mississippi snapping turtle; have bear's claws, alligator's teeth, and the devil's tail; can whip *any man*, by G——d." This was too much for the first and at it they went like two bulls and continued for half an hour, when the alligator was fairly vanquished by the horse.[16]

The upper town and the upper classes were not immune to the pugnacious conduct popularly associated with the lower town's history. Indeed, as the landing became more commercialized in the middle years, street fighting seemed to be more prevalent atop the bluff. In the invaluable Johnson diary for the years 1835–51 over a hundred fights are recorded and sometimes sketched. Quarrels originating over anything from a horse race to ownership of a cheap hat led to fisticuffs, gouging, kicking, and biting, as well as resort to weapons including "chairs, iron bars and sticks, bricks, umbrellas, sword canes, whips, bowie knives, dirks, and pistols." As noted earlier, Negroes were seldom involved, surprisingly, in these disturbances. Combatants represented all white classes, with numerical superiority only slightly favoring the transients and resident Irishmen. The *Free Trader* in 1836 lamented the "many sad consequences resulting from wearing weapons," a practice that had "become almost a passion." A year later the Natchez Fencibles, the principal militia unit, was required to suppress Irish rivermen who rioted in protest against

[16] Schultz, *Travels on an Inland Voyage*, 141.

the city's tax on flatboats.¹⁷ A few months afterward Johnson noted the violent nature of the genteel element:

An Election Came On to day for Major General of 2d Division of Militia of this State, Judge Quitman & Mr Besancon has a fight, Mr Besancon made a thrust at him that would have killed him had not a piece of Silver in the Pocket of the Judge arrested the Progress of the sword, They were Seperated by the Sheriff or some other Gentleman or two—Dr Benbrook and Mr Rivers has a fight The Dr Struck Rivers first with a stick, then Rivers struck him with a Large walking Cane with Both hands a hold of it which Knocked the Dr as flat [as] a flounder, and Struck him twice after that whilst he was down, As soon as he Came to his sinses he hallowed Murder Like a man that was getting murdered.¹⁸

Ever since the establishment of the municipal government the city had employed at least one full-time constable. A sudden rise in violence in the upper town led to the employment in 1838 of a police force of nine men, armed with "short swords." Undoubtedly the enlarged patrol served to curb some of the disturbances and constituted a step toward better protection of life and property. Two years later, however, a disgusted citizen assailed the police as "not worth a baubee" because promptly upon the stroke of midnight the patrol captain "makes it convenient to turn himself and comrades into some convenient place and snore out the balance of the night."¹⁹

In his diary entries for 1841 William Johnson recorded twenty-six fights, five of which involved fatalities. Besides a host of the foreign population, the participants included various prominent persons, among them planters Robert Dunbar and Peter Little, lawyer Ralph North, merchant T. A. Doniphan, probate judge Covington Rawlings, physician Volney Metcalfe, and attorney-politician John Claiborne. Occasions for fights that year included

¹⁷ *Johnson's Diary*, 9; Davis and Hogan, *Barber of Natchez*, 144–45; Natchez *Mississippi Free Trader*, December 8, 1836.

¹⁸ *Johnson's Diary*, 191.

¹⁹ Natchez *Mississippi Free Trader*, March 29, 1838; Natchez *Courier*, August 13, 1840.

militia elections, accusations of lying, horse races, a teacher's flogging of a student, and a lawyer's failure to pay his hotel bill. Fists, whips, and bricks seemed to have been the most popular weapons that year.[20]

Since the Spanish era the favorite dueling ground had been the Vidalia sand bar across the river from Natchez. In territorial times the duelists who exchanged shots on the bar included Benjamin Farrar, William Shields, Ferdinand Claiborne, and Abijah Hunt. The most famous duel there occurred in 1827 when Dr. Thomas H. Maddox faced planter Samuel L. Wells. The party of seconds, assistants, and physicians on each side numbered five, including some of the most respected men of Natchez and Alexandria. Maddox, who wrote the following account of the incident, said the quarrel originated "from some cause which I do not recollect at this time":

I fired across my breast; how he fired I do not know. Two rounds were fired without effect, and the affair was then settled by Mr. S. L. Wells withdrawing all offensive language. We shook hands, and were proceeding to my friends in the edge of the woods to take a glass of wine as a cement. Dr. Denny and myself were a few paces ahead of the rest of the party, when Gen. Cuney, James Bowie, and Jeff. Wells came running down on us; Gen. Cuney saying to Col. Crain that this was a good time to settle their difficulties, he, Cuney, and James Bowie drawing their pistols. Col. Crain saw at a glance how things stood; therefore he shot the one whom he conceived to be "Major General" [Cuney] of the party through the breast, as I believe, and it was so said at the time, for Bowie exclaimed that he was glad that there was so much powder in the pistols, as all the balls passed out. Col. Crain, after shooting at Bowie, who had also shot at him, wheeled around and passed over a little wash in the sand bar, and he and Cuney fired simultaneously at each other, when Cuney fell, mortally wounded, and then Col. Crain, with an empty pistol in his hand, turned to meet James Bowie, who was rushing upon him with his famous "Bowie" knife, and when within reach of his arm, he, Col.

[20] *Johnson's Diary,* 319–58.

Crain, struck him over the head with his empty pistol and brought him to his knees. As he arose, I caught hold of him and he threw me off and faced Wright and the two Blanchards, who had arrived on the field from the edge of the woods. I, at that time, had a pistol pointed at me, but it was not fired, and, being totally unarmed myself, I ran to the edge of the woods, a few paces off, to get my shot gun; and on returning, met Mr. S. L. Wells, who called to me and said: "Doctor, for God's sake don't do any further damage, for it is all over," and on my arrival at the seat of war, to my surprise, I found my friend, Maj. Wright, dead, and Gen. Cuney dying from excessive hemorrhage, Bowie badly wounded, and Alfred Blanchard slightly wounded.[21]

This incident inaugurated a wild four-year period of dueling around Natchez. In fact, less than a month after the Wells-Maddox encounter two well-to-do Natchez planter-attorneys, Aylette Buckner and William Dangerfield, met at the same spot; in the exchange Dangerfield lost his life. An argument over residence requirements for voting in 1828 culminated in Judge James Maury's wounding of John Bonnell. This fray was much disputed in the newspapers since Bonnell retreated into the crowd after firing first and missing. He later admitted that he had violated the strict *code duello*: "After losing my fire, to have remained in a totally defenseless condition and suffer Mr. M. to close upon me with a sword and pistol, requires more of the Hotspur than I find in the composition of my nature." From Bonnell's description it seems that Maury also violated the rules.[22]

In 1832 the new state constitution expressly forbade dueling, and subsequent legislation levied heavy fines upon both challengers and attendants. Moreover, state laws prohibited duelists from holding public office and required the survivor of a duel to pay all debts of the person he killed. Nevertheless, Johnson men-

[21] MS in Thomas H. Maddox Papers, UNC. John Nevitt, who was host to the Maddox party beforehand and witnessed the melee, also left a brief account. See Nevitt Record Book, entry of September 19, 1827. Another description of the incident is in Quitman diary, VI, entry of September 19, 1827, Quitman Papers, UNC.

[22] Natchez *Southern Galaxy*, September 11, 1828.

tioned seven duels in the years 1835–51, and there were probably
several later ones.[23]

An anonymous "Natchezite" published an article in 1826 entitled "The Moral Character of Natchez Defended" in reply to a
Vicksburg editorial attacking his home town. He admitted
that "against the moral character of no city in the U.S. has the
tongue of slander performed its office with more fidelity than it
has against that of Natchez." This he attributed to the fact that
most visitors rarely ventured beyond the landing. He traced the
editorial to the fact that Natchez was "somewhat in the way of
the prosperity of Vicksburg." "Natchezite" contended that Vicksburg was "more vile and wicked" than Natchez, the latter posses-
sing "a spirit of peace and harmony rarely found in a frontier
community."[24] English reform leader James S. Buckingham
visited both towns in 1839 and reached the same conclusion:
Formerly "deemed the worst point along the whole valley for the
haunt of gamblers, thieves, and ruffians of every country and
state," Natchez had yielded to Vicksburg "the palm of pre-
eminence in this respect."[25] Charles A. Murray, another English
visitor in the 1830's, commented that the lower town, once considered "the most abandoned sink of iniquity in the whole Western country," was "much improved."[26]

Nevertheless, occasional incidents offered reminders of the wild
days of yore. In 1852 Captain "Roaring Jack" Russell of the
steamboat *Constellation* tied his landing ropes to a "house of
robbers" at the landing and threatened to pull the structure into
the river if the occupants did not return the money they had
stolen from his passengers. As the paddle wheels began to churn,
the thieves hastily surrendered the loot. Two years later, thirteen
fugitive slaves from the country murdered the crew of a flatboat

[23] Henry S. Foote, *Casket of Reminiscences* (Washington, 1874), 180–86;
Davis and Hogan, *Barber of Natchez*, 167; Wilmuth S. Rutledge, "Dueling in
Antebellum Mississippi," *JMH*, XXVI (August, 1964), 181–91.

[24] Natchez *Gazette*, October 28, 1826.

[25] Buckingham, *Slave States of America*, I, 449.

[26] Murray, *Travels in North America*, II, 176–77.

at the landing and stole its cargo.[27] The rarity of such episodes by the 1850's, however, allowed Vicksburg undisputed supremacy in squalor, vice, and general rowdiness.

More damaging to the town's reputation than its vice was the persistent recurrence of epidemic diseases. Yellow fever hit the town almost yearly during the late summer and early fall months, reaching epidemic proportions in 1823, 1826, 1837, 1839, and 1853. It exacted death tolls of 312, 150, 207, 235, and over 750 people, respectively, in those years. John Quitman wrote in 1823 that whole families had been "exterminated." The mere word that there were cases of "Yellow Jack" at the landing in 1825 resulted in an almost complete exodus, with weeds growing ten feet high on the main streets by late September. The epidemic of 1837 killed 39 citizens in one week, including 5 physicians and the chairman of the city's health board. Extant family letters frequently include week-by-week reports on the town's "healthiness." William Minor, for example, rejoiced in 1827 that the town was "untimed healthy as late as the 23rd of August" and cautiously predicted that "the town may entirely escape the season." Yellow fever produced death, confusion, and despair, paralyzing commercial, political, and church activities and bringing the life of the community to a standstill for weeks. Some northern insurance companies exacted higher premiums from Natchez citizens who remained at home during the summer while others refused altogether to insure them.[28] Joseph Stratton, longtime Presbyterian minister at Natchez, left a vivid description of the impact of the devastating scourge of 1853:

Up to that date I had never witnessed a visitation of the yellow fever in a general and unequivocal form. The security in which we had allowed ourselves to fall was suddenly broken that year by the appearance of several cases of this dreaded disease, as early as August;

[27] Philip Paxton [Samuel A. Hammett], *A Stray Yankee in Texas* (New York, 1853), 407–408; Natchez *Courier*, April 19, 1854; Ingraham, *South-West*, II, 41–42; Lyell, *Second Visit to the United States*, II, 163; Wood, *Autobiography*, I, 429.

[28] Natchez *Ariel*, September 29, 1825; Natchez *Mississippi Free Trader*, October 5, 1837; Natchez *Courier*, December 2, 1839; William Minor to Mrs. Katherine Minor, September 27, 1827, Minor Papers, LSU; John Quitman to Albert Quitman,

and in a short time its presence in the city was acknowledged by the public authorities. Many of you will remember the panic which ensued. The portion of the population which could escape fled, as from an invading foe, to such places of shelter as they could find in the country. The residue, consisting to a large extent of unacclimated persons, remained to wait their fate. There were few of them whom the pestilence did not reach; and many of them it carried to the grave. For nearly four months the places of business were generally closed. The grass literally sprung up in our untrodden streets; and the silence, not of a Sabbath, but of a funeral hour, hung over our usually bustling city. . . . The scourge slowly withdrew itself; the last victim was a beautiful and gifted young lady, who had in a false confidence returned from her retreat to the town, and whom we laid in her grave on the 6th of December; and then, as I believe generally happens after such appalling disturbances of the public composure, the tide of life and business and pleasure flowed back again as buoyantly as tho eternity had not been flashing its light upon the vanity of them all.[29]

The Natchez Charitable Association was born in August, 1853, just as the disease was reaching epidemic proportions. It became the most valuable relief agency in the area for the next seven years. Robert Walker, a small merchant of no kinship to politician Robert John Walker, became the president and guiding force behind the society as it endeavored to raise funds to help victims of the epidemic. The town was divided into ten districts, and members were appointed in each district to report weekly on needs. Between August, 1853, and February, 1854, the association raised and expended $9,341 upon provisions for yellow fever patients and orphans. St. Mary's Orphan Asylum and the Protestant Orphanage (the Female Charitable Society's home) were each given $1,250 during those months. The hardworking district relief chairmen were all downtown busi-

October 1, 1823, Quitman Papers, Mississippi Archives; De Bow's Review, VI (1848), 226; Board of Health Minute Book, I, sundry entries of 1818–22 and 1854–60, City Clerk's Records.
   [29] Stratton, Memorial of a Quarter-Century's Pastorate, 55–56.

nessmen, and most had served as selectmen.[30] Few of the aristocrats would have been available for such duties had they been so disposed, for most had fled to the North or to their country estates. In later years when less severe attacks of yellow fever, cholera, and smallpox struck the town, Walker's group continued to function with efficiency and generosity. Ironically, Robert Walker the merchant was of more valuable service to his town than was Robert Walker the politician.

In spite of their cooperation in relief efforts, many businessmen continued to oppose the quarantine measures of the city's board of health. Enlightened physicians like John Monette and Luke Blackburn were able to convince only a few that ship arrivals had more to do with the appearance of the dreaded "Yellow Jack" than did building excavations. Chafing over the merchants' success in withdrawing the quarantine during a light epidemic, young Rebecca Mandeville wrote in October, 1858: "The yellow fever still increases but is mostly confined to the poorer classes, and now that the Quarantine is drawn up I suppose that it will be worse than ever—for that was all that kept strangers from coming here."[31] Few businessmen of that day would have agreed with the wisdom of the girl's statement.

Epidemical crises were only the most conspicuous of many occasions when doctors and patients revealed ignorance of the causes and cures of illnesses. In 1844 the popular "Thomsonians," who practiced "botanic" medicine at their Natchez Botanic Hospital, won a court decision permitting them to continue work without further pressure from the county board of medical censors. Druggists regularly prescribed without authorization from licensed physicians. One of their most profitable remedies was the imported leech, which, upon proper application to the nape of the neck, was guaranteed to cure a number of ills from com-

[30] Natchez Charitable Association Minute Book, entries of August 24 and September 16, 1853, and March 7, 1854, City Clerk's Records.

[31] *Johnson's Diary*, 59, 691–92; Sydnor, *Wailes*, 138–40; Board of Health Minute Book, I, entries of September-November, 1858, City Clerk's Records; Rebecca Mandeville to Henry D. Mandeville, October 17, 1858, Mandeville Papers, LSU.

mon colds to toe aches and skin rashes. Druggist P. H. McGraw happily advertised that he had "two thousand French Leeches, warranted of the best quality, imported and for sale"; his rival, W. H. Fox, was selling "real Hungary Leeches."[32] Quitman's daughter Louisa wrote him in 1845 describing an illness of her sister and Dr. Samuel Cartwright's treatment, which may have been mild for that era: "In the afternoon she slept constantly, frequently starting up suddenly, after tea her mind appeared to be wandering, mother became alarmed and sent again for the Doctor. He told us that her head was affected and that leeches must be applied. He gave her a dose of medicine which she threw up, with a shiny, tough looking substance. He prescribed castor oil and spirits of wormwood to be taken twice, and also some powders. . . . This morning she is much better."[33]

The greatest threat to property in Natchez was fire. After several devastating conflagrations in 1825 the *Ariel* editor penned an urgent appeal for more and better fire-fighting equipment: "Must we await to be enveloped with the smoking ruins of our homes . . . before we awake from dreams of fancied safety? . . . We hear from all parts of the most distressing occurrences by fire."[34] Five major fires are recorded in Johnson's diary, 1836–40, besides innumerable smaller ones: twenty-eight buildings burned in 1836; five in 1837; four in 1839; one entire downtown block in 1839; and twenty buildings at the landing in 1840. Sometimes the fire bells tolled for conflagrations on steamboats, as in 1835 when the steamboat *Walk in the Water*, along with 1,200 bales of cotton, a runaway boy, a pet bear, and a barkeeper, burned at the landing. By 1847 the city's fire-fighting program consisted of three volunteer companies and four full-time salaried firemen, which, if judged by the complaints in the newspapers, was still far from adequate.[35] The sense of fear and insecurity

---

[32] Davis and Hogan, *Barber of Natchez*, 179, 186.
[33] Louisa Quitman to John A. Quitman, June 11, 1845, Quitman Papers, UNC.
[34] Natchez *Ariel*, December 19, 1825.
[35] Natchez *Mississippi Free Trader*, December 11, 1835; Davis and Hogan, *Barber of Natchez*, 172–75; Selectmen Minute Book, IV, entry of July 21, 1847, City Clerk's Records.

which gripped the citizens as fire bells echoed through their flimsy structures was exceeded only by the horror of "Yellow Jack."

Although not a direct threat to the upper town, flooding at the landing and in the flat plantation stretches across the river produced temporary confusion and turmoil in Natchez. Livestock herds were hastily transported through the narrow streets atop the bluff en route to drier pastures east of the town. Residents from Concordia Parish and Natchez under-the-Hill crowded into whatever public and private quarters they could find in the upper town until the muddy Mississippi waters receded. Beginning in 1809, the great river hurled widespread floods upon the bottom lands west and south of Natchez every second year with disastrous regularity for the next two decades. The worst antebellum inundations in the Natchez area came in 1811, 1815, 1828, and 1840. After the flood of 1828, which marked the all-time high for the Mississippi before 1897, the *Southern Galaxy* pleaded for the "serious attention of our Legislature" to the need for levees constructed with public funds, but nothing of significance was done. In the 1830's the legislature authorized boards of police in the Delta counties to build levees with funds obtained through a special tax upon landowners with frontage on the river. Levee building began in earnest in the early 1850's when Congress transferred title to several million acres of unsold lowlands along the Mississippi to the state governments of Mississippi and Louisiana for flood-control projects. Up until this time little of the state's levee-building efforts benefited Natchez since most of the local citizens' overflow lands lay in Concordia Parish. Because of the high degree of Mississippi ownership of those lands, the Louisiana legislature was also slow to act.[36]

Ranking next to the yellow fever epidemic of 1853 as the

[36] Monette, "The Mississippi Floods," 442–48; William D. Jenkins, "The Mississippi River and the Efforts to Confine It in Its Channels," *PMHS*, VI (1902), 294–304; Natchez *Southern Galaxy*, September 26, 1829; Bettersworth, *Mississippi*, 248–49.

worst single disaster to strike the town was the tornado which hit suddenly on May 7, 1840. Conservative estimates placed the property loss at five million dollars. The death toll at Natchez was at least three hundred, with another six hundred suffering serious injuries. Scores more died as the twister continued several miles into the countryside to the east. One steamboat docked at Natchez under-the-Hill when the tornado hit was found adrift two weeks later near Baton Rouge with fifty-one bodies aboard. Eight years later Sir Charles Lyell, the English geologist, could still find numerous evidences of the tornado's havoc and was told that the disaster had seriously "checked the progress of Natchez."[37] According to Horatio Eustis, who was visiting at Henry Chotard's "Somerset," just east of town, on the day of the catastrophe, the tornado

demolished entirely the lower town leaving but one house standing there. In the upper town which is built mostly of brick many of the larger edifices, such as the Hotels, the churches, and the railroad Depot, were either levelled with the dust or so minced that the walls must come down. The force of the wind was incredible. Iron spikes were borne by the blast with such force and direction as to be driven up to their heads, into the walls of houses. Other walls were pierced (even interior partitions) by pieces of shingles lanced from roofs a hundred rods distant. Men who were able to clutch hold of something firmer, were stripped perfectly naked. The present estimate of lives lost, is about 300, principally at the landing on the river bank where nearly every flat boat and steamboat was sunk or destroyed. The hurricane [tornado] passed just at the dinner hour [about 1:15 P.M.] of the town, or the loss, on land, would have been greater. . . . Contributions are daily arriving for the relief of the distressed, but years must pass before the town can be rebuilt as before, and the trees, which furnished a grateful shade in the principal streets, cannot be replaced. Much damage was done to some of the plantations in the uplands, and negroes killed. How far it extended into the interior is not yet ascer-

[37] Natchez *Mississippi Free Trader*, May 23, 1840; Natchez *Courier*, May 30, 1840; Lyell, *Second Visit to the United States*, II, 152–53.

tained. Poor Natchez has now suffered from fire, pestilence and storm within the circuit of a year.[38]

The reader must disabuse himself of romantic notions if he is to comprehend the way of life in antebellum Natchez. The types of pleasures and vices in which both commoners and aristocrats indulged were dictated mainly by an overpowering sense of boredom and monotony. This feeling can hardly be appreciated even after a visit to a small backwoods town of today. Likewise, the antebellum residents' sense of insecurity of life and property, born of recurrent incidents of human violence and natural catastrophe, permeated all social classes to a depth that cannot today be adequately probed. The pleasures, vices, and disasters of antebellum Natchez, however, were not unique. The reader who has examined life in other frontier communities and river towns will be impressed more by the similarities than by the contrasts in conditions at Natchez when compared with other antebellum towns of the West and Southwest. Natchez was neither an infamous den of iniquity nor a romantic abode permeated by genteel ideals. As early as the 1820's the atmosphere of its lower town could not be markedly differentiated from that of the section atop the bluff. Rather, the way of life of its citizens, rich and poor, white and black, was characterized by the common urges for release from boredom and assurance of security.

[38] Horatio Eustis to General A. Eustis, May 17, 1840, Horatio Eustis Papers, Mississippi Archives.

CHAPTER XI

Exciting Times and Excitable

Citizens

FOR A TOWN ISOLATED FROM THE MAIN centers of population, antebellum Natchez was unusually alert to national issues. The views of its citizenry were generally in line with majority opinion in the Old South. But the town was unique among small Southern communities in the large number of activists it produced in the expansionist and state-rights movements, especially in the years before 1850.

Over the cracker barrels in Natchez stores, expansionist talk, whether about Texas, Cuba, or elsewhere, produced more interest than discussion of the city's problems. Texas had claimed a special place in Natchez hearts ever since the late 1790's when Philip Nolan, Walter Burling, and other local traders brought back news of the Southwest's fine horses and fertile plains. Dr. James Long, a Natchez physician, led two foolhardy, disastrous expeditions of local volunteers to liberate Texas in 1819–21. A number of Natchez residents moved to eastern Texas when the Mexican government opened lands for American settlement in the mid-1820's. Duncan Walker, a prominent local attorney, was imprisoned and tortured by the Mexicans in 1835 for allegedly inciting revolution in Texas. Two years later Robert Walker, his brother, introduced the resolution in the United States Senate for recognition of the Republic of Texas. Senator Walker was also an ardent advocate of annexation of the Lone Star Republic.[1]

The inexplicable popularity of Texas in Natchez eyes was exploited politically by John A. Quitman as well as by Walker.

[1] James E. Winston, "Mississippi and the Independence of Texas," *Southwestern Historical Quarterly*, XXI (July, 1917), 36–37; Shenton, *Walker*, 22–24.

In 1835 Quitman presided over a large public meeting in Natchez to raise funds for the beleaguered Texans. Through benefit dramas and other mediums the townsfolk soon raised over $14,000 for the Texas coffer. The next spring Quitman and nearly one hundred Natchez volunteers marched off to assist the Texans in their war of independence. Though Quitman's warriors did not get beyond Nacogdoches before the hostilities ended, they returned home in May, 1836, to receive accolades worthy of the conquerors of an empire. Quitman had satisfied his own expansionist urge temporarily, assured himself that his investment in 23,000 acres of Texas lands was safe, and reinforced his popular support for future political ventures.[2]

Meanwhile, Felix Huston, a Natchez attorney who had accompanied the Quitman expedition, was appointed temporary commander of the Texas army for several months after Sam Houston became president of the new republic. Huston was thus enshrined forever in his fellow townsmen's hearts as a hero of the Texas Revolution. On the other hand, Santa Anna, the "villain," encountered loud jeers when he stopped briefly at the Natchez landing while en route to a meeting with President Jackson.[3]

The Mexican army invaded South Texas again in 1842, and the old Natchez sympathy for the Texans was rekindled, with Quitman happily returning to the crusade. For the next four years he made speeches encouraging local men to go to the aid of Texas and journeyed to Washington to lobby for annexation of Texas in 1845. When the Mexican War broke out in 1846, Quitman was appointed a brigadier general and authorized to raise a force of

[2] Natchez *Mississippi Free Trader*, April 1 and 8, 1836, and May 20, 1848; Winston, "Mississippi and the Independence of Texas," 38; James H. McLendon, "John A. Quitman in the Texas Revolution," *Southwestern Historical Quarterly*, LII (October, 1948), 163–83; McLendon, "John A. Quitman," 131, 133–36.

[3] *Johnson's Diary*, 154; William R. Hogan, *The Texas Republic: A Social and Economic History* (Norman, 1946), 281–82. Huston's only distinction (if so it was) as commander of the Texas army came in his unsuccessful efforts to launch an invasion of Mexico. Prior to taking command, he engaged in a duel with Albert Sidney Johnston, wherein the future Confederate general was seriously wounded.

Mississippi militiamen to serve in the conflict. The Mississippians, including over two hundred from Natchez, distinguished themselves in the Monterrey and Mexico City campaigns. With the capture of the Mexican capital, Quitman was appointed military governor of the city until the withdrawal of American troops a few weeks later.[4]

Returning to Natchez in November, 1846, Quitman was received more wildly than ever, and there was much talk of running him for governor. Free-Negro Johnson quipped: "Gen. Quitman was Glorified to day—in fine state." Captain James Cox toasted the general at a dinner: "When the American cannon and rifle, on the afternoon of September 13th, roared at the gates of the City, Mexico cried out, 'Who's dat knocking at the door?' The answer was 'John A. Quitman, a Natchez Fencible.'"[5] The image of Quitman the military hero was undoubtedly attractive to voters in his successful gubernatorial bid three years later.

The new excitement in Natchez by the end of 1848 was the California gold rush. As in towns throughout the nation, numbers of Natchez men, chiefly young bachelors, abandoned their jobs to make the arduous trek to California. Absalom F. Dantzler, one such youth, wrote to his older brother in Natchez that the next day he expected to discover his first gold in the Sacramento Valley: "I think that I am now in the high way to fortune and will reap a rich reward for all the troubles, dangers, and hardships that I have passed through in geting [sic] here."[6] The largest stake claimed by Natchez residents, or ex-residents, was that of the New Almaden quicksilver mining syndicate, formed by William Gwin and Robert Walker. Gwin, who had lived in Natchez briefly, moved to California in 1849 and quickly won

<hr />

[4] Natchez *Mississippi Free Trader*, April 7, 1842; Natchez *Courier*, April 1, 1842, and October 19, 1847; Adjutant General Richard Jones to Brigadier General John A. Quitman, July 15, 1846, Quitman Papers, Mississippi Archives; McLendon, "John A. Quitman," 197–287; James E. Winston, "Annexation of Texas and the Mississippi Democrats," *Southwestern Historical Quarterly*, XXV (July, 1921), 21–22.

[5] *Johnson's Diary*, 595; Natchez *Courier*, November 30, 1847.

[6] Absalom F. Dantzler to "Brother," September 13, 1849, Dantzler Papers, Duke.

political success. The New Almaden enterprise, however, brought him and Walker numerous claims suits but no profits. Although newspaper notices of local citizens departing for California in 1848–49 are frequent, no evidence was found that any of the emigrants discovered there "the highway to fortune."[7]

The expansionist impulse in Natchez was directed next toward Cuban filibustering. Quitman recruited volunteers and funds in Natchez for General Narciso Lopez's several attempts to invade Cuba in 1849–51. John Henderson, a Natchez commission merchant and state senator, was also active in the Lopez ventures and boasted that "over half of all the cash advanced to the enterprise" of Lopez in 1851 came from his firm. Quitman and Henderson were indicted in 1850 on charges of violating the federal neutrality law. Though the charges were dismissed after several mistrials, Quitman resigned as governor and Henderson as state senator in early 1851. During their trials the Natchez *Courier* hurled invectives against the federal government for falsely accusing "innocent Americans" who had not taken part in a "military expedition" since the Mexican War.[8]

Undeterred, Quitman and his cohorts made several trips to New York in 1852–54, where they plotted with a Cuban rebel junta for a much larger invasion than the disastrous one of 1851, which had cost Lopez and many volunteers their lives. But in June, 1854, Quitman, Henderson, Felix Huston, and Joseph Thacher, all of Natchez, were arraigned before a federal grand jury on new charges of violating the neutrality statute.[9] The *Courier* again was quick to come to their defense, castigating President Pierce's inconsistent policy on filibusters.[10]

The charges against the men were dropped because of lack of evidence, whereupon they resumed their invasion plans. By

[7] Natchez *Mississippi Free Trader*, December 29, 1848, and May 5, 1849; Shenton, *Walker*, 128–29.
[8] Natchez *Courier*, March 19, 1851; Claiborne, *Quitman*, II, 70; Ray Broussard, "Governor John A. Quitman and the Lopez Expeditions of 1851–1852," *JMH*, XXVIII (May, 1966), 103–20.
[9] McLendon, "John A. Quitman," 331–40.
[10] Natchez *Courier*, June 10, 1854.

October, 1854, Quitman believed that he could count on 3,000 volunteers for the Cuban attack, including 250 men from Natchez. The main supply depot and rendezvous point was a country store on Bayou Boeuf in Louisiana. A supply of a thousand cannon, four thousand pounds of gunpowder, five hundred muskets, and seven hundred barrels of grapeshot was stored there for the invasion. But for unexplained reasons, probably depletion of funds, Quitman and his Natchez friends suddenly withdrew from the scheme, and the most ambitious of all Cuban filibusters was never launched.[11] Thereafter the Natchez citizens became more absorbed in the mounting sectional conflict. The final words on filibustering to appear in Natchez newspapers was an editorial in the *Free Trader* in 1858 warning that, if the federal government did not become more aggressive on expansion into Latin America, the South would take the initiative, "and any attempt to suppress them in their action will only lead to bitter sectional strife and dissention [*sic*]."[12]

The excitability of the Natchez populace over expansionist issues and filibusters was equalled by their emotional intensity over presidential elections. The presence of a wealthy, influential Whig minority and an active Democratic majority in Natchez produced some heated, colorful campaigning during presidential-election seasons. As was probably true in most communities, voters were attracted or repelled more by personalities and campaign gimmicks than by platforms and profound issues.

An almost blind hero-worship of Andrew Jackson gripped most of the townsmen, somewhat obscuring party loyalties at times. As noted earlier, Jackson polled heavy majorities in Natchez pre-

[11] Ezra and Maunsel Bennett's Bayou Boeuf store daybook, X, entries of December 16, 1854–February 12, 1855, Ezra Bennett Papers, Louisiana State University at Alexandria; McLendon, "John A. Quitman," 341–45. In the summer of 1855 John L. Ford of Texas tried to interest Quitman in a filibustering expedition against Mexico: "I will cheerfully consent to follow *your* lead. My anxiety is for the South. I desire to see the Slave States in possession of material guarantees for the present security of slavery and for the future expansion of the area of slave territory." Quitman rejected the proposition. John L. Ford to Quitman, July 2, 1855, Quitman Papers, University of Virginia.

[12] Natchez *Mississippi Free Trader*, January 5, 1858.

cincts in each of his three presidential races. Editor Andrew Marschalk summed up the general feeling about "Old Hickory": "Mr. Adams may be admired by his friends as a politician, but Andrew Jackson is beloved by his as a man." From 1816 onward the anniversary of Jackson's victory at New Orleans, January 15, was celebrated in Natchez mainly as a memorial to a man. His appeal was based more on his many local acquaintances and his military record than on his position in national politics. It will be recalled that military traditions and punctillio had long been of social significance, even though few in Natchez could prove what rank their grandfathers held in the British army or where the Natchez Rifles were at New Orleans. Many Natchez Whigs, such as Adam L. Bingaman, found no discrepancy in idolizing the man and despising his party. Seargent Prentiss once remarked in disgust about the Democrats' exploitation of Jackson's personal appeal: "The sum and substance of all the arguments of the party—*Hurrah for Jackson!*" When the old general died in 1845, Dr. Samuel Cartwright eulogized him before a large assembly in Natchez comprised of both Whigs and Democrats. The Democratic *Free Trader* commented that on the subject of Jackson the man, "party spirit was forgotten and party differences were thrown aside."[13]

Opposition to Jackson was relatively mild around the town prior to the South Carolina nullification controversy. A few aristocrats, led by wealthy Stephen Duncan, constituted the anti-Jackson faction. Even their objections concerned mainly the threat of democratic excesses if his despicable backwoods-following gained control of the state government. The following circular of 1828 epitomizes this feeling:

The partizans of Mr. Adams, we are not; yet it would be doing him great injustice, not to accord him . . . (when compared with his only competitor) superior fitness for the chief magistracy of our Union. . . .

[13] *Mississippi Statesman and Natchez Gazette,* February 22, 1827; Prentiss (ed.), *Memoir of S. S. Prentiss,* I, 166; Natchez *Mississippi Free Trader,* July 15, 1845.

Of General Jackson we would speak with a respect becoming ourselves, and due to his important services in the late war. . . .
Finally, we believe our union to be the work of our political
safety. . . . We, therefore, dread the election of General Jackson, as
much (if possible) on account of *the violence of many of his ad-
herents,* as of his own peculiar unfitness for the station. . . .

Respectfully,

Stephen Duncan	Alvarez Fisk
Beverly R. Grayson	Adam L. Bingaman
Samuel Gustine	Felix Huston
Francis Surget	James K. Cook[14]

Writing to his brother in 1826, Thomas Shields, a local Adams
supporter, sensed how much the personality factor would play
in the next presidential election as far as Natchez citizens were
concerned: "There is an organized opposition to the present
administration & I regret to see it—Whatever tends to the public
good . . . ought to be supported without a reffereance to any one
man or set of them watever."[15] Shields' criterion was seldom
applied by Natchez voters, however, when the candidate was
the "Hero of New Orleans."

Nevertheless, famous Whig politicians were also widely feted
when they came to Natchez. Henry Clay, an intimate of William
St. John Elliott and other Natchez aristocrats, visited the town
on numerous occasions, always welcomed with extravagant ceremonies and social events. His more timely visits came in 1842
and 1844, prefatory to his race against James K. Polk for the
presidency. When General Zachary Taylor visited the community in 1847 as the conquering hero and Whig presidential
aspirant, Johnson reported that his reception was "a warm and
enthusiastic one." The *Courier* claimed on that occasion that "all
was enthusiasm, all was joy, all was gladness." Among Taylor's
most avid followers were Bingaman, who won a $200 bet on his

[14] Broadside by Stephen Duncan and others, January 7, 1828, Wailes Papers,
Mississippi Archives.
[15] Thomas Shields to William F. Shields, March 26, 1826, William F. Shields
Papers, Mississippi Archives.

election, and attorney George Winchester, who led the Adams County Rough and Ready Club in the Whig campaigning in 1848. When Taylor died in 1850, a solemn mock funeral was held in Natchez, attended by a large crowd.[16]

A zenith in Natchez fervor over national campaigns, however, had been reached in 1840 when Whig leaders made a major effort to carry the area for William Henry Harrison. The opposing Democrats' key weapon was a personal visit by Jackson early that year. But Whigs, by some means, grabbed the main positions on the welcoming and program committees; Quitman, for example, headed the arrangements committee, and Bingaman delivered the major address. For obvious reasons, Jackson's reception at Natchez was that of a military hero rather than of a Democratic campaigner for Martin Van Buren. Not only were local Democrats disappointed over the complete de-emphasis of the political nature of the ex-President's visit, but also they were downcast when his stay was cut short by a lung hemorrhage. By that summer the Whig campaign was obviously the more spirited and better organized. Bingaman headed the Adams County Tippecanoe Club, whose members built a picturesque log cabin on the commons and held frequent rallies there.[17] The *Courier* said of one such meeting: "The Whigs of Natchez rallied at the Cabin by hundreds on Sat. night. Old Saratoga [a cannon on the bluff] sent forth her best thunder, and shouts of triumph went up most cheerily. Speeches were made by Thomas Armat, Esq., H. D. Mandeville, Esq., Colonel A. L. Bingaman and Simon Murchison, Esq. Mr. Mandeville was uncommonly happy and eloquent."[18]

Another effective device of the Tippecanoe Club that year was a huge ball, which was rolled around the streets while its pushers sang "Hail to the ball which in grandeur advances" and shouted "Harrison and two dollars a day and roast beef." Barber William

[16] Natchez *Courier*, December 24, 1847, and September 19, 1848; Diary of William J. Minor, entry of June 5, 1847, Minor Papers, LSU; *Johnson's Diary*, 600, 740.
[17] Natchez *Mississippi Free Trader*, January 16 and April 8, 1840; Jackson *Mississippian*, December 22, 1836.
[18] Natchez *Courier*, September 1, 1840.

Johnson, a Democratic sympathizer, gleefully noted just before election day: "The Greate Humb Bug Ball was stollen Last Night by Some one that has more sense than the man who made it, and Demolished the thing, and rolled it down the Bluff."[19] When the celebrating over Harrison's victory was done, however, Natchez Whigs still faced the sober reality that the governor's chair, the congressional seats, and a majority of the places in the state legislature were held by Democrats.

The rise of sectionalism within the nation during the years 1820–60 was reflected rather gradually in the changing outlook of the Natchez citizenry. No strong sectional feeling was evident during the Missouri controversy of 1819–21. In one of its few references to the Missouri Compromise debates Marschalk's *Mississippi State Gazette* calculated the amount of time spent by the members of Congress in speeches on the Missouri issues and chided them for forgetting that "Time is Money," which could be better invested in more important matters. Richard C. Langdon's *Mississippi Republican* was one of the few Southern newspapers which generally favored some form of congressional control over slavery in the territories. The paper assumed that the Northern position was based "only on principles of humanity —on a deep interest for the honor and character of the nation and regard for the future safety of the Southern States—What other motives can they have?" The three Mississippians in Congress, including Thomas Williams and Christopher Rankin of Natchez, voted in favor of most of the Compromise measures.[20] Eden Brashears, a Natchez shopkeeper, probably expressed the sentiments of most of his fellow townsmen when he wrote: "The People of that Territory ought to be the best Judges, as to what would be most to their Interests and advantages—and the less Legislating on this subject the better for the present."[21]

[19] Port Gibson *Correspondent*, November 27, 1840; *Johnson's Diary*, 304.
[20] Natchez *Mississippi State Gazette*, April 1, 1820; Natchez *Mississippi Republican*, January 11, 1820; Glover Moore, *The Missouri Controversy, 1819–1821* (Lexington, 1953), 248–49.
[21] Eden Brashears to John McKee, February 6, 1820, William Hughes and Family Papers, Mississippi Archives.

The first strong excitement in Natchez concerning state-rights was aroused by the South Carolina nullification crisis. The Tariff of 1828 caused mixed feelings to be voiced in Natchez. The *Natchez*, an organ of the community's Clay-Adams faction, advocated a high protective tariff, while the opposing *Gazette* called the Tariff of 1828 "the great landmark, in the South, that divides the two parties." In 1830 Charles Green lost in his bid for a United States Senate seat after championing the tariff in his campaign. Quitman and George Winchester of Natchez joined other anti-Jackson leaders elsewhere in the river counties, including George Poindexter and William L. Sharkey, in trying to exploit the President's recalcitrant position toward South Carolina in order to foment popular opposition to the Democratic party in Mississippi. Shifting his allegiance from Adams and Clay to Calhoun, Quitman busily recruited members into his newly-founded Mississippi States Rights Association. In the spring of 1832, however, Julius Reed claimed that "the State is Jackson, Natchez is Clay or at least contains a powerful Clay party, Woodville & vicinity are I suspect in consequence of Poindexter's influence becoming Calhoun." Another observer commented that "Jackson's party is the strongest as yet, a reason of which is that Calhoun is considered a nullifier."[22]

By early 1833 the groundswell of support for South Carolina had subsided. In January Walker delivered a tirade against disloyalty to the Jackson administration and led several "Union" rallies at Natchez. A few weeks later the Mississippi legislature adopted a resolution prepared by a committee led by Bingaman that denounced South Carolina's "reckless precipitancy." In May, Hiram Runnels, who was critical of the "wild heresies of nullification," won the gubernatorial race. By 1834–35 widespread support for the nullification movement had completely disappeared in Mississippi, except for a few die-hards in the Quitman camp. Among the more obvious reasons for the demise

[22] *Natchez*, August 14, 1830; Natchez *Gazette*, September 22, 1830; Reed to Watson, May 29, 1832, Watson Papers, Duke; Allen Stewart to Duncan McLaurin, November 23, 1831, Duncan McLaurin Papers, Duke.

were complacency lulled by growing prosperity, Jackson's persisting personal popularity, and absorption of public interest in the Jackson-Biddle bank feud and in the opening of the Choctaw lands in northern Mississippi.[23]

It is impossible to guage the nature and extent of Quitman's state-rights organization as the membership list is unavailable. While at its apex, however, his almost fanatical crusading must have been persuasive, judging from Nevitt's experience:

> July 14 [1832] Rode to Natchez and from thence to the old Court house to hear Judge Quitman on subject Nullification supposed they were nullifying doctrines determined not to support him for [constitutional] convention. . . .
>
> July 19 Rode to Natchez attended public Meeting to hear John A. Quitman on nullification Made a Speech Myself after explanation agreed to vote for Mr. Q. for convention.[24]

In late 1834, over a year after the South Carolina furor had quieted on the national scene and within Mississippi generally, Quitman was energetically attempting to organize a national state-rights party.[25] Although his latest movement was stillborn, he never forsook the beliefs which he had enunciated in an earlier letter to a friend:

> I trust in God that the sovereign state of Mississippi will not sustain the political principles of the President's proclamation [on nullification]—They are to my mind dangerous, vitally dangerous to the sacred rights of the states and strike a fatal blow at the federative character of our Union—They go to consolidate all powers in the National Government, and to erect over the ruins of the State governments, a

---

[23] Cleo Hearon, "Nullification in Mississippi," *PMHS*, XII (1912), 65–71; Miles, *Jacksonian Democracy in Mississippi*, 61–69. See also James E. Winston, "The Mississippi Whigs and the Tariff, 1834–1844," *MVHR*, XI (September, 1924), 200–26; Edwin A. Miles, "Andrew Jackson and George Poindexter," *JSH*, XXIV (February, 1958), 51–66.

[24] Nevitt Record Book, entries of July 14 and 19, 1832.

[25] A Quitman supporter reported too optimistically at the time that "the State rights and ante [sic] proclamation and force bill party is rapidly advancing in strength in Miss." Isaac Caldwell to Poindexter, January 29, 1834, Claiborne Papers, Mississippi Archives.

supreme and arbitrary national power against the enactments of which there will [be] no redress, no appeal but to revolution. . . . Carolina tho' she may be wrong, has taken the field in our cause—If she is to be sacrificed, we may as well prepare our necks also for the yoke of colonial bondage—A great national government of unlimited powers extending over a diversity of climates and interests can not exist without becoming an engine of the most grievous oppression upon the South. I wish I were in the Legislature. I should glory in martyrdom in such a cause.[26]

With the issue of congressional authority over territorial slavery mounting again by 1849, the *Free Trader* proclaimed early that year: "The time for talking or threatening . . . [is] past; we must lay down our platform broadly and openly, and say to our Northern brethren, 'thus far and no farther.' " By that autumn an explosive Southern nationalist movement was gaining momentum, spearheaded in Mississippi by Quitman, Jefferson Davis, and A. G. Brown. In October a state convention met and, among other resolutions, called for secession if Congress adopted the Wilmot Proviso, which would prohibit slavery in the territories acquired from Mexico. The next month Quitman, now a Democrat and stumping on a state-rights platform, won the governorship. In his inaugural address in January, 1850, he viciously assailed the Clay resolutions which had recently been introduced in Congress and would ultimately constitute the nucleus of the Compromise of 1850.[27]

As the congressional debates on Clay's resolutions continued through the spring and summer of 1850, varied sentiments were found among the citizens of Natchez. Most Whigs tended to endorse the resolutions. At a well-attended pro-Compromise meeting in Natchez, Bingaman offered a set of proposals which, according to Quitman, "embodied a condensation of more foolishness than any similar production he had ever seen." Later that summer Quitman frantically organized a Southern Rights As-

[26] Quitman to Nathan G. Howard, January 14, 1833, Howard Papers.
[27] Natchez *Mississippi Free Trader*, February 10, 1849; Cleo Hearon, "Mississippi and the Compromise of 1850," *PMHS*, XIV (1914), 60–63.

sociation in a vain effort to promote effective opposition to the Compromise of 1850. As mentioned earlier, Quitman received strong support from the Natchez Democrats but was intensely opposed by the town and county Whigs.[28]

In November, 1850, Quitman called a special legislative session, which endorsed his recommendation for a state convention in November, 1851, to reconsider the affinity between Mississippi and the United States with regard to state sovereignty. Meanwhile Quitman resigned the governorship because of his impending trial on filibustering charges. He returned to his law practice in Natchez and revived his anti-Compromise activities. Now, however, he encountered a strong Unionist party, hastily organized by conservatives, mainly Whigs, and backing Henry S. Foote for governor in the approaching election. In June the Democrats nominated Quitman again for governor. Thus, while the Foote-Quitman campaign was underway, at the same time secessionist and unionist forces were vying for seats in the November state convention.[29]

The *Free Trader,* which avidly supported Quitman and state rights, argued that the Compromise of 1850 would result in the South's prostration before "the unmeasurable numerical, commercial and territorial aggrandizement of the North." Time would work against the South. If secession were postponed, the *Free Trader* maintained, the North would grow stronger proportionally "in people and economic power," lure the border states to its side, and thus prevent the South's withdrawal from the Union. The *Courier* countered that the Union was "of inestimable value to Mississippi" and should be preserved at any reasonable cost, which the Compromise purported to do. At Port Gibson the *Herald* proposed that "the secession of the State of Mississippi from the Union should be immediately followed by the secession of the Southwestern submission counties from the

---

[28] Jackson *Mississippian,* May 3 and September 13, 1850; Hearon, "Mississippi and the Compromise of 1850," 115–28.

[29] Natchez *Mississippi Free Trader,* February 12 and March 19, 1851; McLendon, "John A. Quitman," 313–15; Hearon, "Mississippi and the Compromise of 1850," 178–86.

State." The *Republican* at Woodville supported the *Free Trader* on state sovereignty as "the best protection" of the institution of slavery against the onslaughts of the abolitionists.[30]

When the election of convention delegates occurred in September, the Unionists carried forty-one of fifty-nine counties, including all but one (Franklin) of the southwestern counties. Stung by this popular rejection of his principles, Quitman withdrew from the governor's race. His substitute on the Democratic ticket, Jefferson Davis, was then defeated by Foote two months later. Oddly enough, Adams and three other river counties gave majorities to Davis, though all had opposed state-rightism in September. As expected, the Unionist-dominated convention suppressed efforts at secession and adopted a series of mild resolutions denying the constitutionality of secession but warning the North against further aggressions. Governor Foote predicted that "Quitman and Quitmanism are dead in Mississippi forever." His rejoicing was premature, however, because the radical Democrats swept back into office in the next state elections. Yet, for the time being, the explosion was averted, and even Quitman ranted less about the immediate need for secession.[31]

When the imbroglio of the Kansas-Nebraska Act arose in 1854, the *Courier* discouraged support of the measure: "Before the first five hundred slave-holders reach those regions, fifty thousand Northern men and foreign emigrants . . . [will] have flocked there [and] formed territorial laws for [slavery's] exclusion." The *Free Trader,* speaking for the town's Democracy, refused to admit that the measure incorporated the doctrine of popular sovereignty. The act appeared to be "a triumph of the territorial principles for which the great majority of the people of the South contended,"

[30] Natchez *Mississippi Free Trader,* October 9, 1851; Natchez *Courier,* September 11, 1851; Port Gibson *Herald,* October 14, 1851; Woodville *Republican,* September 4, 1851.

[31] Diary of Jason Niles, XV, entries of November 10–17, 1851, Jason Niles Papers, UNC; Jackson *Mississippi State Gazette,* September 19, 1851; Henry S. Foote to Howell Cobb, July 9, 1851, in *Annual Report of the American Historical Association, 1911* (2 vols.; Washington, 1912), II, 242.

but if popular sovereignty were allowed, then it would become "a mere snare for the South."[32]

While Whigs and Democrats in Natchez were discussing the issue of "Bleeding Kansas," as most Americans were doing, the town became more personally involved when President Buchanan announced the appointment of Robert J. Walker as Kansas territorial governor in March, 1857. Many Natchez folk undoubtedly wondered what their expatriate would do. In his first Kansas address in May, Walker shocked fire-eaters by pleading for cooperation, acceptance of any constitution that was put to a fair vote, and resignation to slavery's natural limits. The Mississippi legislature branded him "an apostate" when Walker opposed the pro-slavery Lecompton Constitution as unfairly adopted. The Woodville *Republican* agreed with him on the hopelessness of slavery in Kansas and called for the South to "let Kansas go."[33] But the *Free Trader* defiantly retorted by asking if the Woodville editor considered the "success of the Democratic party of more importance than the honor, equality and existence of the South?" The *Free Trader* "preferred to see the party rent into ten thousand atoms and sent hurling into eternal oblivion before it would consent to 'Let Kansas Go,' if it is to be accomplished through the treachery of a Democratic Administration or officials. We love the South more than party."[34]

Meanwhile Walker, caught between dissatisfied elements in Kansas and Washington, North and South, piously stated that he hoped to "leave my Kansas policy as a legacy to my country, & silence the voice of faction, which so falsily [sic] charges me with wishing to disturb the equilibrium of our Government, in the treasonable hope of Sectional aspirations."[35] By the time of Walker's resignation as Kansas territorial governor in December,

[32] Natchez *Courier*, June 15 and 20, 1854; Natchez *Mississippi Free Trader*, March 21, 1854.

[33] Percy L. Rainwater, *Mississippi: Storm Center of Secession, 1856–1861* (Baton Rouge, 1938), 47; Woodville *Republican*, August 4, 1857.

[34] Natchez *Mississippi Free Trader*, August 14, 1857.

[35] Robert J. Walker to President James Buchanan, August 3, 1857, Robert J. Walker Papers, Mississippi Archives.

1857, few persons at Natchez, Democrat or Whig, cared any longer to claim their former townsman.

Conservative forces in Mississippi, especially in the Natchez area, were bereft of adroit leadership in the critical late 1850's when the controlling radical Democrats were rushing the state toward disunion. The impotence of Whiggery at Natchez is pointed up by the impressive majority given to A. G. Brown in the gubernatorial election of 1857 by the town's voters. By then the *Free Trader* was the most inflammatory of the state's fire-eating organs. Threats and fiery pronouncements appeared in nearly every issue in the last years before secession. As early as 1857 the *Free Trader* was convinced that civil war was inevitable because "two distinct and rival systems of society and civilization are bound together in this Confederacy, the Northern and the Southern. . . . When the curtain falls over the campaign of 1860, it will hide only the victor and the dead." Flaying such Unionists as Foote, Howell Cobb of Georgia, and Sam Houston of Texas for ignoring the uniqueness of Southern nationalism, the *Free Trader* emphasized that the signs of an impending national rupture were already evident in 1857: "We read it in the volcanic upheavings of the Southern heart, here and there, from Virginia to Texas; we read it in the ominous cloud, yet scarcely bigger than a man's hand, which hangs over the Federal Capitol; we read it in that susurrus which, sighing through the forest, presages the coming storm—we read the prophecy of a sectional convulsion, wider, deeper, and more decisive than we have yet seen."[36]

In February, 1860, the legislature elected seven men to represent Mississippi at a Southern state-rights conference which was to assemble in Atlanta. Attorney Samuel S. Boyd of Natchez was one of the seven. But, since only Mississippi and South Carolina sent delegations to Atlanta, the meeting to discuss Southern grievances did not transpire. Despite this disappointment to the fire-eaters, disunionist talk continued to spread. In April the Mississippi delegates at Charleston joined other Southern Demo-

[36] Natchez *Mississippi Free Trader*, February 6 and July 14, 1857.

crats in walking out of the national Democratic convention. That summer in Natchez the supporters of Stephen Douglas, John Bell, and John C. Breckinridge worked zealously to garner votes for their respective presidential candidates. A "super rally" was held on the public square in September with all three tickets represented, but the Bell men, or Constitutional Unionists, were reported to be in the majority. A few days later a young men's Union Club was organized to boost Bell, and a reading room was open where propaganda of the Constitutional Unionist cause was available. A large Northern Democratic rally was held in late September to promote Douglas. The supporters of Breckinridge, the Southern Democratic candidate, also held rallies in Natchez, but their attendance was noticeably weaker than those of the Bell and Douglas forces.[37]

Early that fall the *Courier* joined the Vicksburg *Whig* in disseminating news of an alleged conspiracy among the Breckinridge forces to foment a secessionist movement prior to the voting in November. But when Duncan proposed in the *Courier* that "nothing can prevent the election of Lincoln but the withdrawal of both Breckinridge and Douglas," the *Whig* responded that "such a man [Duncan] is an actual dead weight upon the cause of Southern rights." Duncan also said that secession was a "monstrous idea" because, without tariffs on imports, direct taxes would consume a fourth of the production of the slave states. He concluded: "If the Union is to be dissolved, I, for one, would be for selling out my possessions immediately." To this the *Free Trader* retorted that "500-slave, 4,000-bale planters like Duncan" had always been opposed to democracy. But he and his kind would not influence elections, the Democratic organ continued, because the nabob's vote did not mean any more than that of "the humblest mechanic who advocates correct principles."[38]

[37] Natchez *Courier*, February 14, March 3, September 10, 12, and 25, 1860.

[38] *Ibid.*, September 19 and October 6, 1860; Vicksburg *Whig*, October 20, 1860; Natchez *Mississippi Free Trader*, September 25, 1860. See also Percy L. Rainwater, "An Analysis of the Secession Controversy in Mississippi, 1854–1861," *MVHR*, XXIV (June, 1937), 38; Ollinger Crenshaw, *The Slave States in the Presidential Election of 1860* (Baltimore, 1945), 268.

Although Duncan was undoubtedly expressing the feelings of most of the Natchez aristocrats, his sentiments must have been shared by a large number of the town and county voters of lower classes as well. A significant majority of the Natchez and Adams County voters cast ballots in favor of Bell and Douglas in November and for Cooperationist (anti-secession) delegates in December's state convention election. No precinct breakdown for the popular voting in the presidential contest was recorded for Adams County, and so the Natchez votes cannot be delineated. But Adams County, including Natchez, gave Bell 448 votes, Breckinridge 376, and Douglas 158. In other words, 61 per cent of the voters did not choose the secessionists' favorite, Breckinridge. The next month an overwhelming 73 per cent of the Natchez precinct ballots went to the Cooperationist candidates for the coming state convention to consider secession.[39]

Attorney Josiah Winchester, who, along with Alexander Farrar, represented Adams County at the state convention in January, 1861, commented before his election that disunion was similar to "committing suicide for fear we shall die a natural death." Foreseeing further sectional clashes between the upper and lower regions of the South if a separate nation was established, he concluded: "And what will be the final result? Another split and a new secession!"[40] Benjamin Wailes, a Whig who had long lamented the rise of the radical Democrats in his state, observed in stoical resignation: "All we can do however I fear will be of little avail. The spirit of anarchy is abroad in the land and we are drifting to a state of anarchy, disorder and ruin."[41]

At the secession convention in Jackson, January 7–23, 1861, Winchester and Farrar joined delegates from three other river counties in vainly supporting the Yerger Amendment, which would have pressed for "further guarantees within the present Union" instead of immediate secession. The Adams County men

[39] Adams County aggregate returns, presidential election of November, 1860, SSA, Series F; Adams County precinct returns, election of state convention delegates, December, 1860, *ibid.*
[40] Natchez *Courier*, November 24, 1860.
[41] Sydnor, *Wailes*, 294–95.

also were in a small minority, consisting mainly of southwestern representatives, who voted for the Brooke Amendment, which would have required a plebescite for ratification of a secession ordinance. Both amendments were defeated by nearly 3-to-1 margins. In the vote on the secession ordinance itself on January 9, both Winchester and Farrar cast ballots against adoption of the fateful document.[42]

In their actions at Jackson the county's delegates probably had the support of a majority of the people they represented, certainly of the citizens of Natchez. The dichotomized reasoning of the typical Natchez voter was such that he could sometimes support state-rights radicals and yet reject secession. A Democrat and owner of few or no slaves, he was accustomed to opposing Whigs and upper-class interests. Nevertheless, as a member of the town's commercial class he was reluctant to sever the lucrative trade linkage with the North, which had brought him greater prosperity than most of his agrarian brethren enjoyed elsewhere across the state. The typical Natchez voter was not a nabob, but he was a man of property. Compared to most backwoods Mississippians, he enjoyed success and security, and he wanted to protect his interests. Thus in the final great test the commoner of Natchez ironically found himself allied with the nabobs, whom he despised as much as did the backwoods yeomen.

The attitudes and behavior of the aristocrats of Natchez during the final three decades of the antebellum period were characterized by escapism and exclusiveness. Like the knight who ignored the pleas of his starving serf and galloped off to join the latest crusade against the Islamic infidels, the Natchez men of wealth indulged in fantasies and ignored realities. They enjoyed flights into filibustering, expansionism, and national party cam-

[42] *Journal of the State Convention and Ordinances and Resolutions Adopted in January, 1861, with an Appendix* (Jackson, 1861), *passim.* Several former Natchez residents were members of the Louisiana secession convention. John Perkins, Jr., who once lived at "The Briers," served temporarily as convention chairman and later headed the committee which drafted the Louisiana secession ordinance. Calhoun, "History of Concordia Parish," *LHQ,* XVI (January, 1933), 98–102.

paigns, but, with few exceptions, remained stolidly apart from state and municipal politics. Perhaps, in their frustration they conceived of themselves as anachronisms in a state that had long since dispensed with rule by gentlemen. A vivid illustration of how the aristocrat viewed the sort of man who held power in Mississippi in the late antebellum era may be found in Englishman William H. Russell's report of an interview with Governor John J. Pettus on the eve of the Civil War. Blunt and uncultured, the chief executive of Mississippi dropped "a portentous plug of tobacco just outside of the spittoon, with the air of a man who wished to show he could have hit the centre if he liked." In braggart tones he informed Russell that "the sovereign State of Mississippi can do a great deal better without England than England can do without her." To the Englishman's astonishment, Pettus went on to extol the democratic virtues and superior culture which he and his radical Democratic supporters had brought to Mississippi.[43]

The retreat from reality among Natchez aristocrats that began with the rise of Jacksonian Democracy and culminated in the triumph of the radicals at the secession convention cost Natchez and the state its most sane leadership during a critical period. With the aristocrats sullenly withdrawing into their own world or foolishly supporting filibusters, Natchez lost forever its opportunity to become a major metropolis, and Mississippi was led to ruin. On his death bed in 1862 Benjamin Wailes expressed the sentiment of the Natchez aristocracy: "In the unhappy state of our Country I may have already lived too long."[44]

[43] William H. Russell, *My Diary North and South* (Boston, 1863), 89.
[44] Diary of Benjamin L. C. Wailes, entry of March 2, 1862, Wailes Papers, Duke.

Bibliography

MANUSCRIPTS

Duke University, Durham, North Carolina

Absalom F. Dantzler Papers.
John C. Knight Papers.
Duncan McLaurin Papers.
Mississippi Free Trader and Natchez Gazette Subscription Book, 1848–1852.
Haller Nutt Papers.
George Poindexter Papers.
Benjamin L. C. Wailes Papers.
Henry Watson, Jr., Papers.

Library of Congress, Washington, D.C.

Archives Nationales, Paris, Colonial Series C 13a, French transcripts.
Archivo General de Indias, Seville, Papeles Procedentes de Cuba, photostats and English transcripts.
British Public Records Office, Colonial Office Papers, Class V, photostats and transcripts.
John F. H. Claiborne Papers.
Andrew Ellicott Papers.
Andrew Jackson Papers.
Mississippi Miscellaneous Papers.

Benjamin L. C. Wailes Papers.
Robert J. Walker Papers.

Louisiana State University, Department of Archives, Baton Rouge

Thomas Affleck Papers.
John Bisland and Family, Papers.
Eli J. Capell Plantation Records.
Francisco L. H. (Baron de) Carondelet Papers.
Commercial Bank of Natchez Papers.
Lemuel P. Conner Papers.
Stephen Duncan Papers.
Eggleston-Roach Papers.
Alexander K. Farrar Papers.
Galveztown Papers.
Manuel Gayoso de Lemos Papers.
David Hunt and Family Papers.
John C. Jenkins Diary.
William Johnson Papers.
Eleanor Percy Ware Lee Papers.
Henry D. Mandeville Papers.
William N. Mercer Papers.
Ayres P. Merrill Papers.
William J. Minor and Family Papers.
John W. Monette Papers.
Joseph D. Shields Papers.
Joseph B. Stratton Diary.
Josef Vidal Papers.

Mississippi Department of Archives and History, Jackson

Richard Abbey Papers.
Adams County Court of General Quarter Sessions of the Peace Papers.
Bank of the State of Mississippi Papers.
Ferdinand L. Claiborne Papers.
John F. H. Claiborne Papers.
John F. H. Claiborne Miscellaneous Papers.
Robert Cochran Papers.
Levin Covington Daybook.
Edward Dickinson Daybook.
Drake-Satterfield Papers.
William Dunbar Papers.
Stephen Duncan Papers.
Horatio Eustis Papers.

Robert G. Hazard Papers.
David Holmes Papers.
Nathan G. Howard Papers.
William Hughes Papers.
Abijah and David Hunt Papers.
Jefferson College Papers.
Charles P. Leverich Papers.
Mansion House Daybook.
Andrew Marschalk Papers.
Mississippi Provincial Archives: English.
Mississippi Territorial Archives, Series A, B, and D.
John W. Monette Papers.
Joseph A. Montgomery and Family Papers.
Natchez and Vicksburg Theatrical Papers.
Natchez Protection Insurance Company Papers.
Natchez Steamboat Company Stock Certificate Book.
George Poindexter Papers.
John A. Quitman Papers.
George Rapalje Notebook.
Secretary of State Archives, Series F.
William F. Shields Papers.
Robert L. Stanton Papers.
Trinity Episcopal Church (Natchez) Records.
Edward Turner Papers.
Benjamin L. C. Wailes Papers.
Robert J. Walker Papers.
William N. Whitehurst Papers.
Robert Williams Papers.

Natchez City Clerk's Office

Accounts and Records, I (1804–70).
Board of Health Minute Book, I (1818–22, 1854–60).
Board of Selectmen Minute Books, I–V (1811–72), except for III
  (1822–46), which is missing.
Census of the City of Natchez, 1837, MS schedules.
Common Council Minute Book, I (1803–1806). Vol. II is missing.
Mayor's Court Minute Book, I (1803–1805).
Natchez Charitable Association Minute Book (1853–58).
Record of Accounts Allowed by the Board of Selectmen, I (1815–26).
Treasurer's Reports, I (1803–26).

Natchez Chancery Clerk's Office (Adams County)

Adams County Court Minute Book, I (1817–33).
Deed Record, Books A–M (1780–1860).
Division of Real Estate Record, I (1814–50).
Guardian's Bonds, I (1802–26).
Inventories and Appraisements, I (1803–18).
Letters of Administration, I (1803–19).
Orphans Court Minute Book, I–II (1803–20).
Record of Wills, I–III (1802–71).
Spanish Records of the Natchez District, A–G (1780–98), MS translation by David Harper, 1818, from original 40 vols. of Spanish Records, also in Chancery Clerk's Office.

National Archives, Washington, D.C.

Consular Letters, New Orleans (1796–1807).
U. S. Censuses (1810–60), MS Population and Slave Schedules, Mississippi, Adams County, City of Natchez.

North Carolina Department of Archives and History, Raleigh

Archivo General de Indias, Seville, Papeles Procedentes de Cuba, photostats and English transcripts.

University of North Carolina, Southern Historical Collection, Chapel Hill

John F. H. Claiborne Papers.
William Dunbar Account Book.
Peter Hagner Papers.
Mary Susan Ker Papers.
Thomas H. Maddox Papers.
James W. Metcalfe Papers.
Stephen Minor, and Family Papers.
Jason Niles Diary.
John A. Quitman Papers.
Frederic Seip Papers.

University of Texas, Austin

Everard G. Baker Diary, Ramsdell Microfilms.
U. S. Censuses (1850–60), MS Schedule VI (Social Statistics), Mississippi, Ramsdell Microfilms.

University of Virginia, Charlottesville

John A. Quitman Papers.

Other Manuscripts

Everard G. Baker Diary, typescript in private possession of Barnes F. Lathrop, Austin, Texas.
Baptismal Records, First Presbyterian Church, Natchez.
Ezra Bennett Papers, Louisiana State University at Alexandria.
Forman Genealogical Papers, in private possession of family of late Miss Pearl V. Guyton, Natchez.
Dunbar Hunt Papers, in private possession of family of late Miss Pearl V. Guyton, Natchez.
MS Cemetery Records of Adams County, in private possession of Mrs. Edith W. Moore, Natchez.
Natchez Female Charitable Society Minute Book (1816–20), Protestant Children's Home, Natchez.
John B. Nevitt Record Book (1826–32), typescript in private possession of Barnes F. Lathrop, Austin, Texas (original in Southern Historical Collection, University of North Carolina).
Dawson A. Phelps MS on Colonial Natchez, Pasadena, Texas.
Session Minute Book, I (1817–72), First Presbyterian Church, Natchez.

NEWSPAPERS

Natchez

Ariel.
Chronicle.
Courier.
Courier and Journal.
Gazette.
Mississippi Free Trader.
Mississippi Free Trader and Natchez Gazette.
Mississippi Herald.
Mississippi Herald and Natchez Gazette.
Mississippi Journal and Natchez Advertiser.
Mississippi Messenger.
Mississippi Republican.
Mississippi Republican and Natchez Intelligencer.
Mississippi State Gazette.
Natchez.
Natchez Courier, & Adams, Jefferson & Franklin Advertiser.
Southern Galaxy.

Other than Natchez

Grand Gulf *Advertiser*.
Jackson *Mississippian*.
Jackson *Mississippi State Gazette*.
Little Rock *Arkansas State Gazette and Democrat*.
New Orleans *Louisiana Courier*.
New Orleans *Picayune*.
Port Gibson *Correspondent*.
Port Gibson *Herald*.   *3 2*
Rodney *Southern Telegraph*.
Vicksburg *Register*.
Vicksburg *Whig*.
Vidalia *Concordia Intelligencer*.
Washington *Republican*.
Washington *Republican and Natchez Intelligencer*.
Woodville *Republican*.

PERIODICALS

American Philosophical Society *Transactions* (Philadelphia; First
    Series).
De Bow's Review of the Southern and Western States (New Orleans;
    title varies).
Louisiana and Mississippi Almanac (Natchez).
Southern Cultivator (Augusta).
Southern Planter (Washington, Miss.).
Southwestern Farmer (Raymond, Miss.).
South-Western Journal (Natchez).

PUBLIC DOCUMENTS

*Acts Passed at the Third Session of the General Assembly of the Mis-
    sissippi Territory* (Natchez, 1802).
*An Act for the More Healthy Police of the City of Natchez and to
    Provide against Infectious and Pestilential Disease* (Natchez, 1818).
Carter, Clarence (ed.), *The Territorial Papers of the United States*,
    Vols. V–VI, *The Territory of Mississippi, 1798–1817* (Washington,
    1937–38).
Grant, W. L., and James Munro (eds.), *Acts of the Privy Council of
    England, Colonial Series, 1613–1783*, Vols. IV–VI (London, 1911–
    12).
Hutchinson, Anderson (comp.), *Code of Mississippi: Being an Analyti-
    cal Compilation of the Public and General Statutes for the Territory*

and State, with Tabular References to the Local and Private Acts, from 1789 to 1848 (Jackson, 1848).

Journal of the Convention of the State of Mississippi Held in the Town of Jackson [1832] (Jackson, 1832).

Journal of the Convention of the Western Part of the Mississippi Territory, Begun and Held at the Town of Washington, on the Seventh Day of July, 1817 (Port Gibson, 1831).

Journal of the State Convention and Ordinances and Resolutions Adopted in January, 1861, with an Appendix (Jackson, 1861).

Kinnaird, Lawrence (ed.), "Spain in the Mississippi Valley, 1765–1794: Translations of Materials from the Spanish Archives in the Bancroft Library," in *Annual Report of the American Historical Association, 1945*, Parts I–III (3 vols.; Washington, 1946).

Laws of the State of Mississippi Passed at a Called Session of the Mississippi Legislature, Held in the City of Jackson, October, 1852 (Jackson, 1852).

McBee, May W. (comp.), *The Natchez Court Records, 1767–1805: Abstracts of Early Records* (2 vols.; Ann Arbor, 1953).

McCain, William D. (ed.), *Journal of the House of Representatives, Second General Assembly, Second Session, October 3–November 19, 1803* (Hattiesburg, 1940).

—— (ed.), *Sargent's Code: A Collection of the Original Laws of the Mississippi Territory Enacted 1799–1800 by Governor Winthrop Sargent and the Territorial Judges* (Jackson, 1939).

McMurtrie, Douglas C. (ed.), *Mississippi Banking Act of 1809* (Chicago, 1936).

Mississippi House Journals (Jackson, 1826–50).

Mississippi Session Acts, 1836 (Jackson, 1837).

Mississippi Historical Records Survey, *Transcription of the County Archives of Mississippi, No. 2: Adams County* (2 vols.; Jackson, 1942).

Nasatir, Abraham P., and Ernest R. Liljegren (eds.), "Materials Relating to the History of the Mississippi Valley, from the Minutes of the Spanish Supreme Council of State, 1787–1797," *Louisiana Historical Quarterly*, XXI (January, 1936), 5–75.

Ordinances of the City of Natchez with the Acts of the Legislature of the State of Mississippi in Regard to Said City; Containing All Ordinances in Force Up to the 9th June, 1829 (Natchez, 1829).

Poindexter, George (comp.), *The Revised Code of the Laws of Mississippi, in Which Are Comprised All Such Acts of the General As-*

sembly, of a Public Nature, as Were in Force at the End of the Year
1823: With a General Index (Natchez, 1824).

Rowland, Dunbar (ed.), _Mississippi Provincial Archives: English_
Dominion, 1763–1766 (Nashville, 1911).

—— (ed.), _Mississippi Territorial Archives, 1798–1803_ (Nashville,
1905).

—— (ed.), _Official and Statistical Register, Centennial Edition, 1917_
(Madison, 1917).

Rowland, Dunbar, and Albert G. Sanders (eds.), _Mississippi Provin-_
cial Archives: French Dominion (3 vols.; Jackson, 1927–32).

Shortt, Adam, and Arthur G. Doughty (eds.), _Documents Relating to_
the Constitutional History of Canada, 1759–1791 (2nd rev. ed., 2
vols.; Ottawa, 1918).

Toulmin, Harry (comp.), _The Statutes of the Mississippi Territory,_
Revised and Digested by the Authority of the General Assembly
(Natchez, 1807).

Turner, Edward (comp.), _Statutes of the Mississippi Territory,_
Digested by the Authority of the General Assembly (Natchez,
1816).

U.S. Congress, _American State Papers: Documents, Legislative and_
Executive [1789–1838] (38 vols.; Washington, 1832–61).

——, _Statutes at Large of the United States . . . 1789–1873_ (17 vols.;
Boston, 1845–73).

PUBLISHED SOURCES

Annual Report of the Managers and Officers with the Annual Address
Before the Natchez Orphan Asylum, Delivered at the Asylum by
Rev. Jos. B. Stratton, with a History of the Institution (Natchez,
1855).

Annual Reports of the Board of Visitors and the Board of Examiners
of the Natchez Institute, 1854 (Natchez, 1854).

Ashe, Thomas, _Travels in America_ (London, 1808).

Audubon, John J., _Journal of John James Audubon Made During His_
Trip to New Orleans in 1820–1821, ed. Howard Corning (Cambridge, Mass., 1929).

Baily, Francis, _Journal of a Tour in Unsettled Parts of North America,_
_in 1796 & 1797_ (London, 1856).

Baldwin, Joseph G., _The Flush Times of Alabama and Mississippi: A_
Series of Sketches (New York, 1853).

Bassett, John S. (ed.), _Correspondence of Andrew Jackson_ (7 vols.;
New York, 1926–33).

Bates, Albert C. (ed.), *The Two Putnams, Israel and Rufus: In the Havana Expedition 1762 and in the Mississippi River Exploration 1772–73 with Some Account of the Company of Military Adventurers* (Hartford, 1931).

Besancon, Lorenzo A., *Besancon's Annual Register of the State of Mississippi for the Year 1838* (Natchez, 1838).

Bossu, Jean-Bernard, *Travels in the Interior of North America, 1751–1762,* ed. Seymour Feiler (Norman, 1962).

Brackenridge, H. M., *Views of Louisiana, Containing Geographical, Statistical, and Historical Notes* (Baltimore, 1817).

Bronner, Edwin R. (ed.), "A Philadelphia Quaker Visits Natchez, 1847," *Journal of Southern History,* XXVII (November, 1961), 513–20.

Brown, Samuel R., *The Western Gazeteer; or Emigrant's Directory* (Albany, 1817).

Buckingham, James S., *The Slave States of America . . .* (2 vols.; London, 1842).

Burnett, Edmund C. (ed.), *Letters of Members of the Continental Congress* (8 vols.; Washington, 1921–36).

—— (ed.), "Papers Relating to Bourbon County, Georgia," *American Historical Review,* XV (January, 1910), 291–98.

Calder, Isabel (ed.), *Colonial Captivities, Marches and Journeys* (New York, 1935).

Carter, Clarence E. (ed.), *The Correspondence of General Thomas Gage with the Secretaries of State, 1763–1775* (2 vols.; New Haven, 1931–33).

Cartwright, Samuel A., *Essays, Being Inductions Drawn from the Baconian Philosophy Proving the Truth of the Bible and . . . of the Decree Dooming Canaan to Be the Servant of Servants . . . in a Series of Letters to the Rev. William Winans* (Vidalia, La., 1843).

Champomier, P. A., *Statement of the Sugar Crop Made in Louisiana, 1854* (New Orleans, 1855).

Charlevoix, Pierre F. X de, *Journal d'un voyage fait par ordre du Roi dans l'Amérique Septentrionale, adressé à Madame la Duchesse de Lesdiguiéres* (2 vols.; Paris, 1744).

Charter and Statutes of Jefferson College, Washington, Miss., as Revised and Amended; Together with a Historical Sketch of the Institution (Natchez, 1840).

Claiborne, John F. H., *Life and Correspondence of John A. Quitman, Major-General, U.S.A., and Governor of the State of Mississippi* (2 vols.; New York, 1860).

——, *Mississippi as a Province, Territory and State* (Jackson, 1880).

————, "A Trip Through the Piney Woods," *Publications of the Mississippi Historical Society,* IX (1906), 487–538.

Collot, George H. V., *A Journey in North America . . .* (3 vols.; London, 1796; reprint, 3 vols.; Florence, 1924).

Compte Rendu, Congres International des Américanistes, 15th Session (2 vols.; Quebec, 1907).

Constitution and Bye-Laws of the Natchez Academy (Natchez, 1829).

Cook, Francis A. (ed.), *Cemetery and Bible Records: A Publication of the Mississippi Genealogical Society* (10 vols.; Jackson, 1954–63).

Cruzat, Helen H. (trans.), "The Concession at Natchez [1731]," *Louisiana Historical Quarterly,* VIII (July, 1925), 389–97.

———— (trans.), "Louisiana in 1724: Banet's Report to the Company of the Indies, Dated Paris, December 20, 1724," *Louisiana Historical Quarterly,* XII (January, 1929), 121–33.

Cuming, Fortescue, *Sketches of a Tour to the Western Country* (Pittsburgh, 1810).

Darby, William A., *The Emigrant's Guide to the Western and Southwestern States and Territories* (New York, 1818).

Davis, Edwin A., and John C. L. Andreassen (eds.), "From Louisville to New Orleans in 1816: Diary of William Newton Mercer," *Journal of Southern History,* II (August, 1936), 390–402.

Davis, Reuben, *Recollections of Mississippi and Mississippians* (Boston, 1891).

Dow, Lorenzo, *History of Cosmopolite: Lorenzo's Journal, Containing His Experience and Travels from Childhood to 1815, Being Upwards of Thirty-Seven Years; Also, His Polemical Writings* (Philadelphia, 1815).

Dunbar, William, *Discoveries Made in Exploring the Missouri, Red River and Washita, by Captains Lewis and Clark, Doctor Sibley, and William Dunbar, Esq. With a Statistical Account of the Countries Adjacent. With an Appendix by Mr. Dunbar* (Natchez, 1806).

Du Pratz, Antoine S. Le Page, *Histoire de la Louisiane, contenant la découverte de ce vaste pays; sa description geographique; un voyage dans les terres; l'histoire naturelle, les moeurs, coûtumes & religion des naturels, avec leurs origines; deux voyages dans le nord du nouveau Mexique, dont un jusqu'á la mer du Sud; ornée de deux cartes & de 40 planches en taille douce* (3 vols.; Paris, 1758).

Ellicott, Andrew, *The Journal of Andrew Ellicott, Late Commissioner on Behalf of the United States during Part of the Year 1796, the Years 1797, 1798, 1799, and Part of the Year 1800; for Determining the Boundary Between the United States and the Possessions of His Catholic Majesty in America* . . . (Philadelphia, 1803).

Fearon, Henry B., *Sketches of America: A Narrative of a Journey of Five Thousand Miles Through the Eastern and Western States of America; Contained in Eight Reports Addressed to the Thirty-Nine English Families by Whom the Author Was Deputed, in June 1817, to Ascertain Whether Any, and What Part of the United States Would Be Suitable for Their Residence. With Remarks on Mr. Birkbeck's "Notes" and "Letters"* (London, 1818).

Featherstonhaugh, George W., *Excursion Through the Slave States, from Washington on the Potomac to the Frontier of Mexico; with Sketches of Popular Manners and Geological Notices* (2 vols.; London, 1844).

Flint, Timothy, *Recollections of the Last Ten Years* (Boston, 1826).

Foote, Henry S., *Casket of Reminiscences* (Washington, 1874).

Forman, Samuel S., *Narrative of a Journey Down the Ohio and Mississippi in 1798–90*, ed. Lyman C. Draper (Cincinnati, 1888).

French, Benjamin F. (ed.), *Historical Collections of Louisiana Embracing Many Rare and Valuable Documents Relating to the Natural, Civil and Political History of That State* (7 vols.; New York, 1846–75).

Fulkerson, Howard S., *Random Recollections of Early Days in Mississippi* (Vicksburg, 1885).

Gibson, George H. (ed.), "The Mississippi Market for Woolen Goods: An 1822 Analysis," *Journal of Southern History*, XXXI (February, 1965), 80–90.

Gould, E. W., *Fifty Years on the Mississippi, or, Gould's History of River Navigation* (St. Louis, 1889).

Gratz, Simon (ed.), "Letters of Thomas Rodney," *Pennsylvania Magazine of History and Biography*, XLIII (1919), 1–23, 117–42, 208–27, 332–67; XLIV (1920), 47–72, 170–89, 270–84, 289–308; XLV (1921), 34–65, 180–203.

Hall, James, *A Brief History of the Mississippi Territory, to Which Is Prefixed, a Summary View of the Country Between the Settlements on Cumberland River & the Territory* (Salisbury, N.C., 1801).

Hamilton, William B., and William D. McCain (eds.), "Wealth in the Natchez Region: Inventories of the Estate of Charles Percy, 1794 and 1804," *Journal of Mississippi History*, X (October, 1948), 290–316.

Harrell, Laura D. S. (ed.), "Diary of Thomas Rodney, 1804," *Journal of Mississippi History*, VII (April, 1945), 111–16.

Henderson, John, *Paine Detected, or the Unreasonableness of Paine's Age of Reason* (Natchez, 1797).

Hodgson, Adam, *Letters from North America, Written During a Tour in the United States and Canada* . . . (2 vols.; London, 1824).

Hogan, William R., and Edwin A. Davis (eds.), *William Johnson's Natchez: The Ante-Bellum Diary of a Free Negro* (Baton Rouge, 1951).

Holmes, Jack D. L. (ed.), *Documentos inéditos para la historia de la Louisiana, 1792–1810* (Madrid, 1963).

Hutchins, Thomas, *An Historical Narrative and Topographical Description of Louisiana and West-Florida Comprehending the River Mississippi with Its Principal Branches and Settlements, and the Rivers Pearl, Pascagoula* . . . *with Directions for Sailing into All the Bays, Lakes, Harbours and Rivers on the North Side of the Gulf of Mexico* . . . (Philadelphia, 1784).

Ideson, Julia, and Sanford W. Higginbothan (eds.), "A Trading Trip to Natchez and New Orleans, 1822: Diary of Thomas S. Teas," *Journal of Southern History*, VII (August, 1941), 378–99.

Imlay, Gilbert, *Topographical Description of the Western Territory of North America* . . . (London, 1797).

Ingraham, Joseph H., *The South-West, by a Yankee* (2 vols.; New York, 1835).

Journal of the Proceedings of a Convention of the Protestant Episcopal Church in the Diocese of Mississippi Held in Natchez (Natchez, 1826).

Ker, Henry, *Travels through the Western Interior of the United States, 1808–1816* (Elizabeth, N.J., 1816).

Kingsford, William, *Impressions of the West and South during a Six Weeks' Holiday* (Toronto, 1858).

La Harpe, Bernard de, *Journal historique de l'établissement des Français a la Louisiane* (New Orleans, 1831).

Le Petit, Mathurin, *Report of the Natchez Massacre by Fra Mathurin Le Petit, S. J.*, trans. R. H. Hart (New Orleans, 1950).

Lewis, Anna (ed.), "Fort Panmure, 1779, as Related by Juan Delaville-beuvre to Bernardo de Galvez," *Mississippi Valley Historical Review*, XVIII (March, 1932), 541–48.

Lloyd, James T., *Lloyd's Steamboat Directory and Railroad Directory, and Disasters on the Western Waters* (Cincinnati, 1856).

Ludlow, Noah M., *Dramatic Life as I Found It* (St. Louis, 1880).

Lyell, Charles, *A Second Visit to the United States of North America* (2 vols.; New York, 1849).

McCain, William D. (ed.), "The Charter of Mississippi's First Bank," *Journal of Mississippi History*, I (October, 1939), 251–63.

McWilliams, Richebourg G. (ed.), *Fleur de Lys and Calumet: Being the Pénicaut Narrative of French Adventure in Louisiana* (Baton Rouge, 1953).

Margry, Pierre (ed.), *Découvertes et établissements des Français dans le Sud de l'Amérique Septentrionale, 1614–1754* (6 vols.; Paris, 1879–88).

Marryat, François, *A Diary in America* (2 vols.; Philadelphia, 1839).

Marshall, Theodora B., and Gladys C. Evans (eds.), "Plantation Report from the Papers of Levin R. Marshall, of 'Richmond,' Natchez, Mississippi," *Journal of Mississippi History*, III (January, 1941), 45–55.

Michaux, François A., *Travels to the West of the Alleghany Mountains . . . in the Year 1802* (London, 1805).

Montulé, Edouard de, *Travels in America, 1816–1817*, trans. Edward D. Seeber (Bloomington, 1951).

Moore, Margaret D. (ed.), "Early Schools and Churches in Natchez," *Journal of Mississippi History*, XXIV (October, 1962), 253–55.

Murray, Charles A., *Travels in North America During the Years 1834, 1835, & 1836* (2 vols.; London, 1839).

The Natchez Almanac for the Year 1853, ed. George W. Fox (Natchez, 1853).

Oehler, Andrew, *The Life, Adventures, and Unparalleled Sufferings of Andrew Oehler, Containing an Account of His Travels . . .* (Trenton, 1811).

Olmsted, Frederick L., *A Journey in the Back Country in the Winter of 1853–4* (New York, 1860).

Padgett, James A. (ed.), "The Reply of Peter Chester, Governor of West Florida, to Complaints Made against His Administration," *Louisiana Historical Quarterly*, XXII (January, 1939), 31–46.

Papers in Relation to the Official Conduct of Governor Sargent. Published by Particular Desire of His Friends (Boston, 1801).

Paxton, Philip [Samuel A. Hammett], *A Stray Yankee in Texas* (New York, 1853).

Pendergrast, Garrett E., *A Physical and Topographical Sketch of the Mississippi Territory, Lower Louisiana, and a Part of West Florida* (Philadelphia, 1803).

Phelps, Dawson A. (ed.), "Excerpts from the Journal of the Rev. Joseph Bullen, 1799 and 1800," *Journal of Mississippi History*, XVII (October, 1955), 254–81.

——— (ed.), "Narrative of the Hostilities Committed by the Natchez

Against the Concession of St. Catherine, 1722," *Journal of Mississippi History*, VII (January, 1945), 3–10.

Phelps, Mathew, *Memoirs and Adventures of Captain Mathew Phelps, Formerly of Harwington in Connecticut, Now Resident in Newhaven in Vermont. Particularly in Two Voyages, from Connecticut to the River Mississippi, from December 1773 to October 1780 . . . Compiled from the Original Journal and Minutes Kept by Mr. Phelps, During His Voyages and Adventures, and Revised and Corrected According to His Present Recollections*, ed. Anthony Haswell (Bennington, Vt., 1802).

Pittman, Philip, *The Present State of the European Settlements on the Mississippi; with a General Description of That River Illustrated by Plans and Draughts*, ed. Frank H. Hodder (Cleveland, 1906).

Posey, Walter B. (ed.), "The First Session Book of the Oldest Presbyterian Church in Mississippi," *Journal of Mississippi History*, X (July, 1948), 132–49.

Postlethwaite, Samuel, "Journal of a Voyage from Louisville to Natchez, 1800," Missouri Historical Society *Bulletin*, VII (April, 1951), 312–29.

Power, Tyrone, *Impressions of America, During the Years 1833, 1834, and 1835 . . .* (2 vols.; London, 1836).

Prentiss, George L. (ed.), *A Memoir of S. S. Prentiss* (2 vols.; New York, 1855).

Rainey, W. H. (comp.), *A. Mygatt & Co.'s New Orleans Business Directory . . . Also a Business Directory of Algiers, Baton Rouge, Natchez, Vicksburg, Bayou Sara, Port Hudson, Woodville, Clinton* (New Orleans, 1858).

Rainwater, Percy L. (ed.), "The Memorial of John Perkins," *Louisiana Historical Quarterly*, XX (October, 1937), 965–89.

Richardson, William, *Journey from Boston to the Western Country and Down the Ohio and Mississippi Rivers to New Orleans, 1815–1816*, ed. William B. Wait (New York, 1940).

Robertson, James A. (ed.), *Louisiana under the Rule of Spain, France, and the United States, 1785–1807* (2 vols.; Cleveland, 1911).

Romans, Bernard, *A Concise Natural History of East and West Florida . . .* (New York, 1775).

Rowland, Eron (ed.), *Life, Letters and Papers of William Dunbar of Elgin, Morayshire, Scotland, and Natchez, Mississippi: Pioneer Scientist of the Southern United States* (Jackson, 1930).

———, "Peter Chester, Third Governor of the Province of West Florida," *Publications of the Mississippi Historical Society, Centenary Series*, V (1925), 17–27.

Schultz, Christian, Jr., *Travels on an Inland Voyage through the States of New York, Pennsylvania, Virginia, Ohio, Kentucky and Tennessee, and through the Territories of Indiana, Louisiana, Mississippi and New Orleans; Performed in the Years 1807 and 1808* (New York, 1810).

Scott, Kenneth (ed.), "Britain Loses Natchez, 1779: An Unpublished Letter," *Journal of Mississippi History*, XXVI (February, 1964), 45–46.

Second Report of the Board of Visitors of the Natchez Institute to the President and Selectmen of the City of Natchez (Natchez, 1846).

Shea, John G. (ed.), *Early Voyages Up and Down the Mississippi, by Cavalier, St. Cosme, Le Seuer, Gravier, and Guignas* (Albany, 1861).

Shields, Joseph D., *Natchez: Its Early History*, ed. Elizabeth D. Murray (Louisville, 1930).

Sparks, William H., *The Memories of Fifty Years* (Philadelphia, 1870).

Stratton, Joseph B., *Confessing Christ: A Manual for Inquirers in Religion* (Philadelphia, 1880).

———, *Memorial of a Quarter-Century's Pastorate* (Philadelphia, 1869).

———, *A Pastor's Valedictory: A Selection of Early Sermons* (Natchez, 1899).

Swearingen, Mack B., "Luxury at Natchez in 1801: A Ship's Manifest from the McDonogh Papers," *Journal of Southern History*, III (May, 1937), 188–90.

Thornton, Mary L. (ed.), "Letter from David Ker to John Steele [1801]," *Journal of Mississippi History*, XXV (April, 1963), 135–38.

Thwaites, Reuben G. (ed.), *Early Western Travels, 1748–1846* (32 vols.; Cleveland, 1904–1907).

——— (ed.), *Jesuit Relations and Allied Documents: Travels and Explorations of the Jesuit Missionaries in New France, 1610–1791* (73 vols.; Cleveland, 1896–1901).

Turner, Frederick J. (ed.), "Carondelet on the Defense of Louisiana, 1794," *American Historical Review*, II (April, 1897), 474–505.

Van Doren, Mark (ed.), *The Travels of William Bartram* (New York, 1940).

Wailes, Benjamin L. C., *Address Delivered in the College Chapel before the Agricultural, Horticultural, and Botanical Society, of Jefferson College . . . on the 24th of April, 1841* (Natchez, 1841).

———, *Memoir of Leonard Covington*, ed. Nellie W. Brandon and W. Magruder Drake (Natchez, 1928).

———, *Report on the Agriculture and Geology of Mississippi, Embracing a Sketch of the Social and Natural History of the State* (Philadelphia, 1854).

Wakefield, Priscilla (ed.), *Excursions in North America* (London, 1806).

Ware, Nathaniel A., *An Exposition of the Weakness and Inefficiency of the Government of the United States of North America* (New York, 1845).

———, *Notes on Political Economy as Applicable to the United States* (New York, 1844).

Wood, William, *Autobiography* (2 vols.; New York, 1895).

Wynne, John H., *General History of the British Empire in America; Containing an Historical, Political, and Commercial View of the English Settlements; Including All the Countries in North America, and the West Indies, Ceded by the Peace of Paris* (2 vols.; London, 1770).

SECONDARY WORKS

BOOKS

Abernethy, Thomas P., *The Burr Conspiracy* (New York, 1954).

———, *The South in the New Nation, 1789–1819* (Baton Rouge, 1961).

Alden, John R., *The Revolution in the South, 1763–1789* (Baton Rouge, 1957).

Alvord, Clarence W., *The Mississippi Valley in British Politics: A Study of the Trade, Land Speculation, and Experiments in Imperialism Culminating in the American Revolution* (2 vols.; New York, 1959).

Arthur, Stanley C., *Audubon: An Intimate Life of the American Woodsman* (New Orleans, 1937).

Beirne, Francis F., *Shout Treason: The Trial of Aaron Burr* (New York, 1959).

Bemis, Samuel F., *Pinckney's Treaty: A Study of America's Advantage from Europe's Distress, 1783–1800* (New York, 1926).

Bettersworth, John K., *Mississippi: A History* (Austin, 1959).

Biographical and Historical Memoirs of Mississippi (2 vols.; Chicago, 1891).

Bishop, J. L., *History of American Manufactures from 1608 to 1860* (3 vols.; Philadelphia, 1861–68).

Boyd, Jesse L., *A Popular History of the Baptists in Mississippi* (Jackson, 1931).

Brigham, Clarence S. (comp.), *History and Bibliography of American Newspapers, 1690–1820* (2 vols.; Worcester, Mass., 1947).

Burson, Caroline M., *The Stewardship of Don Esteban Miró* (New Orleans, 1940).

Butler, Pierce, *The Unhurried Years* (Baton Rouge, 1948).

Cain, John B., *Methodism in the Mississippi Conference, 1846–1870* (Jackson, 1939).

Capers, Gerald M., Jr., *The Biography of a River Town: Memphis, Its Heroic Age* (Chapel Hill, 1939).

Caruso, John A., *The Southern Frontier* (Indianapolis, 1963).

Caughey, John W., *Bernardo de Gálvez in Louisiana, 1766–1783* (Berkeley, 1934).

Claiborne, John F. H., *Life and Times of Gen. Sam Dale, the Mississippi Partisan* (New York, 1860).

Clark, Thomas D. (ed.), *Travels in the Old South: A Bibliography* (3 vols.; Norman, 1955–59).

Coates, Robert M., *The Outlaw Years: The History of the Land Pirates of the Natchez Trace* (New York, 1930).

Cooper, J. Wesley, *Natchez: A Treasure of Ante-Bellum Homes* (Natchez, 1957).

Cox, Isaac J., *The West Florida Controversy, 1798–1813: A Study in American Diplomacy* (Baltimore, 1918).

Crane, Verner W., *The Southern Frontier, 1670–1732* (Philadelphia, 1929).

Craven, Avery O., *The Coming of the Civil War* (Chicago, 1942).

———, *The Growth of Southern Nationalism, 1848–1861* (Baton Rouge, 1953).

Crenshaw, Ollinger, *The Slave States in the Presidential Election of 1860* (Baltimore, 1945).

Davis, Edwin A., and Hogan, William Ransom, *The Barber of Natchez* (Baton Rouge, 1954).

Dickey, Dallas C., *Seargent S. Prentiss: Whig Orator of the Old South* (Baton Rouge, 1945).

Dodd, William E., *Robert J. Walker, Imperialist* (Chicago, 1914).

Eaton, Clement, *A History of the Old South* (New York, 1949; 2nd ed.; 1966).

Ford, James A., *Analysis of Indian Village Site Collections from Louisiana and Mississippi* (New Orleans, 1936).

Fortier, Alcée, *A History of Louisiana* (4 vols.; New York, 1904).

Gates, Paul W., *The Farmer's Age: Agriculture, 1815–1860* (New York, 1960).

Gayarré, Charles E. A., *History of Louisiana* (4 vols.; New York, 1885).

Gerow, Richard O., *Catholicity in Mississippi* (Natchez, 1939).

———, *Cradle Days of St. Mary's at Natchez* (Natchez, 1941).

Gillis, Norman E., *Early Inhabitants of the Natchez District* (Baton Rouge, 1963).

Giraud, Marcel, *Histoire de la Louisiane Française* (3 vols. to date, Paris, 1953–66).

Gray, Lewis C., *History of Agriculture in the Southern United States to 1860* (2 vols.; Washington, 1933).

Green, Thomas M., *The Spanish Conspiracy: A Review of Early Spanish Movements in the South-West* (Cincinnati, 1891).

Gregory, Winifred (ed.), *American Newspapers, 1821–1936: A Union List of Files Available in the United States and Canada* (New York, 1936).

Guyton, Pearl V., *Connelly's Tavern on Ellicott's Hill* (Jackson, 1942).

Hamilton, William B., *Thomas Rodney: Revolutionary and Builder of the West* (Durham, 1953).

Hammond, George P. (ed.), *New Spain and the Anglo-American West* (2 vols.; Lancaster, 1932).

Harrison Robert W., *Alluvial Empire: A Study of State and Local Efforts toward Land Development in the Alluvial Valley of the Lower Mississippi River, Including Flood Control, Land Drainage, Land Clearing, Land Forming* (Little Rock, 1961).

Hawkins, Henry G., *Methodism in Natchez; Including "A Centennial Retrospect or Methodism in Natchez, Miss., from 1799 to 1884," by W. C. Black* (Jackson, 1937).

Hay, Thomas R., and M. R. Werner, *The Admirable Trumpeter: A Biography of General James Wilkinson* (New York, 1941).

Herskovits, Melville J., *The Myth of the Negro Past* (New York, 1941).

Hogan, William R., *The Texas Republic: A Social and Economic History* (Norman, 1946).

Holmes, Jack D. L., *Gayoso: The Life of a Spanish Governor in the Mississippi Valley, 1789–1799* (Baton Rouge, 1965).

Howard, Clinton N., *The British Development of West Florida, 1763–1769* (Berkeley, 1947).

Hunter, Louis C., *Steamboats on Western Waters: An Economic and Technological History* (Cambridge, Mass., 1949).

Jacobs, James R., *The Beginning of the U.S. Army, 1783–1812* (Princeton, 1947).

———, *Tarnished Warrior: Major-General James Wilkinson* (New York, 1938).

James, James A., *Oliver Pollock: The Life and Times of an Unknown Patriot* (New York, 1937).

James, Marquis, *Andrew Jackson: The Border Captain* (New York, 1933).

Johnson, Allen, and Dumas Malone (eds.), *Dictionary of American Biography* (22 vols.; New York, 1928–44). Twenty-two residents of antebellum Natchez have biographical sketches in this work.

Johnson, Cecil, *British West Florida, 1763–1783* (New Haven, 1943).

Jones, John G., *A Complete History of Methodism as Connected with the Mississippi Conference of the Methodist Episcopal Church, South* (2 vols.; Nashville, 1887).

———, *A Concise History of the Introduction of Protestantism into Mississippi and the Southwest* (St. Louis, 1866).

Kane, Harnett T., *Natchez on the Mississippi* (New York, 1947).

Leavell, Z. T., and T. J. Bailey, *A Complete History of Mississippi Baptists* (2 vols.; Jackson, 1904).

Lynch, James D., *The Bench and Bar of Mississippi* (New York, 1881).

Lyon, E. Wilson, *Louisiana in French Diplomacy, 1759–1804* (Norman, 1934).

McCaleb, Walter F., *The Aaron Burr Conspiracy* (New York, 1936).

McMurtrie, Douglas C., *Preliminary Check List of Mississippi Imprints, 1798–1810* (Chicago, 1934).

———, *A Short-Title List of Books, Pamphlets, and Broadsides Printed in Mississippi, 1811–1830* (Chicago, 1936).

Masterson, William H., *William Blount* (Baton Rouge, 1954).

Matthews, Catharine V. C., *Andrew Ellicott: His Life and Letters* (New York, 1908).

Mayes, Edward, *History of Education in Mississippi* (Washington, 1899).

Mellen, T. L., *Life and Labors of William H. Watkins* (Nashville, 1886).

Menn, Joseph K., *The Large Slaveholders of Louisiana——1860* (New Orleans, 1964).

Miles, Edwin A., *Jacksonian Democracy in Mississippi* (Chapel Hill, 1960).

Mississippi Newspapers, 1805–1840: A Preliminary Checklist of Mississippi Newspaper Files Available in the Mississippi Department of Archives and History (Jackson, 1942).

Monette, John W., *History of the Discovery and Settlement of the Valley of the Mississippi* (2 vols.; New York, 1846).

Moore, Edith W., *Natchez Under-the-Hill* (Natchez, 1958).

Moore, Glover, *The Missouri Controversy, 1819–1821* (Lexington, 1953).

Moore, John H., *Agriculture in Ante-Bellum Mississippi* (New York, 1958).

Neitzel, Robert S., *Archeology of the Fatherland Site: Grand Village of the Natchez* (New York, 1965).

Ogg, Frederick A., *The Opening of the Misissippi: A Struggle for Supremacy in the American Interior* (New York, 1904).

Oliver, Nola N., *This Too Is Natchez* (New York, 1953).

Phares, Ross, *Cavalier in the Wilderness: The Story of the Explorer and Trader Louis Juchereau de St. Denis* (Baton Rouge, 1952).

———, *Reverend Devil: A Biography of John A. Murrell* (New York, 1914).

Phillips, Ulrich B., *American Negro Slavery* (New York, 1918).

———, *Life and Labor in the Old South* (Boston, 1929).

Pillar, James J., *The Catholic Church in Mississippi, 1837–1865* (New Orleans, 1964).

Pishel, Robert G., *Natchez: Museum City of the Old South* (Tulsa, 1959).

Posey, Walter B., *The Baptist Church in the Lower Mississippi Valley, 1776–1845* (Lexington, 1959).

———, *The Development of Methodism in the Old Southwest, 1783–1824* (Tuscaloosa, 1933).

———, *The Presbyterian Church in the Old Southwest, 1778–1838* (Richmond, 1952).

Power, Steve, *The Memento: Old and New Natchez, 1700 to 1897* (Natchez, 1897).

Quick, Edward, and Herbert Quick, *Mississippi Steamboatin': A History of Steamboating on the Mississippi and Its Tributaries* (New York, 1926).

Rainwater, Percy L., *Mississippi: Storm Center of Secession, 1856–1861* (Baton Rouge, 1938).

Ranck, James B., *Albert Gallatin Brown, Radical Southern Nationalist* (New York, 1937).

Reber, Thomas, *Proud Old Natchez* (Natchez, 1909).

Rothert, Otto, *The Outlaws of Cave-in-Rock* (Cleveland, 1924).

Rosenberg, Charles G., *Jenny Lind in America* (New York, 1851).

Rowland, Dunbar, *Courts, Judges, and Lawyers of Mississippi* (Jackson, 1935).

———, *History of Mississippi: The Heart of the South* (2 vols.; Chicago, 1925).

———, *Mississippi: Comprising Sketches of Counties, Towns, Events, Institutions, and Persons, Arranged in Cyclopedic Form* (3 vols.; Atlanta, 1907).

———, *Third Annual Report of the Director of the Department of Archives and History of the State of Mississippi* (Nashville, 1905).

Russel, Robert R., *Economic Aspects of Southern Sectionalism, 1840–1861* (Urbana, 1924).

Shenton, James P., *Robert John Walker: A Politician from Jackson to Lincoln* (New York, 1961).

Shields, Joseph D., *The Life and Times of Seargent Smith Prentiss* (Philadelphia, 1883).

Sitterson, J. Carlyle, *Sugar Country: The Cane Sugar Industry in the South, 1753–1950* (Lexington, 1953).

Stephenson, Wendell H., *Isaac Franklin, Slave Trader and Planter of the Old South* (Baton Rouge, 1938).

Stewart, J. Walton, Jr., *History of the First Presbyterian Church* (Natchez, 1955).

Stietenroth, Charles, *One Hundred Years with "Old Trinity" Church, Natchez, Mississippi* (Natchez, 1922).

Surrey, Nancy M., *The Commerce of Louisiana During the French Regime, 1699–1763* (New York, 1916).

Swanton, John R., *Indian Tribes of the Lower Mississippi Valley and Adjacent Coast of the Gulf of Mexico* (Washington, 1911).

———, *The Indian Tribes of North America* (Washington, 1952).

Swearingen, Mack B., *The Early Life of George Poindexter: A Story of the First Southwest* (Chicago, 1934).

Sweet, William W., *The Story of Religion in America* (New York, 1950).

Sydnor, Charles S., *The Development of Southern Sectionalism, 1819–1848* (Baton Rouge, 1948).

———, *A Gentleman of the Old Natchez Region: Benjamin L. C. Wailes* (Durham, 1938).

———, *Slavery in Mississippi* (New York, 1933).

Taylor, George R., *The Transportation Revolution, 1815–1860* (New York, 1951).

U.S. Department of the Interior, *Historical American Buildings Survey No. 17: Outline of the Development of Early American Architecture in Mississippi* (Jackson, 1936).

Van Tassel, David D., *Recording America's Past: An Interpretation of the Development of Historical Studies in America, 1607–1884* (Chicago, 1960).

Wade, Richard C., *The Urban Frontier: The Rise of Western Cities, 1790–1830* (Cambridge, Mass., 1959).
Weaver, Herbert, *Mississippi Farmers, 1850–1860* (Nashville, 1945).
Weems, Robert C., *The Early Economic Development of Mississippi, 1699–1840* (State College, Miss., 1953).
Wender, Herbert, *Southern Commercial Conventions, 1837–1859* (Baltimore, 1930).
Whitaker, Arthur P., *The Mississippi Question, 1795–1803* (New York, 1934).
——, *The Spanish-American Frontier, 1783–1795: The Westward Movement and the Spanish Retreat in the Mississippi Valley* (Boston, 1927).
Winsor, Justin, *The Westward Movement: The Colonies and the Republic West of the Alleghanies, 1763–1798* (Boston, 1897).

ARTICLES

Abbey, Kathryn T., "Efforts of Spain to Maintain Sources of Information in the Colonies before 1779," *Mississippi Valley Historical Review*, XV (September, 1928), 56–68.
——, "Peter Chester's Defense of the Mississippi after the Willing Raid," *Mississippi Valley Historical Review*, XXII (June, 1935), 17–32.
Abernethy, Thomas P., "Aaron Burr in Mississippi," *Journal of Southern History*, XV (February, 1949), 9–21.
Albrecht, Andrew C., "Ethical Precepts among the Natchez Indians," *Louisiana Historical Quarterly*, XXXI (July, 1948), 569–97.
——, "Indian-French Relations at Natchez," *American Anthropologist*, XLVIII (1948), 321–54.
Anderson, Clayton and Company, "Average Annual Spot Price of Cotton Per Pound—Crop Years 1731–2 to 1957–8," *Anderson, Clayton and Co. Press*, XXXIX (March, 1959), 5.
Atkins, Charles H., "Richard Curtis in the Country of the Natchez," *Publications of the Mississippi Historical Society*, III (1900), 147–53.
Bonner, James C., "Plantation Architecture of the Lower South on the Eve of the Civil War," *Journal of Southern History*, XI (August, 1945), 370–88.
Brandon, Gerard, "Historic Adams County," *Publications of the Mississippi Historical Society*, II (1898), 32–39.
Bretz, Julian P., "Early Land Communication with the Lower Mississippi Valley," *Mississippi Valley Historical Review*, XIII (June, 1927), 3–29.

Brough, Charles H., "The History of Banking in Mississippi," *Publications of the Mississippi Historical Society,* III (1900), 317–40.

Broussard, Ray, "Governor John A. Quitman and the Lopez Expeditions of 1851–1852," *Journal of Mississippi History,* XXVIII (May, 1966), 103–20.

Burger, Nash K., "Adam Cloud, Mississippi's First Episcopal Clergyman," *Journal of Mississippi History,* IX (April, 1947), 88–97.

Burger, Nash K., and Charlotte Capers, "Episcopal Clergy of Mississippi, 1790–1940," *Journal of Mississippi History,* VIII (January, 1946), 59–66.

Cabaniss, Francis A., and James A. Cabaniss, "Religion in Ante-Bellum Mississippi," *Journal of Mississippi History,* VI (October, 1944), 191–224.

Calhoun, Robert D., "A History of Concordia Parish, Louisiana," *Louisiana Historical Quarterly,* XV (1932), 44–67, 214–33, 428–52, 618–45; XVI (1933), 92–124.

———, "The John Perkins Family of Northeast Louisiana," *Louisiana Historical Quarterly,* XIX (January, 1936), 70–88.

Campbell, J. A. C., "Repudiation of the Union and Planters Bank Bonds," *Publications of the Mississippi Historical Society,* IV (1901), 493–97.

Carter, Clarence E., "The Beginnings of British West Florida," *Mississippi Valley Historical Review,* IV (March, 1918), 314–41.

———, "Some Aspects of British Administration in West Florida," *Mississippi Valley Historical Review,* I (December, 1915), 369–75.

Caughey, John, "The Natchez Rebellion of 1781 and Its Aftermath," *Louisiana Historical Quarterly,* XVI (January, 1933), 57–83.

———, "Willing's Expedition Down the Mississippi, 1778," *Louisiana Historical Quarterly,* XV (January, 1932), 5–36.

Chappell, Gordon T., "Some Patterns of Land Speculation in the Old Southwest," *Journal of Southern History,* XV (November, 1949), 463–77.

Conrad, Alfred H., and John R. Meyer, "The Economics of Slavery in the Ante-Bellum South," *Journal of Political Economy,* LXVI (April, 1958), 95–122.

Conrad, D. H., "David Holmes: First Governor of Mississippi," *Publications of the Mississippi Historical Society, Centenary Series,* IV (1921), 234–57.

Cotterill, Robert S., "The Beginning of Railroads in the Southwest," *Mississippi Valley Historical Review,* VIII (March, 1922), 318–26.

———, "The Natchez Trace," *Louisiana Historical Quarterly,* VI (April, 1923), 259–68.

————, "The Natchez Trace," *Tennessee Historical Magazine,* VII (January, 1921), 29–36.

Delanglez, John, "The Natchez Massacre and Governor Perier," *Louisiana Historical Quarterly,* XVII (October, 1934), 631–41.

DeRosier, Arthur H., Jr., "William Dunbar, Explorer," *Journal of Mississippi History,* XXV (July, 1963), 165–85.

Diamond, William, "Nathaniel A. Ware, National Economist," *Journal of Southern History,* V (November, 1939), 501–26.

Dickey, Dallas C., "The Disputed Mississippi Election of 1837–38," *Journal of Mississippi History,* I (October, 1939), 217–35.

Drake, W. Magruder, "Mississippi's First Constitutional Convention," *Journal of Mississippi History,* XVIII (April, 1956), 79–110.

————, "A Note on the Jersey Settlers of Adams County," *Journal of Mississippi History,* XV (October, 1953), 274–75.

Dungan, James R., " 'Sir' William Dunbar of Natchez, Planter, Explorer, and Scientist, 1792–1810," *Journal of Mississippi History,* XXIII (October, 1961), 221–34.

Eichert, Magdalen, "Some Implications Arising from Robert J. Walker's Participation in Land Ventures," *Journal of Mississippi History,* XIII (January, 1951), 41–46.

Free, Joseph M., "The Ante-Bellum Theatre of the Old Natchez Region," *Journal of Mississippi History,* V (January, 1943), 14–27.

French, Warren G., "A Sketch of the Life of Joseph Holt Ingraham," *Journal of Mississippi History,* XI (July, 1949), 155–71.

Galloway, Charles B., "Elizabeth Female Academy—the Mother of Female Colleges," *Publications of the Mississippi Historical Society,* II (1899), 169–78.

————, "Lorenzo Dow in Mississippi," *Publications of the Mississippi Historical Society,* IV (1901), 233–44.

————, "Thomas Griffin: A Boanerges of the Early Southwest," *Publications of the Mississippi Historical Society,* VII (1903), 153–70.

Gates, Paul W., "Southern Investments in Northern Lands before the Civil War," *Journal of Southern History,* V (May, 1939), 155–85.

Gates, William B., "The Theatre in Natchez," *Journal of Mississippi History,* III (April, 1941), 71–129.

Gillson, Gordon, "Louisiana: Pioneer in Public Health," *Louisiana History,* IV (Summer, 1963), 207–32.

Grafton, Thomas, "The Scotch at Union Church," *Publications of the Mississippi Historical Society,* IX (1908), 263–71.

Green, John A., "Governor Perier's Expedition Against the Natchez Indians," *Louisiana Historical Quarterly,* XIX (July, 1936), 547–77.

Hale, Edward E., "The Real Philip Nolan," *Publications of the Mississippi Historical Society*, IV (1901), 281–329.

Haman, T. L., "Beginnings of Presbyterianism in Mississippi," *Publications of the Mississippi Historical Society*, X (1909), 204–16.

Hamilton, Peter J. "British West Florida," *Publications of the Mississippi Historical Society*, VII (1904), 399–426.

Hamilton, William B., "Jefferson College and Education in Mississippi, 1798–1817," *Journal of Mississippi History*, III (October, 1949), 259–76.

——, "The Southwestern Frontier, 1795–1817: An Essay in Social History," *Journal of Southern History*, X (November, 1944), 389–403.

——, "The Theater in the Old Southwest: The First Decade in Natchez," *American Literature*, XII (January, 1941), 471–85.

Hamilton, William B., and Ruth K. Nuermberger, "An Appraisal of J. F. H. Claiborne with His Annotated 'Memoranda' (1829–1840)," *Journal of Mississippi History*, VII (July, 1945), 155–62.

Hansen, Marcus L., "The Population of the American Outlying Regions in 1790," in *Annual Report of the American Historical Association, 1931*, Vol. I (Washington, 1932), 398–408.

Harrell, Laura D. S., "Horse Racing in the Old Natchez District, 1783–1830," *Journal of Mississippi History*, XIII (April, 1951), 123–37.

Haskins, Charles H., "The Yazoo Land Companies," in American Historical Association *Papers*, V (1891), 395–407.

Haynes, Robert V., "The Disposal of Lands in the Mississippi Territory," *Journal of Mississippi History*, XXIV (October, 1962), 226–52.

——, "The Southwest and the War of 1812," *Louisiana History*, V (Winter, 1964), 41–51.

Hearon, Cleo, "Mississippi and the Compromise of 1850," *Publications of the Mississippi Historical Society*, XIV (1914), 7–229.

——, "Nullification in Mississippi," *Publications of the Mississippi Historical Society*, XII (1912), 37–71.

Hearsey, Clem G., "The Vengeance of the Natchez," *Louisiana Historical Quarterly*, XII (April, 1929), 266–87.

Holmes, Jack D. L., "Law and Order in Spanish Natchez, 1781–1798," *Journal of Mississippi History*, XXV (July, 1963), 186–201.

——, "Livestock in Spanish Natchez," *Journal of Mississippi History*, XXIII (January, 1961), 15–37.

——, "Robert Ross' Plan for an English Invasion of Louisiana in 1782," *Louisiana History*, V (Spring, 1964), 161–77.

Howard, Clinton N., "Colonial Natchez: The Early British Period," *Journal of Mississippi History,* VII (July, 1945), 156–86.

——, "Some Economic Aspects of British West Florida, 1763–1768," *Journal of Southern History,* VI (May, 1940), 201–21.

James, James A., "Spanish Influence in the West during the American Revolution," *Mississippi Valley Historical Review,* IV (December, 1917), 193–208.

James, D. Clayton, "Municipal Government in Territorial Natchez," *Journal of Mississippi History,* XXVII (May, 1965), 148–67.

Jamison, Lena M., "The Natchez Trace: A Federal Highway of the Old Southwest," *Journal of Mississippi History,* I (April, 1939), 82–99.

Jenkins, William D., "The Mississippi River and the Efforts to Confine It in Its Channel," *Publications of the Mississippi Historical Society,* VI (1902), 283–306.

Johnson, Cecil, "The Distribution of Land in British West Florida," *Louisiana Historical Quarterly,* XVI (October, 1933), 639–53.

——, "Expansion in West Florida, 1770-1779," *Mississippi Valley Historical Review,* XX (March, 1934), 481–96.

Jordan, H. Donaldson, "A Politician of Expansion: Robert J. Walker," *Mississippi Valley Historical Review,* XIX (December, 1932), 362–81.

Kellogg, Louise P., "France and the Mississippi Valley: A Résumé," *Mississippi Valley Historical Review,* XVIII (June, 1931), 3–22.

Leavell, Z. T., "The Ante-Bellum Historical Society of Mississippi," *Publications of the Mississippi Historical Society,* VIII (1904), 227–37.

——, "Early Beginnings of Baptists in Mississippi," *Publications of the Mississippi Historical Society,* IV (1901), 245–53.

Leftwich, George J., "Robert J. Walker," *Publications of the Mississippi Historical Society,* VI (1902), 359–72.

——, "Some Main Travelled Roads," *Publications of the Mississippi Historical Society, Centenary Series,* I (1916), 463–76.

Liljegren, Ernest R., "Jacobism in Spanish Louisiana, 1792–1797," *Louisiana Historical Quarterly,* XXII (January, 1939), 47–97.

McLemore, Richard A., "The Division of the Mississippi Territory," *Journal of Mississippi History,* V (April, 1943), 79–82.

McLendon, James H., "The Development of Mississippi Agriculture," *Journal of Mississippi History,* XIII (January, 1951), 75–87.

——, "John A. Quitman, Fire-Eating Governor," *Journal of Mississippi History,* XV (January, 1953), 73–89.

———, "John A. Quitman in the Texas Revolution," *Southwestern Historical Quarterly*, LII (October, 1948), 163–83.

Matthias, Virginia P., "Natchez-Under-the-Hill as It Developed Under the Influence of the Mississippi River and the Natchez Trace," *Journal of Mississippi History*, VII (October, 1945), 201–21.

Miles, Edwin A., "Andrew Jackson and Senator George Poindexter," *Journal of Southern History*, XXIV (February, 1958), 51–66.

———, "The Mississippi Press in the Jackson Era, 1824–1841," *Journal of Mississippi History*, XIX (January, 1957), 1–20.

Monette, John W., "The Mississippi Floods," *Publications of the Mississippi Historical Society*, VII (1903), 427–78.

———, "The Progress of Navigation and Commerce on the Waters of the Mississippi River and the Great Lakes, 1700–1846," *Publications of the Mississippi Historical Society*, VII (1903), 479–523.

Moody, V. Alton, "Early Religious Efforts in the Lower Mississippi Valley," *Mississippi Valley Historical Review*, XXII (September, 1935), 161–76.

Moore, Edith W., "Natchez Homes," *Natchez Democrat*, 1959 Pilgrimage edition

———, "Natchez Homes," *Natchez Times*, 1959 Pilgrimage edition.

Moore, John H., "Mississippi's Ante-Bellum Textile Industry," *Journal of Mississippi History*, XVI (April, 1954), 81–98.

Morgan, Madel J., "Andrew Marschalk's Account of Mississippi's First Press," *Journal of Mississippi History*, VIII (July, 1946), 146–48.

Morrison, J. K., "The Early History of Jefferson College," *Publications of the Mississippi Historical Society*, II (1899), 179–88.

Nacbin, Jac, "Spain's Report of the War with the British in West Florida," *Louisiana Historical Quarterly*, XIV (July, 1931), 468–81.

Olden, Samuel B., Jr., "Hotels, Inns, and Taverns in Mississippi, 1830–1860," *Journal of Mississippi History*, V (July, 1943), 171–84.

Otken, Charles H., "Richard Curtis in the Country of the Natchez," *Publications of the Mississippi Historical Society*, III (1900), 147–53.

Owen, Thomas M., "Federal Courts, Judges, Attorneys, and Marshals in Mississippi, 1798–1898," *Publications of the Mississippi Historical Society*, II (1899), 147–56.

Phelps, Dawson A., "Stands and Travel Accommodations on the Natchez Trace," *Journal of Mississippi History*, XI (January, 1949), 1–54.

———, "Travel on the Natchez Trace: A Study of Its Economic Aspects," *Journal of Mississippi History*, XV (April, 1953), 155–64.

Posey, Walter B., "The Advance of Methodism into the Lower Southwest," *Journal of Southern History,* II (November, 1936), 439–52.

———, "The Early Baptist Church in the Lower Southwest," *Journal of Southern History,* X (May, 1944), 161–73.

———, "Influence of Slavery upon the Methodist Church in the Early South and Southwest," *Mississippi Valley Historical Review,* XVII (March, 1931), 530–42.

———, "The Slavery Question in the Presbyterian Church in the Old Southwest," *Journal of Southern History,* XV (August, 1949), 311–24.

Rainwater, Percy L., "An Analysis of the Secession Controversy in Mississippi, 1854–1861," *Mississippi Valley Historical Review,* XXIV (June, 1937), 35–42.

Rawson, Donald M., "Democratic Resurgence in Mississippi, 1852–1853," *Journal of Mississippi History,* XXVI (February, 1964), 1–27.

Riley, Franklin L., "A Contribution to the History of the Colonization Movement in Mississippi," *Publications of the Mississippi Historical Society,* IX (1906), 331–414.

———, "Life and Literary Services of Dr. John W. Monette," *Publications of the Mississippi Historical Society,* IX (1906), 199–237.

———, "Life of Col. J. F. H. Claiborne," *Publications of the Mississippi Historical Society,* VII (1903), 217–44.

———, "Sir William Dunbar, the Pioneer Scientist of Mississippi," *Publications of the Mississippi Historical Society,* II (1899), 85–111.

———, "Spanish Policy in Mississippi after the Treaty of San Lorenzo," *Publications of the Mississippi Historical Society,* I (1898), 50–66.

———, "Transition from Spanish Rule," *Publications of the Mississippi Historical Society,* III (1901), 261–67.

Rowland, Dunbar, "Mississippi's First Constitution and Its Makers," *Publications of the Mississippi Historical Society,* VI (1902), 79–90.

Rowland, Eron, "Mississippi's Colonial Population and Land Grants," *Publications of the Mississippi Historical Society, Centenary Series,* I (1916), 405–28.

———, "The Mississippi Territory in the War of 1812," *Publications of the Mississippi Historical Society, Centenary Series,* IV (1921), 7–233.

Rutledge, Wilmuth S., "Dueling in Antebellum Mississippi," *Journal of Mississippi History,* XXVI (August, 1964), 181–91.

Seal, Albert G., "John Carmichael Jenkins: Scientific Planter of the Natchez District," *Journal of Mississippi History,* I (January, 1939), 14–28.

Seibert, Wilbur H., "Loyalists in West Florida and the Natchez District," *Mississippi Valley Historical Review*, II (March, 1916), 469–74.

Shepherd, William R., "Wilkinson and the Beginnings of the Spanish Conspiracy," *American Historical Review*, IX (April, 1904), 494–98.

Sitterson, J. Carlyle, "The William J. Minor Plantations: A Study in Ante-Bellum Absentee Ownership," *Journal of Southern History*, IX (February, 1943), 59–74.

Stephenson, Wendell H., "A Quarter Century of a Mississippi Plantation: Eli F. Capell of 'Pleasant Hill,'" *Mississippi Valley Historical Review*, XXIII (December, 1936), 355–74.

Swearingen, Mack B., "Thirty Years of a Mississippi Plantation: Charles Whitmore of 'Montpelier,'" *Journal of Southern History*, I (May, 1935), 198–211.

Sydnor, Charles S., "The Beginning of Printing in Mississippi," *Journal of Southern History*, I (February, 1935), 49–55.

———, "The Free Negro in Mississippi Before the Civil War," *American Historical Review*, XXXII (July, 1927), 771–79.

———, "Historical Activities in Mississippi in the Nineteenth Century," *Journal of Southern History*, III (July, 1937), 156–74.

Taylor, Garland, "Colonial Settlement and Early Revolutionary Activity in West Florida Up to 1779," *Mississippi Valley Historical Review*, XXII (December, 1935), 351–60.

Weems, Robert C., Jr., "The Makers of the Bank of Mississippi," *Journal of Mississippi History*, XV (April, 1953), 137–54.

Williams, Frederick D., "The Congressional Career of J. F. H. Claiborne," *Journal of Mississippi History*, XVII (January, 1955), 24–42.

Winston, James E., "Annexation of Texas and the Mississippi Democrats," *Southwestern Historical Quarterly*, XXV (July, 1921), 21–32.

———, "Mississippi and the Independence of Texas," *Southwestern Historical Quarterly*, XXI (July, 1917), 36–45.

———, "The Mississippi Whigs and the Tariff, 1834–1844," *Mississippi Valley Historical Review*, XI (September, 1924), 200–26.

Woodson, Carter G., "Free Negro Owners of Slaves in the United States in 1830," *Journal of Negro History*, IX (January, 1924), 42–53.

DISSERTATIONS AND THESES

Armstrong, Helen P., "Public Welfare and Private Programs Administered in Natchez and Adams County, Mississippi, 1798–1822" (unpublished M.A. thesis, University of Chicago, 1943).

Chambers, Moreau B. C., "History of Fort Panmure at Natchez, 1763–1785" (unpublished M.A. thesis, Duke University, 1942).

Cole, Fred C., "The Early Life of Thomas Affleck, 1813–1841" (unpublished M.A. thesis, Louisiana State University, 1936).

Cunnnigham, Mary C., "The Development and Appreciation of Historical Architecture at Natchez, Mississippi" (unpublished M.A. thesis, George Peabody College for Teachers, 1937).

French, Warren G., "Joseph Holt Ingraham, Southern Romancer, 1809–1860" (unpublished M.A. thesis, University of Texas, 1948).

Gladney, Louise, "History of Pleasant Hill Plantation, 1811–1867" (unpublished M.A. thesis, Louisiana State University, 1932).

Hamilton, William B., "American Beginnings in the Old Southwest: The Mississippi Phase" (unpublished Ph.D. dissertation, Duke University, 1938 [1937]).

Hatfield, Joseph T., "The Public Career of William C. C. Claiborne" (unpublished Ph.D. dissertation, Emory University, 1962).

Haynes, Robert V., "A Political History of the Mississippi Territory" (unpublished Ph.D. dissertation, Rice Institute, 1958).

Horton, William B., "The Life of David Holmes" (unpublished M.A. thesis, University of Colorado, 1935).

Kinnaird, Lawrence, "American Penetration into Spanish Territory to 1803" (unpublished Ph.D. dissertation, University of California, Berkeley, 1928).

Lang, Herbert H., "Nineteenth Century Historians of the Gulf States" (unpublished Ph.D. dissertation, University of Texas, 1954).

McLendon, James H., "John A. Quitman" (unpublished Ph.D. dissertation, University of Texas, 1949).

McMillan, Lucy M., "Natchez, 1763–1779" (unpublished M.A. thesis, University of Virginia, 1938).

McPherson, Hallie M., "William McKendree Gwin, Expansionist" (unpublished Ph.D. dissertation, University of California, Los Angeles, 1931).

Miles, Edwin A., "Robert J. Walker—His Mississippi Years" (unpublished M.A. thesis, University of North Carolina, 1949).

Morris, A. B., "R. J. Walker in the Kansas Struggle" (unpublished M.A. thesis, University of Chicago, 1916).

Seal, Albert G., "John Carmichael Jenkins, Scientific Planter of the Natchez District" (unpublished M.A. thesis, Louisiana State University, 1937).

Stokes, Beatrice M., "John Bisland, Mississippi Planter, 1776–1821" (unpublished M.A. thesis, Louisiana State University, 1941).

Taylor, Arvilla, "Horse Racing in the Lower Mississippi Valley to 1860" (unpublished M.A. thesis, University of Texas, 1953).

Tick, Frank H., "The Political and Economic Policies of Robert J.

Walker" (unpublished Ph.D. dissertation, University of California, Los Angeles, 1947).

Volstorff, Vivian V., "William Charles Cole Claiborne: A Study in Frontier Administration" (unpublished Ph.D. dissertation, Northwestern University, 1932).

Weems, Robert C., Jr., "The Bank of Mississippi: A Pioneer Bank of the Old Southwest, 1809–1844" (unpublished Ph.D. dissertation, Columbia University, 1951).

Whitwell, Joseph W., "The Public Life of William M. Gwin in Mississippi" (unpublished Ph.D. dissertation, University of Texas, 1930).

Williams, Frederick D., "The Career of J. F. H. Claiborne, States' Rights Unionist" (unpublished Ph.D. dissertation, University of Indiana, 1953).

Williams, Robert W., Jr., "The Mississippi Career of Thomas Affleck" (unpublished Ph.D. dissertation, Tulane University, 1954).

Wingfield, C. L., "The Sugar Plantations of William J. Minor, 1830–1860" (unpublished M.A. thesis, Louisiana State University, 1950).

NOTE: Other secondary works on Natchez which were consulted but not used in the preparation of this study include Nola N. Oliver, *Natchez: Symbol of the Old South* (New York, 1940); Theodora B. Marshall and Gladys C. Evans, *They Found It in Natchez* (New Orleans, 1940); Richard F. Reed, *Natchez Country* (Natchez, n.d.); Elizabeth D. Murray, *Early Romances of Historic Natchez* (Natchez, 1938); Katherine G. Miller, *Natchez of Long Ago* (Natchez, 1938); Georgia W. Newell and Charles C. Compton, *Natchez and the Pilgrimage* (Kingsport, Tenn., 1935); Catherine Van Court, *The Old House* (Richmond, 1950); Theodora B. Marshall, *Come to Natchez* (Natchez, n.d.); Theodora B. Marshall and Gladys C. Evans, *A Day in Natchez* (Natchez, 1946).

Index

Weeks, Levi G., 239–40
Weier, William, 245
Weldon, George, 163
Welfare and relief: overseers of the poor, 84; orphan indentures, 168; orphanages, 219–20; Natchez Charitable Association, 268–69
Wells, Jefferson, 264–65
Wells, Samuel L., 264–65
West, Benjamin: paintings exhibited, 230
West, Cato: and Ellicott-Gayoso, 68, 71; in territory, 101, 102, 103, 104–108
West, Wellington, 180
West Feliciana Rail Road Company, 190
West Florida: British, 12, 13, 24, 25–27; negotiations of 1782–83, pp. 28–29; as liability, 29–30
Westphalia: Quitman visits, 191–92
Wetasil, Luis, 35
Wheat, 7
Whig (Vicksburg), 290
Whigs: alleged stronghold of, 100; local leaders, 117, 129–30, 152, 177, 236, 278; elections and voting strength, 177–35 *passim*; and "bank war," 201; *Courier* favors, 230, 231; decline, 231, 289; visits of national leaders, 280–81; and Compromise of 1850, pp. 285–87
White, James, 59, 64
White Cliffs: *See* Ellis' Cliffs
White family, 137, 153
White Horse Tavern, 188
Whitehurst, William N., 226n
Whitmore, Charles, 186
Wiley, Calvin, 223
Wilkins, James: in territorial politics, 110–12, 131; Junto leader, 113, 121; defeated, 116, 121; land speculation, 120; becomes Whig, 130 n; mer-

chant-planter, 149–50, 158, 159; commercial interests, 196, 205–206; banker, 199–200, 201; mentioned, 180, 228, 256
Wilkins family, 137
Wilkinson, James: trading and separatist activities, 48, 58–60; mentioned, 76
Wilkinson County: created, 103; political influence, 119–20; mentioned, 115, 119, 121, 153, 246
Williams, David, 48
Williams, Robert, 106–108
William, Thomas H., 106, 113, 282
Willing, James: merchant, 19, 21; raid, 21–24, 29
Willson, A. L., 177–78
Winans, William, 175, 247
Winchester, George, 42n, 124–25, 281, 283
Winchester, Josiah, 134, 291–92
Winn, Baylor, 181
Wood, Henry, 205
Wood, John, 131
Wood, Robert W., 96
"Woodlawn," 157
Woodville, Miss.: business and trade, 83, 146, 190, 198, 211, 213; leaders, 119–20; lyceum, 233
Woodville Manufacturing Company, 146
Woolley, Melling, 45n
Wynne, John H., 16

Yazoo Act, 63–64
Yazoo Indians, 3–4, 10, 56
Yellow fever: city officials and, 85–86; Thompsons and, 136–37, 150; delays Institute opening, 221; physicians study, 233, 236, 239; Van de Velde stricken by, 244; epidemics, 267–69
Yerger Amendment: to secession ordinance, 291